Sustainable Logistics

Logistics refers to the processes that start with resources and their acquisition, storage, and transportation to their destination. The concept is crucial in business—particularly for the manufacturing sector—to understand, manage, and control how resources are handled and progress through the whole supply chain. Now, there is a strong trend to focus on sustainability and eco-friendly solutions in logistics. Processes based on both technology and management need innovations and detailed implementation steps to achieve a satisfactory level of sustainability.

This book explores how and where innovations can be implemented to provide a broad approach to sustainability in logistics. It addresses the main challenges affecting modern and sustainable logistics and supply chains and is organized according to six main themes: supply chain management; information intelligent hubs (e.g., warehouses and cities); sustainable transportation; technology for logistics; reverse logistics; and city logistics. The key results presented are based on both extensive types of research and business cases. The overarching advanced logistics and supply chain concepts at the heart of this book contribute to a sustainable intelligent logistics and transport system by making it more efficient, reliable, environmentally friendly, and competitive.

Essentially, this book presents the most current research related to sustainability in logistics activities and addresses the theoretical background of sustainability and its significance for logistics, the challenges in supply chains and transportation, and possible solutions for more sustainable logistics systems.

Sustainable Logistics

How to Address and Overcome the Major Issues and Challenges

Edited by Joanna Domagała, Aleksandra Górecka, Monika Roman

Routledge
Taylor & Francis Group

A PRODUCTIVITY PRESS BOOK

First published 2023
by Routledge
605 Third Avenue, New York, NY 10158

and by Routledge
4 Park Square, Milton Park, Abingdon, Oxon, OX14 4RN

Routledge is an imprint of the Taylor & Francis Group, an informa business

Library of Congress Cataloging-in-Publication Data
A catalog record for this book is available from the British Library.

ISBN: 978-1-032-30297-3 (hbk)
ISBN: 978-1-032-30296-6 (pbk)
ISBN: 978-1-003-30436-4 (ebk)

DOI: 10.4324/9781003304364

Typeset in Garamond
by Apex CoVantage, LLC

Contents

Figures

Tables

Foreword by Wojciech J. Florkowski, PhD

The premise of sustainability has penetrated into every corner of social, policy, and economic activity. This outstanding book offered by a team of authors from Polish, Slovenian, Croatian and Finnish universities tackles a timely issue of supply logistics. Initiated by a team of editors from Warsaw University of Life Sciences, Joanna Domagała, Aleksandra Górecka, and Monika Roman, the collection of chapters tackles logistics as a dimension of sustainability that has received piecemeal attention. Expanding trade stimulated research interest in logistics, while also trying to reduce resource exploitation and minimize detrimental environmental effects. Decision-making in logistics requires understanding and application of solutions consistent with the sustainability principle driven by policies and changing attitudes in society at large. Split into three sections, the book directs attention to the theoretical foundations of sustainable logistics, sustainable management of supply chains, and challenges faced in applying sustainable logistics in practice. Each part is a collection of chapters focused on modern-day issues.

Section I addresses innovative developments in sustainable logistics, transportation, warehousing, and waste management. With logistics centers popping up in Central and Southern Europe, the underlying concepts of managing distribution, storage, and waste generation and disposal are of utmost importance. Section II shifts the focus to supply-chain management by distinguishing the global and micro-context. The section examines the newest technology and use of autonomous vehicles and digital technology applications enhancing the flexibility of business models applied in supply chains. Recognizing special logistical requirements, a chapter appraises pricing that internalizes external transportation costs of fresh fruit and vegetables to improve sustainability and competitiveness. Section III illustrates how sustainable logistics have or can be applied as well as major challenges. Those issues include the use and influence of digitalization and the internet on smart, sustainable logistics, attempts to lower emissions through decarbonization in shipping, and the potential of telematics to transform the urban landscape. A separate chapter investigates the concept of food-sharing using the example of Warsaw, Poland, anticipating positive food redistribution effects.

Sustainability requires continuous effort and adoption of innovative technologies as well as evolving practices if it is to make a difference in future economies, and logistics plays an essential role in assuring sustainable production and distribution. The emphasis on the unique dimension of sustainability as it relates to supply logistics makes this book a timely contribution to the literature. The book facilitates the understanding of options in sustainable logistics and will make it a desired reading for students, managers, policymakers, and organizations pursuing a path to sustainable development and growth.

Wojciech J. Florkowski, PhD
The University of Georgia, USA

Foreword by Altuğ Murat Köktaş, PhD

In a globalized world with complex businesses, logistics is perceived as the significant motor of international-goods exchange and people mobility. The development of logistics processes influences the goods flow and the fluent passenger movement. On the other hand logistics processes, particularly transportation, can cause several external effects on the environment.

Sustainable Logistics: How to Address and Overcome the Major Issues and Challenges presents the importance of sustainable solutions in the main areas of logistics, which are: Supply chain, transportation; warehouses; reversed logistics; and city logistics. The increasing number of vehicles and their exploitation affects the environment very intensely. This issue is described based on different cases and sustainable city transportation, digitalization of transportation processes, and decarbonization of container maritime transport.

The trend to go green is underlined. The green logistics approach aims at minimizing the negative influence of logistics flows on the ecosystem. Authors suggest innovative ways on how to reduce greenhouse gas emissions in the supply chain. Sustainable Supply-Chain Management (SSCM) in the context of energy use is an important strategy that helps organizations achieve a competitive advantage and improve overall performance, and therefore the authors describe this issue too.

Apart from the standard logistics management and operational issues, the authors also focus on the reactions of the logistics sector during the COVID-19 pandemic. Emerging problems related to the prohibition of the movement of people and the need to adapt to the prevailing conditions of the transport of goods changed the logistics sector, which did not escape the authors' attention, and is widely described.

The book is an excellent example of a combination of academic knowledge and business implementations as it includes the theoretical aspects of shifting the main processes in the logistics and the supply chains into a higher level of sustainability based on innovations implementation.

Altuğ Murat Köktaş
Necmettin Erbakan University, Konya, Turkey

Preface

Sustainable logistics is an important issue, which has caught the attention of practitioners, academicians and researchers. Logistics refers to the processes starting from resource acquisition, storage, and transportation to their final destination. The concept is now broadly implemented in business, particularly by enterprises in the manufacturing sectors to understand, manage and control how resources are handled and moved along the whole supply chain. In the 21st century, there is a strong trend to focus on sustainability and eco-friendly solutions in logistics. The processes based on both technology and management need innovative implementation to achieve a satisfactory level of sustainability.

This book presents and discusses the main challenges posed by sustainable logistics in a manner relevant to both practitioners and scholars. It is important to learn how companies should introduce the principles of sustainable development in the area of logistics. The key findings are based on extensive research and business cases. The overarching advanced logistics and supply-chain concept at the heart of this book endeavors to contribute to a sustainable, intelligent logistics and transport system by making it more efficient, reliable, environmentally friendly, and competitive.

This book aims to bring together the theory and practice of sustainable logistics. It looks at the current state of sustainable logistics, including a comprehensive overview of both research and practical applications. The book is divided into three parts: the first covers theoretical foundations of innovative and sustainable logistics, the second covers sustainable supply-chain management, and the third covers applications and challenges in sustainable logistics. Details of the chapters are summarized below.

The first section contains four chapters. **Chapter 1** discusses the main direction of developing innovative and sustainable logistics. This chapter primarily focuses on novel technologies such as IoT and blockchain that can revolutionize the supply chain by eliminating the intermediaries and, consequently, how firms operate, generate value, attract new customers and investors, etc. **Chapter 2** presents the theoretical background of innovations and their importance for modern transportation systems. Additionally, examples of the technologies used in the aviation business in the 21st century are presented. **Chapter 3** focuses on a systematic literature review of green warehousing. This chapter provides a comprehensive overview and classification of the existing research on green warehousing, summarizes and synthesizes the available knowledge on this topic, and identifies key trends, including green warehouse management, the environmental impact of the warehouse building, and energy-saving initiatives in warehousing. In **Chapter 4**, following a review of the literature and applied solutions described, the author identifies the main research directions and ongoing changes in reverse logistics from a sustainable waste-management perspective. Based on the conducted analysis, thematic clusters were created in the research on reverse logistics.

The second section contains five chapters. The aim of **Chapter 5** is to discuss the theoretical foundations of the global supply chains and critically review the diversified strands of literature underlying it. Particularly, the author answers the following research questions: What is the genesis of the supply chain and value chain concepts? what are the differences between the many diversified strands of literature underlying the chain concepts? and how well can different strands of literature address the present need to incorporate more resiliency and robustness into global supply chains? **Chapter 6** discusses the applicability of autonomous vehicles in global supply chains based on selected global 3PL leaders and determines the main benefits of implementing autonomous vehicles in supply chains. The research methodology of this chapter is based on desk research. Scientific and professional literature is used to prepare the theoretical framework, while the analytical part is based on case studies of leading 3PL providers. The primary purpose of **Chapter 7** is to present the positive impact of implementing optimal logistics models in micro and small companies so that they can provide inbound logistics to retail businesses and create sustainable value in the food industry. The chapter discusses specific problems of contemporary logistics efficiency with an analysis based on the COVID-19 environment, offering a sustainable distribution model in the food-processing industry as a national strategic branch. The aim of **Chapter 8** is to appraise the pricing of international transport of fresh fruits and vegetables through the internalization of external costs as an essential indicator of sustainability. This chapter uses a systematic literature review, and secondary and primary data. **Chapter 9** shows the sharing-economy concept and its effects on economic growth and development with a particular focus on the supply-chain industry. Based on the case-study analysis of international companies, the authors analyze the current application of the sharing-economy practice in the supply-chain industry and forecast the possible prospect of its impact from the business perspective and the perspective of economic growth and development.

The third section contains five chapters. The aim of **Chapter 10** is to present assumptions of sustainable logistics with the use of Internet-of-Things solutions. In the framework of undertaken discussion, an analysis of the practical implementations of this type of system is carried out. Solutions from the area of land, water, and air transport are compared. **Chapter 11** presents the importance of the digitalization of transport documentation in logistics companies. The process is described in the example of the GreenTransit system. This platform is used to digitalize all documentation occurring in the transport process. The primary purpose of **Chapter 12** is to assess the prospects of the green initiative combined with the perspective of container carriers' implementation of greenhouse gas-reduction strategy and investigate the impact of these regulations on carriers' competitiveness. Based on the recent scientific and professional research papers, the authors frame the theoretical background of the topic, while the analytical part is based on the interviews with employers related to the greenhouse gas-reduction operations and case-study analysis. **Chapter 13** presents a multi-aspect analysis of suburban transportation. This chapter determines the influences of auto telematics transformation on the risk of driving, risk management, driving behavior, time of day, driving location, and the functioning of the city. The aim of **Chapter 14** is to present the perception and experience of dwellers regarding food-sharing locations and food-sharing applications. The research used analyzed source materials and the CAWI method. The chapter shows the popularity of the applications, themes, and obstacles to their use.

This book provides the theoretical background and practical issues related to sustainable logistics. The editors believe that the collection of chapters is relevant and beneficial to the needs of professionals, researchers, and post-doctoral and graduate students. The authors of this book try to stimulate new research directions, and show the issues and challenges related to sustainable logistics. It brings together conceptual thinking and empirical research on the nature, meaning, and perspectives of sustainable logistics.

Editors

Joanna Domagała, PhD, is an associate professor in the Department of Logistics, Institute of Economics and Finance, Warsaw University of Life Sciences (WULS). The main fields of her scientific interest are enterprise efficiency, internationalization, globalization of the food industry sectors, logistics systems in agribusiness, management, and planning of logistics in enterprises, and supply-chain management. She is the author or co-author of more than 150 scientific publications. She has participated in foreign internships at the University of Georgia (USA) and Shanghai Ocean University (China). She has been a reviewer and a guest co-editor for many international journals. She is a member of the Polish Logistics Society, European Association of Agricultural Economists, and Association of Agricultural Economists and Agribusiness. She is the head of Postgraduate Studies in Logistics.

Monika Roman, PhD, is an assistant professor in the Department of Logistics, Institute of Economics and Finance, Warsaw University of Life Sciences (WULS). Her research interests include several topics: Spatial economies, agricultural economics, quantitative methods, transport, logistics systems in agribusiness, and optimization of logistics processes in enterprises. She is the author or co-author of more than 60 scientific publications. She has participated in foreign internships at University College Cork (Ireland), the National University of Life and Environmental Sciences of Ukraine, and the Czech University of Life Sciences Prague. She has been a reviewer and a guest co-editor for several international journals. She is a member of the Polish Logistics Society, Polish Society of Production Management, and Association of Agricultural Economists and Agribusiness.

Aleksandra Górecka, PhD, is an assistant professor in the Institute of Economics and Finance, Warsaw University of Life Sciences (WULS). Her main field of research is transport infrastructure, transport economics, and economic development. She participated in more than 30 mobilities (e.g., Germany, Slovenia, Croatia, Austria, Czech Republic), and numerous national and international conferences, hence her scientific relations allowed her to contribute to international joined research. She is the author or co-author of over 40 papers and three research books. She was also the reviewer of many Polish and foreign journals.

Contributors

Maria Bajak is an assistant at the Department of Marketing of the Cracow University of Economics, Poland. Her research focuses on the use of the Internet of Things in marketing communication, sustainable development, and social marketing. She gained her professional experience, among others, in an IT company, where she had practical contact with projects concerning digital technologies in business. For her scientific activity during her master's studies, she was awarded the title of finalist in the Student Nobel Prize competition in 2020. She is an author of numerous publications on marketing communication, new technologies in business, and corporate social responsibility.

Agata Balińska, PhD, is an assistant professor in the Institute of Economics and Finance, Warsaw University of Life Sciences (WULS). Her scientific research concerns the development of tourism, territorial development, consumer behavior, and the sharing economy. She is the author and co-author of over 140 scientific publications, including: Experiences of Polish Tourists Traveling for Leisure Purposes during the COVID-19 Pandemic, *Sustainability* 2021; Pro-Environmental Forms of Transport in the Experience and Perception of Tourists Visiting Warsaw, *Journal of Environmental Management and Tourism*, 2020, (iii) Sharing economy in the tourism economy: theoretical and empirical context, 2021, Warsaw University of Life Sciences, ISBN 978-83-8237-009-6, 126 pp.-monography.

Sandra Bonča, PhD, holds a bachelor's and master's degree in economics and a Ph.D. in the economics of renewable natural resources. She is currently working in the private sector.

Zoran Ježić, PhD, is an associate professor, at the Faculty of Economics and Business in Rijeka and relates to the courses National Economy, Human Resource Management, Economics of Education, and Economic Growth and

Development. He is a regular member and chairman of the Supervisory Board of the Croatian Economic Association (ZDE), a member of the Croatian section of the European Regional Science Association, the Alumni Association of the Faculty of Economics of the University of Rijeka and chairman of the Technical Board of the certification program Business Friendly Certification South East Europe (BFC SEE), which awards a certificate for an entrepreneur-friendly environment to cities and municipalities in South East Europe.

Irena Jędrzejczyk, PhD, is a full professor of economic science. She has had many years of experience in teaching, research, and administration. Her field of interest has been the economy, business management, finances, and investment. She earned her MA and her PhD at the University of Economics in Cracow, Poland and she completed her Habilitation and her professorship at the University of Economics in Katowice—Silesia. She spent many years as a research scholar at the University in Trier, Germany, and the University of Zurich, Switzerland. She was first appointed as head of the Educational Centre of Insurance and Risk management, coordinator and project manager of JEP No 11015 TEMPUS PHARE, head of the Department of Insurances Market Studies at the University of Economics in Katowice—Silesia, head of Branche of Finance Markets Studies at the University of Life Sciences, Warsaw, coordinator and project manager of JEP No: DKS/DEF-III/ POPT/04/185/08. Since 2017, Professor Jędrzejczyk has worked as researcher and teacher at the Management Department, Faculty of Management and Transport, the University of Bielsko-Biała in Silesia, Poland.

Oskar Juszczyk is a PhD student in the Industrial Management Department at the School of Technology and Innovations of the University of Vaasa. He holds an MSc in Economics and Organization of Enterprises from Warsaw University of Life Sciences (WULS-SGGW), Poland, and Paris 13 Sorbonne University, France. His main research focus is the commercialization of renewable energy technologies, energy transition policies, innovative energy technologies related to digitalization, strategic and operational management tools as well as the intersectoral collaboration supporting the implementation of sustainable energy solutions.

Leonardo Lovričić is a master of economics in International Business with further intention to enroll in PhD studies. Employed within Liburnia Group as Logistics Manager, with special focus on international shipping and chartering, dealing with standardized and heavy-lift cargo globally. His research interests are in the area of automatization and digitalization processes in shipping, with the highlight on blockchain technologies and environmentally responsible business practices.

Marko Lukavac is a PhD student at the Faculty of Economics and Business, University of Rijeka, Croatia. At first, he worked as a teaching assistant at the Department of Economics at the University of Zadar in order to acquire new skills and knowledge as a base for future academic development, and now he is setting up a private consultant business in the fields of accounting and EU funds. He is additionally occupied with managing a family business with a tradition of more than three decades in the segment of the food-processing industry. He continues his Ph.D. in economics which he treats as the link and catalyst between the business and policymakers' needs and expectations. His research focuses on equal and sustainable development opportunities for society, and he has published several scientific papers in this field.

Dejan Miljenović, PhD, is an assistant professor of the Faculty of Economics and Business at the University of Rijeka, Croatia. He is referred to as a social economist specializing in socioeconomic sustainability. Within the Erasmus program, he is a regular visiting professor at the University of Ljubljana, School of Economics and Business, and an editor of journals specializing in the topic of Sustainability Economics, making additional effort to actively bring this actualized topic regularly to business practice, managers and students. His field of research includes analysis of the Triple Bottom Line (TBL), Stakeholder Management, Sustainable Value Added (SVA), Social Entrepreneurship, and analysis, recently being a scientific consultant for the issues of business carbon efficiency in the sector of logistics and energy facilitation.

Helga Pavlić Skender, PhD, is an associate professor at the Faculty of Economics and Business in Rijeka, Croatia. Her field of work relates to the courses Business Logistics, International Forwarding and Logistics, and Transport and Maritime Economics. Her research interest covers the area of transportation, international logistics, and supply chains.

Michał Pietrzak is a full professor at Warsaw University of Life Sciences, Institute of Economics and Finance. He is an economist and strategic management researcher and practitioner. He is the vice-chairman of the committee responsible for the strategy of this university. His main areas of interest include economics (in particular: New institutional economics and hybrid organizations, e.g., cooperatives, chains, and networks,) as well as strategic management, organizational learning, and logistics. His consultancy experience covers strategic analyses, strategy development, and Balanced Scorecard implementation for many industries and sectors, e.g., automotive, energy, chemistry, professional services, municipal services, public agencies, and universities. He was also Head of the MBA program and postgraduate studies for many years.

Piotr Pietrzak, PhD, is an assistant professor at the Warsaw University of Life Sciences (WULS—SGGW), in the Management Institute. His research interests include several topics: Public management, efficiency measurement, strategic management, process management, and digital management. He is the author of over 70 articles and four books. He has published work in journals such as the *International Journal of Innovation and Learning, Human Systems Management*, and *Foundations of Management.*

Elizabeta Ribarić holds a master's degree from the Faculty of Economics and Business at the University of Rijeka, Croatia. Her research interest covers the area of sustainable supply chains and modern technologies.

Adam Sadowski, PhD, is an associate professor in logistics at the Institute of Logistics and Informatics of the University of Lodz. He received his Ph.D. in economics at the University of Lodz, Poland. His research interests include reverse logistics, supply-chain management, supply-chain digitalization, military logistics, and simulation issues. His work has been published in such journals as *Electronic Commerce Research, Journal of Big Data, International Journal of Productivity and Performance Management*, and others.

Khuram Shahzad, PhD, is an assistant professor of Digital Innovation Management at the School of Technology and Innovations/InnoLab Research Platform of the University of Vaasa in Finland. His research interests focus on digital technologies and innovations, open innovation, R&D and innovation ecosystems, blockchain, digital transformation, and supply-chain management. His research work has been published in several journals of international repute.

Sebastian Stolarczyk holds a bachelor's degree in logistics from Warsaw University of Life Science. He started his adventure in the logistics industry at secondary school, from which he graduated with the title of Logistics Technician, the EPICOR ISCALA certificate in company logistics management, and the international ELA certificate. He studies Finance and Accounting at the Warsaw University of Life Sciences. He is a cofounder of the start-up GreenTransit, which created a platform for the digitalization of transportation documents. His responsibilities include seeking new ways of development, finances, and current activities.

Josu Takala has experience in the industry from ABB 1979–1992 and academia. He graduated from Tampere University of Technology M.Sc in 1980 and PhD in 1988, PhD HC 2009 from Technical University of Košice, Slovakia, and Universiti Tun Hussein Onn Malaysia 2015. He has been a Professor in Industrial Management at the University of Vaasa, Finland since 1988, and visiting/adjunct professor in various universities in Finland and abroad. His field is decision-making on operative sustainable competitive strategies. He has 650 scientific articles, Co- and Special-Issue Editorships, he has been invited as Speaker and Chairman in conferences, he participates in activities within university-society relationships and programs, and he possesses ownerships in about ten startups.

Andrej Udovč is a full professor of Agricultural Economics and Rural Development at the Biotechnical Faculty, University of Ljubljana. He is the head of the Chair for Agrometheorology, Agricultural land management, Agricultural Economics, and Rural Development. His main research interests pertain to farm management, the coexistence of rural economies and high-value natural landscapes, and common-pool resources management.

Petra A. Zaninović, PhD, is a researcher and teaching assistant, Faculty of Economics and Business, at the University of Rijeka, Croatia. She has participated in several international scientific conferences and published articles in scientific journals in the field of economics and business. Her research interests are in the area of trade logistics and supply chains.

INNOVATIVE AND SUSTAINABLE LOGISTICS

Theoretical Foundations

I

Chapter 1

Innovative and Sustainable Logistics: Main Direction of Development

Khuram Shahzad, Oskar Juszczyk, and Josu Takala

School of Technology and Innovations, University of Vaasa, Finland

Contents

1.1 Introduction

The current image of the supply chains appears to be increasingly complex, where multinational business entities compete to gain their share of the market

DOI: 10.4324/9781003304364-2

(Saberi et al., 2019). The globalization of supply chains which has resulted in a "flat world" (Friedman, 2005) makes this network even more intricate because of divergent regulations as well as various customer behavioral patterns. This complexity causes difficulties in information and risk management, where fraudulent practices cause challenges in terms of trust. Therefore, there is a necessity of increasing the excellence of information distribution and transparency (Ivanov et al., 2018).

Such trackability of the whole production and logistics process is becoming a requirement for the growing share of environmentally conscious stakeholders and end customers. It can make a radical change in the competitive advantage of a given company, especially in the sectors of agriculture (Kamilaris et al., 2019; Kamble et al., 2020), medicine (Rotunno et al., 2014; Radanović & Likić, 2018), energy (Andoni et al., 2019; Teufel et al., 2019), or luxurious goods (Maurer, 2017).

It is challenging to achieve it in the modern supply chains, which are formed in centralized management-information systems, such as enterprise resource planning (ERP), that are imperfect in terms of reliability. Such centralized information systems rely heavily on trust given to a single authority for processing and storing valuable and sensitive data, which makes them susceptible to malfunction, cyberattacks, or even corruption (Dong et al., 2017).

Over the past few years, there has been an increasing pressure from all sectors of society on supply chains to follow the idea of sustainability. Therefore, sustainable supply chains should generate added value according to the triple-bottom-line approach that proposes harmony in consideration of economic, societal, and environmental aspects (Elkington, 1998, 2004). Following that concept, organizations perceive sustainability as a fundamental principle of smart management (Savitz & Weber, 2006), and following the triple-bottom-line strategy can not only benefit the natural environment and society but can provide long-lasting economic prosperity and a competitive advantage for the company (Carter & Rogers, 2008). However, in order to successfully achieve sustainable practices, there is a need to confirm and verify the processes, activities, and end-products that follow the specific sustainability criteria and proofs for such actions. Moreover, the triple bottom line comes with its supporting facets of sustainability that can serve companies to improve the quality of their risk management, transparency, strategy, and culture (Gladwin et al., 1995; Hart, 1995).

Hence, there is a need for better information sharing within the supply chains, which are currently not fully capable of supporting data required for the timely provenance of goods and services in a safe manner that is comprehensible and solid enough to ensure trust. Consequently, the future-oriented supply chains should improve their transparency, reliability, resilience, and operations integrity (Sivula et al., 2021). The solution that may provide such features could be blockchain technology. The application of such an innovative technology makes these improvement targets more logistically, economically, and technologically feasible (Abeyratne & Monfared, 2016). Blockchain, by being a distributed "trustless" database, is a disruptive technology that enhances global-scale transactions as well as operation decentralization amidst different supply chain actors and could make a critical—perhaps even revolutionary—impact on supply-chain management (Helo, 2020).

There have been already several applications of blockchain in different industries that have improved the transparency, integrity, and interoperability of the performed transactions. From a sustainable supply-chain-management point of view, the example of Provenance can be mentioned, which is a provider of blockchain technology in the seafood sector. In this specific supply chain, the visibility and legitimacy of sustainable standards are decisive (Steiner & Baker, 2015). The use cases show the potential applications of blockchain have been deliberated broadly in the professional, academic, and popular literature in terms of the topics related to environmental, economic, or societal performance dimensions.

Even though there is a growing number of use cases over the recent years, blockchain technology, as it is highly disruptive in nature, faces many challenges for its widespread implementation within global supply chain systems. While being in its infancy stage of development, blockchain is restricted by multifarious barriers of, for example, behavioral, structural, technological, or regulatory aspects. These numerous bottlenecks as well as measures to overcome them will be discussed more thoroughly later in this chapter.

The main goal of this chapter is to estimate the potential of blockchain technology applicability in the sustainable supply-chain-management theory and practice. In order to do so, we will introduce the main features of blockchain technology first. Then, we will discuss the possible benefits coming from its implementation by supply chains and how it could revolutionize the current outlook of supply-chain management, based on current literature. Further on, we provide a conceptual framework for blockchain-based sustainable supply chains. We will focus specifically on sustainable supply chains and how blockchains could positively impact sustainable practices. This will be followed by the presentation of various barriers to the adoption of blockchain in sustainable supply chains together with the proposition of several actions to tackle these challenges. Lastly, we will conclude the Chapter with its theoretical and practical implications as well as the direction toward future development.

1.2 Literature Review

To provide the conceptual background for this chapter, the review of the existing literature is presented to shed light on the concepts of sustainability in logistics and supply-chain management. Then, basic features of blockchain technology and its potential impact on the supply chains and more, specifically on the concept of sustainable supply-chain management, are discussed.

1.2.1 Sustainability in Logistics and Supply Chains

The most commonly used definition of sustainability is developed by Brundtland Commission: "Development that meets the needs of the present without compromising the ability of future generations to meet their needs." This broad concept includes recognizing the environmental impact of business activities all over the world (Erlich & Erlich, 1991), providing global food security (Lal et al., 2002), fulfilling basic human needs (Savitz & Weber, 2006), or enhancing the preservation of nonrenewable resources (Whiteman & Cooper, 2000). Such a macroeconomic perspective causes challenges in its understanding and application by organizations, where their specific situation affects the determination of present and future needs. Moreover, it provides limited guidance for the firms on how to decide which technological and organizational resources are necessary to meet those needs, and to efficiently balance cooperation liabilities with stakeholders within and outside of the company—including society and the natural environment (Hart, 1995; Starik & Rands, 1995). Furthermore, it is troublesome for the companies to establish their distinctive roles in such a broad concept (Stead & Stead, 1996). Therefore, a more microeconomic approach was introduced in the operations management and engineering literature by mainly considering the environmental dimension of sustainability, with limited apprehension of societal and economic aspects (Shrivastava, 1995; Starik & Rands, 1995). Still, this viewpoint continues a long-term perspective of sustainability, as Shrivastava (1995) depicts sustainability as providing the "potential for reducing long-term risks associated with resource depletion, fluctuations in energy costs, product liabilities, as well as pollution and waste management." Interestingly, the engineering literature proves more inclusive, and has directly considered all three dimensions of sustainability, claiming that organizational sustainability is "a wise balance among economic development, environmental stewardship, and social equity," (Sikdar, 2003) which includes "equal weightings for economic stability, ecological compatibility and social equilibrium" (Góncz, 2007).

In the context of supply-chain management from the logistics perspective, authors have scrutinized particular societal and environmental issues, such as environmental-logistics strategies, environmental purchasing, improvement of fuel efficiency, limiting greenhouse gas (GHG) emissions in transport, the safety of various means of transportation, etc. More lately, Carter and Jennings (2002) have provided a conceptual framework for integrating environmental and social issues within a theory of Logistics Social Responsibility (LSR), which relates to the issues discussed previously, such as natural environment, human rights, safety, etc., to the logistics management field. They follow their research by including purchasing impact of LSR, which they call Purchasing Social Responsibility (PSR). According to their definition, PSR is a second-tier concept composed of first-tier dimensions discussed earlier, which are: Environment, safety, diversity, philanthropy, and human rights (Carter & Jennings, 2004). Although there are numerous definitions of sustainable logistics, the foundations have always focused mainly on environmental and/or social aspects, leaving the economic dimension unconsidered.

Having that in mind, the triple-bottom-line concept emerged including three components of environmental, societal, and economic value creation, where each of them is considered simultaneously from the microeconomic perspective (Elkington, 1998, 2004). This seminal theory has shed new light on the theory of sustainability and is still present in the literature as a foundation for future concepts.

Next, we are going to discuss the notion of supply-chain management, which was described by Mentzer et al. (2002) as "the systemic, strategic coordination of the traditional business functions and the tactics across these business functions within a particular company and across businesses with the supply chains, for the purposes of improving the long-term performance of the individual companies and the supply chain as a whole," whereas Lambert (2006) perceives it as "the integration of key business processes from end-user through original suppliers that provides products, services, and information that add value for customers and other stakeholders." Basing on these classifications and by including the elements of sustainability discussed above,

Carter and Rogers (2008) define sustainable supply-chain management (SSCM) as "the strategic, transparent integration and achievement of an organization's social, environmental, and economic goals in the systemic coordination of key inter-organizational business processes for improving the long-term economic performance of the individual company and its supply chains." This definition also strictly relates to the triple-bottom-line concept and the previously mentioned supporting features of sustainability—risk management, transparency, strategy, and culture.

1.2.2 Blockchain Technology

Blockchain (or distributed ledger technology—DLT) is a technology that ensures digital information distribution in a shared database that contains a continuously expanding log of transactions and their chronological order. In other words, it is a ledger that may contain digital transactions, data records, and executables that are shared among blockchain participating agents (Nakamoto, 2008; Andoni, 2019). Blockchain technology is distinct from other previously known information systems by its four main features: Non-localization (decentralization), security, auditability, and smart execution (Teufel et al., 2019). It is a highly innovative technology that is the result of a decade's efforts from "an elite group of computer scientists, cryptographers, and mathematicians" (Tucker, 2019).

The basic process within blockchains is structured as follows. First, the agent creates a new transaction to be included in the blockchain. This freshly created transaction is shared with the network for verification and auditing. When the transaction is approved by the majority of nodes based on predetermined and multilaterally established rules, this activity can be transferred to the chain as a new block. A record of that transaction is stored in several distributed nodes to ensure security. In the meantime, the smart contract, as a crucial component of blockchain, facilitates trustworthy transactions to be conducted without third parties' involvement (Cong & He, 2019; Saberi et al., 2019).

To show the substantial change in current information systems, a comparison with the Internet could help the readers to realize the potential impact of blockchain technology on existing structures. Principally, the Internet (as opposed to blockchain), was designed to transfer information (not value) as well as to process and relocate copies of things (not original information). Therefore, in blockchains, value is generated through transactions recorded in a distributed ledger which is secured by arranging a verifiable, time-stamped record of transactions, which results in secure and auditable information

(Arora & Arora, 2018). These digital transactions go through a verification process that is agreed upon by the network consensus rules. When the new record passes this whole process, it is verified and included in the blockchain, and then multiple copies are generated in a distributed way to form a trustworthy chain.

One of the most essential features of blockchain is decentralization, which significantly increases information validity. Adding, updating, or removing information in the centralized information systems is not only inefficient and costly, but such systems are more vulnerable to hacking, corruption, or critical errors (Casino, 2019). Blockchain, by providing decentralized information sharing systems, significantly improves trust of the performed transactions, as there is no longer a need to estimate the credibility of the middlemen (who are removed) or of any parts of transactions in that network, and this information is easily accessible and verified. This results in another substantial benefit coming from blockchain utilization, which is the transparency of information whilst protecting the anonymity of participants, e.g., through cryptographic systems (Wang et al., 2019). Moreover, this structure allows limiting any human or behavioral misconduct such as dishonesty or sluggishness, ensuring the integrity of the system.

Determined by a specific technology application, blockchain construction can be contrasting when forming public (permissionless) or private (permissioned) information systems and ledgers. Both public and private blockchain networks are decentralized and distributed between their users to track all peer-to-peer transactions without the intermediary customarily trusted to authorize them (Yang et al., 2020). However, in private or closed blockchains, the partners know each other and there is no anonymity, which creates a need to introduce certifiers who are responsible for certifying network participants and maintaining these private networks. In public or open blockchains, cryptographic methods are applied to ensure trust among many anonymous users to allow them to access the network and perform operations inside of it. To continue this comparison, let us discuss a few key differentiating aspects. Private blockchains have higher transaction processing rates with fewer authorized participants. Therefore, a shorter time is needed to achieve the network consensus and more transactions can be processed within a second. By contrast, public blockchains have a significantly limited transaction processing rate. The consensus mechanisms such as Bitcoin's Proof-of-Work (PoW) in public blockchains require the entire network to reach a consensus on the state of transactions. Moreover, public blockchains' information privacy is more prone to risk due to their inherent nature. Alternatively, private blockchains have stronger data security foundations where any modification can be made basically when all nodes agree that the data can be transformed by the consensus mechanism (Yang et al., 2020).

In the meantime, the innovative transactional applications that enhance trust, transparency, and auditability are possible through blockchain applications, and these applications are ruled by smart contracts. Smart contracts are software solutions for storing principles and regulations during the negotiation of terms and actions between participants. It serves to automatically verify if preestablished rules and conditions have been fulfilled, and then executes transactions. Smart contracts could mitigate informational asymmetry and expand welfare and consumer surplus through enhanced access and competition, yet distributing information during consensus generation might encourage larger complicity (Cong & He, 2019).

Blockchain has gained popularity as a trading platform for Bitcoin, which is a digital cryptocurrency (Nakamoto, 2008). However, it has been spread across different industries as a tool for improvement in computing and information-flow aspects, also with numerous implications for innovative supply chains and logistics (Abeyratne & Monfared, 2016; Maurer, 2017; Cole et al., 2019, Pournader et al., 2020). Therefore, we will discuss the applications of blockchain in supply chains and possible multidimensional benefits coming from blockchain technology implementation.

1.3 Conceptual Framework

In this section, we will present a conceptual foundation for the chapter. Based on the literature review, we provide insight into blockchain-based sustainable supply chains. The whole process of building the framework is depicted in Figure 1.1.

In order to perform deductive reasoning, we will start with the applications of blockchain technology in supply chains. Next, we will apply blockchain technology into the context of sustainability, which will strongly support and directly lead us to the central concept of sustainable supply-chain management implementing blockchain. Because of its automation and decentralization, we will discuss the idea of blockchain as a governance mechanism as well.

Lastly, as it is an emerging technology in its early stages of development and practical application, we will examine the main barriers and challenges

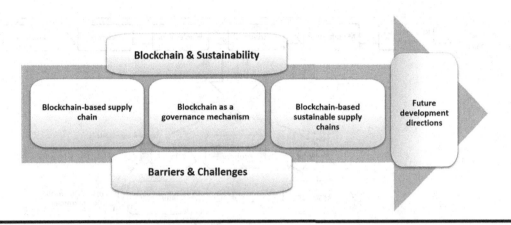

Figure 1.1   A Conceptual Framework for Blockchain-Based Sustainable Supply Chains.
Source: Own elaboration.

to a widespread blockchain implementation in supply chains. This whole process will help us to critically review the pros and cons of deploying blockchain in sustainable supply chains as well as limitations in the recent literature which will allow us to propose future directions for research and further development of that concept in theory and practice.

1.3.1 Blockchain-Based Supply Chains

Blockchain, as a highly innovative technology, can provide new solutions for the structure, operations, and management of supply chains. Its capability of ensuring dependability, traceability, and validity of information, as well as connection with smart contracts creating a trustless environment for transactions could result in major alterations in the current image and understanding of modern and future supply chains. This possibly revolutionary impact can be seen in Figure 1.2.

Dissimilar to certain public blockchain applications like Bitcoin or Ethereum, blockchain-based supply chains might require a closed, private, permissioned blockchain with multiple participants. However, the possibility of open, public, permissionless blockchains may still be possible and thus, the determination of privacy level will be one of the key initial decisions (Saberi, 2019).

Primarily, new actors' groups might appear to support blockchain integration into supply chains. According to Abeyratne and Monfared (2016), there would be a need to include:

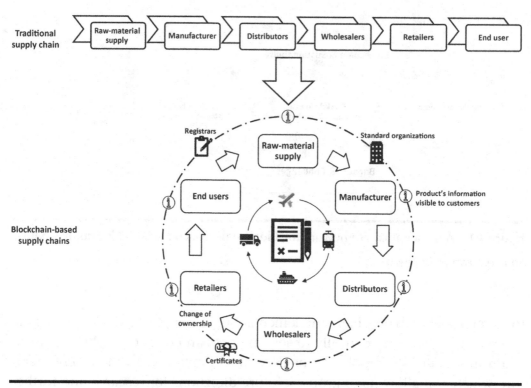

Figure 1.2 Supply Chain Transformation.

Source: Adapted from Saberi et al., 2019.

1) *registrars,* who form unique identities to network participants,
2) *standards organizations,* which develop standards frameworks, policies, and technological criteria,
3) *certifiers,* who give certifications to supply chain network participants, and
4) *actors,* containing producers, retailers, or end-customers, that need to be certified by an authorized auditor or certifier to ensure the system's trust.

Moreover, the influence of blockchain on supply-chain material and product flows can be observed as well. Each product could have a digital blockchain existence so that all interested participants would have direct access to product details. For security measures, only authorized users of blockchain would have that access through the digital key. The information about the materials or products could be of a different nature, such as their ownership and localization status, type, origin, or quality. Each product would have a digital information tag that connects the physical compound with its virtual identity in blockchain (Pournader et al., 2020).

Especially important in the context of ownership, access to the trading platforms granted to certified actors may be an important rule, whereas getting that access might require smart contract agreements and consensus mechanisms. Before the ownership is changed (by a sale or transfer), both sides would sign a digital contract or meet the standards of the smart contract to validate the transaction. After performing this exchange, its details are updating the blockchain register. Blockchain provides the automatic update of transactional data once the transaction is performed, which leads us to another important feature of blockchain—cost- and time-efficient automation of processes within supply chains (Abeyratne & Monfared, 2016).

As already mentioned, blockchain can provide detailed information on key product characteristics, such as the nature (what it is), the quality (how good it is), the quantity (how many units are available), the location (where it is) and the ownership (who owns it at any time). In that context, blockchain removes the need for a trusted central organization in these processes and provides the access to direct, verifiable, and constantly updated information about the product across its life cycle.

Blockchain, by providing reliability and transparency, facilitates material and information flow across the supply chain, with distributed and automated governance exigencies. This may cause an essential alteration from an industrial, product-oriented economy to an information and customization-centered economy. It is claimed that products will be more dependent on knowledge and information sharing rather than on components' features (Pazaitis et al., 2017). This can also result in increased customers' trust, as they could verify all the necessary information about the given product.

Smart contracts, being a set of pre-agreed rules, facilitates information flow between the participants of a blockchain-based supply chain. A smart contract can manage actors' certification, by providing precise and up-to-date information on access statutes, requirements, and limitations for a particular participant. The current state of rules cannot be changed without consensus mechanisms. Smart contracts can be useful in procurement as well, because of their ability to legally update the automated record of the transactions between trading partners. Therefore, smart contracts have a huge potential to provide substantial business process improvements in supply chains (Saberi, 2019).

To conclude this section, blockchains could bring many benefits to the supply-chain management, by impacting process and product management as well as financial transactions between supply-chain participants. A main possible utility of blockchain in supply chains is the removal of the middlemen from the transaction processes, and providing new trading possibilities which would boost the efficiency of trading processes between business partners and allow cost reduction of the end product, which could result in substantial savings (Fanning & Centers, 2016; Kamilaris, 2019). Lastly, the automation of financial transactions through smart contracts would facilitate their security, interoperability, and integrity as preestablished financial management mechanisms would allocate the funds to specific projects and departments in a well-timed and cost-effective manner, through their ability to mix currencies and resources in the optimized way (Tapscott & Tapscott, 2017).

1.3.2 Blockchain and Sustainability

As part of increasing environmental awareness in general on a global scale, organizations are heading towards sustainability which, besides environmental goals such as pollution reduction, also involves care for economic and social sectors as part of an overall strategy to improve organizational operations and their performance in the supply chain. Thus, sustainable supply-chain management offers several benefits to all participants by adopting more efficient production and transportation means, and reducing delays and costs. However, achieving sustainability has been limited due to inherent inefficiencies in traditionally oriented processing involving data and material flows such as inaccurate data, material waste, and the inability to meet requirements involving supply and demand in terms of quality, quantity, and timing, in particular for those of end-customers. This has resulted in the centralized nature of supply chains, with a lack of transparency and traceability across organizations. Therefore, as a technological solution, blockchain can be leveraged to deliver benefits, for example, tracking the origin of raw materials, production locations, product carriers, storage, and retailers which can be done using IoT combined solutions (Juszczyk & Shahzad, 2022). It allows to hold employees and ultimately businesses with their supply chains accountable by providing visibility into its tamper-resistant ledger. Such solutions enable decentralized systems, peer-to-peer trading of natural resources and permits, supply-chain monitoring and origin tracking, new financing models such as democratizing investment, and realization of nonfinancial value such as natural capital (Dorri et al., 2017; Tian, 2017).

Blockchain enables efficient tracking and transparency of defective and substandard goods (Saberi et al., 2019). It also helps to verify the provenance of a product and related sustainability practices, that is, if there are any fraudulent and unethical labor practices involved (Nyman, 2019). Such possibility of efficient tracking also helps to track the sustainability of supply chains, for example by calculating the carbon footprints of the products (Saberi et al., 2019). The verifiable and transparent management of resources enables an increase in the environmental sustainability of the supply chain. This could be maintained and even increased by using a tokenized ecosystem where resources, materials, and shipments are linked to tokens that in turn are verifiable and traceable. When a supply chain's practices are ideal from an environmental standpoint and verified through the blockchain, the organization would be rewarded with tokens. This ecosystem could draw more organizations into the ecosystem which would turn their supply chains more environmentally sustainable.

Blockchain can promote circular economy practices which include reducing materials and waste, reusing products, and recycling. The traceability and transparency features mean that operating costs decrease, and so can waste decrease. Blockchain can be used to incentivize new behaviors by verifying social sustainability claims, tokenizing sustainable purchases, and creating new systems for pricing and trading. Each step and transaction of the supply chain can be traced and its sustainability can be evaluated. While Köhler and Pizzol (2020) stated that there is no strong evidence as such that blockchain would increase sustainability, if we think about the main advantages of blockchain, i.e., transparency, traceability, authenticity, and trust, it can support a sustainable supply chain in various ways (Saberi et al., 2019). For example, having better information available about product freshness can help reduce food waste. Another example is how blockchain can enable certifications, including sustainability certifications, to be easily issued and tracked in a trustworthy way. In that sense, it can also help tackle human rights issues. Nevertheless, the design of the blockchain solution has a great influence on achieving specific sustainability objectives; it enables more efficient tracking of social and environmental conditions of supply chains (Saberi et al., 2019; Köhler & Pizzol, 2020).

Blockchain helps organizations in ensuring an environmentally green and sustainable supply chain. It is often difficult to verify that products are produced in an environmentally friendly way. If there is proof available that the products are manufactured with the use of renewable energy and sustainable material sources, consumers are more willing to buy the products. For example, in the furniture industry, Ikea has a table in their catalog claiming that it is made from a sustainable woodcut in Indonesia. Ikea must have an efficient tracking system to ensure that the product is indeed made from a specific material. It is a difficult process but can be accomplished with the use of blockchain technology and the origins of the product can be tracked through the whole supply chain (Saberi et al., 2019). Another aspect that blockchain can help to achieve is social sustainability. Saberi et al. (2019) stated that the food and beverage industries are just a few examples that face a lot of pressure from consumers related to sustainability nowadays. Blockchain can help organizations to ensure that only suppliers that provide proof of sustainable practices are allowed, which can be validated as product, ingredient information, and certificates need to be recorded in the blockchain. Varriale et al. (2021) stated that blockchain can also help in preventing the violation of human rights. This is necessary, especially in luxury products such as diamonds where corruption and illegal practices are common. The transparency offered by blockchain can help in achieving better sustainability, and control suppliers to avoid human rights violations, child labor, inhuman working conditions, and corruption.

1.3.3 Blockchain as a Governance Mechanism

Unlike traditional organizational governance where rules and conditions are enforced through economic governance, i.e., contractual governance or through sociological governance, i.e., relational governance (Shahzad et al., 2018), blockchain functions as an autonomous system of formal rules—a self-automated governance mechanism, relying on a set of protocols and code-based rules that are inevitably applied by the underlying blockchain-based network (Lumineau et al., 2021). Since blockchain does not directly depend on the enforceability of external legal obligations, smart contracts are placed in a blockchain-based network that facilitates the enforcement of rules by their embedded codes and algorithms (Catalini & Boslego, 2019). Blockchain also negates the concept of dependence, expectations of partner's behavior, and/or judgment based on their history, as it facilitates collaboration beyond these notions of expectations in behaviors and integrity is established without any direct contact between parties but through the system's immutability. In this vein, scholars such as Lumineau et al. (2021) comprehensively differentiated blockchain governance with contractual and relational governance based on defining features, regulatory principles, modes of enforcement, and form. They argued that, in blockchain, the identity of collaborating parties is less important and blockchain governance is distinct from both contractual and relational governance which facilitates hindering opportunism and boosting cooperation.

Thus, a holistic understanding of blockchain governance, its processes, implementation, and practices in the industrial ecosystem is required for further research in order to produce a clear understanding for both research and practice. It necessitates exploring and mapping the usage of blockchain technology by firms to automate transactions as well as revising and renewing their business model in order to achieve a successful innovation-management process. Blockchain can help in breaking silos among different actors in the supply chain and has the potential to make it an integrated ecosystem that is fully transparent to all the players involved.

1.3.4 Challenges and Barriers to Adopting Blockchain in the Supply Chain

Kshetri (2021) mentioned that blockchain has several challenges on its way before entering mass adoption. One major issue is the lack of standards, regulations, and laws. Global supply chains operate in an environment where different countries have different regulations and standards on how to operate, and most of the processes are managed by human beings in an old-fashioned way with lots of documents. Data in the blockchain needs to follow different regulatory requirements, and it is not yet clear what can be recorded in the blockchain and how the data needs to be managed in a secure way that is aligned with the requirements. Kshetri (2021) further identified common barriers to blockchain adoption including lack of institutional capacities, low degree of digitization, lack of technological expertise and absorptive capacity, and rank effect and barriers faced by small companies. The lack of institutional capacities relates to a lack of consistent societal, political, and economic operational context involving environments with diverse laws, regulations, and institutions where supply chains operate across the globe. Also, in developing countries, for instance, person-dependent patron-client relationships, which are often informal, reach from the state structures to local levels and determine which path will be taken in practice with respect to official laws and regulations. A low degree of digitization is another issue typical in developing countries as high-degree computerization is a core requirement for blockchain and the digitalization of supply chains overall. This means a lack of digital devices as well as Internet access, which together inhibit the introduction of the solutions.

Furthermore, since blockchain is in its infancy and developing in several industrial sectors, the available use cases are limited and industry-specific, and it becomes difficult to generalize its value for everyone by only looking at some pilot projects. In such a scenario, several concerns regarding its scalability and operability in the context of the supply chain arise, as there exist chain limitations with the ever-increasing number of transactions and a huge amount of information in blocks. A lack of technological maturity also hinders the blockchain to run efficiently as this has to do with the scalability aspect of the technology (Hackius & Petersen, 2017). The concern of the cost of developing, maintaining, and implementing blockchain in the supply chain is another factor that triggers an uncertainty as it is not just a question of developing in-house but acquiring or outsourcing from external sources to fit with the requirements of a firm's supply chain. Queiroz and Wamba (2019) highlighted that replacing a mature system to implement blockchain can pose several infrastructural challenges along with the cost of such changes. The ability to connect blockchains with the existing infrastructure of the companies, in order to function effectively, creates uncertainty as the technological usability remains low. Thus, it becomes unclear whether the technology will develop in the future and if so, how it will happen (Hackius & Petersen, 2020). Similarly, for small companies, it might be challenging to implement blockchain as it requires infrastructural changes and investments (Queiroz & Wamba, 2019), which small companies usually lack.

As traditional supply-chain operations face several challenges such as damage, erroneous data entry, order mismanagement, etc., the effective implementation and smooth functioning of blockchain in supply-chain systems requires the integration of various supply-chain players. As blockchain requires every transaction to be processed and validated through each node, weak infrastructure and political and institutional arrangements in developing countries restrict flawless implementation (Kshetri, 2021; Min, 2019). Although the transparency, visibility, and immutability of blockchain are great advantages in supply chains, data duplication in certain nodes or individual tampering might hurt the whole chain (Queiroz & Wamba, 2019). Furthermore, the mass adoption of blockchain technology is considered to be a challenge at the moment as the technology itself is not ready yet. Since the size of supply networks has grown massively, the capacity of blockchains to deal with a huge number of transactions seems to prevent scaling up. As several alternative solutions exist and excel in dealing with such large sets of data in the supply chain, the suitability of blockchain with legacy systems can pose several challenges for firms. For example, global supply chains are complex; one cannot just employ blockchain in operations to solve a certain supply-chain problem as it requires the whole supply-chain parties to integrate and comply with diverse laws, regulations, and institutions (Hackius et al., 2020; Kshetri, 2021). This might also slow down the development of blockchain in supply-chain operations because of the large number of participants involved. Also, each participant would want to have their own ways of working applied and many participants will have to change their existing way of working.

Regulating disruptive technologies is one of the main barriers when organizations want to implement blockchain. For blockchain, there are only a few standards placed while requiring more standards to execute the system efficiently and securely. Also, the legislation is changing at a rapid pace and questions remain as to whether the solutions will comply with the future laws (Hackius et al., 2020). In addition to that, the lack of support from governments in the form of regulatory frameworks and policies promoting standards restricts the adoption of the blockchain (Choi et al., 2020). The legality of smart contracts is still unclear because of the nature of encrypted code that courts may not be able to recognize. Even cryptocurrencies are still being monitored and policies are in the process of being established.

Another barrier that is restricting the adoption of blockchain into supply chains is the lack of understanding of the technology that stakeholders have (Jabbar et al., 2021). Currently, there is a low level of understanding that exists among both industry leaders and consumers. Blockchain technology contains complex elements that are sometimes difficult to understand, and several people stamp it as illegitimate due to the recent frauds and scandals reported. Furthermore, lagging to adopt technology is not an unknown phenomenon and is often studied by scholars. Costs, complexity, and skills are existing barriers to technology adoption. Walsh et al. (2021) studied the resistance to a blockchain system by assessing managers' resistance to the change. In short, perceived benefits decrease resistance, however there are challenges in understanding the full benefits because of a lack of knowledge about blockchain technology (Walsh et al., 2021).

Kshetri (2021) states that another issue is that there is a relatively low level of digitalization in the supply chain and the technical requirements to start using blockchain. To adopt blockchain, a high degree of computerization is required from the participants and many of them are in developing countries. In such countries, there are challenges related to digitalization, and simply not enough resources to implement blockchain in their operations. In addition to this, the overall level of skills regarding blockchain is still rather low. As of 2018, there were approximately 20 million software developers in the world, but only 0.1% of them knew about blockchain codes. It requires a lot to implement a high-quality blockchain ecosystem that includes a wide network consisting of different countries and operations. Similarly, Chang et al.

(2020) state that one of the main barriers to the larger adoption of blockchain in supply-chain management is that most organizations are too suspicious of the technology. Blockchain is easily considered a synonym for cryptocurrencies, and organizations are suspicious about the safety of the system and the actual benefits that can be gained when implementing it in real-life projects. For now, not many users see the benefits clearly as there are too many threats such as fear of unintentional data compromise because the regulations and standards are not implemented yet.

One notable challenge related to blockchain adoption is also that it is unclear whether it is needed and how beneficial it is compared to the current centralized data-sharing and management models. It costs a lot to set up a blockchain network as it needs to be integrated with the existing systems. In addition to the costs, and complexity, it remains unclear whether it is scalable enough to handle all the transactions and whether the performance and level of costs are sufficient to replace the old systems.

1.3.5 Overcoming the Challenges

Overcoming these challenges boils down to recognizing the limitations of implementing blockchain solutions, particularly on a large scale. Blockchain could be leveraged in improving operational efficiency by optimizing existing business processes to recognize its benefits, if any. As blockchain technology is young and future research is required to develop new traceability applications, small-scale experimentations can be performed to quantitatively stress the need for blockchains in the supply chain (Sunny et al., 2020). Moreover, as experiments are conducted and relevant experience is acquired, technological enablers become more applicable and available. With better capabilities combined with lower prices as well as the establishment of a more comprehensive digital infrastructure across the globe, implementation of blockchain solutions on a wider scale can be achieved for the benefit of all. The issue of ensuring appropriate inputs into blockchain remains among the main concerns, which requires the establishment and application of comprehensive governance based on the decentralization principles for input validation in blockchain to minimize the incentives to act based on adverse motivations when participating in blockchain-based cooperation.

Moreover, there is still a lot of work to do with the features and operations of smart contracts, and those developments are expensive and troublesome. The programmed codes with bugs can cost a lot to organizations, so they must be precise, but also simple and cost-efficient. Regarding key management, in a smart contract every user has public and private keys, which are used for authentications; it can be challenging to store the private keys. Further, a smart contract platform to keep up with the growth of organizations must be scalable. However, current platforms are not capable and scalable enough and have different limitations, such as time intervals and block sizes required to generate new blocks (Omar et al., 2020). Similarly, these platforms are not equipped to prepare and handle unseen future events, such as natural disasters or any unexpected change of circumstances. This obstacle could be handled by combining the smart contract with artificial intelligence, big data, or machine learning, however, the combined technologies are not mature enough (Omar et al., 2020). People can resist when a new platform or technology is set to be implemented in an organizational setting. Similarly, Omar et al. (2020) argued that people are used to the old technologies and ways to work and are afraid of the risks, and do not want to try new possibilities. Also, the privacy of data plays a role, as each country has its own laws and legal requirements which make it difficult for smart contracts to be implemented effectively (Khan et al., 2021). Also, due to the fact that the supply chain involves various entities in different stages, having multiple decision makers complicates the management and therefore leads to information inequality. Lack of information sharing and traceability makes the process, collaboration among parties, sense, and response events more difficult to chart.

In order to ensure product safety and quality, there is a need for greater transparency throughout the entire supply chain. As the customers have more knowledge in different fields, they demand to know the provenance of the product before they commit to buying it. It is vital to build trust and strong relationships with the customers and all of the partners throughout the supply-chain process.

Data loss is one challenge that the implementation of smart contracts has, due to the fact that the systems are mainly heterogeneous and categorized under different administrative domains. One challenge is the governance-related issues, where it is important to know how governments should regulate such contracts and how such heterogeneous regulations will be emerged. For example, it is important to know how certain transactions will be taxed and how the privacy and anonymity of data will be addressed as it can be challenged. When a large number of transactions takes place simultaneously and a hacker gains unauthorized access to the blockchain, they can create false contracts that might be left unnoticed and accepted, which can lead to many types of losses, of which the financial losses are the most obvious (Rouhani & Deters, 2019).

1.4 Conclusions and Future Development Directions

In this opening chapter, we have gone straight to the future to suggest an innovative technology solution that may revolutionize the whole supply chain. In response to the global changes in the environment, society and business areas, it is imperative for all of the actors in the supply chain to follow the sustainable path of operations.

Therefore, in the literature review, we have introduced the concept of sustainability and linked its development all the way to sustainable supply-chain management. Next, we have shed some light on the principles and basic features of blockchain technology, as it is still an emerging technology with relatively low levels of common understanding by society.

This theoretical foundation has led us to present a conceptual framework for blockchain application in sustainable supply chains. We have achieved it by mixing the concepts of blockchain-based supply chains together with blockchain utilization in sustainability. The supporting element of our framework was blockchain as a governance mechanism, which can drastically change the current administration of supply chains. As blockchain is still in its infancy stage of development, we have identified major barriers to its widespread implementation within supply chains and proposed practical measures to overcome these numerous challenges. Therefore, this conceptual framework provides both theoretical and practical implications by analyzing extant seminal literature in the field of sustainable supply-chain management together with proposing future research directions. Practitioners from the logistics, blockchain technology, digitalization, and supply-chain areas can utilize this framework as a guide toward the successful implementation of blockchain in future-oriented sustainable supply chains.

As it is claimed that blockchain could revolutionize the current approach toward supply-chain management, future research should further investigate the impact of blockchain and its long-lasting benefits (Pournader et al., 2020). By providing disintermediation and supply-chain transparency, blockchain can support a trust-free environment for conducting business, which could dramatically change the interrelations between producers and end customers and cause the rethinking of the current trust-based theories in the supply chain (Saberi et al., 2019). As it is claimed that blockchain-based systems may require business model innovation, an interesting area of future research is the influence of blockchain's application on the current business models (Nowiński & Kozma, 2017; Shahzad, 2020). Moreover, as shown in the chapter, blockchain would provide new governance mechanisms, which will put the existent supply-chain governance structures into question. Furthermore, as the main feature of blockchain is to improve information sharing, a more advanced information processing theory would help to better understand technical nuances related to the blockchain-based supply chains.

Importantly, as we have discussed sustainability in supply chains, further research is recommended to analyze the blockchain-enabled sustainable supply chains from the environmental, economic, and societal aspects and to measure each performance accordingly (Kshetri, 2021).

Lastly, blockchains, through providing decentralization, transparency, and smart contracts, might bring a very open and dynamic approach to performance systems which would allow more operational relationships while decreasing the importance of strategic alliances. It will strongly stimulate the supply-chain risk management as well, by bringing efficiency improvements which would serve to reduce delays and overall risk levels across the supply chain (Fu & Zhu, 2019). Hence, such a possible significant influence of blockchain on current structures requires deeper investigation.

Acknowledgments

This research is a part of the BizPub research project funded by the foundation for Economic Education (Liikesivistysrahasto) under the grant number 200264.

References

Abeyratne, S. A., & Monfared, R. P. (2016). Blockchain ready manufacturing supply chain using distributed ledger. *International Journal of Research in Engineering and Technology*, 5(9), 1–10.

Andoni, M., Robu, V., Flynn, D., Abram, S., Geach, D., Jenkins, D., & Peacock, A. (2019). Blockchain technology in the energy sector: A systematic review of challenges and opportunities. *Renewable and Sustainable Energy Reviews*, 100, 143–174.

Arora, A., & Arora, M. (2018). Digital-information tracking framework using blockchain. *Journal of Supply Chain Management Systems*, 7(2), 1.

Carter, C. R., & Jennings, M. M. (2002). Logistics social responsibility: An integrative framework. *Journal of Business Logistics, 23*(1), 145–180.

Carter, C. R., & Jennings, M. M. (2004). The role of purchasing in the socially responsible management of the supply chain: A structural equation analysis. *Journal of Business Logistics, 25*(1), 145–186.

Carter, C. R., & Rogers D. S. (2008). A framework of sustainable supply chain management: Moving toward new theory. *International Journal of Physical Distribution & Logistics Management, 38*(5), 360–387.

Casino, F., Dasaklis, T. K., & Patsakis, C. (2019). A systematic literature review of blockchain-based applications: Current status, classification, and open issues. *Telematics and Informatics, 36*, 55–81.

Catalini, C., & Boslego, J. (2019). *Blockchain Technology and Organization Science: Decentralization Theatre or Novel Organizational Form?* Working Paper, Massachusetts Institute of Technology, Cambridge.

Chang, Y., Iakovou, E., & Shi, W. (2020). Blockchain in global supply chains and cross border trade: A critical synthesis of the state-of-the-art, challenges and opportunities. *International Journal of Production Research, 58*(7), 2082–2099.

Choi, T. M., Guo, S., & Luo, S. (2020). When blockchain meets social media: Will the result benefit social media analytics for supply chain operations management? *Transportation Research Part E: Logistics and Transportation Review, 135*, 101860.

Cole, R., Stevenson, M., & Aitken, J. (2019). Blockchain technology: Implications for operations and supply chain management. *Supply Chain Management: An International Journal, 24*(4), 469–483.

Cong, L. W., & He, Z. (2019). Blockchain disruption and smart contracts. *The Review of Financial Studies, 32*(5), 1754–1797.

Dong, F., Zhou, P., Liu, Z., Shen, D., Xu, Z., & Luo, J. (2017). Towards a fast and secure design for enterprise-oriented cloud storage systems. *Concurrency and Computation: Practice and Experience, 29*(19), 4177.

Dorri, A., Kanhere, S. S., Jurdak, R., & Gauravaram, P. (2017). *Blockchain for IoT Security and Privacy: The Case Study of a Smart Home.* 2017 IEEE International Conference on Pervasive Computing and Communications Workshops (PerCom Workshops) (pp. 618–623). IEEE. DOI: 10.1109/ PERCOMW.2017.7917634; https://www.ieee.org/about/index.html?utm_ source=dhtml_footer&utm_medium=hp&utm_campaign=learn-more

Elkington, J. (1998). *Cannibals with Forks: The Triple Bottom Line of the 21st Century.* Stoney Creek, CT: New Society Publishers.

Elkington, J. (2004). Enter the triple bottom line. In A. Henriques & J. Richardson (eds.), *The Triple Bottom Line: Does It All Add Up?* (pp. 1–16) London: Earthscan.

Erlich, P. R., & Erlich, A. H. (1991). *The Population Explosion.* New York, NY: Touchstone.

Fanning, K., & Centers, D. P. (2016). Blockchain and its coming impact on financial services. *Journal of Corporate Accounting & Finance, 27*(5), 53–57.

Friedman, T. L. (2005). *The World Is Flat.* New York, NY: Farrar, Strauss and Giroux.

Fu, Y., & Zhu, J. (2019). Big production enterprise supply chain endogenous risk management based on blockchain. *IEEE Access, 7*, 15310–15319.

Gladwin, T. N., Kennelly, J. J., & Krause, T. (1995). Shifting paradigms for sustainable development: Implications for management theory and research. *Academy of Management Review, 20*(4), 874–907.

Góncz, E., Skirke, U., Kleizen, H., & Barber, M. (2007). Increasing the rate of sustainable change: A call for a redefinition of the concept and the model for its implementation. *Journal of Cleaner Production, 15*(6), 525–537.

Hackius, N., & Petersen, M. (2017). *Blockchain in Logistics and Supply Chain: Trick or Treat? In Digitalization in Supply Chain Management and Logistics: Smart and Digital Solutions for an Industry 4.0 Environment.* Proceedings of the Hamburg International Conference of Logistics (HICL), Vol. 23 (pp. 3–18). Berlin: epubli GmbH.

Hackius, N., & Petersen, M. (2020). *Translating High Hopes into Tangible Benefits: How Incumbents in Supply Chain and Logistics Approach Blockchain.* IEEE Access, 8, 34993–35003.

Hart, S. L. (1995). A natural-resource-based view of the firm. *Academy of Management Review, 20*(4), 986–1014.

Helo, P., & Shamsuzzoha, A. (2020). Real-time supply chain: A blockchain architecture for project deliveries. *Robotics and Computer-Integrated Manufacturing, 63*, 101909.

Ivanov, D., Dolgui, A., & Sokolov, B. (2018). The impact of digital technology and industry 4.0 on the ripple effect and supply chain risk analytics. *International Journal of Production Research, 57*(3), 1–18.

Jabbar, S., Lloyd, H., Hammoudeh, M., Adebisi, B., & Raza, U. (2021). Blockchain-enabled supply chain: Analysis, challenges, and future directions. *Multimedia Systems, 27*(4), 787–806.

Juszczyk, O., & Shahzad, K. (2022). Blockchain Technology for Renewable Energy: Principles, Applications and Prospects. *Energies, 15*(13), 4603.

Kamble, S. S., Gunasekaran, A., & Sharma, R. (2020). Modeling the blockchain enabled traceability in agriculture supply chain. *International Journal of Information Management, 52*, 101967.

Kamilaris, A., Fonts, A., & Prenafeta-Boldú, F. X. (2019). The rise of blockchain technology in agriculture and food supply chains. *Trends in Food Science & Technology, 91*, 640–652.

Khan, S. N., Loukil, F., Ghedira-Guegan, C., Benkhelifa, E., & Bani-Hani, A. (2021). Blockchain smart contracts: Applications, challenges, and future trends. *Peer-to-Peer Networking and Applications*, 1–25.

Köhler, S., & Pizzol, M. (2020). Technology assessment of blockchain-based technologies in the food supply chain. *Journal of Cleaner Production, 269*, 122193.

Kshetri, N. (2021). Blockchain and sustainable supply chain management in developing countries. *International Journal of Information Management, 60*, 102376.

Lal, R., Hansen, D. O., & Uphoff, N. (2002), *Food Security and Environmental Quality in the Developing World.* Boca Raton, FL: CRC Press.

Lambert, D. M. (2006). *Supply Chain Management: Processes, Partnerships, Performance* (2nd ed.). Sarasota, FL: Supply Chain Management Institute.

Lumineau, F., Wang, W., & Schilke, O. (2021). Blockchain governance: A new way of organizing collaborations? *Organization Science, 32*(2), 500–521.

Maurer, B. (2017). *Blockchains Are a Diamond's Best Friend: Zelizer for the Bitcoinmoment.* In: F. F. W. Nina Bandelj & Viviana A. Zelizer (eds.), *Money Talks: Explaining How Money Really Works* (pp. 215–230). Princeton: Princeton University Press.

Mentzer, J. T., DeWitt, W., Keebler, J. S., Min, S., Nix, N. W., Smith, C. D., & Zacharia, Z. G. (2002). Defining supply chain management. *Journal of Business Logistics, 22*(2), 1–25.

Min, H. (2019). Blockchain technology for enhancing supply chain resilience. *Business Horizons, 62*(1), 35–45.

Nakamoto, S. (2008). *Bitcoin: A Peer-to-Peer Electronic Cash System.* Retrieved from: https://bitcoin.org/bitcoin.pdf Available [April 4, 2022].

Nowiński, W., & Kozma, M. (2017). How can blockchain technology disrupt the existing business models? *Entrepreneurial Business and Economics Review, 5*(3), 173–188.

Nyman, T. (2019). *Increased Transparency and Prevention of Unethical Actions in the Textile Industry's Supply Chain through Blockchain.* Aalto University. Retrieved from: https://aaltodoc.aalto.fi/handle/123456789/39341 Available [April 1, 2022].

Omar, I. A., Jayaraman, R., Salah, K., Simsekler, M. C. E., Yaqoob, I., & Ellahham, S. (2020). Ensuring protocol compliance and data transparency in clinical trials using Blockchain smart contracts. *BMC Medical Research Methodology, 20*(1), 1–17.

Pazaitis, A., De Filippi, P., & Kostakis, V. (2017). Blockchain and value systems in the sharing economy: The illustrative case of backfeed. *Technological Forecasting and Social Change, 125*, 105–115.

Pournader, M., Shi, Y., Seuring, S., & Koh, S. L. (2020). Blockchain applications in supply chains, transport and logistics: A systematic review of the literature. *International Journal of Production Research, 58*(7), 2063–2081.

Queiroz, M. M., & Wamba, S. F. (2019). Blockchain adoption challenges in supply chain: An empirical investigation of the main drivers in India and the USA. *International Journal of Information Management, 46*, 70–82.

Radanović, I., & Likić, R. (2018). Opportunities for use of blockchain technology in medicine. *Applied Health Economics and Health Policy, 16*(5), 583–590.

Rotunno, R., Cesarotti, V., Bellman, A. Introna, V., & Benedetti, M. (2014). Impact of track and trace integration on pharmaceutical production systems. *International Journal of Engineering Business Management, 6*(25). DOI: 10.5772/58934.

Rouhani, S., & Deters, R. (2019). Security, performance, and applications of smart contracts: A systematic survey. *IEEE Access, 7*, 50759–50779.

Saberi, S., Kouhizadeh, M., Sarkis, J., & Shen, L. (2019). Blockchain technology and its relationships to sustainable supply chain management. *International Journal of Production Research, 57*(7), 2117–2135.

Savitz, A. W., & Weber, K. (2006). *The Triple Bottom Line.* San Francisco, CA: Jossey-Bass.

Shahzad, K., Ali, T., Takala, J., Helo, P., & Zaefarian, G. (2018). The varying roles of governance mechanisms on ex-post transaction costs and relationship commitment in buyer-supplier relationships. *Industrial Marketing Management, 71*, 135–146.

Shahzad, K. (2020, July). Blockchain and organizational characteristics: towards business model innovation. In *International Conference on Applied Human Factors and Ergonomics* (pp. 80–86). Springer, Cham.

Shrivastava, P. (1995). The role of corporations in achieving ecological sustainability. *Academy of Management Review, 20*(4), 936–960.

Sikdar, S. K. (2003). Sustainable development and sustainability metrics. *AIChE Journal, 49*(8), 1928–1932.

Sivula, A., Shamsuzzoha, A., & Helo, P. (2021). Requirements for blockchain technology in supply chain management: An exploratory case study. *Operations and Supply Chain Management: An International Journal, 14*(1), 39–50.

Starik, M., & Rands, G. P. (1995). Weaving an integrated web: Multilevel and multisystem perspectives of ecologically sustainable organizations. *Academy of Management Review, 20*(4), 908–935.

Stead, E., & Stead, J. G. (1996). *Management for a Small Planet: Strategic Decision Making and the Environment* (2nd ed.). Thousand Oaks, CA: Sage.

Steiner, J., & Baker, J. (2015). *Blockchain: The Solution for Transparency in Product Supply Chains.* Retrieved from: www.provenance.org/whitepaper Available [February 10, 2022].

Sunny, J., Undralla, N., & Pillai, V. M. (2020). Supply chain transparency through blockchain-based traceability: An overview with demonstration. *Computers & Industrial Engineering, 150*, 106895.

Tapscott, A., & Tapscott, D. (2017). How blockchain is changing finance. *Harvard Business Review, 1*(9), 2–5.

Teufel, B., Sentic, A., & Barmet, M. (2019). Blockchain energy: Blockchain in future energy systems. *Journal of Electronic Science and Technology*, 100011.

Tian, F. (2017). *A Supply Chain Traceability System for Food Safety Based on HACCP, Blockchain & Internet of Things.* 2017 International Conference on Service Systems and Service Management (pp. 1–6). IEEE, June.

Tucker, C. (ed.) (2019). *Blockchain: The Insights You Need from Harvard Business Review*, HBR Insights Series. Brighton, MA: Harvard Business Press.

Varriale, V., Cammarano, A., Michelino, F., & Caputo, M. (2021). Sustainable supply chains with blockchain, IoT and RFID: A simulation on order management. *Sustainability, 13*(11), 6372.

Walsh, C., O'Reilly, P., Gleasure, R., McAvoy, J., & O'Leary, K. (2021). Understanding manager resistance to blockchain systems. *European Management Journal, 39*(3), 353–365.

Wang, L., Shen, X., Li, J., Shao, J., & Yang, Y. (2019). Cryptographic primitives in blockchains. *Journal of Network and Computer Applications, 127*, 43–58.

Whiteman, G., & Cooper, W. H. (2000). Ecological embeddedness. *Academy of Management Journal, 43*(6), pp. 1265–1282.

Yang, R., Wakefield, R., Lyu, S., Jayasuriya, S., Han, F., Yi, X., & Chen, S. (2020). Public and private blockchain in construction business process and information integration. *Automation in Construction, 118*, 103276.

Chapter 2

Modern Transportation Systems: The Field for Innovations Implementation

Aleksandra Górecka

Warsaw University of Life Sciences—SGGW, Poland

Contents

2.1 Introduction

For a successful modern economy, the issue of fundamental importance is the ability to guarantee the smooth and efficient transportation of people and goods. To achieve it, it is necessary to implement innovations in the transportation system. Those nowadays are focused on three main areas: Decreasing costs, increasing safety, time-saving, and environmental protection. Cutting-edge technologies, environmental regulations, and the emergence of autonomous vehicles mean that companies in the sector must constantly adapt. The aim of the chapter is to present the importance of innovations for modern transportation systems. The investigation included in this chapter is based on the example of the selected three

DOI: 10.4324/9781003304364-3

groups of innovations (current novelties, COVID-19 response innovations, and innovations for sustainability) implemented in the air business sector in the 21st century.

This chapter is organized as follows: Section 2.2 provides the theoretical background of innovations. In Section 2.3 I presented the importance of innovation in the transportation sector. Section 2.4 reviews selected innovations in the aviation business in the 21st century. Section 2.5 concludes and suggests the field for future investigation.

2.2 Innovations—the Theoretical Background

Modern economic science is on its way to a synthetic theory of innovation that presents innovative activity against the background of the overall process of socioeconomic development. In view of the above, the development is the result of the implementation of innovative solutions, which is forced by the need for companies to respond to the occurring phenomena and dynamically developing and complex processes (Barańska-Fischer & Blażlak, 2016). Innovation becomes a significant factor in the development, causing positive changes that determine the development of the company or economy (Ortega et al., 2021; Ryley et al., 2013; Załoga & Liberadzki, 2010). The first to introduce the concept of innovation to economic sciences was Schumpeter, who in his work from 1912, entitled "The Theory of Economic Development," presented a unique understanding for the turn of the 19th and 20th century: An understanding of the essence of entrepreneurship, associating it with a "new combination" of production factors. He emphasized that only when factors are combined for the first time can such an action be described as entrepreneurial. The repetition of this combination in the course of the normal running of an enterprise is just a mere routine (Schumpeter, 1949). Schumpeter's basic premise was also that innovation is only something new that has been applied for the first time since its invention. According to him, further uses of the invention were imitations and should not be called innovations (Musiał & Chrzanowski, 2018). The conditions for the existence of innovation in Schumpeter's view were as follows:

1) The introduction on the market of a good which is not yet known to the general consumer or which is of a new and better quality;
2) the use of improved production methods, which must be the result of new inventions, but may simply consist of improved ways of trading in goods;

3) the opening of a new market to the products of a particular industry operating in a particular country, whether or not such a market previously existed;

4) gaining new sources of supply for raw materials and semifinished goods— as in the previous case, it is not important whether a given source previously existed or not;

5) better organization of a given area of the economy.

Innovation was considered very important in the development of a company, and profit was to be the reward for innovation.

In the 1970s, Galbraith (1979) pointed out the definition of innovation as a change that is specific and novel and, most importantly, is carried out in a completely deliberate manner. He emphasized the planned nature of innovation in large companies and corporations. It is determined in advance what is to be invented and what improvements in production processes will have to be made in order to technologically improve them. These activities take place according to predetermined schedules and budgets since the vast majority of them require specialized knowledge, organization, and financial support. Innovation in manufacturing processes inevitably entails the substitution of labor for capital, leading to increased certainty of corporate revenue. Overall, it seems that the innovations that Galbraith would be willing to accept would be to create an increasing sense of security in doing business (Musiał & Chrzanowski, 2018).

Currently, innovation is considered an effective tool to achieve the set goals in an enterprise. Referring to this definition, stimulating innovation concerns not only systems but also the management and culture of the organization (Mirabito & Joe Layng, 2013). Nowadays, the positive aspect of implementing innovation into an enterprise is not only to make more profits, which will only come in after some time of innovation, but to survive and thrive in today's turbulent environment. This involves a great deal of effort on the part of companies, which must demonstrate a willingness to act and be creative (Urbancová, 2013).

The importance of innovation, as a major driver of economic growth, began to be recognized by the European Union (European Commission, 1995), as well as by the OECD in the late 20th century (OECD, 2009, 2011). The institutions defined and divided innovation into (OECD, 2005):

1) Product innovation—introducing a new product or improving an existing one with different materials, components, or specifications;

2) process innovations—reducing overhead costs thus improving quality of production or supply;

3) marketing innovations—introduction of visual, price, or promotional changes in a given product;

4) organizational innovations—improvement of the enterprise potential through reduction of various costs and increase of job satisfaction.

Product innovations are nowadays equated with technological solutions while processing, marketing, and organizational innovations are identified as non-technological innovations. These are less visible, and moreover, are generally less expensive than the others (Hyard, 2013).

Green Paper on Innovation (European Commission, 1995) was the basis for the formulation of European innovation policy in subsequent years. Innovation was considered to be synonymous with the adoption and use of novelties in the socioeconomic sphere, and it was pointed out that the new solutions resulting from innovation can meet the needs of both society as a whole and individuals.

2.3 Innovations in the Transport Sector

The introduction of unfamiliar goods, new methods of distribution, the development of new industries, and concern for the sourcing of raw materials are the foundations of the innovation stream. Numerous areas of business are experiencing transformations that deserve to be called progress. The movement of material goods and the provision of services are areas where progress is made visible through logistics. Here, the modern interpretation of transport services means eliminating the storage of goods to a minimum and reducing costs, mainly documentation.

The transport and infrastructure industry is under increasing pressure to innovate in the way it provides services to customers, with advances in technology acting as a catalyst. In the current century, the most significant determinant for the implementation of innovations in the transport sector is struggling for its sustainability. This is the reason for the fact that the transport sector is presented as a key one for general sustainable development due to the social and economic benefits it covers while minimizing its negative effects on society, the economy, and the environment. Sustainable transport is fundamentally defined through the impacts of the system on the economy, environment, and overall social well-being, and measured by system effectiveness, efficiency, and the impacts of the system on the natural environment (Baran & Górecka, 2019; OECD, 2004). From the technical perspective, the components for evaluating sustainability include the particular vehicles used for road, water, or air transport, the source of energy, and the infrastructure used to accommodate the transport (roads, railways, airways, waterways, canals, and terminals). Transport operations and logistics are also involved in the evaluation (Jeon & Amekudzi, 2005). From the perspective of economics, innovations arise through the mechanisms affecting the demand and supply (European Bank for reconstruction and development, 2019):

1) Reduction of the need for travel through substitution,
2) improvement of the efficiency and convenience of travel by creating new modes,
3) improvement of route planning, more efficient vehicles, in-vehicle services, and so on,
4) improvement of the efficiency of infrastructure construction, operation, and management,
5) improvement of the efficiency of transport operators through more competition, new services, and new market structures,
6) externalities such as reduced emissions, productivity gains, and better information for public planning.

2.4 Aviation—Range of Possibilities for Innovations

The aviation sector is said to be the driving force of global technology development and innovations. Robotics, artificial intelligence, machine learning, and biometrics represent only a few examples of the 21st-century technologies implemented to improve the efficiency of air transport. Original solutions in the aviation industry are applied by airlines, airports, and aircraft producers. At the airports, innovations influence operations such as passengers, baggage, and cargo handling, and lead to achieving their maximum safety level while ensuring comfort for passengers and timely aircraft handling, i.e., increasing airport capacity and security. Apart from technologies, the whole sector is exceptionally innovative in terms of organizational and management techniques. Kleczkowska (2021) investigated the best Asian airports included in "World's Top 100 Airports 2020" and concluded that the most numerous groups of innovations were those focused on marketing and airport image (65%), maintaining the comfort of passengers (20%), and processing and management improvement (1%). The tables below present an overview of the most popular innovations in aviation and the purposes of their application (Table 2.1).

Table 2.1   The Examples of Innovations in the Aviation Sector.

Innovation	Innovation type	Implementation/ testing examples	Purpose
Robot for the production of meals	Processing/ management innovations	e.g. Etihad, KLM Royal Dutch Airlines	■ Manage food waste inflight.
Self-driving autonomous guide robots	Processing innovation	e.g. British Airways, Heathrow Airport, Incheon Airport, Munich Airport, Rotterdam The Hague Airport	■ Improvement of baggage-handling efficiency; ■ Enhancement of ergonomic working conditions for ground staff.
Fully functional digital twin	Processing innovation	e.g. AirAsia	■ Improvement of operational decision making, based on the holistic view of airport operations; ■ Help set up robust schedules; ■ Management and solving disruptions.
Virtual reality (VR) & immersive experiences	Marketing innovation	e.g. Aigle Azur, Austrian Airlines, British Airways, Emirates, Etihad, Evelop	■ Quick creation of visual assets including photography, film, and 360° content to be used across marketing channels.
Inflight Connectivity	Product innovation	e.g. testing in AirAsia, Norwegian, Qatar Airways	■ High-quality Wi-Fi up in the air.

Source: Own elaboration based on www.futuretravelexperience.com. Available: March 15, 2022.

In 2021, apart from environmental challenges, the aviation industry mainly focused on the reaction to the COVID-19 crisis and rebuilding the business, therefore many new solutions for ensuring health safety were launched. Fabre (2021) indicated four main fields of challenges for the aviation industry that must be solved by different types of innovations that will support airport operations and management in the future, and these are:

1) Achieving efficiency of low-touch operations by automation and digitization techniques,
2) gaining leaner operations, and adapting to fluctuating passenger numbers through cloud technology and business intelligence,
3) challenges for regional airports to attract passengers as in international and hub airports by digital experience for seamless interoperation across travel systems,
4) difficulties of airline supply chains solved by blockchain technology.

Those innovations which are strictly connected with the COVID-19 pandemic are shown in Table 2.2.

The ongoing processes of liberalization, deregulation, amendments to legal regulations as well as infrastructure investments strongly affect the natural environment and therefore, innovations implemented in this sector are also focused on supporting sustainability. Hence, striving for sustainability continued high on the development agenda for airlines and airports, and an important part of the aviation sector is research into techniques and technologies to reduce consumption of natural resources and environmental pollution, and integrate air transport with other transport modes within an integrated and sustainable system (European Commission, 2014). Several initiatives are supposed to lead to a decrease in environmental pollution from aviation. The assumption of air-transport sustainability forced the airlines and aircraft manufacturers to investigate more and more advanced technologies allowing for the replacement of fossil fuels with alternative energy sources. Another reason is to find a business hedge against fluctuations in fossil-fuel prices that have been observed over the past few decades.

The International Air Transport Association (IATA) has introduced the Sustainable Alternative jet Fuels (SAF) strategy which was explained as the intermediate shift of the aviation business into fully alternative, low-emission fuels. The new fuels and energy sources, such as solar jet fuel, power-to-liquid engines, and electrically powered aircraft, would play a major role in aviation starting from approximately 2040 to 2050. However, before employing these technologies, which are currently being tested, IATA claims that drop-in fuels remain the only sustainable alternative to fossil jet fuels for at least two to three decades before aviation sustainability is achieved (IATA, 2015). The data of E4Tech (Bauen et al., 2020) presents the savings in CO_2 using SAF (cf. Table 2.3).

Table 2.2   Innovations Addressing the Needs of the COVID-19 Crisis.

Innovation	Innovation type	Implementation/ testing examples	Purpose
The end-to-end contactless airport experience	Process innovation	e.g. AirAsia, Etihad, Bangalore Int. Airport Ltd.	■ Reduction of the interaction between passengers and staff.
Touchless check-in	Process innovation	e.g. American Airlines, Avalon Airport, Avinor, Japan Airlines	■ Reduction of the interaction between passengers and staff.
Inflight entertainment based on the BYOD model (bring your own device)	Organizational innovation	e.g. Southwest Airlines	■ Minimizing the spread of viruses.
Just Walk Out technology	Process innovation	e.g. Dallas Love Field Airport	■ Reduction of the interaction between passengers and staff by the contactless walk-through shopping experience.
E-commerce service	Process innovation	e.g. AirAsia	■ Reduction of the interaction between passengers and staff by contactless purchasing of duty-free products and having them delivered to their doorstep the next day.
Contactless food & beverage (f&b)	Process/ organizational innovation	e.g. Chicago Midway, Dallas/Fort Worth Airport, Los Angeles Int., Philadelphia, Schiphol, Transavia	■ Reduction of the interaction between passengers and staff by contactless ordering of a meal through a web platform before the flight.
Digital health passports & vaccination visas	Process innovation	e.g. SunExpress	■ Shortening the time of passenger handling and health-checking process.
COVID-19 test centers	Process innovation	e.g. Dublin Airport, Heathrow, Schiphol, Los Angeles Int., San Francisco	■ Speeding up the process of covid-testing.

Table 2.2 *(Continued)* Innovations Addressing the Needs of the COVID-19 Crisis.

Innovation	Innovation type	Implementation/ testing examples	Purpose
APEX Health Safety initiative	Management innovation	e.g. Air Canada, Alaska Airlines, Etihad, JetSmart, Qatar Airways, Saudia, Singapore Airlines, Spirit, Sri Lankan, Turkish Airlines, United Airlines, Virgin Atlantic	■ Awarding airlines for their efforts in ensuring the highest standards of cleanliness and sanitization.
Advanced self-service and biometrics	Process innovation	e.g. Lufthansa Group, US airports, Dubai Int. Airport; Etihad, Hollywood Int. Airport	■ Reduction of the face-to-face interaction between airline staff & passengers.
Robots with ultraviolet light technology for cleaning	Process innovation	e.g. G. R. Ford Int. Airport, Hamad Int. Airport, Heathrow Airport, JetBlue, Gatwick, Helsinki, Qatar Airways, Pittsburgh Int. Airport	■ Improving health safety and comfort of passengers.
Floor-scrubbing robot	Process innovation	e.g. Cincinnati/ Northern Kentucky Int. Airport	■ Improving health safety and comfort of passengers.
Non-face-to-face automatic body temp. robots	Process innovation	Incheon Int. Airport	■ Reduction of the face-to-face interaction between airline staff & passengers.
Video analytics and virtual queueing	Process innovation	e.g. J.F. Kennedy Int. Airport, Stuttgart Airport	■ Monitoring social distancing from curbside to check-in and through the security checkpoint in the terminal.
Home check-in, baggage disinfection services	Process innovation	Dubai Airport	■ Improving health safety and comfort of passengers.

Source: Own elaboration based on www.futuretravelexperience.com. Available: March 15, 2022.

Table 2.3   Greenhouse-Gas Emissions of SAF.

Technology	Stock	Savings in CO2 vs. jet fuels
The FT—Fischer Tropsch—process converts solid biomass (including residual waste) into synthetic gas and then processes the gas into a mixture of hydrocarbons including road and aviation fuels.	Wood residues/straw	95%
The HEFA—Hydrotreated Esters and Fatty Acids—process converts oils into a fuel similar to the refinement of crude fossil oil.	Conventional oil crops (palm oil, soy, rapeseed)	20%–54%
	Jatropha	66%
	Camelina	85%
	Animal fat	89%
	Algae	98%

Source: Own elaboration based on Bauen et al. (2020).

Apart from SAF, there are several environmentally focused initiatives, mostly launched by startups. Here, the artificial-intelligence algorithms programmed in the software help to create a fuel-saving strategy. While investigating the flight parameters from aircraft black boxes, it turned out to be possible to reduce fuel consumption by up to several dozen kilograms during one flight. This means not only a significant reduction in greenhouse-gas emissions into the atmosphere but also millions in savings for airlines (MM Magazyn Przemysłowy, 2022).

2.5 Conclusions

Innovativeness is a measure of the level of modern management and its purpose is the search for solutions that bring convenience for people, improvement of management efficiency, and protection of the natural environment. Innovations have continued to drive the aerospace industry from the beginning of its operation. The same is true today, in the modern age, as it was said by Schumpeter, that innovations are still major factors for business development. Product, process, organizational, and marketing novelties are equally important for the airlines and the airport to achieve success

in the market. In the chapter, I presented examples of 21st-century technologies that either have been introduced by air-transport companies or
are being tested by research institutes to be introduced in the future. There
was a huge issue to classify them into the exact groups of innovations, as
some represent together product and marketing innovations; on the other
hand, some can be included in organizational and process innovations.
Nevertheless, innovations are perceived as ventures that enable the aviation
industry's sustainable growth by meeting all requirements and regulations
while ensuring financial stability, and responding to customer needs which
ultimately results in the development of the sector which is in line with
Schumpeter's theory.

In 2020, the COVID-19 pandemic reality, with all the problems and difficulties related to suspensions and bans on passenger flights, designated that
investments in searching for innovations in passengers' health safety were
the exclusive factor that allowed airports and airlines to remain in business.
Although from the academic and business perspective, it is a vast challenge to
investigate whether the costs incurred by companies of "COVID-19 innovations"
actually ensured the effective operation of the air business enterprises. This
understanding of innovations is in line with Galbraith's perspective.

The huge limitation of the chapter is the access to reliable sources about
innovations that have been implemented in the aviation-industry companies,
especially those that constitute the know-how of the companies.

References

Baran, J., & Górecka, A. K. (2019). Economic and environmental aspects of inland
transport in EU countries. *Economic Research-Ekonomska Istraživanja*, *32*(1),
1037–1059. DOI: 10.1080/1331677X.2019.1578680

Barańska-Fischer, M., & Blażlak, R. (2016). Innowacje w biznesie. Wybrane zagadnienia
[Business innovation: Selected issues]. *Monografie Politechniki Łódzkiej*, Łódź.

Bauen, A., Bitossi, N., German, L., Harris, A., & Leow, K. (2020). Sustainable aviation fuels. *Johnson Matthey Technological Review*, *64*(3), 263–278. DOI:
10.1595/205651320X158167560120

European Bank for reconstruction and development. (2019). *Disruptive Technology
and Innovation in Transport: Policy Paper on Sustainable Infrastructure*.
Retrieved from: www.ebrd.com/documents/transport/disruptive-technology-
and-innovation-in-transport.pdf Available [May 25, 2022].

European Commission. (1995). *Green Paper on Innovation*. Document drawn
up on the basis of COM(95) 688 final, Bulletin of the European Union
Supplement 5/95.

European Commission. (2014). *Understand the Policy of the European Union: Transport.* Luksemburg: Publications Office of the European Union.

Fabre, S. (2021). *The Air Transport Industry Must Take Sustainability into Its Transformation.* Retrieved from: www.timesaerospace.aero/news/air-transport/air-transport-industry-must-take-sustainability-into-its-transformation Available [February 20, 2022].

Galbraith, J. K. (1979). *The Nature of Mass Poverty.* Cambridge, MA, (USA): Harvard University Press.

Hyard, A. (2013). Non-technological innovations for sustainable transport. *Technological Forecasting & Social Change, 80,* 1375–1386.

IATA. (2015). *IATA Sustainable Aviation Fuel Roadmap.* Retrieved from: www.iata.org/contentassets/d13875e9ed784f75bac90f000760e998/safr-1-2015.pdf Available [March 16, 2022].

Jeon, C. M., & Amekudzi, A. (2005). Addressing sustainability in transportation systems: Definitions, indicators, and metrics. *Journal of Infrastructure Systems, 11,* 31–50. DOI: 10.1061/(ASCE)1076–0342(2005)11:1(31).

Kleczkowska, A. (2021). *Airport Innovations on the Example of Eastern Asian Airports.* The Bechelor Thesis. Warsaw University of Life Sciences, Institute of Economics and Finance, Department of Logistics.

Mirabito, M. M., & Joe Layng, T. V. (2013). Stimulating innovation (or making innovation meaningful again). In: M. Murphy, S. Redding, & J. Twyman (eds.), *Handbook on Innovations in Learning.* Philadelphia: Center On In Learning.

MM Magazyn Przemysłowy. (2022). *Innowacyjne rozwiązanie dla przemysłu lotniczego* [Innovative Solution for the Aviation Industry]. Retrieved from: https://magazynprzemyslowy.pl/artykuly/innowacyjne-rozwiazanie-dla-przemyslu-lotniczego Available [February 15, 2022].

Musiał, G., & Chrzanowski, I. H. (2018). *Schumpeter-Lange-Galbraith. Innowacje w teorii i praktyce* [Schumpeter-Lange-Galbraith: Innovations in Theory and Practice]. Zeszyty Naukowe Uniwersytetu Ekonomicznego w Katowicach, Katowice.

OECD. (2004). *Assessment and Decision Making for Sustainable Transport. European Conference, of Ministers of Transport.* Paris: OECD Publications Service.

OECD. (2005). *Oslo Manual: Guidelines for Collecting and Interpreting Innovation Data* (3rd ed.). OECD & Eurostat. Retrieved from: https://ec.europa.eu/eurostat/documents/3859598/5889925/OSLO-EN.PDF/60a5a2f5-577a-4091-9e09-9fa9e741dcf1?version=1.0 Available [February 20, 2022].

OECD. (2009). *Responding to the Economic Crisis-Fostering Industrial Restructuring and Renewal,* Industry and Innovation, July.

OECD. (2011). *Innovation and the Transfer of Environmental Technologies.* Paris: OECD Studies of Environmental Innovation.

Ortega, A., Gkoumas, K., Tsakalidis, A., & Pekár, F. (2021). Low-emission alternative energy for transport in the EU: State of play of research and innovation. *Energies, 14*(22), 7764. DOI: 10.3390/en14227764

Ryley, T., Elmirghani, J., Budd, T., Miyoshi, Ch., Mason, K., Moxon, R., Ahmed, I., Qazi, B., & Zanni, A. (2013). Sustainable development and airport surface access:

The role of technological innovation and behavioral change. *Sustainability*, 5(4), 1617–1631. DOI: 10.3390/su5041617

Schumpeter, J. A. (1949). *The Theory of Economic Development: An Inquiry into Profits, Capital, Credit, Interest, and the Business Cycle*. Cambridge, MA: Harvard University Press.

Urbancová, H. (2013). Competitive advantage achievement through innovation and knowledge. *Journal of Competitiveness*, 5(1), 3.

www.futuretravelexperience.com Available [March 15, 2022].

Załoga, E., & Liberadzki, B. (2010). Innowacje w transporcie. Korzyści dla użytkownika [Transport innovations: User benefits]. *Zeszyty Naukowe nr 603 Ekonomiczne Problemy Usług Nr 59*. Wydawnictwo Naukowe Uniwersytetu Szczecińskiego.

Chapter 3

Green Warehousing: A State-of-the-Art Literature Review

Joanna Domagała

Warsaw University of Life Sciences—SGGW, Poland

Contents

DOI: 10.4324/9781003304364-4

3.1 Introduction

Nowadays, the rapid growth of logistics operations associated with, among other things, long-haul freight transportation, intensive intracity distribution, and the growth of online sales generates negative externalities in daily operations (Lindholm & Blinge, 2014), including emissions, congestion, traffic accidents, noise, vibrations, infrastructure failures, and waste of resources (United Nations, 2011). A rapid increase in negative externalities can bring about irreversible consequences for the economy and the entire ecosystem.

On the other hand, awareness of climate change and issues of sustainability has also been growing rapidly. Consumers are demonstrating increasing interest in going green, and additional regulatory pressure is forcing companies to manage all operations from an environmental perspective (Mutingi et al., 2014). In order to address environmental aspects, as well as to gain a competitive advantage, many companies are implementing or considering implementing Green Supply-Chain Management (GSCM) (Bititci et al., 2012).

Like any logistics activity, warehouses contribute to the production of greenhouse gases (GHGs). Warehousing operations account for approximately 11% of the total GHG emissions generated by the logistics sector worldwide (Doherty & Hoyle, 2009). As a result, companies are increasingly paying attention to the environmental issues of warehouses in addition to operational and economic goals, especially since certain European governments have also set specific energy efficiency targets.

Research on sustainability in logistics and supply-chain management has been growing steadily in recent years (Seuring & Müller, 2008; Hassini et al., 2012; Schaltegger et al., 2014). Even though the concept of GSCM is increasingly attracting the attention of researchers and practitioners, Green Warehouse issues have so far only been addressed in a few independent literature-review publications.

Therefore, a literature review was conducted and systematized to analyze warehouse operations in terms of environmental sustainability. The main purpose of the chapter is to present the results of the bibliometric analysis of scientific research on the issue of "Green Warehouse (GW)." In particular, the conducted research will indicate:

1) Dynamics of changes in researchers' interest in GW issues;
2) key/influential scientists, publications, and journals in the GW field;
3) distribution of research by geography (countries and research institutions);
4) keywords clustering and research problems in the GW field;
5) research gaps and future research opportunities.

Therefore, the novelty of this paper lies in the systematization of the literature review and the visualization of the relationships between GW-related research topics. The research will identify emerging research subareas as well as gaps in GW research that can improve the analysis of GW issues both theoretically and practically. It is also expected that the conducted analyses will provide researchers and practitioners with a more in-depth understanding of Green Warehouse research and practical activities. The approach proposed in the research can also be applied as a tool to further collect, analyze, and expand GW-related knowledge.

The chapter is organized as follows. Section 3.1 is the introduction. Section 3.2 provides a short literature review of the GSCM studies. In Section 3.3, the outline of the research method is introduced. Section 3.4 presents the results of the data collection and the results of five parts of scientometric analysis. Section 3.5 proposes the taxonomy of GW research based on the keywords clustering and discusses the knowledge branches in detail. Section 3.6 concludes by highlighting the limitations of this review and proposing directions for future research.

3.2 Literature Review

Due to the growing importance of implementing the concept of sustainability in the management of enterprises, the implementation of mechanisms for assessing and improving the environmental performance of processes related to the delivery of the product to the final consumer becomes necessary. Such an approach is related to the concept of green supply-chain management (Gavronski et al., 2011).

The first green supply-chain (GSC) concept was developed in 1989 when Kelle and Silver (1989) mentioned the use of reusable products and then introduced green operations concerning the concept of reverse logistics. As a result of the quality revolution of the 1980s and the supply chain revolution of the 1990s, companies began to implement sustainability (Srivastava, 2007). In the late 1990s, many researchers conducted comprehensive reviews and studies on Green Supply-Chain Management (GSCM) (Barros et al., 1998; Sarkis & Cordeiro, 2001; Pakurár et al., 2020).

GSCM is the integration of sustainability issues in design, procurement, manufacturing, distribution, sales, and marketing, as well as product end-of-life management (Handfield et al., 1997; Srivastava, 2007; Green et al., 2012; Grabara et al., 2020).

According to Darnall et al. (2008), GSCM practices include environmental activities to provide environmentally friendly products or services and reduce costs in the value chain. GSCM involves both implementing and monitoring environmental management programs and further controlling the implemented practices through various Rs (reduce, reuse, recycle, rethink, etc.) to minimize waste.

According to Malviya and Kant (2015), GSCM is a holistic approach that incorporates environmental awareness in the supply chain and supports companies to improve their sustainability. In addition, GSCM is a strategic management tool that enhances the environmental performance of the manufacturing industry. It also improves other sustainability goals (Hassan et al., 2016).

Therefore, green supply-chain management covers environmentally responsible activities related to planning and controlling the flow of raw materials, components, and finished products from suppliers to the end consumer. Green supply-chain management enables the cooperation and communication between partners necessary to implement environmentally responsible practices in their operations (Zhu et al., 2008), and thus contributes to the performance of the cooperating entities.

The operation of any supply chain has environmental consequences (Large & Gimenez Thomsen, 2011). The environmental impact of green supply chains is primarily positive. Furthermore, the introduction of environmentally friendly practices into the supply chain contributes to cost reductions (e.g., emissions-related costs) and improved customer service (Walton et al., 1998), although the paradoxes of green logistics include a higher level of environmental costs than other costs generated by the logistics system (Bajdor, 2012).

GSCM is gaining popularity in various industries such as the automotive industry, chemicals, textiles, oil and gas exploration, pharmaceuticals, metal manufacturing, FMCG goods, electronics, construction, plastics, and tourism (Thierry et al., 1995; Srivastava, 2007; Green et al., 2012; Hasan et al., 2019; Liu et al., 2020).

The GSCM literature deals with various aspects, including sustainable supply chain, (Fahimnia et al., 2015; Zhang & Yousaf, 2020), GSCM (Srivastava, 2007; Green et al., 2012; Tseng et al., 2019; Liu et al., 2020), sustainable business (Bocken & Geradts, 2020), green marketing (Nekmahmud & Fekete-Farkas, 2020; Szczepańska-Woszczyna & Kurowska-Pysz, 2016), and green business (Hasan et al., 2019; Urbański & Haque, 2020). In addition, some studies focus on the methodological part of the GSCM literature (Soda et al.,

2016). Several literature review articles on GSCM have also been published (Srivastava, 2007; Ahi & Searcy, 2013; Fahimnia et al., 2015; Bajdor & Grabara, 2011; Malviya & Kant, 2015; de Oliveira et al., 2018; Badi & Murtagh, 2019; Tseng et al., 2019).

Some authors include "green warehouse" as an environmentally sustainable supply-chain process (Rostamzadeh et al., 2015; Kumar et al., 2015). However, while the topic of GSCM has been extensively reviewed in the literature, the topic of GW has only been addressed in a few independent literature-review publications. Nonetheless, following the global trend, increasing attention should be given to green and sustainable warehouse processes, including research into management concepts, technology, and equipment to reduce the carbon footprint of warehouses (Wiedmann & Minx, 2008).

There is no single formal definition of the term green warehouse in the literature. In this chapter, the term green warehouse (GW) will be used to describe a management concept that integrates and implements environmentally friendly measures in warehouses to minimize energy consumption, energy costs, and greenhouse-gas emissions.

3.3 Research Methods and Data

3.3.1 Methods and Analysis Tools

The study uses bibliometric methods. According to Pritchard (1969), bibliometrics is a set of research techniques that can be used to analyze publications (Klincewicz, 2009). There is a distinction between evaluative bibliometrics, concerning the evaluation of scientific centers or researchers, which is based mainly on article-citation indices (Solla Price, 1976; Bornmann & Daniel, 2014), and descriptive bibliometrics, which is used to analyze trends in scientific research and identify relevant researchers or research centers (Klincewicz, 2012). The descriptive approach will be used for the planned analyses, which will facilitate a synthetic analysis of the literature and enable us to identify mainstream developments in the area of Green Warehouse (GW).

Various tools and techniques were used for the bibliometric analysis. Trend analysis was applied to the rate of changes in the number of publications and citations during the studied period. We also used citation analysis, which concerns substantive relationships between publications (Klincewicz, 2012).

A higher impact factor indicates a higher level of interest from other authors in the publication. Citations also reflect the degree of transfer and dissemination of knowledge by authors representing different research centers. The study also used the co-word analysis method, which is based on counting the frequency of word pairs appearing in the analyzed text. The co-occurrence of words may signal the existence of subareas of research or identify premises guiding the further development of a given research area. The analysis can be performed at the level of different text elements: Titles, abstracts, keywords, the actual text of the publication, or based on various combinations of these elements. For this study, the cluster analysis method developed by S. Zhu et al. (2009) was also applied. The method was applied using the VOSviewer (Visualizing Scientific Landscapes) software version 1.6.17. VOSviewer is open-source software used for bibliometric network analysis. It was developed at the Center for Science and Technology Studies (CWTS) by Leiden University in the Netherlands. The software enables users to work on text files containing descriptions of bibliographic records exported, among other sources, from Web of Science (WoS) and Scopus databases. The study also used data-analysis tools available in the Web of Science database.

3.3.2 Data Collection and Research Tasks

Data for the study were collected from the Web of Science database on January 10, 2022. Next to Scopus, Web of Science is recognized as the world's most comprehensive bibliographic database in terms of subject coverage. This database thematically covers the natural sciences, social sciences, humanities, medical sciences, as well as the arts.

A key issue in performing database queries is identifying keywords that identify all publications that are relevant to research purposes (Aveyard, 2014). Ries et al. (2017) studied the most commonly used keywords about green warehouses, which is why their study was taken as a basis for identifying keywords in this paper.

The keywords were divided into two groups. The first group included concepts related to warehousing, e.g., "warehouse*," "automated storage," "material handling," and "order-picking." The second group of terms was related to environmental sustainability, e.g., "green," "environment*," "emission," "eco," "sustain*," "carbon," "CO2," and "energy." To run the query in the Web of Science database, each keyword from the first group was combined with each keyword from the second group. Articles that contained at least one search term from both groups in the article title were accepted for further analysis. This resulted in a set of 202 publications, which underwent a further cleanup process. Four limiting criteria were considered.

1) Time range of publication—publications from 1990 until 2021 were considered;
2) type of publication—only publications in peer-reviewed scientific journals and books were considered;
3) the language of publication—only publications in English were considered;
4) articles that did not focus on the topic of GW were eliminated.

After applying the above limitations, the data set consisted of 103 publications.

A set of five research questions was then formulated:

1. What is the overall trend in terms of publications and interest in the topic of the green warehouse?
2. Which authors/researchers, in light of the data analyzed, are most relevant when it comes to green-warehouse research?
3. Which journals, in light of the data analyzed, are most relevant when it comes to publishing green-warehouse research results?
4. Which science and research centers/countries, in light of the data analyzed, are key in terms of publishing green-warehouse research results?
5. What are the main research areas on the topic of the green warehouse?

3.4 Results

3.4.1 General Trend in GW Publications

In the WoS database, the first publication on green warehouse issues appeared in 1971. It was a paper by Kucera et al. (1971) titled "Carbon monoxide from engines in warehouse operations," published in *American Potato Journal*. The publication concerned the evaluation of carbon-monoxide production by forklift internal-combustion engines in warehouses. Tests compared gasoline engines and LP gas engines, equipped with regular and catalytic mufflers and with the fuel system at normal and 10% rich air-fuel ratios.

Table 3.1 presents the basic bibliometric indices, while Figure 3.1 shows the number of publications and citations in the WoS database for the green

Table 3.1 Basic Bibliometric Indicators.

Basic bibliometric indicators	
number of records: 103	number of authors: 333
number of countries: 47	number of institutions: 202
number of citations: 1101	number of journals: 77

Source: Own elaboration based on the created database.

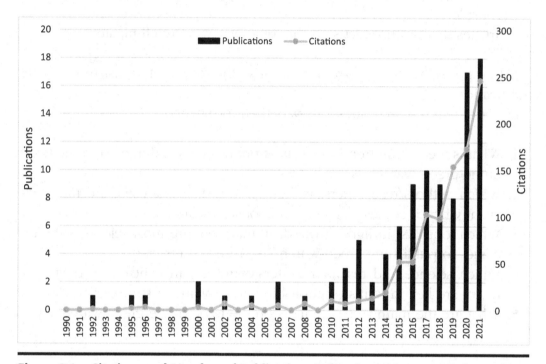

Figure 3.1 Citations and Number of Publications Related to a Green Warehouse in the Period 1990–2021 in WoS.

Source: Own elaboration based on the created database.

warehouse from 1990 to 2021. The data in the figure confirms the ever-growing interest in the topic being analyzed. Three subperiods of green-warehouse publication development can be distinguished:

1) 1990–2009, when a total of ten publications appeared;
2) 2010–2015, when an average of four articles were published per year (22 publications in total);
3) 2016–2021, when an average of twelve articles were published per year (71 publications in total).

This significant increase in the number of publications, as well as citations, in recent years can be attributed to the increased attention around the integration of sustainability topics (including environmental aspects in particular) and logistics operations, which is also forcing businesses to look for new opportunities to reduce the carbon footprint of warehouses (Tambovcevs & Tambovceva, 2012; Satolo et al., 2013). Moreover, the obtained results indicate that there has been a recent increase in interest in the topic of GW, confirming the usefulness of systematizing literature review, summarizing the key findings on the topic, and identifying future research directions that could develop the field further. The largest number of publications corresponded to such research topics as engineering, environmental sciences, green sustainable-science technology, energy fuels, engineering manufacturing, and management (Table 3.2).

Table 3.2   Fifteen Top Research Areas in the Green Warehouse.

Research areas	No. of papers in WoS
Engineering Industrial	17
Environmental Sciences	16
Green Sustainable-Science Technology	15
Energy Fuels	14
Engineering Manufacturing	14
Management	12
Operations Research Management Science	10
Construction Building Technology	8
Engineering Mechanical	8
Thermodynamics	8
Computer-Science Interdisciplinary Applications	7
Engineering Civil	7
Engineering Environmental	7
Automation Control Systems	6
Environmental Studies	6

Source: Own elaboration.

3.4.2 Analysis of Authorship and Collaboration

In the next step, the distribution of authors' scientific productivity was examined. The results presented in Table 3.3 confirm that a small number of authors published between three to five articles, while most authors published one GW article. The largest number of publications about GW was published by Meneghetti A. and Monti L., and it was five articles.

The contribution of individual authors to the development of GW research can be primarily evaluated by taking the number of citations of their publications in the created database as a criterion. From Table 3.4, it can be seen

Table 3.3 Most Productive Authors by the Number of Papers.

Rank	Ranking by the number of publications	
	Author	*No. of papers in WoS*
1	Meneghetti, A.	5
1	Monti, L.	5
3	Lerher, T.	4
4	Zajac, P.	3
5	Bortolini, M.	2
5	Dal Borgo, E.	2
5	Digiesi, S.	2
5	Facchini, F.	2
5	Gamberi, M.	2
5	Glock, C.H.	2
5	Grosse, E.H.	2
5	Gultekin, H.	2
5	Gunthner, W.A.	2
5	Gurel, S.	2
5	Kumar, S.	2
5	Mashud, A.M.	2
5	Mossa, G.	2
5	Pilati, F.	2
5	Sarkar, B.	2
5	Wang, Y.	2
5	Zanoni, S.	2
5	Zrnic, N.	2

Source: Own elaboration.

Table 3.4   Top Ten Cited Papers in the GW Literature.

Authors	Title	Total Citations	Publication Year
Meneghetti, A.; Monti, L.	Greening the food supply chain: an optimisation model for sustainable design of refrigerated automated warehouses	66	2015
Lerher, T.; Edl, M.; Rosi, B.	Energy efficiency model for the mini-load automated storage and retrieval systems	48	2014
Chen, X.; Wang, X.; Kumar, V.; Kumar, N.	Low carbon warehouse management under the cap-and-trade policy	42	2016
Battini, D.; Glock, Ch. H.; Grosse, E. H.; Persona, A.; Sgarbossa, F.	Human energy expenditure in order picking storage assignment: A bi-objective method	41	2016
Khouri, S.; Boukhari, I.; Bellatreche, L.; Sardet, E.; Jean, S.; Baron, M.	Ontology-based structured web data warehouses for sustainable interoperability: requirement modeling, design methodology, and tool	40	2012
Rai, D.; Sodagar, B.; Fieldson, R.; Hu, X.	Assessment of CO_2 emissions reduction in a distribution warehouse	38	2011
Ely, E.; Moorehead, B; Haponik, E.	Warehouse workers' headache: emergency evaluation and management of 30 patients with carbon monoxide poisoning	38	1995
Fawcett, T.; Moon, R.; Fracica, P.; Mebane, G.; Theil, D.; Piantadosi, C.	Warehouse workers headache—carbon-monoxide poisoning from propane-fueled forklifts	35	1992
Zhu, K.; Li, X.; Campana, P. E.; Li, H.; Yan, J.	Techno-economic feasibility of integrating energy storage systems in refrigerated warehouses	30	2018
Ene, S.; Kucukoglu, I.; Aksoy, A.; Ozturk, N.	A genetic algorithm for minimizing energy consumption in warehouses	26	2016

Source: Own elaboration.

that in 2015, the paper published by Meneghetti and Monti got the highest number of citations (66), followed by the paper by Lerher, Edl, and Rosi (48) in 2014.

3.4.3 Analysis of Publication Sources

Of the 103 peer-reviewed articles, 94 were published in scientific journals (90.4%) and the remaining 10 in books (9.6%). Two journals can be considered the leaders in terms of the number of GW publications in the WoS database: *Sustainability*, and *Journal of Cleaner Production*, which published six and five articles on the topic of GW, respectively (Table 3.5), accounting

Table 3.5   Scientific Journals with the Largest Number of Publications on GW Issues in the WoS Database.

The title of the scientific journal	No. of papers in WoS
Sustainability	6
Journal of Cleaner Production	5
International Journal of Production Research	4
Ashrae Journal	3
Computers Industrial Engineering	3
Energy and Buildings	3
International Journal of Logistics Research and Applications	3
Applied Energy	2
Ecoproduction	2
Energies	2
Energy	2
Energy Consumption in Refrigerated Warehouses	2
FME Transactions	2
International Journal of Advanced Manufacturing Technology	2
International Journal of Computers Communications & Control	2
Robotics and Computer-Integrated Manufacturing	2

Source: Own elaboration.

jointly for more than 10% of the total number of publications. In addition to these journals, we identified one journal that published four articles, and four journals that published three articles each. The remaining journals published one or two articles on the topic of GW.

Considering the total citations of articles in each position, five journals with at least 40 citations were noted. It is worth noting that the *International Journal of Production Research* is the leader in this view. The second place is taken by the *International Journal of Advanced Manufacturing Technology*, while the third place is taken by the *Journal of Cleaner Production*. The subject areas of these journals are broad and enable authors to publish research from the broadly understood area of GW.

3.4.4 Analysis of Publications by Country/Research Center

Taking into account the mechanisms of aggregation of data from records (bibliographic descriptions of articles), it is possible to analyze the publication output through the lens of geography, specifying the country or scientific center of origin of authors with the largest number of publications on a given topic. Authors publishing GW articles most often come from China, Italy, and the United States. They are followed by authors from countries such as Germany and the United Kingdom (Table 3.6).

Given the fact that GW is a multidisciplinary issue and requires knowledge from different research fields, it can be assumed that researchers are interested in collaborating to share and complement this knowledge. Therefore, the analysis also identified the strength of cooperation between countries. The largest collaborations were carried out by UK researchers working with researchers from nine countries. Researchers from India and China were slightly less cooperative.

The spatial distribution also shows the scientific centers with authors of the largest number of publications on the analyzed subject. A wide dispersion of scientific research was observed in the perspective of the centers where it is conducted and then published. Most centers produced one article on GW. Two centers produced five articles each, six centers produced three articles each, and twenty centers produced two articles. In such a case, it is difficult to talk about the occurrence of institutional focus, and focus of a given center on the topic of GW. A list of the strongest science centers is shown in Table 3.7. Two centers are more productive in this perspective:

Table 3.6 Spatial Distribution (by Country) of Authors Most Frequently Publishing in the Area of the Green Warehouse.

Countries	No. of papers in WoS
China	16
Italy	15
USA	15
England	8
Germany	8
India	7
Poland	6
Turkey	6
Slovenia	5
Canada	4
France	4
Iran	4
Saudi Arabia	4
Serbia	4
South Korea	4

Source: Own elaboration.

Table 3.7 Institutions of Authors Most Frequently Publishing in the Area of the Green Warehouse.

Research center	No. of papers in WoS
University of Maribor	5
University of Udine	5
Middle East Technical University	3
Technical University of Munich	3
University of Belgrade	3
University of Padua	3
Wroclaw University of Science Technology	3

Source: Own elaboration.

The University of Maribor and the University of Udine, with five articles published at each.

3.4.5 *Analysis of the Main Research Areas*

The last and most important element of the conducted bibliometric analysis was the co-word analysis, which served as cluster analysis, reflecting research subareas in the GW field. The analysis was conducted in the following steps:

Step 1: Searching for records in the WoS database based on set criteria
co-word analysis was performed for the resources of the Web of Science
· database. The criteria for searching records in the database are described
  in subsection 3.3.2.
Step 2: Exporting bibliographic descriptions
This step's purpose was to export the record details—author, title, source, abstract—to a text file.
Step 3: Developing relationship maps and cluster analysis
Maps were developed using VOSviewer by importing the entire text file
  with saved records from the WoS database. The map generation process
  included the following steps:

1) Term extraction, with an indication of terms whose recurrence in
   bibliographic descriptions is at a level of at least five. In the studied case, 623 terms were identified, of which 55 terms occurred a
   minimum of five times. VOSviewer uses Binary Counting for this
   purpose;
2) for a set of 55 words, a relationship map, a cluster map of research
   areas, and a citation-intensity map of analyzed terms were developed.

Step 4: Analysis of the obtained results.

The results of the analyses are presented in Figure 3.2.

The co-word analysis made it possible to identify five research clusters related to the topic of GW: (i) optimization of warehouse building construction/design concerning environmental impact; (ii) impact of warehouse automation on environmental issues; (iii) reduction of carbon footprint in warehouses; (iv) energy efficiency in warehouses; (v) sustainable warehouse management.

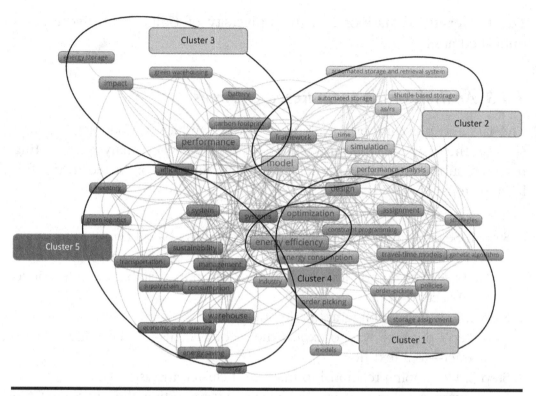

Figure 3.2   Co-Word Cluster Map.

Source: Own elaboration using VOSviewer based on the created database.

3.5 Discussion

Cluster 1. Optimization of Warehouse Building Construction/Design Concerning Environmental Impact

Business operations have a huge impact on the environment, and buildings (including warehouse buildings) around the world generate more than 40% of total CO2 emissions through heating, cooling, and electricity. Warehouse buildings, throughout their life cycle, from construction to demolition, contribute to energy and natural-resource consumption (Rai et al., 2011). Energy consumption in warehouses is also related to the external conditions in which the building operates. In some regions of the world, summer energy consumption in a warehouse building can increase by more than 100% during the day (Huang & Gurney, 2016). According to a report by Cushman and Wakefield (2020) titled "Industrial goes green," as many as 82% of tenants of warehouse facilities express interest in green solutions used in buildings. Companies are increasingly recognizing the benefits of investing in modern systems designed to reduce resource consumption.

The topic cluster on warehouse design and construction analyzed issues related to building design and optimal use of installations and systems (e.g., lighting or heating) to reduce energy consumption and greenhouse-gas emissions.

Using simulation software, Cook and Sproul (2011) assessed the energy requirements of a retail warehouse building in Sydney. Simulation results showed that lighting is a major factor affecting energy consumption in warehouses. The simulation demonstrated a reduction in warehouse energy consumption of up to 73% by incorporating various changes to the warehouse building, such as a sawtooth roof, in conjunction with efficient T5 fluorescent lighting and automatic daylighting controls. Other savings were made by adding insulation to the building, using natural ventilation and selective glazing to limit heat transfers into and out of the building.

Rai et al. (2011) evaluated how various design decisions and building materials, particularly insulation, affect greenhouse-gas emissions in warehouse buildings.

Fikiin et al. (2017) studied refrigerated warehouses for food products. The authors analyzed the feasibility of integrating renewable energy sources (RES) and innovative Cryogenic-Energy Storage (CES) technology. The results confirmed that a conventional cold-storage facility for chilled and frozen products can be transformed into a smart-energy center by using innovative cryogenic-energy storage technology.

On the other hand, Accorsi et al. (2017) proposed a multi-objective model of designing a warehouse building intended to determine the most efficient building parameters (width, length, and height), and minimize the cycle time, total cost, and carbon footprint of the warehouse. The developed model was used to design a warehouse for an Italian food-and-beverage company. The model balanced building dimensions, storage capacity, and material-handling efficiency using Pareto frontier analysis. The proposed best balance solution limits the total cost and carbon footprint increment below 1% compared to their single-objective optima, while the cycle time worsening is limited to 4% compared to the optimal cycle-time solution.

Seifhashemi et al. (2018) conducted research in Australia and noted that the energy consumption of commercial buildings in warmer climates is higher than the national average. The authors evaluated how the use of cool-roof technology affects energy consumption in warehouses. The results showed that this technology has many advantages in terms of reducing energy consumption and saving energy costs, improving the thermal comfort of the building, and reducing the energy demand for cooling warehouses in all evaluated climate zones.

Cluster 2. Impact of Warehouse Automation on Environmental Issues

In this topic cluster, automated storage and retrieval systems (AS/RS) were evaluated from a sustainable-storage perspective. Based on the citation-intensity map, the most cited papers within this cluster were Lerher et al. (2014) and Tappia et al. (2015).

Meneghetti and Monti (2015) proposed an optimization model for the design of sustainable AS/RS systems in refrigerated warehouses, taking into account investment costs, operating costs, energy consumption, and GHG emissions. Fichtinger et al. (2015) also developed an integrated simulation model to evaluate the relationships between inventory management, warehouse management, and GHG emissions in automated AS/RS warehouses.

Meneghetti and Monti (2013) also investigated how AS/RS device movements can be designed to be energy efficient. A subsequent paper by Meneghetti et al. (2015) investigated AS/RS device-control policy models based on a time criterion and an energy-consumption criterion. They paid particular attention to rack shapes and dimensions, which play an important role in terms of energy consumption. The results showed that the energy demand of AS/RS systems is related to the rack height. The best energy efficiency in the simulation was achieved for the average rack height.

On the other hand, Lerher et al. (2014) proposed an energy-efficiency model for AS/RS mini loads. The authors considered the throughput, speed, and engine power of an S/R machine, as well as energy consumption and greenhouse-gas emissions. Comparing these different AS/RS mini-load models, the results showed that energy consumption and GHG emissions increase as the speed of the AS/RS devices increases.

Tappia et al. (2015) compared automated storage solutions in terms of AVS/RS (autonomous vehicles) and storage and retrieval systems (AS/RS). Their results indicated that autonomous vehicle technology has lower costs compared to AS/RS.

Stöhr et al. (2018) developed a comparative method to evaluate the energy efficiency of three AS/RS systems, i.e., mini load-crane, horizontal carousel, and shuttle systems.

Cluster 3. Reduction of Carbon Footprint in Warehouses

As part of this topic cluster, Ries et al. (2017) analyzed how different design aspects of a warehouse, such as building performance and technology used, affect greenhouse-gas emissions. The researchers used empirical data from the US. They used factor analysis to identify specific scenarios for reducing greenhouse-gas emissions.

The primary focus of this research area has been the carbon footprint generated by forklift operations. Boenzi et al. (2015) developed a decision support system that considers minimizing greenhouse-gas emissions from material-handling activities in warehouses. The model considers forklift emissions in the transportation, picking, storage, and retrieval processes and identifies the storage method, as well as the type of forklift, which minimizes the energy required during material-handling operations. In another study, Facchini et al. (2016) built a forklift-selection simulation model considering the technical characteristics of major forklift models and their GHG emissions. Two sources of forklift fuel were considered, e.g., fossil-fuel and electricity. The simulation results showed that electric forklifts are preferred in cases of light/medium-weight units and are less emissive than fuel-powered forklifts.

On the other hand, Dadhich et al. (2015) used life-cycle analysis (LCA) to identify GHG emissions in the drywall supply chain. The results showed that the highest carbon emissions associated with warehousing come from handling operations due to the use of diesel forklifts and electricity consumption from warehouse lighting. The authors concluded that the implementation of cross-docking and the use of renewable energy sources—wind energy, in particular—are major decarbonization initiatives.

Cluster 4. Energy Efficiency in Warehouses

Within this topic cluster, special attention was paid to energy efficiency in lighting systems, warehouse heating, and air-conditioning and ventilation systems. The energy efficiency of warehouses was also evaluated according to the level of automation of warehouse processes. Indeed, energy consumption can be converted into greenhouse-gas emissions (Ries et al., 2017).

Pudleiner and Colton (2015) identified a set of warehouse building energy-efficiency metrics that can be used for net-zero-energy building design. This means that every unit of energy consumed by a building must be offset by the generation of a unit of renewable energy. A vaccine warehouse was studied. The parameters studied were exterior wall insulation, window properties, infiltration, natural ventilation, lighting, and furnishings. Building control parameters and their control have been shown to have a greater impact on reducing energy consumption than architectural-design parameters.

On the other hand, Dhooma and Baker (2012) used an energy audit to analyze the final energy consumption of warehouses. They considered different types of end-use, i.e., lighting, equipment, and HVAC. The results showed how energy can be stored according to end-use type, especially for HVAC and lighting.

Fekete et al. (2014) proposed the application of an energy-consumption monitoring process to material-handling processes, developing key performance indicators from a technological, organizational, and economic perspective. The approach presented in the publication follows the SECA (Standardized Energy-Consuming Activities) scheme. The results of the study case showed that the main consumption in warehouses comes from lighting (36%) and material-handling equipment (32%), and that the cost of energy consumption affects the total cost of the material-handling process by up to 7%.

It can be seen that the analyzed cluster 4 is contained in cluster 1, which means that energy efficiency is also affected by the level of automation of warehouse operations. In this context, Freis et al. (2016) developed mathematical models to determine energy demand in warehouses and presented the results of a case study based on three different types of warehouses: manual, semiautomated, and fully automated. The results confirmed that in a manual warehouse, heating and cooling systems consume most of the energy, while in semiautomated and fully automated warehouses, material-handling equipment consumes the largest portion of energy. Makris et al. (2006) studied the order-picking problem, focusing on the trade-off between energy consumption and product-picking time, and developed a routing algorithm based on the traveling-salesman problem (TSP) that minimizes energy consumption. On the other hand, Burinskiene et al. (2018) identified the main areas of energy and time wastage in warehouses and developed a mathematical model to improve the efficiency of warehouse processes. Zaja͵c (2011) developed a mathematical model to increase the energy efficiency of the process of transporting goods within a warehouse, taking into account the energy consumption of lifting and transporting pallets and driving forklifts. Similarly, Ene et al. (2016) proposed a genetic algorithm (GA) for solving the order-grouping and routing problems with an approach that considered two objectives: Minimizing travel time and energy consumption in a manual warehouse.

Cluster 5. Sustainable Warehouse Management

This topic cluster ranges from environmental guidelines to an analysis of available initiatives, environmental certifications, and sustainability standards to reduce greenhouse-gas emissions in warehouses. Aspects of business ethics and corporate social responsibility were also examined in this area. Tan et al. (2010) and Amjed and Harrison (2013) analyzed the relationships between social, economic, and environmental issues through key sustainability indicators in warehouses. On the other hand, Bank and Murphy (2013) proposed sustainability indicators for warehouse processes that fit into the Sustainable Logistics Initiatives (SLI) developed by the International Warehouse Logistics Association. Electricity consumption, recycling, liquid-fuel consumption, and water consumption were identified as the main SLI environmental indicators. Similarly, Rüdiger et al. (2016) investigated a method for evaluating GHG emissions from storage and handling activities by considering a set of environmental performance indicators (EPIs).

Building certification is also an important issue in sustainable warehouse management. In his work, Żuchowski (2015) compared four methodologies for warehouse building certification, i.e., Building Research Establishment Environmental Assessment Methodology (BREEAM), Haute Qualité Environnementale (HQE), Deutsche Gesellschaft für Nachhaltiges Bauen (DGNB), and Leadership in Energy and Environmental Design (LEED).

Another issue explored in this topic cluster is the adoption of sustainability standards and observance of cap-and-trade emission policies. Chen et al. (2016) discussed the impact of cap-and-trade policies on warehouse-management decisions by examining the role of green technology investments. The authors used data from a retailer's warehouse to assess greenhouse-gas emissions. The results highlighted that carbon cap pricing, as well as cap-and-trade emission policies, can effectively reduce the carbon footprint of warehouses.

3.6 Conclusions and Implications for Theory and Practice

Due to the rise of global warming and change in biodiversity, there is increased pressure on firms to improve environmental performance. Moreover, there is an increased environmental awareness among the stakeholders which stimulates the firms to minimize the negative environmental impact of firms' operations

(Ming-Lang et al., 2019). Given the impact of the carbon tax on company competitiveness (Lin & Li, 2011), in the coming years, green storage management will become an inevitable requirement that has the potential to lead to significant improvements in both operational efficiency and energy efficiency while promoting the use of renewable energy sources. ·

The conducted research allows us to formulate the following conclusions. First, the importance of GW has been increasing over time, which means that environmental aspects in the warehousing area are playing an increasingly important role. The study reveals that the University of Maribor and the University of Udine are top contributing institutions in the GW area. This study reveals that Meneghetti and Monti are the most influential authors in the GW area in several publications and citations. Moreover, *Sustainability* is found to be the most popular journal regarding its impact and the number of papers it publishes in this area. The study also reveals that China, Italy, and the USA are dominating this discipline in terms of their impact and number of publications.

The most frequently researched topics in GW were energy conservation in warehousing, the environmental impact of warehouse construction and equipment, and sustainable warehouse management (with a focus on environmental aspects).

The author is aware of the existing limitations of the conducted bibliometric analysis. These mainly stem from:

1) Limitation to a selected bibliographic database (Web of Science) with monographs and reports excluded. It would also be worth it to analyze the resources of the Scopus and GoogleScholar databases, which, according to Mingers and Lipitakis (2010), for the social sciences, are characterized by a higher coverage rate of publications of various types. For the GS database, however, there are issues of reliability and transparency of the data;

2) language restriction related to searching foreign databases for English-language texts only;

3) time limitation; the study covered the period from 1990 to 2021.

Therefore, analyses that were: Conducted on other data sets; taken from other databases; conducted at other times; on data retrieved using other phrases; in other search fields; involving other types of documents; and conducted with other conditions for exclusion from the data set, may yield different results and lead to different interpretations.

The bibliometric analysis of publications referring to GW in the title was, to the best of the author's knowledge, one of the few studies conducted in this area. However, the results obtained should be regarded as preliminary and in need of verification, mainly due to the limitations stated above. From a practical point of view, the results of this review show that the importance of the carbon footprint of a warehouse and the waste of resources such as fuel, electricity, and water can no longer be ignored. It is hoped that the analyses presented in this review will systematize the available knowledge on GW and increase the awareness of researchers and practitioners concerning warehouse sustainability.

In practice, steps are being taken toward low-carbon warehousing and can be achieved without significant capital investment. For example, simulation models and sustainability guidelines exist to reduce warehouse greenhouse-gas emissions, ranging from optimizing warehouse building design, lighting systems, and installed equipment, to designing automated solutions for efficient energy use. However, more research is needed to encourage new investment in GW facilities. Further research directions may include, for example, full life-cycle warehouse emissions testing. There is a lack of research on big data. Only a few papers consider big data for evaluating GW performance. It might be useful to study the overall energy consumption of a warehouse, including all end-use types. An important direction would be researching environmental certifications and cap-and-trade emission policies of warehouses.

References

Accorsi, R., Bortolini, M., Gamberi, M., Manzini, R., & Pilati, F. (2017). Multi-objective warehouse building design to optimize the cycle time, total cost, and carbon footprint. *The International Journal of Advanced Manufacturing Technology*, *92*(1–4), 839–854.

Ahi, P., & Searcy, C. (2013). A comparative literature analysis of definitions for green and sustainable supply chain management. *Journal of Cleaner Production, 52*, 329–341.

Amjed, T. W., & Harrison, N. J. (2013). *A Model for Sustainable Warehousing: From Theory to Best Practices*. Proceedings of the International Decision Sciences Institute and Asia Pacific DSI Conference, United States (pp. 1–28).

Aveyard, H. (2014). *Doing a Literature Review in Health and Social Care: A Practical Guide*. London (UK): McGraw-Hill Education.

Badi, S., & Murtagh, N., (2019). Green supply chain management in construction: A systematic literature review and future research agenda. *Journal of Cleaner Production, 223*, 312–322.

Bajdor, P. (2012). Comparison between sustainable development concept and green logistics: The literature review. *Polish Journal of Management Studies, 5*, 236–244.

Bajdor, P., & Grabara, J. K. (2011). Implementing "green" elements into the supply chain: The literature review and examples. *Annales Universitatis Apulensis: Series Oeconomica, 13*(2), 584.

Bank, R., & Murphy, R. (2013). *Warehousing sustainability standards development.* IFIP International Conference on Advances in Production Management Systems (pp. 294–301). Berlin, Heidelberg: Springer.

Barros, A. I., Dekker, R., & Scholten, V. (1998). A two-level network for recycling sand: A case study. *European Journal of Operational Research, 110*(2), 199–214.

Battini, D., Glock, Ch. H., Grosse, E. H., Persona, A., & Sgarbossa, F. (2016). Human energy expenditure in order picking storage assignment: A bi-objective method. *Computers and Industrial Engineering, 94*(C), 147–157. DOI: 10.1016/j.cie.2016.01.020

Bititci, U., Garengo, P., Dörfler, V., & Nudurupati, S. (2012). Performance measurement: Challenges for tomorrow. *International Journal of Management Reviews, 14*(3), 305–327.

Bocken, N. M., & Geradts, T. H. (2020). Barriers and drivers to sustainable business model innovation: Organization design and dynamic capabilities. *Long Range Planning, 53*(4), 101950.

Boenzi, F., Digiesi, S., Facchini, F., Mossa, G., & Mummolo, G. (2015). Greening activities in warehouses: A model for identifying sustainable strategies in material handling. *Annals of DAAAM & Proceedings, 26*(1), 980–988.

Bornmann, L., & Daniel, H.-D. (2014). What do citation counts measure? A review of studies on citing behavior. *Journal of Documentation, 64*(1), 45–80. DOI: 10.1108/00220410810844150

Burinskiene, A., Lorenc, A., & Lerher, T. (2018). A simulation study for the sustainability and reduction of waste in warehouse logistics. *International Journal of Simulation Modelling, 17*(3), 485–497.

Chen, X., Wang, X., Kumar, V., & Kumar, N. (2016). Low carbon warehouse management under cap-and-trade policy. *Journal of Cleaner Production, 139*, 894–904.

Cook, P., & Sproul, A. (2011). Towards low-energy retail warehouse building. *Architectural Science Review, 54*(3), 206–214.

Cushman & Wakefield. (2020). *Industrial Goes Green.* Retrieved from: https://industrial.pl/aktualnosci/reports/421-industrial-goes-green-zielone-rozwiazania-w-polskich-magazynach-raport Available [March 20, 2022].

Dadhich, P., Genovese, A., Kumar, N., & Acquaye, A. (2015). Developing sustainable supply chains in the UK construction industry: A case study. *International Journal of Production Economics, 164*, 271–284.

Darnall, N., Jolley, G. J., & Handfield, R. (2008). Environmental management systems and green supply chain management: Complements for sustainability? *Business Strategy and the Environment, 17*(1), 30–45.

de Oliveira, U. R., Espindola, L. S., da Silva, I. R., da Silva, I. N., & Rocha, H. M. (2018). A systematic literature review on green supply chain management: Research implications and future perspectives. *Journal of Cleaner Production, 187,* 537–561.

Dhooma, J., & Baker, P. (2012). An exploratory framework for energy conservation in existing warehouses. *International Journal of Logistics Research and Applications, 15*(1), 37–51.

Doherty, S., & Hoyle, S. (2009). Supply chain decarbonisation: The role of logistics and transport in reducing supply chain carbon emissions. *World Economic Forum,* Geneva.

Ely, E., Moorehead, B., & Haponik, E. F. (1995). Warehouse workers' headache: Emergency evaluation and management of 30 patients with carbon monoxide poisoning. *The American Journal of Medicine, 98*(2), 145–155. DOI: 10.1016/ s0002-9343(99)80398-2

Ene, S., Küçükoğlu, İ., Aksoy, A., & Öztürk, N. (2016). A genetic algorithm for minimizing energy consumption in warehouses. *Energy, 114,* 973–980.

Facchini, F., Mummolo, G., Mossa, G., Digiesi, S., Boenzi, F., & Verriello, R. (2016). Minimizing the carbon footprint of material handling equipment: Comparison of electric and LPG forklifts. *Journal of Industrial Engineering and Management, 9*(5), 1035.

Fahimnia, B., Sarkis, J., & Davarzani, H. (2015). Green supply chain management: A review and bibliometric analysis. *International Journal of Production Economics, 162,* 101–114.

Fawcett, T. A., Moon, R. E., Fracica, P. J., Mebane, G. Y., Theil, D. R., & Piantadosi, C. A. (1992). Warehouse workers' headache: Carbon monoxide poisoning from propane-fueled forklifts. *Journal of Occupational Medicine: Official Publication of the Industrial Medical Association, 34*(1), 12–15.

Fekete, P. L., Martin, S., Kuhn, K., & Wright, N. (2014). The status of energy monitoring in science and industry by the example of material handling processes. *Business, Management and Education, 12*(2), 213–227.

Fichtinger, J., Ries, J. M., Grosse, E. H., & Baker, P. (2015). Assessing the environmental impact of integrated inventory and warehouse management. *International Journal of Production Economics, 170,* 717–729.

Fikiin, K., Stankov, B., Evans, J., Maidment, G., Foster, A., Brown, T., Radcliffe, J., Youbi-Idrissi, M., Alford, A., Varga, L., Alvarez, G., Ivanov, I. E., Bond, C., Colombo, I., Garcia-Naveda., G., Ivanov, I., Hattori, K., Umeki, D., Bojkov, T., & Kaloyanov, N. (2017). Refrigerated warehouses as intelligent hubs to integrate renewable energy in industrial food refrigeration and to enhance power grid sustainability. *Trends in Food Science & Technology, 60,* 96–103.

Freis, J., Vohlidka, P., & Günthner, W. A. (2016). Low-carbon warehousing: Examining impacts of building and intra-logistics design options on energy demand and the CO2 emissions of logistics centers. *Sustainability, 8*(5), 448.

Gavronski, I., Klassen, R. D., Vachon, S., & Machado do Nascimento, L. F. (2011). A resource-based view of green supply management. *Transportation Research Part E, 47*(6), 872–885.

68 ■ *Sustainable Logistics*

Grabara, J., Dabylova, M., & Alibekova, G. (2020). Impact of legal standards on logistics management in the context of sustainable development. *Acta Logistica*, 7(1), 31–37.

Green, K. W., Zelbst, P. J., Meacham, J., & Bhadauria, V. S. (2012). Green supply chain management practices: Impact on performance. *Supply Chain Management: An International Journal*, 17(3), 290–305.

Handfield, R. B., Walton, S. V., Seegers, L. K., & Melnyk, S. A. (1997). Green value chain practices in the furniture industry. *Journal of Operations Management*, 15(4), 293–315.

Hasan, M. M., Nekmahmud, M., Yajuan, L., & Patwary, M. A. (2019). Green business value chain: A systematic review. *Sustainable Production and Consumption*, 20, 326–339.

Hassan, M. G., Abidin, R., Nordin, N., & Yusoff, R. Z. (2016). GSCM practices and sustainable performance: A preliminary insight. *Journal of Advanced Management Science*, 4(5), 430–434.

Hassini, E., Surti, C., & Searcy, C. (2012). A literature review and a case study of sustainable supply chains with a focus on metrics. *International Journal of Production Economics*, 140(1), 69–82. DOI: 10.1016/j.ijpe.2012.01.042

Huang, J., & Gurney, K. R. (2016). The variation of climate change impact on building energy consumption to building type and spatiotemporal scale. *Energy*, 111, 137–153.

Kelle, P., & Silver, E. A. (1989). Forecasting the returns of reusable containers. *Journal of Operations Management*, 8(1), 17–35.

Khouri, S., Boukhari, I., Bellatreche, L., Sardet, E., Jean, S., & Baron, M. (2012). Ontology-based structured web data warehouses for sustainable interoperability: Requirement modeling, design methodology and tool. *Computers in Industry*, 63, 799–812.

Klincewicz, K. (2009). Zastosowanie bibliometrii w naukach o zarządzaniu. [Application of bibliometry in management sciences]. *Problemy Zarządzania*, 7(4), 130–156.

Klincewicz, K. (2012). Bibliometria a inne techniki analityczne [Bibliometry and other analytical techniques]. In: K. Klincewicz, K. Żemigała, & M. Mijal (eds.), *Bibliometria w zarządzaniu technologiami i badaniami naukowymi* [Bibliometry in technology and research management] (pp. 34–40). Warszawa: Ministerstwo Nauki i Szkolnictwa Wyższego.

Kucera, H. L., Mewes, J. R., & Orr, P. H. (1971). Carbon monoxide from engines in warehouse operations. *American Potato Journal*, 49(3), 93–97.

Kumar, N., Agrahari, R. P., & Roy, D. (2015). Review of green supply chain processes. *IFAC-PapersOnLine*, 48(3), 374–381.

Large, R. O., & Gimenez Thomsen, C. (2011). Drivers of green supply management performance: Evidence from Germany. *Journal of Purchasing & Supply Management*, 17, 176–184.

Lerher, T., Edl, M., & Rosi, B. (2014). Energy efficiency model for the mini-load automated storage and retrieval systems. *The International Journal of Advanced Manufacturing Technology*, 70(1–4), 97–115.

Lin, B., & Li, X. (2011). The effect of carbon tax on per capita CO2 emissions. *Energy Policy, 39*(9), 5137–5146.

Lindholm, M. E., & Blinge, M. (2014). Assessing knowledge and awareness of the sustainable urban freight transport among Swedish local authority policy planners. *Transport Policy, 32*, 124–131.

Liu, J., Hu, H., Tong, X., & Zhu, Q. (2020). Behavioral and technical perspectives of green supply chain management practices: Empirical evidence from an emerging market. *Transportation Research Part E: Logistics and Transportation Review, 140*, 102013.

Makris, P. A., Makri, A. P., & Provatidis, C. G. (2006). Energy-saving methodology for material handling applications. *Applied Energy, 83*(10), 1116–1124.

Malviya, R. K., & Kant, R. (2015). Green supply chain management (GSCM): A structured literature review and research implications. *Benchmarking: An International Journal, 22*(7), 1360–1394.

Meneghetti, A., & Monti, L. (2013). Sustainable storage assignment and dwell-point policies for automated storage and retrieval systems. *Production Planning & Control, 24*(6), 511–520.

Meneghetti, A., Dal Borgo, E., & Monti, L. (2015). Rack shape and energy efficient operations in automated storage and retrieval systems. *International Journal of Production Research, 53*(23), 7090–7103.

Meneghetti, A., & Monti, L. (2015). Greening the food supply chain: An optimisation model for sustainable design of refrigerated automated warehouses. *International Journal of Production Research, 53*(21), 6567–6587.

Mingers, J., & Lipitakis, E. A. E. C. G. (2010). Counting the citations: A comparison of web of science and Google scholar in the field of business and management. *Scientometrics, 85*, 613–625. DOI: 10.1007/s11192-010-0270-0

Ming-Lang, T., Kuo-Jui, W., & Ming, K. L. (2019). Data-driven sustainable supply chain management performance: A hierarchical structure assessment under uncertainties. *Journal of Cleaner Production, 227*(5), 760–771.

Mutingi, M., Mapfaira, H., & Monageng, R. (2014). Developing performance management systems for the green supply chain. *Journal of Remanufacturing, 4*(1), 6.

Nekmahmud, M., & Fekete-Farkas, M. (2020). Why not green marketing? Determinates of consumers' intention to green purchase decision in a new developing nation. *Sustainability, 12*(19), 7880.

Pakurár, M., Khan, M. A., Benedek, A., & Oláh, J. (2020). The impact of green practices, cooperation and innovation on the performance of supply chains using statistical method of meta-analysis. *Journal of International Studies, 13*(3), 111–128.

Pritchard, A. (1969). Statistical bibliography or bibliometrics. *Journal of Documentation, 25*(4), 348–349.

Pudleiner, D., & Colton, J. (2015). Using sensitivity analysis to improve the efficiency of a Net-Zero Energy vaccine warehouse design. *Building and Environment, 87*, 302–314.

Rai, D., Sodagar, B., Fieldson, R., & Hu, X. (2011). Assessment of CO2 emissions reduction in a distribution warehouse. *Energy, 36*(4), 2271–2277.

Ries, J. M., Grosse, E. H., & Fichtinger, J. (2017). Environmental impact of warehousing: A scenario analysis for the United States. *International Journal of Production Research, 55*(21), 6485–6499.

Rostamzadeh, R., Govindan, K., Esmaeili, A., & Sabaghi, M. (2015). Application of fuzzy VIKOR for evaluation of green supply chain management practices. *Ecological Indicators, 49*, 188–203.

Rüdiger, D., Schön, A., & Dobers, K. (2016). Managing greenhouse gas emissions from warehousing and transshipment with environmental performance indicators. *Transportation Research Procedia, 14*, 886–895.

Sarkis, J., & Cordeiro, J. J. (2001). An empirical evaluation of environmental efficiencies and firm performance: Pollution prevention versus end-of-pipe practice. *European Journal of Operational Research, 135*(1), 102–113.

Satolo, E. G., Lima, C. R. C., & Simon, A. T. (2013). Sustainability within logistics operations: A Brazilian experience. *International Refereed Journal of Engineering and Science, 2*(12), 23–28.

Schaltegger, S., Burritt, R., Beske, P., & Seuring, S. (2014). Putting sustainability into supply chain management. *Supply Chain Management, 19*(3), 322–331.

Seifhashemi, M., Capra, B. R., Milller, W., & Bell, J. (2018). The potential for cool roofs to improve the energy efficiency of single-story warehouse-type retail buildings in Australia: A simulation case study. *Energy and Buildings, 158*, 1393–1403.

Seuring, S., & Müller, M. (2008). From a literature review to a conceptual framework for sustainable supply chain management. *Journal of Cleaner Production, 16*(15), 1699–1710. DOI: 10.1016/j.jclepro.2008.04.020Soda, S., Sachdeva, A., & Garg, R. K. (2016). Literature review of multi-aspect research works carried out on the concept and implementation of GSCM. *International Journal of Industrial and Systems Engineering, 23*(2), 223–253.

Solla Price, D. (1976). A general theory of bibliometric and other cumulative advantage processes. *Journal of the American Society for Information Science, 27*(5), 292–306. DOI: 10.1002/asi.4630270505.

Srivastava, S. K. (2007). Green supply-chain management: A state-of-the-art literature review. *International Journal of Management Reviews, 9*(1), 53–80.

Stöhr, T., Schadler, M., & Hafner, N. (2018). Benchmarking the energy efficiency of diverse automated storage and retrieval systems. *FME Transactions, 46*(3), 330–335.

Szczepańska-Woszczyna, K., & Kurowska-Pysz, J. (2016). Sustainable business development through leadership in SMEs. *Engineering Management in Production and Services, 8*(3), 57–69.

Tambovcevs, A., & Tambovceva, T. (2012). Logistic system integration with environmental management system, a case study of international company. *World Academy of Science, Engineering and Technology, 6*(8), 1–11.

Tan, K. S., Daud Ahmed, M., & Sundaram, D. (2010). Sustainable enterprise modelling and simulation in a warehousing context. *Business Process Management Journal, 16*(5), 871–886.

Tappia, E., Marchet, G., Melacini, M., & Perotti, S. (2015). Incorporating the environmental dimension in the assessment of automated warehouses. *Production Planning & Control, 26*(10), 824–838.

Thierry, M., Salomon, M., Van Nunen, J., & Van Wassenhove, L. (1995). Strategic issues in product recovery management. *California Management Review, 37*(2), 114–136.

Tseng, M. L., Islam, M. S., Karia, N., Fauzi, F. A., & Afrin, S., (2019). A literature review on green supply chain management: Trends and future challenges. *Resources, Conservation and Recycling, 141*, 145–162.

United Nations (2011). *Transport and Communications Bulletin for Asia and the Pacific, No. 80 Sustainable Urban Freight Transport; Economic and Social Commission for Asia and Pacific.* Bangkok, Thailand: United Nations Building. Retrieved from: www.unescap.org/publications/transport-and-communications-bulletin-asia-and-pacific-no-80-sustainable-urban-freight Available [September 20, 2021].

Urbański, M., & Haque, U. A. (2020). Are you environmentally conscious enough to differentiate between greenwashed and sustainable items? A global consumers perspective. *Sustainability, 12*(5), 1786.

Walton, S. V., Handfield, R. B., & Melnyk, S. A. (1998). The green supply chain: Integrating suppliers into environmental management processes. *Journal of Supply Chain Management, 34*(2), 2–11.

Wiedmann, T., & Minx, J. (2008). A definition of 'carbon footprint'. *Ecological Economics Research Trends, 1*, 1–11.

Zając, P. (2011). The idea of the model of evaluation of logistics warehouse systems with taking their energy consumption under consideration. *Archives of Civil and Mechanical Engineering, 11*(2), 479–492.

Zhang, X., & Yousaf, H. A. U. (2020). Green supply chain coordination considering government intervention, green investment, and customer green preferences in the petroleum industry. *Journal of Cleaner Production, 246*, 118984.

Zhu, K., Li, X., Campana, P. E., Li, H., & Yan, J. (2018). Techno-economic feasibility of integrating energy storage systems in refrigerated warehouses. *Applied Energy, 216*(C), 348–357.

Zhu, Q., Sarkis, J., & Lai, K. (2008). Green supply chain management implications for 'closing the loop'. *Transportation Research Part E, 44*(1), 1–18.

Zhu, S., Takigawa, I., Zeng, J., & Mamitsuka, H. (2009). Field independent probabilistic model for clustering multi-field documents. *Information Processing and Management, 45*(5), 555–570.

Żuchowski, W. (2015). Division of environmentally sustainable solutions in warehouse management and example methods of their evaluation. *LogForum, 11*(2), 171–182.

Chapter 4

Reverse Logistics for Sustainable Waste-Management Processes

Adam Sadowski

University of Lodz, Poland

Contents

DOI: 10.4324/9781003304364-5

4.1 Introduction

Over the past three decades, research in logistics has moved towards one of the biggest challenges for operations management, which is the waste stream arising in all phases of physical flows. Even though reverse logistics has many definitions, approaches, conceptualizations, and practical applications, there is still a lot of ambiguity in its definition in the intellectual structure (Bernon et al., 2011; Islam et al., 2021; Presley et al., 2007; Suzanne et al., 2020; Wang & Hsu, 2010). The overall reverse logistics model covers diverse waste streams and the environmental problems associated with them. As a result, the thematic scope of the research is very broad and dynamically changing along with the emergence of new global challenges, such as worn electric car batteries (Alamerew & Brissaud, 2020). At the same time, the picture of the contribution of reverse logistics to waste management is "blurred" as the following terms are used in parallel: Closed-loop logistics (Tornese et al., 2018; Wang et al., 2019), green logistics (Eng-Larsson & Kohn, 2012), reverse supply chain (Battaïa & Gupta, 2015; Blackburn et al., 2004; Guide et al., 2006), green supply chain (Homayouni et al., 2021), closed-loop supply chain (Gaur et al., 2017; Van Wassenhove, 2019), sustainable logistics (Arampantzi & Minis, 2017; Frota Neto et al., 2008; Lee et al., 2010), or environmental logistics (Sarkis, 2021). In many publications, these terms appear simultaneously and are used interchangeably, which adds significant difficulty to the mapping of this research area (Jemai et al., 2020). For this reason, the research in this chapter is limited to reverse logistics only, abandoning the broader conceptualization of existing knowledge in the areas of logistics, supply-chain management, and management trainability.

The complexity of reverse logistics and its ambiguity also makes the intellectual structure diverse, multifaceted, and multithreaded. Thanks to the use of techniques within the framework of bibliometric methodology, network analysis is a widely recognized approach in the scientific community, used to present the current and future developing thematic areas. It also shows the interdependence between studies, researchers, institutions, and countries. The identification of these clusters gives a clear picture of the intellectual structure and offers an in-depth look into a complex network of connections. The chapter provides an assessment of the research area, taking into account more than 1,000 published articles on reverse logistics. Using rigorous bibliometric tools (e.g., citation and co-citation analyses), clusters describing previous research achievements and the future potential direction of changes in research topics in reverse logistics were identified.

The remaining part of the chapter is organized as follows. Section 2 presents definitions of reverse logistics, showing their evolution and diversity. Section 3 discusses the methodology and data used in the bibliometric analysis. Section 4 contains the results of the bibliometric analysis. Section 5 shows research limitations. The final section contains conclusions and presents the main insights on the intellectual structure of reverse logistics.

4.2 Reverse Logistics Definitions

There are many different perspectives on reverse logistics, which find expression in the number of its definitions. Although the earliest definitions of reverse logistics appeared in the early nineties as a product "going the wrong way down a one-way street because the great majority of product shipments flow in one direction" (Lambert & James, 1982, p. 19), more accurate, process- and function-oriented ones were formulated later (Murphy & Poist, 1988; Stock, 1992, 1998). The Council of Supply Chain Management Professionals (CSCMP) provides the following frequently used definition: "reverse logistics is a specialized segment of logistics focusing on the movement and management of products and resources after the sale and delivery to the customer. It includes product returns for repair and/or credit." Definitions of reverse logistics differ significantly, as far as the scope of problems and processes that constitute its essence is concerned.

A more comprehensive definition is provided by Rogers & Tibben-Lembke (1999, p. 2). It states that "reverse logistics is the process of planning, implementing and controlling the efficient, cost-effective flow of raw materials, in-process inventory, finished goods, and related information from the point of consumption to the point of origin to recapture or create value or proper disposal." The unique character of reverse logistics compared to forward logistics has contributed to its evolution and the creation of original empirical research paths. In this way, both the thematic scope of reverse logistics and its subject matter have broadened. This, in turn, has led to the development of a large and diverse body of knowledge in the field of reverse logistics (Agrawal et al., 2015; De Brito & Dekker, 2004; Huscroft et al., 2013). However, the current large body of knowledge in the field of reverse logistics has not led to a clear demarcation between this concept and other related concepts such as Green Logistics (GL) (Bensalem & Kin, 2019; Rajagopal et al., 2015).

4.3 Methodology and Data

4.3.1 Research Methodology

The research uses bibliometric analysis based on the definition of bibliometrics. Bibliometrics is defined as a "quantitative study of physical published units, or of bibliographic units, or the surrogates for either" (Broadus, 1987, p. 376). Although the first discussion on the use of bibliometrics began in the early fifties, its use for research on intellectual achievements and its structure in the areas of "business, management and accounting" and "decision sciences" occurred much later. The use of bibliometric methods requires the widespread availability of large codified datasets on scientific achievements.

The universality of access to bibliographic databases is important for the replication of analyses by different researchers and the verification of the correctness of conclusions drawn from the research. Currently, researchers can use publicly available databases, such as Scopus or the Web of Science, which collect enormous amounts of information useful for the analysis of scientific achievements. The increase in the amount of codified knowledge in databases has triggered the emergence of software designed to use these knowledge resources. Currently available bibliometric software includes graphmaker programs such as Citnetexplorer, Bibexcel, BibliometrixR, HistCite, Gephi, Leximancer, Pajek, and VOSviewer. In this study, the latest version of VOSviewer, 1.6.17, was used to draw up bibliometric maps to illustrate the characteristics of publications. VOSviewer helps visualize bibliometric results using bibliometric indicators in a researcher-friendly manner. It allows for the direct use of Scopus data to generate a network visualization, which constitutes the software's advantage and speeds up the process of creating visualizations.

The bibliometric methodology has been used in research in various areas of logistics and SCM, including the foundation of logistics and the supply-chain management (Georgi et al., 2013), urban logistics (Dolati Neghabadi et al., 2019), reverse logistics and closed-loop supply-chain management (Bensalem & Kin, 2019; Campos et al., 2017; Kazemi et al., 2019), reverse logistics and corporate social responsibility (Bensalem & Kin, 2019), and supply-chain management (Kotzab et al., 2021; Pournader et al., 2021; Seyedghorban et al., 2020). It is used in the area of logistics and supply-chain management in three main areas of analysis. These areas include all available bibliographic resources, selected journals, and one scientific journal.

In this study, to conduct a review of the past, present and future of the RL research field, co-citation analysis, bibliographic coupling, and co-word analysis were selected as analysis techniques (e.g., notable words in the implications and future research directions of full texts). We used the procedure proposed by Donthu et al. (2021), which includes four stages: Defining the purpose and scope of bibliometric analysis, selecting techniques for analysis, collecting data, conducting analysis, and gathering insight. In the final stage, the study used science mapping to show the intellectual structure of reverse logistics through clustering and visualization.

4.3.2 Data Collection

Scopus (www.scopus.com) and the Web of Science (www.webofknowledge.com) are the two major search engines for searching scholarly sources that offer a significant variety of documents. Scopus, in particular, offers a wide range of coverage of literature and is commonly used for bibliometric analysis (e.g., co-citation analysis and co-word analysis) (Pournader et al., 2021). This was the reason for using this particular database as a source of data on the existing intellectual achievements in the area of reverse logistics. Scopus is a source-neutral abstract and citation database curated by independent subject-matter experts. The results of the search show that there are 3,908 records for the query TITLE-ABS-KEY ("reverse logistics"). The largest number of records corresponds to subject areas, such as engineering and business, management and accounting, computer science, and decision sciences (Table 4.1).

Subsequently, after a thorough screening of the abstracts of the articles, only articles from the areas of Business, Management, Accounting, and Decision Sciences were qualified for the next stage. Such types of records as conference papers, reviews, book chapters, conference reviews, books, editorials, errata, or notes were removed. Our search results show that there are 1,109 articles published in these areas. For 1,109 articles, the total number of footnotes is 27,883, which demonstrates the size of intellectual achievements in the area of reverse logistics. Although the footnotes also contain influential studies, articles, and books, they were not included in the analysis. The research includes the yearly distribution of the bibliographic records of RL articles over 29 years. A significant increase in the number of articles, which began in the mid-2000s, can also be observed.

In 1992, the first Stock's white paper (1992) was published, starting a scientific discourse in the field of reverse logistics. As in the research conducted by Wang et al., the year 1992 was adopted as the starting point for bibliometric analysis (Wang et al., 2017). To show significant changes in the development

Table 4.1 Top Ten Subject Areas in Reverse Logistics.

Rank	Subject area	Number of records
1	Engineering	1,950
2	Business, Management and Accounting	1,457
3	Computer Science	1,176
4	Decision Sciences	986
5	Environmental Science	650
6	Mathematics	434
7	Social Sciences	400
8	Energy	284
9	Economics, Econometrics, and Finance	277
10	Materials Science	102

Source: Own elaboration.

of reverse logistics, we divided the 29 years into three periods, which differ in the intensity of the increase in articles. The first one (A), covers the years 1992–2004 and corresponds to the first research in the area of reverse logistics. The second one (B), covering the years 2005–2013, is characterized by a sharp increase in publications and a regular upward trend. The last period (C), covering the years 2014–2021, like the preceding one, shows an upward trend in the number of publications, with years in which there was a significant decrease in the number of published articles. The division of a dataset into periods is commonly used in bibliometric research and allows for more accurate capture of publication trends. In our research, we adopted about a decade as one in which changes in the development of the discipline are visible. However, shorter, five-year periods were also used for analysis in reverse-logistics research (Wang et al., 2017, p. 670).

4.4 Data Analysis and Results

4.4.1 General View

The general upward trend in the number of articles published in the area of reverse logistics can also be observed. It is interesting to present the most significant authors, institutions, and journals as well as the most cited authors and journals in the RL field. Table 4.2 presents the ten most important journals in which articles on RL have been published. During period A, the largest number of articles were published in the *European Journal of Operational Research* (ten), with a total of 68 articles, representing 14.7% of all articles. During period B, the most, 11.4%, of all articles from the RL area were published in the *International Journal of Production Research*. In the last analyzed period, C, the most publications, 19.2%, were published in the *Journal of Cleaner Production*. Throughout the understudied period 1992–2021, we can observe a considerable change in the profile of journals that publish articles on RL research. At the same time, almost 30% of the latest research is concentrated on one of the following three journals: The *Journal of Cleaner*

Table 4.2   Top Ten Most Productive Journals in Reverse Logistics.

Rank	1992–2004 (68 papers)		2005–2013 (422 papers)		2014–2021 (619 papers)	
1	European Journal of Operational Research	10	International Journal of Production Research	1	European Journal of Operational Research	10
2	International Journal of Production Economics	8	International Journal of Production Economics	2	International Journal of Production Economics	8
3	International Journal of Physical Distribution and Logistics Management	6	International Journal of Logistics Systems and Management	3	International Journal of Physical Distribution and Logistics Management	6
4	OR Spectrum	5	Computers and Operations Research	4	OR Spectrum	5
5	Interfaces	4	European Journal of Operational Research	5	Interfaces	4
6	International Journal of Logistics Management	4	Journal of Cleaner Production	6	International Journal of Logistics Management	4
7	Journal of Business Logistics	4	International Journal of Physical Distribution and Logistics Management	7	Journal of Business Logistics	4

(Continued)

Table 4.2 *(Continued)*   Top Ten Most Productive Journals in Reverse Logistics.

Rank	1992–2004 (68 papers)		2005–2013 (422 papers)		2014–2021 (619 papers)	
8	Journal of the Operational Research Society	3	Transportation Research Part E: Logistics and Transportation Review	8	Journal of the Operational Research Society	3
9	Omega	3	Omega	9	Omega	3
10	Production and Operations Management	3	International Journal of Business Performance and Supply Chain Modelling	10	Production and Operations Management	3

Source: Own elaboration.

Production, the *International Journal of Production Economics*, and the *International Journal of Production Research*.

Table 4.3 shows the authors who wrote the most articles between 1992 and 2012. The largest number of articles (eight) in period A was published by Fleischmann, M., and in period B: Adenso-Díaz, B. Kannan, G., Ravi, V., and Shankar, R. In the last period (2014–2021), the largest number of articles (fifteen) were published by Govindan, K. At the same time, we can note that the names of these authors do not repeat in the rankings, which is related to the dynamics of the development of the RL field. The only author to appear twice in periods A and B is Van Wassenhove, L.N.

4.4.2 Co-citation Analysis

Co-citation analysis forms clusters of scholarly sources that are frequently co-cited in a pool of articles (Small, 1973). To identify the clusters of reverse-logistics research, co-citation analysis, a widely accepted approach, was used (Fahimnia et al., 2015). It allows researchers to examine the existing links between articles that were published as part of the dataset of all articles in the area of reverse logistics. Co-citation analysis is a technique for science mapping that assumes publications that are cited together frequently are similar thematically (Hjørland, 2013).

The analysis can be used to reveal the intellectual structure of a research field, such as thematically similar research areas. The idea behind clustering through co-citation analysis is that the higher the frequency of the co-citation of each pair of references, the higher the likelihood of these references

Table 4.3 The Most Productive Authors by the Number of Papers.

Rank	1992–2004	Documents	Rank	2005–2013	Documents	Rank	2014–2021	Documents
1	Fleischmann, M.	8	1	Adenso-Díaz, B.	8	1	Govindan, K.	15
2	Daugherty, P.J.	5	1	Kannan, G.,	8	2	Soleimani, H.	9
2	Dekker, R.	5	1	Ravi, V.	8	3	Shankar, R.	7
3	Autry, C.W.	4	1	Shankar, R.	8	4	Singh, S.R.	6
3	Minner, S.	4	2	Kumar, S.	7	5	Agrawal, S.	5
3	Vlachos, D.	4	3	Hazen, B.T.	6	5	Chileshe, N.	5
4	Guide, V.D.R.	3	4	Chan, F.T.S.	5	5	Diabat, A.	5
4	Kiesmüller, G.P.	3	4	Chan, H.K.	5	5	Garza-Reyes, J.A.	5
4	Krikke, H.R.	3	4	Corominas, A.	5	5	Jha, P.C.	5
4	Van Wassenhove, L.N.	3	4	Genchev, S.E.	5	5	Kumar, V.	5
			4	Hall, D.J.	5	5	Rameezdeen, R.	5
			4	Hanna, J.B.	5	5	Singh, R.K.	5
			4	Jayaraman, V.	5	5	Singh, S.P.	5
			4	Li, Y.	5			
			4	Mukhopadhyay, S.K.	5			
			4	Saen, R.F.	5			
			4	Sarkis, J.	5			
			4	Tang, O.	5			
			4	Van Wassenhove, L.N.	5			

Source: Own elaboration.

forming a cluster and converging to a similar topic. Each cluster, therefore, contains a set of co-cited references that have a strong connection among them and a weaker connection to the rest of the clusters. Co-citation analysis only focuses on highly cited publications, which makes it useful for identifying the most important works that form the basis of a given field. These works are usually the starting point for the development of a given field of knowledge.

Table 4.4 presents the ten most important articles in the entire set of articles in the area of reverse logistics. It can be assumed that they had a huge impact on the dynamics of the development of the intellectual structure, giving rise to various research paths, including niche ones. Co-citation analysis revealed the existence of five thematic clusters (Figure 4.1).

Table 4.4   Top Ten Cited RL Papers.

Rank	References	Title	Number of citations
1	(Dowlatshahi, 2000)	"Developing a theory of reverse logistics"	74
2	(Carter & Ellram, 1998)	"Reverse logistics: a review of the literature and framework for future investigation"	72
3	(Govindan et al., 2015)	"Reverse logistics and the closed-loop supply chain: A comprehensive review to explore the future"	41
4	(Fleischmann et al., 2001)	"The impact of product recovery on logistics network design"	37
5	(Rogers & Tibben-Lembke, 2001)	"An examination of reverse logistics practices"	32
6	(Daugherty et al., 2002)	"Information support for reverse logistics: the influence of relationship commitment"	30
7	(Srivastava, 2008)	"Network design for reverse logistics"	30
8	(Jayaraman et al., 2003)	"The design of reverse distribution networks: models and solution procedures"	27
9	(Pokharel & Mutha, 2009)	"Perspectives in reverse logistics: a review"	26
10	(Ravi & Shankar, 2005)	"Analysis of interactions among the barriers to reverse logistics"	25

Source: Own elaboration.

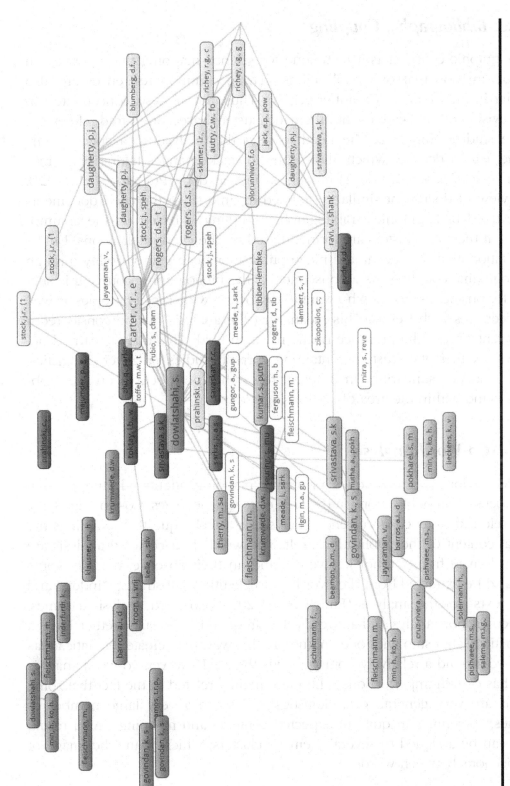

Figure 4.1   Co-Citations Cluster Map.

Source: Own elaboration.

4.4.3 Bibliographic Coupling

Bibliographic coupling is a technique for science mapping that operates on the assumption that two publications sharing common references are also similar in their content (Weinberg, 1974). Thus, the analysis concentrates on the division of publications into thematic clusters based on shared references. Some studies emphasize the need to refer the analysis to a specific time frame, e.g., a decade, which allows one to track changes taking place in a given field (Martyn, 1964). However, as indicated by Prathap et al. (2021), this view of document similarity is fixed in time since the cited documents have fixed bibliographies. Bibliographic coupling is based on the assumption that thematic clusters are formed based on the cited publications. Unlike co-citation analysis, recent and niche publications can gain visibility through bibliographic coupling. As a consequence, the bibliographic coupling is suitable for business scholars who want to discover a wide range of topics as well as recent research trends. This means that the analysis can be considered a representation of the presence of the research field. The analysis carried out shows six thematic clusters containing current studies on reverse logistics. They evidence similarities in different researcher perspectives on the problems found within the area of reverse logistics.

4.4.4 Co-Word Analysis

In the previous two techniques for science mapping, attention in the research was focused on publications in the area of reverse logistics. Co-word analysis, also referred to as co-occurrence analysis, is a technique that examines the actual content of the publication itself. The words in a co-word analysis are often derived from "author keywords" and, in their absence, notable words can also be extracted from "keywords," "article titles," "abstracts," "index," and "full texts" for the analysis (Emich et al., 2020). Co-word analysis assumes, like co-citation analysis, that words that frequently appear together have a thematic relationship with one another. In this way, they create thematic areas focused around a relatively homogeneous theme. However, co-word analysis also has certain imperfections. These are mainly related to the fact that some words are very general, e.g., "logistics" occurs in a very large number of articles, sometimes in quite unexpected contexts and meanings. As a result, they can be assigned to several thematic clusters, which "blur" the image of connections between words.

The use of co-word analysis can be treated as a strategic discovery of topics in which research in a given field is concentrated. As emphasized by Chang et al. (2015), co-word analysis can be used as a supplement to enrich the understanding of thematic clusters derived from co-citation analysis of bibliographic coupling. Therefore, research assumes that co-word analysis sets the future directions of research areas. Figure 4.2 shows the visualization of keywords for the thematic area of reverse logistics.

Keyword-frequency analysis was carried out for the entire set of keywords (4,575 words) in the article set. After setting the parameter of the occurrence

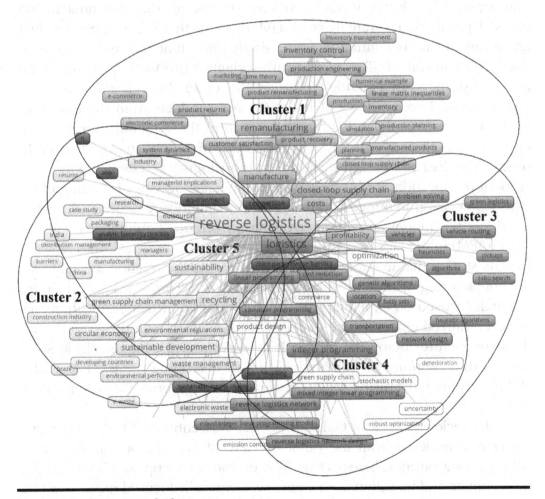

Figure 4.2   A Co-Word Cluster Map.

Source: Own elaboration.

of a word in the set to a minimum of ten, a total of 155 keywords were obtained. The visualization shows five thematic clusters. The most common keywords in the set of all documents are "reverse logistics" (778), "logistics" (258), "supply chains" (165), "remanufacturing" (118), "recycling" (114), "decision making" (96), "sustainable development" (94), "closed-loop supply chain" (80), "sustainability" (78), and "integer programming" (77). In parentheses, the frequency of occurrence of a given word in the whole set is given.

Cluster 1. Remanufacturing and the Closed-Loop Supply Chain

The top-middle cluster includes articles discussing the remanufacturing of used products. Jayaraman et al. (1999) prove that recoverable product environments are becoming an increasingly important segment of the production environment. The ecologically oriented production environment offers customers an extended product life cycle through remanufacturing or repair. Reverse flows of materials and products from the customer to the remanufacturer and forward flows from the remanufacturer to the customer are characterized by a specific type of supply chain. Their complexity requires the design of a closed-loop logistics system, taking into account the location of objects as well as managerial uses of the model for logistics decision making. Another article (Majumder & Groenevelt, 2001) considers the model of remanufacturing an original-equipment manufacturer (OEM) in the face of competition. In the model, they take into account various stimuli that make manufacturers increase the fraction available for remanufacturing or reduce remanufacturing costs. This trend also includes research focused on explaining the operation of coordination mechanisms in decentralized channels and decentralized decision-making systems with the manufacturer being the leader. It is important to compare these solutions with a centrally coordinated system to determine the level of profitability of remanufacturing used products into new ones (Savaskan et al., 2004).

In the review studies of Guide Jr. & Van Wassenhove (2009), remanufacturing is considered from the point of view of closed-loop supply chains with a strong business perspective. The evolutionary approach involves the development and transition from a narrow, technically focused niche area to a fully recognized subfield of supply-chain management. We can find a similar nature of review in the research conducted by Souza (2013), which presents a review and tutorial of the literature on closed-loop supply chains. It contains reverse flows of used products (postconsumer use) back to manufacturers. This article discusses base models with underlying assumptions, results, and comments on extensions. Finally Atasu et al. (2013) discuss the impact of the collection cost structure on the optimal reverse-channel choice of manufacturers who remanufacture their products.

Cluster 2. Sustainability and Waste Management

The bottom-left cluster encompasses articles taking a general perspective on sustainability and waste management. Nagurney and Toyasaki (2005) developed an integrated framework for the modeling of the reverse supply-chain management of electronic waste, which includes recycling. They describe the behavior of the various decision makers: Recyclers, processors, as well as consumers associated with the demand markets. Sarkis et al. (2010) drew attention to social and ethical dimensions of sustainability, particularly as they apply to reverse logistics. The environmental implications of reclamation, reuse, and recycling to save landfill space, fuel, and costs are becoming more important for organizations, especially in the context of social sustainability. In their research, Chaabane et al. (2012) presented a framework for a sustainable supply-chain design that considers life-cycle assessment (LCA). The proposed framework distinguishes between solid and liquid wastes, as well as gaseous emissions resulting from various production processes and transportation systems. At the same time, current legislation and emissions-trading schemes (ETS) must be harmonized at a global level to drive a meaningful environmental strategy.

Hsu et al. (2013), using survey data collected from ISO 14001 certified organizations, indicated that crucial drivers motivating firms to adopt green supply-chain management can be measured by a second-order construct related to the implementation of the firm's green supply-chain initiatives. In their research, they pointed to green purchasing, design-for-environment, and reverse-logistics initiatives as key to the adoption of the green supply-chain concept. Finally, Brandenburg et al. (2014) provide content analysis of 134 carefully identified papers on quantitative, formal models that address sustainability aspects in the forward Supply Chain (SC).

Cluster 3. Quantitative Methods in Reverse Logistics

The bottom-right cluster remains in the line of research and application of quantitative methods in reverse logistics. The basis of the researchers' interest is the recovery of used products due to growing environmental concerns. Fleischmann et al. (1997) subdivide the reverse-logistics field into three main areas, namely distribution planning, inventory control, and production planning. They drew attention to the implications of emerging reuse efforts as well as a review of mathematical models proposed in the literature. They also pointed to differences and similarities about classical "forward" logistics methods. In other articles (Fleischmann et al., 2000, 2001), the authors identify the general characteristics of product recovery networks and compare them with traditional logistics structures. They also derive a classification scheme for different types of recovery networks. The articles present a generic facility location model to analyze the impact of product return flows on logistics networks. They point out that the efficient implementation of closed-loop supply chains requires changes in logistics structures for the arising flows of used and recovered products (Melo et al., 2009). Supply-chain performance measures, optimization techniques, and aspects related to the structure of the supply-chain network, including those specific to reverse logistics, are also addressed. For Sarkis et al. (2010), the key issue is supporting the relationship between the stakeholder and resource-based theory as a complementary theoretical framework. This relationship is supported by the link between institutional theory and the dimensions of dynamic capabilities in resource-based theory about environmentally oriented reverse-logistics practices.

Cluster 4. Green Operations and Supply-Chain Management

The fourth cluster includes articles focused on problems of green supply-chain management (GSCM). Sheu et al. (2005) present an optimization-based model that systematically optimizes the operations of both integrated logistics and corresponding used-product reverse logistics in a given green supply chain. The next article (Laosirihongthong et al., 2013) examines the deployment of proactive and reactive practices in the implementation of green supply-chain management (GSCM). The results of this study demonstrate that reverse-logistics practices (proactive practices) have had low levels of adoption and do not have a significant impact on GSCM performance.

In-depth research conducted by Govindan et al. (2014), using a deductive research approach to derive a conceptual model, identifies the practices with a significant impact on supply-chain sustainability. These are "waste elimination," "supply chain risk management," and "cleaner production." The research provides a taxonomy for lean, resilient, and green supply-chain management practices at three levels: upstream, organization, and downstream. The authors (Govindan and Soleimani (2017; Govindan et al. (2017), taking into account articles published in the *Journal of Cleaner Production* (JCP), clarify the main trends in reverse logistics and closed-loop supply-chain subjects, and also provide a systematic view on developing reverse logistics and closed-loop supply chains. Uncertain business environments provide a comprehensive review of studies in the fields of supply chain network design and reverse-logistics network design.

Cluster 5. Sustainable Supply-Chain Concepts

The last cluster, located in the middle of our map, addresses global concepts of sustainable supply chains. Van Hoek (1999) looks at challenges for research on green supply chains, as a step towards lowering the ecologic footprint of supply chains. Research shows the need for developing a grounded theory, and frameworks that go beyond the partial and fragmented contribution of reversed logistics. Lu et al. (2007) prove that the green supply chain (GSC) is a broad concept that refers to a variety of methods by which companies work with their suppliers to improve the environmental performance of their products or the manufacturing processes of the suppliers or customers. It combines specified environmental performance criteria and helps suppliers recognize the importance of resolving environmental issues. Finally, Quariguasi Frota Neto et al. (2009), by designing a complex recycling logistics network in Germany, posit that visual exploration of the efficient frontier and trade-offs between profitability and environmental impacts are particularly suitable in sustainable supply chains.

To summarize, the study of the five clusters presents different approaches and analytical capabilities used by the article authors. The first cluster focuses on the problems associated with remanufacturing in terms of the effectiveness of closed-loop supply chains. The second cluster offers a broad view of waste management from the perspective of sustainability and the environmental implications of a reverse supply chain. Unlike the first two clusters, the third one primarily exposes the use of quantitative methods in reverse logistics using different theoretical approaches. The fourth cluster focuses on understanding business practices and the decision-making process in green supply-chain management. The final, fifth cluster is more conceptual as it considers and analyzes the existing theoretical framework for sustainable supply chains.

4.5 Discussion and Conclusions

This study presents an analysis of reverse logistics (RL), an emerging research field aimed at solving environmental problems within the framework of supply-chain management. The novel contribution of the chapter is a proposal of a theoretical framework for related concepts that occur in the area of sustainability-oriented supply-chain management. Such concepts as CLSCM, EL, GL, GSCM, SL, SCM, and SSCM refer to the problem of waste, often in an ambiguous way. As in other studies (e.g., Guarnieri et al., 2015), we started with the qualitative analysis of existing achievements in the area of reverse logistics and then directed the research to bibliometric analysis. The use of bibliometric analysis allowed us to determine the links between these concepts and RL.

The results include a five-cluster configuration from the co-citation map, which was identified by a mapping algorithm. It proves that there is relative isolation between the five lines of research. However, studies in clusters 4 and 5 interpenetrate, to a large extent, with other, more clearly designated clusters. This suggests the emergence of new thematic areas, based on more well-established concepts such as reverse logistics. This is evidenced by research conducted by Bensalem & Kin (2019), in which four isolated thematic clusters were identified. The emergence of an additional cluster over three years clearly shows the dynamics of changes occurring in the conducted research and the gradual transition from reverse logistics to new concepts, such as SSCM or GSCM. At the same time, it may indicate a lack of maturity of research on reverse logistics in terms of the debate between a business versus an environmental orientation of the development of modern supply chains. At the same time, the majority of the latest research results are concentrated in one of three journals: *Journal of Cleaner Production, International Journal of Production Economics*, and *International Journal of Production Research*, which profiles the studies and sets research directions in line with the journals' objectives. However, the number of articles in the area of reverse logistics, including 1,109 items published over almost 30 years, demonstrates an upward trend. Three periods: A, B, and C can be distinguished in the increase in the number of publications. The first two, covering the years 1992–2013, show a stable growth rate in the number of publications in the area of reverse logistics. The third period (2014–2021), along with periods of decline in the number of publications, clearly indicate the change and emergence of new concepts within which the problem of waste is considered.

Co-citation analysis clearly shows that the development of the reverse-logistics theory included fundamental axiological problems and their conceptualization, which created a theoretical framework for the development of further research in the following decades. The initial narrow orientation in research, e.g., on used-product remanufacturing, was gradually replaced by a broader SC perspective, which included specific research areas. GL, SL, or GSCM serve as good examples of this.

The study presents some limitations that result from bibliometric methods. Summing up the problems, we can mention a loss of relevant papers, the overrepresentation of theoretical articles, the inclusion of nonrelevant papers, and the exclusion of highly relevant papers. In general, the problem concerns the quality of the initial article database which, when processed, provides a graphical picture of research in a given field in the form of analytical maps. An important issue is also a lack of reference of keywords in co-word analysis to the context in which they were used. Despite these shortcomings, the growing number of published bibliometric studies demonstrates that it is a widely accepted methodology and approach to determining the structure of knowledge in a given area of science. This is especially true for well-established areas of research, such as logistics and SCM, characterized by significant scientific achievements demonstrated in a large number of published articles.

References

Agrawal, S., Singh, R. K., & Murtaza, Q. (2015). A literature review and perspectives in reverse logistics. *Resources, Conservation and Recycling, 97*, 76–92.

Alamerew, Y. A., & Brissaud, D. (2020). Modelling reverse supply chain through system dynamics for realizing the transition towards the circular economy: A case study on electric vehicle batteries. *Journal of Cleaner Production, 254*, 120025. DOI: 10.1016/j.jclepro.2020.120025

Arampantzi, C., & Minis, I. (2017). A new model for designing sustainable supply chain networks and its application to a global manufacturer. *Journal of Cleaner Production, 156*, 276–292. DOI: 10.1016/j.jclepro.2017.03.164

Atasu, A., Toktay, L. B., & Van Wassenhove, L. N. (2013). How collection cost structure drives a manufacturer's reverse channel choice. *Production and Operations Management, 22*(5), 1089–1102. DOI: 10.1111/j.1937-5956.2012.01426.x

Battaïa, O., & Gupta, S. M. (2015). Reverse supply chains: A source of opportunities and challenges. *Journal of Manufacturing Systems, 37*, 587–588. DOI: 10.1016/j.jmsy.2015.11.005

Bensalem, A., & Kin, V. (2019). A bibliometric analysis of reverse logistics from 1992 to 2017. *Supply Chain Forum, 20*(1), 15–28. DOI: 10.1080/16258312.2019.1574430

Bernon, M., Rossi, S., & Cullen, J. (2011). Retail reverse logistics: A call and grounding framework for research. *International Journal of Physical Distribution and Logistics Management, 41*(5), 484–510. DOI: 10.1108/09600031111138835

Blackburn, J. D., Guide, V. D. R., Souza, G. C., & Wassenhove, L. N. Van. (2004). For commercial returns. *California Management Review, 46*(2), 6–23.

Brandenburg, M., Govindan, K., Sarkis, J., & Seuring, S. (2014). Quantitative models for sustainable supply chain management: Developments and directions. *European Journal of Operational Research, 233*(2), 299–312. DOI: 10.1016/j.ejor.2013.09.032

Broadus, R. N. (1987). Toward a definition of "bibliometrics." *Scientometrics, 12*(5–6), 373–379. DOI: 10.1007/BF02016680

Campos, E. A. R. de, Paula, I. C. de, Pagani, R. N., & Guarnieri, P. (2017). Reverse logistics for the end-of-life and end-of-use products in the pharmaceutical industry: A systematic literature review. *Supply Chain Management: An International Journal, 22*(4), 375–392. DOI: 10.1108/SCM-01-2017-0040

Carter, C. R., & Ellram, L. M. (1998). Reverse logistics: A review of the literature and framework for future investigation. *Journal of Business Logistics, 19*(1), 85.

Chaabane, A., Ramudhin, A., & Paquet, M. (2012). Design of sustainable supply chains under the emission trading scheme. *International Journal of Production Economics, 135*(1), 37–49. DOI: 10.1016/j.ijpe.2010.10.025

Chang, Y.-W., Huang, M.-H., & Lin, C.-W. (2015). Evolution of research subjects in library and information science based on keyword, bibliographical coupling, and co-citation analyses. *Scientometrics, 105*(3), 2071–2087. DOI: 10.1007/s11192-015-1762-8

Daugherty, P. J., Myers, M. B., & Richey, R. G. (2002). Information support for reverse logistics: The influence of relationship commitment. *Journal of Business Logistics, 23*(1), 85–106.

De Brito, M. P., & Dekker, R. (2004). A framework for reverse logistics. In: Dekker, R. Fleischmann, M., Inderfurth, K. & Van Wassenhove, L.N. (eds.), *Reverse Logistics* (pp. 3–27). Berlin, Heidelberg: Springer. DOI: 10.1007/978-3-540-24803-3_1

Dolati Neghabadi, P., Evrard Samuel, K., & Espinouse, M. L. (2019). Systematic literature review on city logistics: Overview, classification and analysis. *International Journal of Production Research, 57*(3), 865–887. DOI: 10.1080/00207543.2018.1489153

Donthu, N., Kumar, S., Mukherjee, D., Pandey, N., & Lim, W. M. (2021). How to conduct a bibliometric analysis: An overview and guidelines. *Journal of Business Research, 133*(March), 285–296. DOI: 10.1016/j.jbusres.2021.04.070

Dowlatshahi, S. (2000). Developing a theory of reverse logistics. *Interfaces, 30*(3), 143–155.

Emich, K. J., Kumar, S., Lu, L., Norder, K., & Pandey, N. (2020). Mapping 50 years of small group research through small group research. *Small Group Research, 51*(6), 659–699. DOI: 10.1177/1046496420934541

Eng-Larsson, F., & Kohn, C. (2012). Modal shift for greener logistics: The shipper's perspective. *International Journal of Physical Distribution & Logistics Management, 42*(1), 36–59. DOI: 10.1108/09600031211202463

Fahimnia, B., Sarkis, J., & Davarzani, H. (2015). Green supply chain management: A review and bibliometric analysis. *International Journal of Production Economics, 162*, 101–114. DOI: 10.1016/j.ijpe.2015.01.003

Fleischmann, M., Beullens, P., Bloemhof-Ruwaard, J. M., & Van Wassenhove, L. N. (2001). The impact of product recovery on logistics network design. *Production and Operations Management, 10*(2), 156–173.

Fleischmann, M., Bloemhof-Ruwaard, J. M., Dekker, R., van der Laan, E., van Nunen, J. A. E. E., & Van Wassenhove, L. N. (1997). Quantitative models for reverse logistics: A review. *European Journal of Operational Research, 103*(1), 1–17. DOI: 10.1016/S0377-2217(97)00230-0

Fleischmann, M., Krikke, H. R., Dekker, R., & Flapper, S. D. P. (2000). A characterisation of logistics networks for product recovery. *Omega, 28*(6), 653–666. DOI: 10.1016/S0305-0483(00)00022-0

Frota Neto, J. Q., Bloemhof-Ruwaard, J. M., van Nunen, J. A. E. E., & van Heck, E. (2008). Designing and evaluating sustainable logistics networks. *International Journal of Production Economics, 111*(2), 195–208. DOI: 10.1016/j.ijpe.2006.10.014

Gaur, J., Subramoniam, R., Govindan, K., & Huisingh, D. (2017). Closed-loop supply chain management: From conceptual to an action oriented framework on core acquisition. *Journal of Cleaner Production, 167*, 1415–1424. DOI: 10.1016/j.jclepro.2016.12.098

Georgi, C., Darkow, I. L., & Kotzab, H. (2013). Foundations of logistics and supply chain research: A bibliometric analysis of four international journals. *International Journal of Logistics Research and Applications, 16*(6), 522–533. DOI: 10.1080/13675567.2013.846309

Govindan, K., Azevedo, S. G., Carvalho, H., & Cruz-Machado, V. (2014). Impact of supply chain management practices on sustainability. *Journal of Cleaner Production, 85*, 212–225. DOI: 10.1016/j.jclepro.2014.05.068

Govindan, K., Fattahi, M., & Keyvanshokooh, E. (2017). Supply chain network design under uncertainty: A comprehensive review and future research directions. *European Journal of Operational Research, 263*(1), 108–141. DOI: 10.1016/j.ejor.2017.04.009

Govindan, K., & Soleimani, H. (2017). A review of reverse logistics and closed-loop supply chains: A Journal of Cleaner Production focus. *Journal of Cleaner Production, 142*, 371–384. DOI: 10.1016/j.jclepro.2016.03.126

Govindan, K., Soleimani, H., & Kannan, D. (2015). Reverse logistics and closed-loop supply chain: A comprehensive review to explore the future. *European Journal of Operational Research, 240*(3), 603–626.

Guarnieri, P., Sobreiro, V. A., Nagano, M. S., & Marques Serrano, A. L. (2015). The challenge of selecting and evaluating third-party reverse logistics providers in a multicriteria perspective: A Brazilian case. *Journal of Cleaner Production, 96*, 209–219. DOI: 10.1016/j.jclepro.2014.05.040

Guide Jr., V. D. R., Souza, G. C., Van Wassenhove, L. N., & Blackburn, J. D. (2006). Time value of commercial product returns. *Management Science, 52*(8), 1200–1214. DOI: 10.1287/mnsc.1060.0522

Guide Jr., V. D. R., & Van Wassenhove, L. N. (2009). The evolution of closed-loop supply chain research. *Operations Research, 57*(1), 10–18. DOI: 10.1287/opre.1080.0628

Hjørland, B. (2013). Facet analysis: The logical approach to knowledge organization. *Information Processing & Management, 49*(2), 545–557. DOI: 10.1016/j.ipm.2012.10.001

Homayouni, Z., Pishvaee, M. S., Jahani, H., & Ivanov, D. (2021). A robust-heuristic optimization approach to a green supply chain design with consideration of assorted vehicle types and carbon policies under uncertainty. *Annals of Operations Research.* DOI: 10.1007/s10479-021-03985-6

Hsu, C., Choon Tan, K., Hanim Mohamad Zailani, S., & Jayaraman, V. (2013). Supply chain drivers that foster the development of green initiatives in an emerging economy. *International Journal of Operations & Production Management, 33*(6), 656–688. DOI: 10.1108/IJOPM-10-2011-0401

Huscroft, J. R., Hazen, B. T., Hall, D. J., Skipper, J. B., & Hanna, J. B. (2013). Reverse logistics: Past research, current management issues, and future directions. *The International Journal of Logistics Management, 24*(3), 304–327. DOI: 10.1108/IJLM-04-2012-0024.

Islam, M. S., Moeinzadeh, S., Tseng, M. L., & Tan, K. (2021). A literature review on environmental concerns in logistics: Trends and future challenges. *International Journal of Logistics Research and Applications, 24*(2), 126–151. DOI: 10.1080/13675567.2020.1732313

Jayaraman, V., Guide, V. D. R., & Srivastava, R. (1999). A closed-loop logistics model for remanufacturing. *Journal of the Operational Research Society, 50*(5), 497–508. DOI: 10.1057/palgrave.jors.2600716

Jayaraman, V., Patterson, R. A., & Rolland, E. (2003). The design of reverse distribution networks: Models and solution procedures. *European Journal of Operational Research, 150*(1), 128–149.

Jemai, J., Chung, B. Do, & Sarkar, B. (2020). Environmental effect for a complex green supply-chain management to control waste: A sustainable approach. *Journal of Cleaner Production, 277*, 122919. DOI: 10.1016/j.jclepro.2020.122919

Kazemi, N., Modak, N. M., & Govindan, K. (2019). A review of reverse logistics and closed loop supply chain management studies published in IJPR: A bibliometric and content analysis. *International Journal of Production Research, 57*(15–16), 4937–4960. DOI: 10.1080/00207543.2018.1471244

Kotzab, H., Bäumler, I., & Gerken, P. (2021). The big picture on supply chain integration: Insights from a bibliometric analysis. *Supply Chain Management: An International Journal, ahead-of-p*(ahead-of-print). DOI: 10.1108/SCM-09-2020-0496

Lambert, D. M., & James, R. (1982). Strategic physical distribution management. *RD Irwin.*

Laosirihongthong, T., Adebanjo, D., & Choon Tan, K. (2013). Green supply chain management practices and performance. *Industrial Management & Data Systems, 113*(8), 1088–1109. DOI: 10.1108/IMDS-04-2013-0164

Lee, D. H., Dong, M., & Bian, W. (2010). The design of sustainable logistics network under uncertainty. *International Journal of Production Economics, 128*(1), 159–166. DOI: 10.1016/j.ijpe.2010.06.009

Lu, L. Y. Y., Wu, C. H., & Kuo, T. C. (2007). Environmental principles applicable to green supplier evaluation by using multi-objective decision analysis. *International Journal of Production Research, 45*(18–19), 4317–4331. DOI: 10.1080/00207540701472694

Majumder, P., & Groenevelt, H. (2001). Competition in remanufacturing. *Production and Operations Management, 10*(2), 125–141. DOI: 10.1111/j.1937-5956.2001.tb00074.x

Martyn, J. (1964). Bibliographic coupling. *Journal of Documentation, 20*(4), 236. DOI: 10.1108/eb026352

Melo, M. T., Nickel, S., & Saldanha-da-Gama, F. (2009). Facility location and supply chain management: A review. *European Journal of Operational Research, 196*(2), 401–412. DOI: 10.1016/j.ejor.2008.05.007

Murphy, P. R., & Poist, R. F. (1988). Management of logistical retromovements: An empirical analysis of literature suggestions. *Journal of the Transportation Research Forum, 29*(HS-040 801).

Nagurney, A., & Toyasaki, F. (2005). Reverse supply chain management and electronic waste recycling: A multitiered network equilibrium framework for e-cycling. *Transportation Research Part E: Logistics and Transportation Review, 41*(1), 1–28. DOI: 10.1016/j.tre.2003.12.001

Pokharel, S., & Mutha, A. (2009). Perspectives in reverse logistics: A review. *Resources, Conservation and Recycling, 53*(4), 175–182.

Pournader, M., Ghaderi, H., Hassanzadegan, A., & Fahimnia, B. (2021). Artificial intelligence applications in supply chain management. *International Journal of Production Economics, 241*(August), 108250. DOI: 10.1016/j.ijpe.2021.108250

Prathap, G., Ujum, E. A., Kumar, S., & Ratnavelu, K. (2021). Scoring the resourcefulness of researchers using bibliographic coupling patterns. *Journal of Informetrics, 15*(3), 101168. DOI: 10.1016/j.joi.2021.101168

Presley, A., Meade, L., & Sarkis, J. (2007). A strategic sustainability justification methodology for organizational decisions: A reverse logistics illustration. *International Journal of Production Research, 45*(18–19), 4595–4620. DOI: 10.1080/00207540701440220

Quariguasi Frota Neto, J., Walther, G., Bloemhof, J., van Nunen, J. A. E. E., & Spengler, T. (2009). A methodology for assessing eco-efficiency in logistics networks. *European Journal of Operational Research, 193*(3), 670–682. DOI: 10.1016/j.ejor.2007.06.056

Rajagopal, P., Kaliani Sundram, V. P., & Maniam Naidu, B. (2015). Future directions of reverse logistics in gaining competitive advantages: A review of literature. *International Journal of Supply Chain Management, 4*(1), 39–48.

Ravi, V., & Shankar, R. (2005). Analysis of interactions among the barriers of reverse logistics. *Technological Forecasting and Social Change, 72*(8), 1011–1029.

Rogers, D. S., & Tibben-Lembke, R. S. (1999). *Going Backwards: Reverse Logistics Trends and Practices* (Vol. 2). Pittsburgh, PA: Reverse Logistics Executive Council.

Rogers, D. S., & Tibben-Lembke, R. S. (2001). An examination of reverse logistics practices. *Journal of Business Logistics, 22*(2), 129–148.

Sarkis, J. (2021). Supply chain sustainability: Learning from the COVID-19 pandemic. *International Journal of Operations & Production Management, 41*(1), 63–73. DOI: 10.1108/IJOPM-08-2020-0568

Sarkis, J., Gonzalez-Torre, P., & Adenso-Diaz, B. (2010). Stakeholder pressure and the adoption of environmental practices: The mediating effect of training. *Journal of Operations Management, 28*(2), 163–176. DOI: 10.1016/j.jom.2009.10.001

Sarkis, J., Helms, M. M., & Hervani, A. A. (2010). Reverse logistics and social sustainability. *Corporate Social Responsibility and Environmental Management, 17*(6), 337–354. DOI: 10.1002/csr.220

Savaskan, R. C., Bhattacharya, S., & Van Wassenhove, L. N. (2004). Closed-loop supply chain models with product remanufacturing. *Management Science, 50*(2), 239–252. DOI: 10.1287/mnsc.1030.0186

Seyedghorban, Z., Tahernejad, H., Meriton, R., & Graham, G. (2020). Supply chain digitalization: Past, present and future. *Production Planning and Control, 31*(2–3), 96–114. DOI: 10.1080/09537287.2019.1631461

Sheu, J.-B., Chou, Y.-H., & Hu, C.-C. (2005). An integrated logistics operational model for green-supply chain management. *Transportation Research Part E: Logistics and Transportation Review, 41*(4), 287–313. DOI: 10.1016/j.tre.2004.07.001

Small, H. (1973). Co-citation in the scientific literature: A new measure of the relationship between two documents. *Journal of the American Society for Information Science, 24*(4), 265–269.

Souza, G. C. (2013). Closed-loop supply chains: A critical review, and future research*. *Decision Sciences, 44*(1), 7–38. DOI: 10.1111/j.1540-5915.2012.00394.x

Srivastava, S. K. (2008). Network design for reverse logistics. *Omega, 36*(4), 535–548.

Stock, J. R. (1992). *Reverse Logistics: White Paper.* Oak Brook, IL: Council of Logistics Management.

Stock, J. R. (1998). *Development and Implementation of Reverse Logistics Programs.* Oak Brook, IL: Annual Conference Proceedings, Council of Logistics Management.

Suzanne, E., Absi, N., & Borodin, V. (2020). Towards circular economy in production planning: Challenges and opportunities. *European Journal of Operational Research, 287*(1), 168–190. DOI: 10.1016/j.ejor.2020.04.043

Tornese, F., Pazour, J. A., Thorn, B. K., Roy, D., & Carrano, A. L. (2018). Investigating the environmental and economic impact of loading conditions and repositioning strategies for pallet pooling providers. *Journal of Cleaner Production, 172*, 155–168. DOI: 10.1016/j.jclepro.2017.10.054

van Hoek, R. I. (1999). From reversed logistics to green supply chains. *Supply Chain Management: An International Journal, 4*(3), 129–135. DOI: 10.1108/13598549910279576

Van Wassenhove, L. N. (2019). Sustainable innovation: Pushing the boundaries of traditional operations management. *Production and Operations Management, 28*(12), 2930–2945. DOI: 10.1111/poms.13114

Wang, H. F., & Hsu, H. W. (2010). A closed-loop logistic model with a spanning-tree based genetic algorithm. *Computers and Operations Research, 37*(2), 376–389. DOI: 10.1016/j.cor.2009.06.001

Wang, J. J., Chen, H., Rogers, D. S., Ellram, L. M., & Grawe, S. J. (2017). A bibliometric analysis of reverse logistics research (1992–2015) and opportunities for future research. *International Journal of Physical Distribution and Logistics Management, 47*(8), 666–687. DOI: 10.1108/IJPDLM-10-2016-0299

Wang, J. J., Lim, M. K., Tseng, M.-L., & Yang, Y. (2019). Promoting low carbon agenda in the urban logistics network distribution system. *Journal of Cleaner Production, 211*, 146–160. DOI: 10.1016/j.jclepro.2018.11.123

Weinberg, B. H. (1974). Bibliographic coupling: A review. *Information Storage and Retrieval, 10*(5), 189–196. DOI: 10.1016/0020-0271(74)90058-8

SUSTAINABLE SUPPLY-CHAIN MANAGEMENT

Chapter 5

Should We Rethink Supply-Chain Management? Insights from Global-Value-Chain Approach

Michał Pietrzak

Warsaw University of Life Sciences—SGGW, Poland

Contents

DOI: 10.4324/9781003304364-7

5.1 Introduction

According to Ansell and Boin (2019, p. 1,079), "modern societies are increasingly faced with 'unknown unknowns,' Black Swans, and mega-crises." Unexpectedly, due to the COVID-19 outbreak and supply shortages experienced in many countries at the beginning of the pandemic, the term "supply chain" became a new buzzword in the public consciousness (Gereffi, 2020). Some critics started to question popular business practices such as just-in-time or lean management spreading worldwide within supply chains, which were demystified as neglecting vital safety margins (Financial Times, 2020, 2021; O'Leary, 2020; Shih, 2020). Other authors even asked if we were witnessing the end of globalization as we knew it, and predicted re-shoring, a greater regionalization of supply chains, or at least more redundancy and diversification of built-in supply chains (Farrell & Newman, 2020; Gereffi, 2020; O'Neil, 2020; Shih, 2020). These concerns were not only due to the pandemic but also due to many other events and processes observed roughly in the last decade: The global financial crisis, the digital revolution, the outbreak of populism, and economic nationalism (Gereffi, 2020). Currently, the world is experiencing another crisis due to Russian aggression in Ukraine.

Overall, it seems that it is becoming clearer and clearer that the current approach to global supply chains should be rethought as there is a need for more viable, resilient, robust, or even "antifragile" (cf. Taleb, 2012) supply chains. Looking for a new approach, I would like to propose a review of different strands of literature that concern the issue of chains. The most criticized business practices in global supply chains were developed mainly in one such strand, namely, supply-chain management (SCM) rooted in logistics and operational management. There are, however, other strands. Among them is the widely recognized value-chain approach proposed in Porter's (1998 [1985]) seminal book. However, there is a less popular but very promising strand of literature, which could be called the socioeconomic strand, which is represented by the world-systems theory, the commodity-chain approach, and the global-commodity-chain (GCC) approach. Finally, the newest and most eclectic approach has appeared, namely the global value chain (GVC). This last approach could be, in my opinion, considered to form the basis of rethinking global supply chains and their improvement in the upcoming post-pandemic era.

The aim of this chapter is to discuss two approaches underlying global supply chains (SCM and GVC) and to find potential for their cross-fertilization. The main research question is: How could the GVC approach complement

SCM to address the present need of incorporating more resiliency in global supply chains regarding the recent challenges and uncertainties faced by the global economy? This chapter is based on literature review and a critical discussion.

The chapter organization is as follows. It starts with a short introduction (5.1). The crucial processes from the point of view of the origins of global supply chains are presented in section 5.2. Then the Supply-Chain Management (SCM) approach, in the context of recent challenges (COVID-19, the war in Ukraine), is discussed (5.3). Section 5.4 presents the genealogy and main thoughts of the global-value-chain approach, while in section 5.5., the main insight that could be drawn for SCM from GVC. In liteterature are used both acronyms GVC and GVCs, however I would like to unify this acronym within the whole text. Thus, I would like to use GVC when I refer to the Global Value Chain approach or to the particular global value chain in singular. I would like to use GVCs when I refer to the global value chains in plural are discussed. Then the implications of these insights are presented (5.6). Finally, this chapter ends with concluding remarks and some research propositions (5.7), which could be further explored in future studies.

5.2 Fragmentation of Production Processes, and the Old and New Globalization

Let us start with the phenomenon of fragmentation or the splitting up of previously vertically integrated production processes (Jones & Kierzkowski, 1990, 2000), which could be generally explained by referring to Stigler's (1951) seminal paper, which was ahead of its time (cf. Odersteijn et al., 2004). Stigler (1951, p. 187) wrote: "the firm is usually viewed as purchasing a series of inputs, from which it obtains one or more saleable products, the quantities of which are related to the quantities of the inputs by a production function.... it is better to view the firm as engaging in a series of distinct operations: purchasing and storing materials; transforming materials into semifinished products and semifinished products into finished products; storing and selling outputs; extending credit to buyers; etc. That is, we partition the firm... into the functions or processes constituting the scope of its activity."

Let us assume that this scope of activity (done under one firm umbrella) covers three processes (P1, P2, and P3), the costs of which are independent of each other. The costs of these processes are different, showing increasing returns to scale (P1), decreasing returns to scale (P2), and behavior according to the classic U-shaped curve (P3). The U-shaped cost curve means that the costs decrease with increasing scale to some extent, but beyond some threshold of the scale costs tend to rise. Due to this different nature of cost behavior, the size of the firm will reflect some kind of compromise between local optima for processes P1–P3. One could ask, however, that since the P1 process has increasing economies of scale, why doesn't this firm just increase the size of its business? The obstacle is, of course, diseconomies of scale resulting from the cost characteristics of other processes. One could continue his/her query and ask why has the company not taken advantage of outsourcing? The firm, through the outsourcing of P1, could leverage increasing returns to scale in this process.

The problem, Stigler (1951) explains, is that the demand for P1's products may be too small relative to the scale needed to attract the interest of a specialized outsourcer. This brings us to the heart of the issue called Smith's Theorem: "As is the power of exchanging that gives occasion to the division of labor, so the extent of this division of labor must always be limited by the extent of that power, or, in other words, by the extent of the market" Smith (2003 [1776], p. 27).

Now globalization comes into the foreground. "As by means of water-carriage, a more extensive market is opened to every sort of industry than what land-carriage alone can afford, so… that industry of every kind naturally begins to subdivide and improve itself" (Smith, 2003 [1776], p. 27). The possibilities of extending markets, since Smith, have developed substantially. The first breakthrough was the steam revolution. "Steam power allowed humans to conquer intercontinental distances and reshape the world in ways that were unimaginable with horse, wind, and water power" (Baldwin, 2019, p. 49). The "Old Globalization" or the "first unbundling," according to Baldwin (2019), has started.

When costs of moving goods are high, only very few of them could economically be shipped over anything but close distance. This problem made production bundled with consumption. "In the pre-globalization world, distance isolated people and production to such an extent that the world economy was little more than a patchwork of village-level economies" (Baldwin, 2019, p. 4). This state started to change when product transportation costs fell. Thus, "Old Globalization" can be thought of as a progressive unleashing of production from a "hostage" of consumption, which started around 1820. While costs of moving goods fell, other costs of distance still mattered, namely the costs of moving ideas and the costs of moving people. Therefore, markets expanded globally, but production clustered locally. This progressive reversal of bundling production and consumption due to the decrease in costs of transportation of products were the "first unbundling" (Baldwin, 2019).

According to Baldwin, this "Old Globalization" process could be divided into three stages: The development of international trade due to falling trade costs (1820–1913); then the confrontation of world powers—with two World Wars and the Great Depression in between them—and, therefore, the recurrence of re-bundling (1914–1945); and the final stage of first unbundling based on trade liberalization (1947's General Agreement on Tariffs and Trade) and transportation innovations, e.g., containerization (1946–1990) (cf. Baldwin, 2019, pp. 47–78). The result of the first unbundling was the boom of international trade and "The Great Divergence" due to the new worldwide division of labor between the global "North" (innovations and value-added products) and the "South" (natural resources, raw materials, and simple commodities).

However, since the 1990s new structural changes have arisen, namely a revolution in information and communication technology (ICT), which "produced a transition from… globalization's first unbundling to… a second unbundling[1]" (Baldwin, 2019, p. 80). ICT capacity grew at a tremendous annual rate of growth: 23% in information storage, 28% in telecommunications, and 58% in computational power. As a result, just the increment of the volume of information between 2006 and 2007 was 1.06×10^{36} times bigger than the sum of all information transmitted in the previous decade (Baldwin, 2019, p. 82). Such capacity development was complemented by the rise of the Internet. While steam power allowed to lower trade costs of moving products, the ICT revolution radically lowered the costs of communication and, therefore, facilitated the easy moving of ideas. The ICT revolution was complemented by the further development of transportation innovations including containerization and, particularly, the development of air cargo (Baldwin, 2019).

Let us go back to Stigler's (1951) work. From a very generally simplified point of view, the development path described above follows Smith's Theorem. Due to extending markets (first from local to domestic ones), splitting previously integrated processes into separate fragments of production (outsourcing) opens up possibilities for exploiting yields from specialization (increasing returns to scale in process P1 in our example). "Although such fragmentation is likely to occur first on… a national basis, significant cuts in the costs of international co-ordination often allow producers to take advantage of differences in technologies and factor prices among countries in designing more global production networks" (Jones & Kierzkowski, 2000, p. 1). Through outsourcing and offshoring, a new phenomenon arises, namely global supply chains, a.k.a. global value chains.[2]

Even though these terms are usually used almost interchangeably, as names of some specific form of interorganizational relations, one should be aware of the difference between the supply-chain-management (SCM) approach to this phenomenon and the global-value-chain (GVC) approach. Both SCM and GVC are separate schools of thought,[3] with different genealogy and theoretical backgrounds. In my opinion, this creates an occasion for the cross-fertilization of both approaches. Here we will focus on challenges faced by SCM due to recent uncertainties (COVID-19, the war in Ukraine) and will try to figure out how the GVC approach could shed light on some challenges connected with them.

5.3 Supply-Chain Management in the Face of the Challenges of Recent Uncertainties

The concept of the supply chain appeared in the 1970s and was initially focused on the integration of logistics operations within enterprises to reduce costs (Camps, 2004). According to Coyle et al. (1996), responsibility for various logistic functions and tasks was traditionally dispersed across various departments of enterprises. Gradually, these responsibilities began to be encapsulated into two broad tasks: Materials management and physical distribution. Finally, all these tasks were integrated into the logistics supply chain (Coyle et al., 1996), which prevents attempts to improve logistics against the problem of suboptimization.[4]

However, logistics students gradually started to think about the supply chain in a broader context, i.e., going beyond the boundaries of a single company (Camps, 2004; Sweeney, 2011) and consisting of a sequence of related enterprises (Lazzarini et al., 2001; van der Vorst, 2004). Integration and matching are at the heart of the supply-chain concept (Christopher, 2011; Storey et al., 2006). According to Fawcett and Magnan (2002), four levels of integration can be identified: Internal (inter-functional), backward (with direct suppliers), forward (with direct buyers), and complete back and forth (from suppliers delivering to direct suppliers, to customers buying from direct customers). Thus, while at its inception the concept of the supply chain concerned the first level, nowadays it is usually interpreted in terms of the fourth level of integration.

In this broader sense, the term supply chain was first used in the early 1980s by Oliver and Weber (1982). The Council of Supply Chain Management Professionals (CSCMP) regards the supply chain as follows: "1) starting with unprocessed raw materials and ending with the final customer using finished goods, the supply chain links many companies together. 2) the material and informational interchanges in the logistics process stretch from the acquisition of raw materials to the delivery of finished products to the end-user. All vendors, service providers, and customers are links in the supply chain" (Supply Chain . . ., 2013, p. 186).

The central issue for the supply-chain concept is to move away from looking at these links separately through an integrated view. In this context, the idea of supply-chain management appears. Supply-chain management, according to the CSCMP definition, includes the planning and coordination of all activities related to procurement, processing, logistics, and cooperation with partners such as suppliers, intermediaries, third-party service providers, and customers—the essence of which is "linking major business functions and business processes within and across companies to create a cohesive and high-performing business model" (Supply Chain . . ., 2013, p. 187). Striving for the integrated coordination of all links in the chain prompts us to consider efficiency and competitiveness not only at the level of its individual links but above all at the level of the entire supply chain (Jarzębowski, 2012; Klepacki & Wicki, 2014; Sweeney et al., 2018).

Typically, the integrated approach to supply-chain management focuses on cost minimization[5] (Camps, 2004). In the case of a nonintegrated (or fragmented) supply chain, product flows between economic entities take place in a series of cycles located at the interface between the links of the chain (van der Vorst, 2004). This way of functioning causes the necessity to buffer each link by securing stocks against the uncertainty resulting from the difficulties in the mutual synchronization of production flows with use/consumption. In particular, the upstream links experience uncertainty regarding the volume of orders, while the downstream links experience uncertainty regarding the stability of supplies. Moreover, as Forester has shown, even slight disturbances in the downstream links of the chain tend to build up as we follow the chain upstream. This phenomenon causes considerable difficulties and overstocking; the more severe, the more the upstream link is considered. It is known as the Forester effect or the bullwhip effect (cf. Forrester, 2013 [1961]; Meadows, 2008; Senge, 2006; Sterman, 2000; van der Vorst, 2004). Thus, the most obvious incentive for the integration of the supply chain is, therefore, the opening and streamlining of information channels and striving to reduce uncertainty thanks to information freely flowing up and down within the chain and, consequently, due to a reduction (ideally—elimination) of inventories and related costs (Baran et al., 2008).

Global supply chains were challenged substantially by the outbreak of the COVID-19 pandemic and its consequences. The end of 2019 and the beginning of 2020 saw the start of the SARS-CoV-2 proliferation, which rapidly spread throughout the world. In March 2020 the pandemic was announced by the World Health Organization. The COVID-19 pandemic has strongly impacted the complex structure of global supply chains. As a consequence of the introduction of pandemic emergencies worldwide (lockdowns, the closures of factories and offices), the many linkages within global supply chains were disrupted. Subsequent variants of SARS-CoV-2 weaken the global recovery.

Mobility restrictions and chain volatility have continued to weigh on activity, up till now. COVID-19—in the third year of the pandemic—continues to fuel uncertainty. According to the very recent report of the International Monetary Fund, supply disruptions cut 0.5%–1% off global GDP growth in 2021, while adding 1% to core inflation. In general, the pandemic could cost the global economy $13.8 trillion in lost economic output by the end of 2024 (International Monetary Fund, 2022).

Very recently we have observed the escalation of the Russian-Ukrainian war, after a full-scale military invasion by Russia. In response, the West imposed substantial sanctions on Putin's regime. While it is too early to fully assess the consequences of these happenings, one could be sure that the impact of this war on the global economy will be huge—and they will cause additional disturbances in global supply chains, which were already strongly hit by the pandemic, and have little room for other shocks. The war in Ukraine will further exacerbate global shortages not only of energy commodities. The prices of oil and gas as well as wheat and corn are soaring dramatically. While this text is being written (at the beginning of March 2022) gas prices have more than quadrupled, oil costs 73% more, wheat is up more than 80%, and corn costs 38% more since the beginning of the year (Zschäpitz, 2022). Moreover, as geopolitical tensions remain extremely high, other global risks could emerge. And, still, there are common concerns about natural disasters caused by the ongoing climate crisis.

According to the research[6] of the Institute of Supply Management (ISM), during the pandemic as much as 75% of companies faced supply-chain disruptions. 64% of respondents reported longer lead times in China; 68% of them see longer lead times in Europe, and between 40%–54% from North American countries, accordingly. This crisis has forced companies to take ad hoc measures. 42% of companies changed their supplier due to the lockdown-related impossibility of delivery. 56% of respondents report holding more inventory than usual (Institute of Supply Management, 2020).

For years, one of the most widely adopted practices of SCM was just-in-time, or more generally—lean management. While implementing lean practices in global chains often proved to be successful regarding efficiency (lower inventory, shorter lead times, better on-time-in-full deliveries, etc.), they are also accused of exposing companies to the risk of chain disruption in a time of uncertainty and unexpected events. According to the McKinsey report, a disruption of the supply chain lasting one or two weeks could occur every two years, while those lasting more than a month can occur about every 3.7 years. Severe disruptions such as the last pandemic can recur every five years (Lund et al., 2020).

The pandemic gave rise to the awareness that global chains' design is inherently fragile due to just-in-time logistics and lean inventories. Some critics have started questioning popular business practices such as just-in-time or lean management, spread worldwide within supply chains, which have been demystified as neglecting vital safety margins (Financial Times, 2020, 2021; O'Leary, 2020; Shih, 2020). SCM was rather focused on efficiency but not necessarily on resilience (cf. Lund et al., 2020).

Some authors have asked if we have witnessed the end of globalization as we know it, and have predicted re-shoring or more regionalization of supply chains, or at least more redundancy and diversification of built-in supply chains (Farrell & Newman, 2020; Gereffi, 2020; O'Neil, 2020; Shih, 2020). Recent problems have led to speculation that companies could shift to more local production and sourcing. The closure of factories in Asia reveals the risk of being dependent on one region. According to the Capgemini Research Institute, the main goal of the surveyed companies is to reduce dependence on Asian suppliers and develop regional ones. 66% of them anticipate significant changes to their supply-chain strategy over the next three years (Capgemini Research Institute, 2021). McKinsey estimates that the production of some 16%–26% of global trade ($2.9 trillion–$4.6 trillion) could move between countries in the medium term due to domestic production, nearshoring, or offshoring to different locations (Lund et al., 2020).

These concerns are not only due to the pandemic but also due to many other crises observed in recent years (Gereffi, 2020). Recent uncertainties provide the opportunity to boost efforts to develop and adopt new approaches to designing and governing supply chains. These crises create incentive to seize the opportunity to make supply chains more resilient. Overall, it seems that it is becoming clearer and clearer that the current approach to global supply chains should be rethought and there is a need for more viable, robust, or even "antifragile" (cf. Taleb, 2012) supply chains.

5.4 Global-Value-Chain (GVC) Approach

The model of vertical connections of enterprises discussed so far (SCM) adopts a business perspective. The theoretical roots of GVC go back to the concept of the "commodity chain,"[7] which was developed based on the world-systems theory and refers to the macroeconomic perspective. The American sociologist, historian, and economist Immanuel Wallerstein, who also draws heavily on the achievements of the French historian Braudel, is the creator of the world-systems theory concerning the genesis (in a historical horizon dating back to the 16th century), the development, and functioning of contemporary capitalism and the prospects for changes in this currently dominant world-system. Wallerstein's theory emphasizes the long horizon of analyses as well as the need to go beyond the national perspective. Basic research units are wider areas (so-called world systems), constituting an economic whole based on the flows of goods (Braudel, 2013 [1985]; Wallerstein, 1974, 2004).

The concept of a world system should have been treated not so much as a system covering the entire globe, but rather as a system that creates a peculiar universe for its participants, which may be relatively limited in geographical scope at a given moment in human history. Historically, there have been many separate world systems in the world (e.g., Europe, the world of Islam, India, China, and Japan). In the modern era, however, there was the territorial expansion of the capitalist system, which nowadays has absorbed the entire globe (Braudel, 2013 [1985]; Wallerstein, 2004).

The fundamental property of world systems is inequality. Economic flows, as a result of an unequal exchange, affect the polarization of the system—the emergence of central and peripheral areas. In the central areas, innovations are created and highly processed goods are produced. Peripheral areas are a source of natural resources, low-processed materials, and a reservoir of cheap labor force. Their development is determined by relations with central areas. It is also possible to distinguish areas of the semi-periphery that may mediate between the center and the periphery. In the modern capitalistic world system, most of the absorbed areas have become the periphery of this system (Wallerstein, 2004). The system's central areas were subject to long-range[8] changes, including shifts in the position of the hegemon from the Netherlands, through Great Britain, to the United States (Braudel, 2013 [1985]).

World systems are based on two pillars: Economic and political. The economic pillar is related to the flows of goods, labor, and capital that integrate a given system. Economic structures are intersected by political structures—states (Braudel, 2013 [1985]; Wallerstein, 1974). "The national economy is a political space modified by the state" (Braudel, 2013 [1985], p. 129). Through political action, states may seek the relative improvement of their position in the world system (Braudel, 2013 [1985]); Wallerstein, 1974).

Historically, two kinds of markets could be distinguished. On the one hand, there were "public markets" (or category-A markets) supervised by authorities that were striving to maintain competition. On the other hand, there were "private markets" (or category-B markets), free from this supervision. Category-A markets consisted of daily local exchanges as well as long-distance trading if it was regular, predictable, routine, and open to smaller players. It gathered producers (farmers, craftsmen)—and customers. Private markets involved direct purchases from a producer (e.g., linen) or a farmer (e.g., wheat, hemp, wool, cattle, poultry), and were popular in England from the 15th century. The purchases were often agreed in advance and made in advance, e.g., the purchase of wheat before harvest (Braudel, 2013 [1985] pp. 28–29, 39, 65–75). Since that time, we can observe the introduction of autonomous trade chains—quite long, freely forming—against traditional market regulations. As the market economy and then capitalism developed, B markets gained an advantage by gradually replacing A markets[9] (Braudel, 2013 [1985]).

In this way, the concept of commodity chains arose from the world-systems theory. The concept was first coined as a "chain of merchandising" by Wallerstein (1974). In subsequent Wallerstein publications, prepared together with Hopkins (Hopkins & Wallerstein, 1977, 1986, 1994), a modified term, "commodity chain," appears, which they define as a network of work and production processes, the result of which is a finished commodity (Hopkins & Wallerstein, 1986). Commodity chains contain combinations of central activities that allow for relatively high rates of return and peripheral activities that generate relatively low profits. It can be observed, however, that the mix of activities carried out in a given country may change over time. Hence, it is advisable to define the goals of the national development program as an increase in the ratio of central processes to peripheral activities carried out in a given country (Bair, 2014).

The Global Commodity Chain (GCC) is a concept related to the work of Gereffi and colleagues (Raikes et al., 2000). It arose out of the previously discussed literature on commodity chains. However, as it developed, it moved away from its roots understood as the world-systems theory. As Bair (2014) notes, in the 1990s, along with the intensification of globalization,[10] the interest in the commodity chain grew as one of the few concepts offering a methodological approach to the analysis of complex international production networks. However, the concept evolved in its way that was separate from its parent theory. There was a redirection of the existing concept explaining development differences at a macro level towards a normative concept and development policy tool at a mesoeconomic level. Thus, the central research issue related to the question of how commodity chains shape inequalities at a global world-system level has been reoriented to the question: How can one support development at a level of subsystems of the world system, namely a particular chain and its links (Bair, 2014)?

It is assumed (Drost, 2011; Raikes et al., 2000) that the origins of GCC as a concept separate from commodity chains are related to the publication of a monograph edited by Gereffi and Korzeniewicz (1994). Most of the authors of this monograph emphasized not the historical context and long cycles, but rather the emergence of new forms of cooperation in the global production system—including geographically dispersed but centrally coordinated activities related to the delivery of goods to final buyers (Raikes et al., 2000). Gereffi (1995) ascribed the world-systems theory with problems grasping the activity of large corporations in the context of specific conditions of local economies and their dynamics. He also pointed to the need of building a bridge to overcome the macro-micro gap in economic development research.

As a part of the emerging GCC concept, three key dimensions of the chain have been identified: The input-output structure (the set of products and services linked together in a sequence of value-adding activities), geographic coverage (spatial dispersion or the concentration of enterprises of various sizes and types involved in the chain) and the governance structure, i.e., the control structure (authority and power relations that determine how financial, material, and human resources are distributed within the chain) (Gereffi, 1994). Soon, the above three dimensions were supplemented with a fourth one—institutional (how do local, national and international conditions and policies influence the process of globalization in individual links of the chain?) (Gereffi, 1995).

The period of development of the GCC concept falls in the 90s of the last century. After this decade, the creators of GCC, namely Gereffi and his associates, deemed it necessary to modify their concept, significantly enough to be emphasized by changing the name to the Global Value Chain (GVC). Together with a group of researchers from various countries and disciplines (including economics, sociology, political science, management, and geography) as well as politicians and activists from non-governmental organizations, they created a project called the Global Value Chains Initiative, under which several workshops were conducted in the years 2000–2004. The aim was to develop a theory that, on the one hand, would be grounded in the existing literature and build consensus among researchers, and, on the other hand, could help decision makers explain and predict control patterns in cross-border value chains (Sturgeon, 2008).

The modification of the term from Global Commodity Chain to Global Value Chain was associated with the replacement of the word "commodity" with the word "value." The motivation for this change was threefold. Firstly, the word "commodity" is often associated with an undifferentiated product such as crude oil and bulk agricultural products (Sturgeon, 2008). Secondly, the word "commodity" suggests a concentration on physical products, while the outcome of the chain may be an intangible asset or service (Drost, 2011). Therefore, as the animators of the first Global Value Chains Initiative workshop Gereffi et al. (2001, p. 3) wrote: "the value chain concept was adopted over several widely used alternatives because it was perceived as the most inclusive of the full range of possible chain activities and end products." Finally, the word "value" refers to Porter's concept,[11] with his idea of adding value through chain activities and financial results as a measure of competitive advantage (cf. Sturgeon, 2008).

With its distant ancestor, namely the world-system theory, GVC shares an interest in the relations of authority and economic power, and a critical attitude to the existing economic structures that create inequalities (Gereffi et al., 2001; Fitter & Kaplinsky, 2001). GVC employs the mesoeconomic perspective and focus on a practical approach, namely on strategies supporting development, in particular on so-called upgrading, i.e., improving the position in the chain (Drost, 2011; Sturgeon, 2008). Contemporarily, the concept of GVC has become an important analytical approach within different strands of social sciences including economics. It helps make sense of the increasingly organizationally and geographically partitioned system of production worldwide (Dünhaupt et al., 2022).

5.5 What New Insights Could Be Drawn for SCM from the GVC Approach?

Despite different names, one could easily find that the object of interest, namely the chain of interconnected firms engaged in fragmented stages of business, which finally produce finished goods, is just the same in GVC as in the case of SCM literature. However, the perspective is quite different. Thus, what are the new insights drawn from the GVC approach, which could be fruitful for SCM?

First of all, from the discussion above, it is clear that the concept of GVC is quite eclectic, with a body of knowledge and possible insights that have grown incrementally through its development. Let us start with the very early stage of this development. There are four issues subject to inquiry in the commodity chain literature: (i) How do states try to shape commodity chains? (ii) what are the relationships between chains and the stratification of the world system, and are they changing? (iii) which links in the chain does the surplus come from and how is it distributed between them? (iv) what relationships are formed between commodity chains and political organizations (Bair, 2014)?

The issue of coordination or governance in global chains has become a particular area of interest within the new research stream of GCCs (Raikes et al., 2000; Stamm, 2004; Sturgeon, 2008). The governance structure is defined as "authority and power relations that determine how financial, material and human resources are allocated and flow within the chain" (Gereffi, 1994, p. 97). Thus, the problem of governance in GCC was equated with relations of authority and power and put a lot of emphasis on leading firms' capability of governing the functioning of chains. Gereffi (1994) popularized a dichotomous classification of governance structures in GCCs: Producer-oriented and buyer-oriented. This proposal—which is a change in comparison to the focus on the state and macroeconomics (typical for the theory of commodity chains) in favor of focusing on enterprises playing the leading role in the chains—met with great interest from researchers and practitioners (Sturgeon, 2008).

Manufacturer-oriented chains are typical for capital-intensive products with high investment in technology, such as cars, airplanes, computers, electrical machinery and equipment, semiconductors, etc. In this type of chain, the leading role is played by large transnational corporations controlling the production system with vertical connections backward and forwards. In the manufacturer-oriented chains, the core competencies are production and R&D, and entry barriers are based on economies of scale. These chains correspond to the model of mass production—Fordism (Gereffi, 1994, 1999a, 1999b).

Buyer-oriented chains are typical for labor-intensive products such as clothing, footwear, toys, consumer electronics, household appliances, furniture, and interior furnishings. In this type of chain, the key role is played by large retailers (e.g., Walmart, Sears), branded distribution channels (e.g., Tommy Hilfiger, Marks & Spencer, C&A), and producers of branded goods (e.g., Nike,

Reebok). In buyer-oriented chains, the key competencies are design and marketing, and entry barriers are based on the economics of scope. These chains correspond to the model of flexible specialization—post-Fordism (Gereffi, 1994, 1999a, 1999b).

The issue of governance is further developed under GVC' umbrella. Some shifts are observed in the meaning of this term and proposed classification. Another dichotomous classification of relations in GVCs was proposed by Humphrey and Schmitz (2000, 2002): (i) Quasi-hierarchical, and (ii) network. Thus, one could find that, in this case, governance does not only mean relations based on power. Sturgeon and Lee (2001) proposed a three-stage classification: (i) The supplier of goods, (ii) the supplier trapped in a relation (captive), and (iii) the solution provider (turnkey).

However, finally, in GVC' literature, currently, a five-element classification of governance structures dominates (Gereffi et al., 2005; Sturgeon, 2008):

1) Markets—simple price-regulated market connections; low switching costs for both partners; product specifications are simple allowing easy fabrication by suppliers with minimal information from buyers; low specificity of assets; knowledge necessary for transactions easy to codify;
2) modular value chains—suppliers make products according to the buyers' specifications of varying complexity; a limited degree of asset specificity; modular value chains occur in a situation of the modular architecture of the final product, which enables the reduction of component variability and the application of uniform specifications and standards; then, such a modular "intermediate" can be exchanged with a limited level of investment in transaction-specific assets and there is little need of monitoring and control (thanks to the codification and even digitization of necessary information flow); the switching cost remains relatively low for both parties;
3) relational value chains—characterized by complex relationships between sellers and buyers including tacit knowledge and a high level of investment in specific assets; reputation-related or family and ethnic ties play a major role; alternatively, interdependence can be governed by mechanisms that impose costs on the party breaking the arrangements (e.g., a credible commitment based on a so-called hostage exchange); switching costs are high for both parties;
4) captive value chains—small suppliers are dependent on much larger buyers, as a result, sellers experience unilaterally high switching costs, becoming, in some way, "prisoners" of the chain; a situation somewhat

similar to modular chains (due to the possibility of codification of knowledge related to transactions), with the difference, however, that the low competences of suppliers require a significant scope of intervention in their operations and control by leading companies, which results in a lock-in relationship; tied suppliers are reliant on complementary processes carried out by other links in the chain; opportunism is constrained by dominance over suppliers and making an exit is not an attractive option for them;

5) hierarchies—links within the same company, regulated by hierarchical authority; they occur when product specifications cannot be codified, products are complex, transactions are strongly saturated with tacit knowledge and, at the same time, there is no access to competent suppliers.

In addition to the governance issues, GVC focus strongly on the question of value-adding and its distribution. This focus is emphasized by the term "global value chain"; here lies an important difference in comparison to SCM. "The value chain is an important construct for understanding the distribution of returns arising from design, production, marketing, coordination and recycling" (Kaplinsky & Morris, 2002, p. 25). The incentive to participate in the value chain is the possibility of gaining rent (supernormal profit). There are four general kinds of rents: Endogenous to the firm (control over scarce technologies, access to better skills of human resources, superior organization, better marketing capabilities/brand names), endogenous to the chain (relational rents due to relations with suppliers and buyers), exogenous to the chain (resource rent—access to scarce natural resources), and finally rents provided by parties external to the chain (access to finance on better terms, access to high-quality infrastructure and policy rents) (Kaplinsky & Morris, 2002).

An important concern of the GVC approach is the matter of the distribution of value.[12] Taking into account the distribution of value within the value chain, one could easily raise the question of power relations and inequalities within GVC. As Kaplinsky and Morris (2002, pp. 14–15) claim, "the debate is polarized between two views—globalization is good for the poor or globalization is harmful to the poor. Yet, this is a way too simplistic perspective, since it is less a matter of globalization being intrinsically good or bad, but rather how producers and countries insert themselves in the global economy." By highlighting the issue of the distribution of gains within a chain, asking for rent, power asymmetries, and inequalities, the global-value-chain approach can help in both understandings (a positive analysis) and identifying and crafting appropriate policies (a normative analysis), which could be implemented by producers (firms, regions, or countries) to increase their share in benefits from participating in a global exchange (Kaplinsky & Morris, 2002).

That is where the "upgrading" term comes into play. The stake in this issue is to insert producers into the GVC in a way, in which they enable a virtuous cycle of sustained-gain growth instead of being trapped in a race to the bottom (so-called immiserizing growth). Upgrading focuses on moving to higher-value activities in GVC to increase gains from participating in global specialization and a division of labor by: Being more efficient (process upgrading), moving into better or more sophisticated products (product upgrading), acquiring new functions to increase the skill content of more complex processes (functional upgrading), and moving into more promising chains/sectors (chain or inter-sectoral upgrading) (Gereffi & Fernandez-Stark, 2011).

The prerequisites for the emergence of GVCs are globalization and the fragmentation of production. The progress of globalization is conditioned by a decline in barriers to the costs of moving goods, moving ideas, and moving people (Baldwin, 2019). However, while these flows of goods, ideas, and people integrate an economic system called the global value chain, it is still intersected by political structures—states, which create an institutional context for links in the chain. According to Gereffi and Fernandez-Stark (2011, p. 11), "institutions include tax and labor regulation, subsidies, education and an innovation policy that can promote or hinder industry growth and development." From this perspective, the role of institutions in supporting or blocking upgrading the position of producers (firms, regions, or countries) in GVCs is hard to overestimate.

It seems that these issues outlined above could also be interesting for researchers representing the SCM approach, if they treat the need of rethinking the supply chains seriously, particularly in a global or, at least, international context.

5.6 Implications

5.6.1 Framework

As one can see, the GVC approach offers some potentially fruitful insight for supply-chain management. The pandemic, as well as geopolitical tensions, and expected further disruptions in global supply chains call for the development and adaptation of new, more resilient approaches to designing and managing them. It seems that the useful, common platform for comparing and cross-fertilizing both GVC and SCM could be system thinking. We would like to propose a framework, which is a compilation of propositions of Kornai (1971) and Bossel (2007), based on system thinking—Figure 5.1. The essence of the concept of the system is that the whole is greater than the sum of its parts (Bertalanffy, 1972). In other words, a system is a set of elements, interconnected by relations that form a whole with features qualitatively different from the sum of elements (Pszczołowski, 1978). Therefore, we cannot fully understand the behavior of a system solely by analyzing its components. It can be said that the system is a product of the interaction of elements that make up a given system. The interactions form the structure of the system, and the structure of the system defines its behavior (Meadows, 2008).

According to Kornai (1971), the economy as a whole, as well as any economic system within it, consists of two components: A real sphere and a control sphere. This distinction could be used as a lens, which we will use to analyze features of any global-value (-supply) chain. When depicting the chain as a system, we will

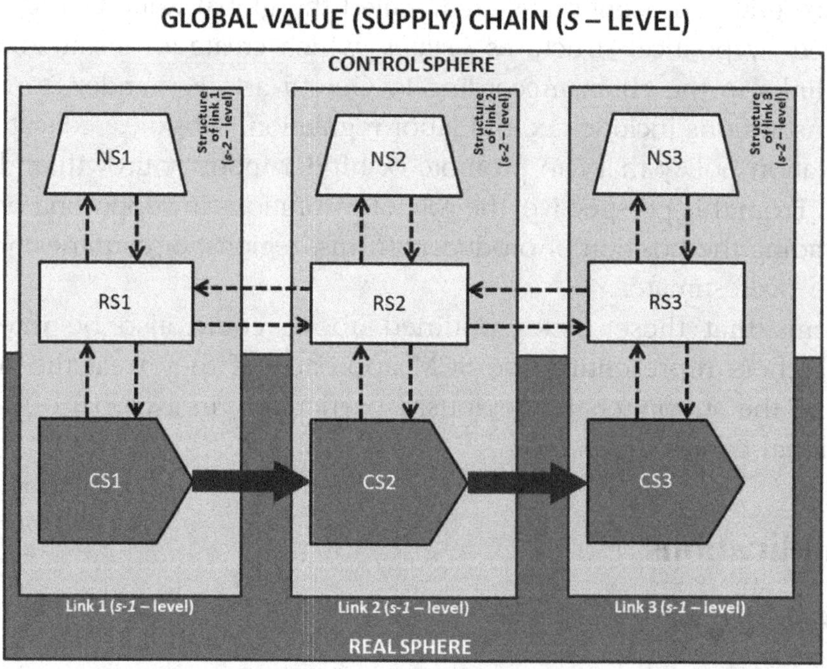

Figure 5.1 Simplified Diagram of a Value (Supply) Chain as an Economic System.

Source: Own based on concepts of Kornai (1971, p. 41) and Bossel (2007, p. 58).

Note: Thick arrows indicate product/service flows, thin dashed arrows indicate information flows; CS denotes causal systems, RS denotes response systems and NS denotes normative systems.

use the hierarchical structure of systems (i.e., systems within systems), which are built from subsystems, which, in turn, are divided into subsystems, etc. (Simon, 1962). Accordingly, we will talk about level *S* considering the whole value chain, level *S-1*, taking into account its links, and level *S-2*—considering the internal structure of these links. Figure 5.1 depicts the global-value (-supply) chain as a systemic whole (a system-level or *S*-level), which covers a set (in our case only three for simplicity) of firms or links in the chain (a subsystem or *S*-1 level). What creates the chain as a system is an interconnectedness between the links. Thus, one could easily find two kinds of connections, which connect the links: Product (or service) flows (as indicated by thick arrows), and information flows (as indicated by thin dashed arrows). In this framework both the chain and its links are treated as economic systems, thus they both could be divided into a real and a control sphere, respectively.

According to the description of the economic system proposed by Kornai, the processes taking place in it can be divided into two categories: The real sphere (*R*) and the control sphere (*C*). The real sphere includes the material processes taking place in the economic system, such as production and delivery (including products and services), sale, and consumption. The control sphere includes the thought processes occurring in the economic system, such as perception, transmission, and the processing of information, preparation, and decision making, which govern the material processes in the real sphere (Kornai, 1971).

As Figure 5.1 depicts each of the subsystems, the *S*-1 level (links of the chain) consists of successive subsystems at an *S*-2 level, namely: The units of the real sphere responsible for the delivery of products or services and the units of the control sphere, which are both connected by information flows occurring within the *S*-1 subsystems. Following Bossel's (2007) nomenclature, I will call these units of the real sphere causal systems (CS), while the units of the control sphere will further be divided into two kinds of units and I will call them response systems (RS) and normative systems (NS).

The causal system (which could also be called a physical system) is, according to Bossel (2007, p. 58), "composed of those processes representing the material functioning of the system." In the causal system, instructions originating from the response system are translated into internal processes or actions influencing the environment. "The response system is an information processing system combining the processes of situation perception and classification, state analysis, problem-solving, policy synthesis, the assessment of outcomes of alternatives and the decision." The normative system will be discussed in 5.6.3.

5.6.2 Asymmetries in Power and Value Distribution

Here, it is important to emphasize the crucial difference between a traditional, economic (neoclassical) vision of interfirm relations and a nontraditional one for the chain approach, which, in this case, is common for both regarded approaches, namely: SCM and GVC. All these visions could be described in the framework from Figure 5.1. In the case of the economic vision, all the exchange relations between suppliers and buyers could be framed on the market model with its interplay of demand and supply resulting from the market-clearing price. The material object of the interchange (thick arrows) is, in the neoclassical model, the undifferentiated commodity, while all the information (thin dashed arrows between links of the chain) needed to govern this mechanism of exchange is embodied in the market price (cf. Figure 5.1 and Table 5.1). Thus, the interfirm relations are separated in Macneil's (1985) meaning, namely the identity of trading partners is unimportant.

The concept of interfirm relations, which form "the chain," includes the idea of strong, non-separated (relational[13]) linkages between chain participants and the activities they perform, so it is important that they create a new whole with features distinct not only from individual companies but also from neoclassical markets. We call such a whole "the chain." Thus, the role of transfer of information (thin dashed arrows) is much broader and much more emphasized in chain approaches (cf. Figure 5.1 and Table 5.1). In the case of SCM, the basic information scope (apart from price information) covers operational information such as inventory levels, production specifications, plans, schedules, etc. What is new, from the GVC perspective, are informational relations in the form of commands or unequal power relations. Such a way of governance arises from asymmetries between exchange parties. Such asymmetries in knowledge or just in economic power create more privileged partners in the chain and allow them to experience some kind of authority (compare the discussion on the governance structure in section 5.5) over other links in the chain, even if they are nominally independent firms—Table 5.1.

According to Galbraith, "the appeal of the competitive model was its solution to the problem of power" (2014 [1952], p 24). However, in global chains, some links, and some fragmented production stages tend to pass "from the hands of the many to the few" (Galbraith, 2014 [1952], p. 33). Braudel (2013 [1985]) claims that as the market economy and capitalism developed, the relatively competitive "public markets" were gradually supplanted by "private markets" (a.k.a. "commodity chains") with the distinctive feature of market power. Also, Gereffi et al. (2005) and Sturgeon (2008) explain that competitive

Table 5.1   Comparison of Neoclassical, SCM, and GVC Approaches to Interorganizational Relationships.

Category		*Economics (neoclassical) approach*	*Supply Chain Management approach*	*Global Value Chain approach*
What is transferred among partners of the exchange?	Goods	Undifferentiated commodity	Differentiated products and services	Differentiated products and services
	Information	Governance by price information	Governance by price information	Governance by price information
		–	Governance by operational information (inventory levels, production specs and plans, etc.)	Governance by operational information (inventory levels, production specs and plans, etc.)
		–	–	Governance by commands due to asymmetries in power, authority, and knowledge
Normative orientors		One orientor (optimization on each firm-level)	One orientor (optimization on a chain level)	Many different basic orientors possible, probable differences between orientors and their relative wage among partners
The role of the state/nation		"Night watchman," tariffs, and other trade barriers	"Night watchman," tariffs, and other trade barriers	"Night watchman," tariffs, and other trade barriers
		–	–	Institutional differences between states and an active policy of upgrading

Source: Own elaboration.

relations (arms-length market linkages) with low switching costs for both partners are only one of many possibilities of governance structures between links in GVC.

Another possibility is, for example, captive relations with small partners experiencing unilaterally high switching costs and, thus, becoming, in some way, "prisoners" of power-based relations. Such asymmetries in power easily lead to inequalities in the distribution of gain from cooperation among GVC members (consider the examples presented in n. 12, the iPhone case in particular). If the firm, region, or country is forced to enter the value chain in an unequal position, there is a risk of being trapped in immiserizing growth—"the situation where there is increasing economic activity (more output and more employment) but falling economic returns" (Kaplinsky & Morris, 2002, p. 21).

Consider the case of the firm from an export processing zone in the Dominican Republic described by Kaplinsky and Morris (2002, p. 19). The firm saw its chance in entering the international value chain of jeans. By investing $150,000 in equipment, the firm was able to sign a contract for sewing materials imported from and cut in the US, based on a design from the US—all under the brand of a multinational company. The initial (January 1990) unit price was $2.18, declining to $2.05 after ten months and further to $1.87 before the end of 1990. Moreover, after one year of cooperation, the contract was terminated and the multinational firm started to source from Honduras.

Considering expectations of decoupling and nearshoring of supply chains due to the COVID-19 experience, one could expect that some firms, regions, or countries would want to take advantage of this new deal and will try to escape from captive relations in value chains due to these shifts. This trend will be reinforced by the increasing role and legitimacy of nation-states, which will be discussed below. Moreover, if the Russian invasion of the Ukraine starts a kind of "New Cold War," such shifts could be even more common worldwide.

5.6.3 Orientors as Normative References

Despite the differences in informational relations among links in the chain, GVC also offer some additional insight. Both neoclassical economics and the SCM approach almost deny the issue of normative systems, or they both marginalize this issue by ad hoc assumptions regarding normative issues. According to Bossel (2007), the response system in performing its tasks has to refer back to the normative system (Figure 5.1). The normative system provides "normative references needed by the response system" (p. 58). A set of such references or criteria that are relevant for the evaluation of the system are called orientors. "Orientors are aspects, terms, or dimensions… that designate important criteria or qualities of system survival and development" (Bossel, 2007, p. 158).

Both economics and the SCM approach treat such normative references as granted. They both assume that there is only one normative orientor steering the economic activity—namely optimization. The difference between these two approaches is that in neoclassical economics the orientor is optimization, as defined on an individual firm level, while in the SCM—as defined on the whole chain level (Table 5.1). One could note that normative systems are relatively autonomous (in the sense that they are independent of other links in the chain). On the other hand, normative systems are dependent[14] on an institutional context in which links of the chain operate. This institutional context is mainly determined locally (nation-state).

The global-value-chain approach, by emphasizing the role of the institutional environment, is much more open to normative issues. The crucial issue here is that institutions fundamentally change the price[15] an economic actor pays due to his/her decisions, and this is what determines their influence on decision making (North, 2011 [1990]). In other words, institutions could affect the role of normative references used by the response system.

As mentioned above, in economics, as well as in many concepts of management (e.g., SCM), what is taken for granted is that economic actors optimize (e.g., maximize profits). In system thinking it is assumed that the overall reason for the existence of the system and, therefore, for all its behavior is viability/ sustainability (Beer, 1995; Bossel, 2007). Such a "supreme orientor" is very general, it would be applicable in any conditions, however, it is much too general to be relevant for system survival and development. Thus, from the "supreme orientor" some "basic orientors" could be drawn, such as efficiency (e.g., profit maximization) or security, etc. (Bossel, 2007; cf. Table 5.1). The complex list of basic orientors is presented in Table 5.2.

The basic orientors match relevant environmental properties (Table 5.2). According to Bossel (2007), the environment of the system has six fundamental

Table 5.2 Supreme and Basic Orientors of the System and Matching Environmental Properties.

Supreme orientors of the system	Basic orientors of the system	Relevant environmental properties accordingly
Viability/ Sustainability	Existence	Normal state
	Effectiveness and efficiency	Resource scarcity
	Freedom of action	Diversity and variety
	Security	Variability
	Adaptability	Change
	Coexistence (Cooperation or competition)	Other actors

Source: Own based on Bossel (2007, pp. 182–187).

properties: A normal state (which can vary in a certain range), resource scarcity, diversity and variety, variability (fluctuations beyond the normal state range), change, and other actors. To be viable and exist sustainably, systems have to match their environment. Therefore, by imposing certain constraints on the system, the environment directs its behavior.

The system has to be able to exist (existence) in a normal range of the environmental state. The fact that resources are not available will, in an infinitive-amounts system, need to be effective in securing scarce resources and be efficient in using them. Due to the diversity and variety of the environment, the system needs to be able to cope selectively and appropriately (freedom of action) with challenges produced in this way. Occasional fluctuations of the environmental state could be detrimental to the further survival of the system. Thus, it must be able to protect itself from such detrimental effects, namely, to be secure, e.g., through redundancy built in the system. Apart from a relatively small variation inside the range of the normal state and occasional fluctuations beyond this range, the environment can shift to a permanently different new normal state. This calls for adaptability, which enables one to cope with such permanent changes, namely, to learn, adapt, and self-organize. The system has to deal with the existence of other actors and, therefore, it needs to coexist with them. Such coexistence can encapsulate the form of cooperation and competition (Bossel, 2007)—cf. Table 5.2.

Normative constraints, namely orientors, reflect the basic interest of the systems and, therefore, shape behavior of it decisively (Bossel, 2007). The choice between the pursuit of any basic orientor, like increasing efficiency, or other normative values, such as security, can be expressed as a function with a negative slope (Figure 5.2). In other words, there is a trade-off between relative roles, which orientors play in decision making. For example, considering security as the orientor in one's actions has its relative "price" as measured by the efficiency needed to give up for the increase of security. If such a price is low (cf. curve A in Figure 5.2), security will play a significant role in the decision making, however, if it is high (cf. curve B in Figure 5.2), its influence on behavior will be much smaller as compared to the role of efficiency. In an extreme case, when the only orientor taken into account is efficiency (which means that function, which expresses the choice between orientors, is identical with the "X" axis—cf. curve C in Figure 5.2)—the cost of considering other orientors (e.g., security) will be infinite. This way of reasoning could be an explanation for why "lean" supply chains focused hard on optimization faced substantial problems due to the disruptions caused by COVID-19.

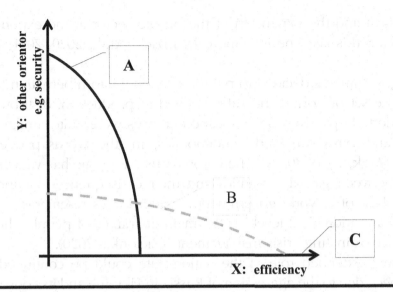

Figure 5.2 Relationship between Efficiency and Other Orientors, E.g., Security.
Source: Own.

5.6.4 The Role of Nation-States

If we would like to rethink how supply chains should be designed and organized, we should identify the root cause of problems we would like to overcome. According to GVC, an important context for how the chain operates is created by institutions. A prominent representative of new institutional economics claims "institutions fundamentally change the price an individual pays" (North, 2011 [1990], p. 22). This is why the institutional context is crucial for the basic orientor set taken into account. One could find that the institutional environment is strongly affected by nations (informal institutions) and by states (formal institutions). This could create substantial differences between a set of orientors between partners cooperating in global chains.

Thus, additional insight arising from the GVC approach, which could be novel and fruitful for SCM, is emphasizing the role of nation-states (Table 5.1). This is particularly important due to the experience of the pandemic when COVID-19 brought back the nation-state into the game. "The nation-state seems to be experiencing a striking renaissance. Borders are back…. Virtually overnight, national capitals have effectively reclaimed sovereignty from the European Union…. They are practically ruling by decree in a war-style fashion…. The coronavirus outbreak seems to be reversing the course of history. Gone is globalization" (Zielonka, 2020). After decades of dominance of neoliberalism and the expansion of the private sector at the expense of the public sector, this last one is being called back (Arak, 2020, 2021; Zielonka, 2020).

Most governments decided to put the economy into hibernation to protect people. The set of norms and rules applied to production, distribution, and consumption, despite how some local differences were quite similar between countries and could be named "pandenomics," in other words, pandemic-time economy (Arak, 2020, 2021). "The coronavirus pandemic has vanished… the distance between global dynamics and their consequences for individuals. Against a lack of a world government… nation-states re-emerge… between the global and individual levels as the main guarantor of people's health and the entity coordinating crisis management" (Zielonka, 2020).

This new, extended role of the nation-state could be continued, as one could expect, due to the aggression of Russia in Ukraine and its consequences. The new challenges have arisen in the face of threats against military security, energetic security, and food security. The war hit the global economy at a difficult time when supply-chain shortages became apparent due to the pandemic. Thus, the war and its consequences could be perceived as the Black Swan that shatters all forecasts. Europe gets 40% of its gas from Russia. One could imagine further sanctions in the form of imposing embargoes on Russian gas and oil, which could, furthermore, drive up already-existing extreme high prices (Zschäpitz, 2022).

These would be political decisions, which would impose huge responsibility on nation-states. It seems to be clear that instead of going back to the new normal after COVID-19 and withdrawal, the extended activity of the state from the economy, we stand on the threshold of an era of even bigger commitment of the nation-state. After "pandenomics," one can predict that nation-states would even go one step further towards something close to a war economy. One could expect that such engagement will impact the normative systems of firms, which are links in global value chains and, therefore, on the design, conduct, and performance of whole chains (cf. Figure 5.1). Apart from such institutional changes, states could get involved directly in active attempts in redesigning supply chains in areas crucial for national security, e.g., by investments in a critical capacity. According to Ralf Fücks from the think tank Zentrum Liberale Moderne, we must rethink globalization to not become dependent on China in key sectors such as medical technology or the 5G network. In the same vein, Maximilian Terhalle from the London School of Economics claims that when we talk about gas, oil, and digital technology, we can no longer see them only as elements of cooperation, but also as a leverage of influence, and if we fail to have such leverage, then as a weak-point (Geiger, 2022).

Let us consider the example of EU counteraction plans about the recent global crisis in the semiconductors industry. Currently, 80% of semiconductors are sourced from Asia, mainly Taiwan, followed by South Korea, Japan, and China. Semiconductors are strategically important in the economy and are called the lubricants of the fourth industrial revolution. This is why this product is the subject of a geostrategic race. The EU has 10% of the global semiconductors sector and plans to increase its share to 20% in 2030 (which means a quadrupling of actual production, as the market itself will redouble: From 500 billion to 1 trillion euros). Thierry Breton, the EU Commissioner for the Internal Market announced the plan to allocate 45–50 billion euros for the production of semiconductors of the most advanced technology (those smaller than two nanometers and five to seven nanometers). About 12 billion euros would go towards R&D (two to three years), while another 30 billion euros would be allocated for building-production capacity (another four years). On the other hand, the US passed the Chips Fair America Act last year, which allocates similar funds (the equivalent of 52 billion euros) to building semiconductor capacity. The US has a 10 % share in semiconductors, while it plans to increase this share to 30% by the end of the decade (Słojewska, 2022).

Let us sum up the implications we can draw from the new insights from the GVC approach. Firstly, we should change the way we perceive the nature of relations between links in supply chains and global supply chains in particular. In thinking about supply chains, we should unleash ourselves from the oversimplistic and somehow naïve neoliberal view that an economic contract is always an expression of economic freedom and, as such, is a guarantor of competitiveness and economic welfare. And, that it is only a question of efficiency, apart from issues of power, inequality, and ethics. Economic exchange can indeed be the trigger of a self-feeding virtuous circle of increasing gains for participating parties—both on a local as well as global scale (this argument is in line with neoclassical economics). It is also true that intensive cooperation between participating parties and, therefore, the open sharing of operational information can be an important factor in increasing efficiency substantially within the whole chain (this argument is in line with the SCM approach). However, we should not be blind to the fact that cooperation in the chain does not eradicate all competition between links of the chain (cf. the idea of co-opetition[16] in Brandenburger & Nalebuff, 1998). We should be able to analyze, design, and improve supply chains seriously taking into account the huge asymmetries of power, privileged and unprivileged parties, differences in added value and its distribution within chains, the abuse of authority over the chain, inequalities, and injustices. And we should also take into account that some parties of the chain will actively attempt to improve their position in the chain and could be supported by states in these attempts.

Secondly, we should, therefore, abandon the view of global supply chains as purely business initiatives. It seems to be clear that contrary to this neoliberal view, the SCM approach should gain some fresh insight from the perspective of the GVC lens. In this lens, it is indispensable to take nation-states into account. According to the GVC approach and its predecessors (GCC, commodity chains, the world-system theory), states try to shape supply chains. The policy of active support of upgrading could be an important part of national-development programs focused on increasing the ratio of high-value-added processes against low-value-added processes typical to peripheral countries. Recently, due to COVID-19 and the perspective of the "New Cold War," one can expect an even more expanding policy of nation-states (as well as their alliances like the EU) towards supporting and redesigning global supply chains. However, nowadays it could be driven not mainly by the upgrading principle (focused on higher value added) but also by the security principle (focused on leveraging chains by possessing influence in the most critical links).

This brings us to the third implication, the normative-issues matter. The main problem with the business strand of literature underlying the chain concept and with SCM literature, in particular, is that it is only focused on the causal system and the response system and neglects the normative system. This strand implicitly takes it as given that the only normative rule is the efficiency principle. This issue was clearly exposed during the pandemic by the failure of practices such as just-in-time and lean management. As previously explained, the normative system provides references for the response system, which, on the other hand, directly steers the behavior of the causal system. Apart from the efficiency orientor, such a reference set can cover many other basic orientors, such as security, adaptability, freedom of action, etc.

The relative relevance of basic orientors of the system could be modified by both external and internal changes. By external changes, I mean influence on the normative system by shifts in the system's institutional environment. This is the way nation-states could influence the design, conduct, and performance of value chains, apart from direct investments and other direct support. By internal changes, I mean modifications of the normative system by itself in the process of learning. This is the way firms could influence the design, conduct, and performance of value chains in which they participate. The attempts to build up critical inventory, diversify sourcing, or even shift towards decoupling and nearshoring are just observable examples of the increase of the relative role of such orientors as security, adaptability, and freedom of action.

5.7 Concluding Remarks

COVID-19, the war in Ukraine, as well as many possible but uncertain yet, future problems will challenge the design, conduct, and performance of global supply chains. Supply-chain management (SCM) is a business-based approach to modeling, designing, and coordinating supply chains (in such numbers, the global ones) rooted in logistics and operational management. This approach and practices such as just-in-time and lean management in particular, which are strongly oriented towards efficiency and optimization within the whole chain, could be reasonably criticized as disregarding other possible basic orientors of the system. Those other orientors such as security turn out to be crucial in times of uncertainty. The refreshed approach to global supply chains is needed. Global value chain (GVC) approach is presented and discussed here. This approach gives rise to some issues, which are neglected or, at least, underestimated by supply-chain management. Therefore, GVC could be insightful in attempts to rethink the design, conduct, and performance of global supply chains aimed at being more resilient, robust, or even "antifragile."

There are threefold implications drawn from these insights, which seem to be the most important. Firstly, global value chains are systems, which are built on inherent duality—namely, creating value is fundamentally a cooperative process, while capturing and distributing value within the chain is a competitive process. Thus, the design and management of the global supply chain could not merely be treated as a coordination issue focused solely on business efficiency, but it is necessary to consider issues of economic power, asymmetries, inequalities, and injustices within the chain. Secondly, we can go astray by treating global supply chains as purely business initiatives in a stateless vacuum. In such a way we could overlook or underestimate the important sources of influence on the chain. This risk has grown bigger recently and will continue to in the future, as global systemic uncertainty has been growing and the role of nation-states in the economy is getting bigger. Thirdly, normative issues matter in governing global chains. Treating firms and whole chains merely as mechanical structures (machines) for earning profits proves to be myopic and was recently painfully tested by COVID-19 and the war in

Ukraine. This calls for a reorientation of normative systems of firms, which could be driven by both the learning process on a business units' level as well as by the institutional context created at a nation-state level (or on a level of state alliances such as the EU).

Thus, the global-value-chain approach could shed some new light on interorganizational cooperation on a global scale and, therefore, GVC could enrich the business-oriented SCM approach. GVC could help rethink the weaknesses of global supply chains exposed by the recent crisis and draw further developments.

This study is conducted in a very general way and lacks any solid empirical research. One could find it as a limitation. However, it seems that this limitation could be justified due to the very preliminary stage of the study. While the global economy is still impacted by the coronavirus pandemic, it has just, very recently, started to experience another and possibly even harder kind of disturbance (the war in Europe). Thus, we urgently need to discuss how to redesign global supply chains in this time of uncertainty. The possible cross-fertilization of both global-value chain and supply-chain management seems to be a valuable part of the future development of such a discussion. Future research could follow two paths. The first one could be a deeper, more detailed study on each of the three implications mentioned previously (namely (i) the issue of power asymmetries and unequal distribution of value added, (ii) the relative role of basic orientors, (iii) the role of nation-states in structuring of the normative system). The second path could be collecting empirical material regarding these three issues, respectively.

Notes

1. Or the "New Globalization" as he named it. Since the ICT revolution lowered the costs of moving ideas, it facilitates the separation of so far integrated production processes or, in other words, the fragmentation of factories. This is why this trend is called "second unbundling" (Baldwin, 2019).
2. As production split around the world, value chains have grown in length and complexity in recent decades. The value of intermediate goods traded worldwide has tripled since 2000 to about $10 trillion per year (Lund et al., 2020).
3. Nevertheless, with a practical orientation as well.
4. Sub-optimization means that decisions or actions in a part of the system are made at the expense of the whole (Supply Chain . . ., 2013, p. 184).
5. However, thanks to the integration of the links in the supply chain, it is also possible to achieve other benefits, beyond cost reduction (Camps, 2004). An illustration of this trend is the definition of the supply chain proposed by Lazzarini

et al. (2001, p. 7)—"a set of sequential, vertically organized transactions representing successive stages of value creation". Gradually, the concept of the supply chain breaks away from its logistics and operational roots and shifts towards a more strategic orientation (cf. Sweeney et al., 2018)—focusing on building a competitive advantage, created within the entire chain. Thus, the concept of Supply Chain Management is more similar to Porter's ideas of the value chain and the value system, introduced in his book "Competitive Advantage" from 1985. Porter (1998 [1985], p. 33) emphasizes that a competitive advantage cannot be fully understood "by looking at a firm as a whole. It stems from many discrete activities a firm performs in designing, producing, marketing, delivering and supporting its product". Thus, the set of these activities creates the "chain". The essence of the company's competitive advantage is the condition that the value for the customer generated by a set of related activities exceeds the sum of the costs resulting from conducting these processes. The difference of these two amounts is the margin, which indicates the size of the advantage. The essence of the value chain as a strategic management tool is to analyze activities related to a given business in terms of their relative cost position and the role they can play in building unique benefits for the client—so-called differentiation (Porter, 1998 [1985]). One could notice that Porter is fully aware that the value chain of a given company is integrated into a wider stream of processes, which he referred to as the value system—"gaining and maintaining a competitive advantage depends on understanding not only the value chain enterprise, but also its adjustment to the entire value system" (Porter, 1998 [1985], p. 34).

6. The survey was conducted with more than 770 respondents.
7. Initially Wallerstein (1974) also used the term "chain of merchandising".
8. The long-term reflected the perspective of the long Kondratieff cycles (Hopkins & Wallerstein, 1994; Raikes et al., 2000; Wallerstein, 2004).
9. According to the McKinsey Global Institute (Lund et al., 2020, p. 21) more than 95 percent of global trade flows through "tightly choreographed value chains".
10. Compared to Baldwin's (2019) notion of "New Globalization" discussed above.
11. Porter's value chain is already mentioned in endnote 5. The "value" in the term value chain is understood as the amount that buyers are willing to pay for a product/service provided to them by a given supplier. The processes carried out by the company not only add value to the customer, but also generate costs. In other words, it means that an increase in value understood in this way proves a relative improvement in a company's competitiveness. This competitiveness is, therefore, a result of the value for the customer added by the individual processes carried out by the company. (Porter, 1998 [1985]).
12. For illustration let us consider three examples of value distribution from both—low-tech and high-tech sectors. In the case of coffee, the $4.40/lb. retail price in 1994 breaks down as follows: 10%/21% for the farmer (depending on the dry or wet process), 20%/9% for the bean processing factory (depending on the dry or wet process), 11% for export, freight and insurance, 8% for the importer, 29% for the final processing factory, and 22% for the retailer (Fitter & Kaplinsky, 2001, p 73). In the case of canned peach, 42.9% stay inside South Africa (12.4%

for peaches, 11.6% for cans, 4.2% for sugar, 14.7 for canning), while 57.1% goes outside South Africa (24.2% for shipping, duties, insurance, landing charges, 6.3% for the importer, and 26.7 for the supermarket) (Kaplinsky, 2000, p. 24). The $499 retail price of Apple's iPhone sold in US stores in 2010 breaks down as follows: $179 (35.9%) for the wholesale value of the iPhone shipped to the US and $320 (64.1%) for the bottom line, which goes to the US for R&D, design, engineering, financing, advertising, logistics etc. and Apple's profits (58.5%). The $179 wholesale value of the iPhone breaks down as follows: $6.50 (3.6% of the wholesale value or 1.3% of the retail price) for the manufacturing costs in China, $10.75 (6% or 2.2%, respectively) for inputs imported to China from the US, and 161.71 (90.3% or 32.4%, respectively) for inputs imported from other countries (Kraemer, Linden & Dedricket al., 2011; Landefeld, 2014).

13. In Macneil's (1985) meaning.
14. This dependence is not depicted in Figure 5.1 because this figure does not show the environment, due to simplicity.
15. And, therefore, the institutional context could influence the relative importance of criteria used in decision-making.
16. Something between cooperation and competition.

References

Ansell, C., & Boin, A. (2019). Taming deep uncertainty: The potential of pragmatist principles for understanding and improving strategic crisis management. *Administration & Society*, *51*(7), 1079–1112. https://doi.org/10.1177/0095399717747655

Arak, P. (2020). *Pandenomics: A State of War*. Retrieved from: https://wszystkoconajwazniejsze.pl/piotr-arak-pandenomics-a-state-of-war/ Available [January 15, 2022].

Arak, P. (2021). *Pandenomia. Czy koronawirus zakończył erę neoliberalizmu?* [Pandenomics: Did the Coronavirus End the Era of Neoliberalism?]. Warszawa: Poltext.

Bair, J. (2014). Editor's introduction: Commodity chains in and of the world-systems. *Journal of World-Systems Research*, *20*(1), 1–10. https://doi.org/10.5195/jwsr.2014.574

Baldwin, R. (2019). *The Great Convergence. Information Technology and the New Globalization*. Cambridge: The Belknap Press of Harvard Univesity Press.

Baran, J., Maciejczak, M., Pietrzak, M., Rokicki, T., & Wicki, L. (2008). *Logistyka. Wybrane zagadnienia* [Logistics: Selected Issues]. Warszawa: Wydawnictwo SGGW.

Beer, S. (1995). *Brain of the Firm: The Managerial Cybernetics of Organization*. Chichester: John Wiley & Sons.

Bertalanffy, von, L. (1972). The history and status of general systems theory. *The Academy of Management Journal*, *15*(4), 407–426. https://doi.org/10.2307/255139

Bossel, H. (2007). *Systems and Models: Complexity, Dynamics, Evolution, Sustainability*. Norderstedt: Books on Demand.

Brandenburger, A. M., & Nalebuff, B. J. (1998). *Co-Opetition*. New York: Currency & Doubleday.

Braudel, F. (2013 [1985]). *Dynamika kapitalizmu* [The Dynamics of Capitalism]. Warszawa: Wydawnictwo Aletheia.

Camps, T. (2004). Chains and networks: Theory and practice. In: T. Camps, P. Diederen, G. J. Hofstede, & B. Vos (eds.), *The Emerging World of Chains and Networks: Bridging Theory and Practice* (pp. 13–32). Den Haag: Reed Business Information.

Capgemini Research Institute. (2021). *The Wake-Up Call: Building Supply Chain Resilience in Consumer Products and Retail for a Post-COVID World*. Retrieved from: www.capgemini.com/wp-content/uploads/2021/03/Supply-Chain-in-CPR_2021-03-10_Web.pdf Available [March 9, 2022].

Christopher, M. (2011). *Logistics and Supply Chain Management: Creating Value-Adding Networks*. Harlow: Prentice Hall.

Coyle, J. J., Bardi, E. J., & Langley, J. (1996). *The Management of Business Logistics*. Cleveland: West Publishing.

Drost, S., Wijk, van J., & Vellema, S. (2011). *Development Value Chains Meet Business Supply Chains: The Concept of Global Value Chains Unraveled*. Rotterdam: Partnerships Resource Centre.

Dünhaupt, P., Herr, H., Mehl, F., & Teipen, C. (2022). Introduction: Governance, rent-seeking and upgrading in global value chains. In: C. Teipen, P. Dünhaupt, H. Herr, & F. Mehl (eds.). *Economic and Social Upgrading in Global Value Chains* (pp. 1–31). London: Palgrave Macmillan.

Farrell, H., & Newman, A. (2020). Will the coronavirus end globalization as we know it? *Foreign Affairs*. Retrieved from: www.foreignaffairs.com/articles/2020-03-16/will-coronavirus-end-globalization-weknow-it Available [March 9, 2022].

Fawcett, S. E., & Magnan, G. M. (2002). The rhetoric and reality of supply chain integration. *International Journal of Physical Distribution & Logistics Management*, *32*(5), 339–361.

Financial Times. (2020). Companies should shift from 'just in time' to 'just in case'. Retrieved from: www.ft.com/content/606d1460-83c6-11ea-b555-37a289098206 Available [March 9, 2022].

Financial Times. (2021). Supply chains: Companies shift from 'just in time' to 'just in case'. Retrieved from: www.ft.com/content/8a7cdc0d-99aa-4ef6-ba9a-fd1a1180dc82 Available [March 9, 2022].

Fitter, R., & Kaplinsky, R. (2001). Who gains from product rents as the coffee market becomes more differentiated? A value chain analysis. *IDS Bulletin, 32*(3), 69–82. https://doi.org/10.1111/j.1759-5436.2001.mp32003008.x

Forrester, J. W. (2013 [1961]). *Industrial Dynamics* (reprint). Eastford: Martino Publishing.

Galbraith, J. K. (2014 [1952]). *American Capitalism: The Concept of Countervailing Power: With a Ne Introduction by the Author* (10th printing). New Brunswick: Transaction Publishers.

Geiger, K. (2022). Jetzt rächt sich Deutschlands Feigheit [Now Germany's cowardice is taking its revenge]. *Die Welt*. Retrieved from: www.welt.de/politik/

ausland/plus237106283/Drohender-Krieg-in-Europa-Jetzt-raecht-sich-Deutschlands-Feigheit.html Available [March 9, 2022].

Gereffi, G. (1994). The organization of buyer-driven global commodity chains: How US retailers shape overseas production networks. In: G. Gereffi & M. Korzeniewicz (eds.), *Commodity Chains and Global Capitalism* (pp. 93–122). Westport: Praeger.

Gereffi, G. (1995). Global production systems and third world development. In: B. Stallings (ed.), *Global Change, Regional Response: The New International Context of Development* (pp. 100–142). Cambridge: Cambridge University Press.

Gereffi, G. (1999a). International trade and industrial upgrading in the apparel commodity chain. *Journal of International Economics, 48*(1), 37–70.

Gereffi, G. (1999b). *A Commodity Chains Framework for Analyzing Gobal Industries.* Mimeo: Duke University. Retrieved from: https://citeseerx.ist.psu.edu/viewdoc/download?doi=10.1.1.608.812&rep=rep1&type=pdf Available [December 15, 2021].

Gereffi, G. (2020). What does the COVID-19 pandemic teach us about global value chains? The case of medical supplies. *Journal of International Business Policy, 3*, 287–301. https://doi.org/10.1057/s42214-020-00062-w

Gereffi, G., & Fernandez-Stark, K. (2011). *Global Value Chain Analysis: A Primer.* Durham: Center on Globalization, Governance & Competitiveness.

Gereffi, G., Humphrey, J., Kaplinsky, R., & Sturgeon, T. J. (2001). Introduction: Globalisation, value chains and development. *IDS Bulletin, 32*(3), 1–7. https://doi.org/10.1111/j.1759-5436.2001.mp32003001.x

Gereffi, G., Humprey, J., & Sturgeon, T. (2005). The governance of global value chains. *Review of Interntional Political Economy, 12*(1), 78–104. https://doi.org/10.1080/09692290500049805

Gereffi, G., & Korzeniewicz, M. (eds.). (1994). *Commodity Chains and Global Capitalism.* Westport: Praeger.

Hopkins, T. K., & Wallerstein, I. (1977). Patterns of development of the modern word-system. *Review, 1*(2), 11–45.

Hopkins, T. K., & Wallerstein, I. (1986). Commodity chains in the world economy prior to 1800. *Review, 10*(1), 157–170.

Hopkins, T. K., & Wallerstein, I. (1994). Commodity chains: Construct and research. In: G. Gereffi & M. Korzeniewicz (eds.), *Commodity Chains and Global Capitalism* (pp. 1–14). Westport: Praeger.

Humphrey, J., & Schmitz, H. (2000). *Governance and Upgrading: Linking Industrial Cluster and Global Value Chain Research.* IDS Working Paper, 120. Brighton: Institute of Development Studies, University of Sussex.

Humphrey, J., & Schmitz, H. (2002). How does insertion in global value chains affect upgrading in industrial clusters? *Regional Studies, 36*(9), 1017–1027. https://doi.org/10.1080/0034340022000022198

Institute of Supply Management. (2020). *COVID-19's Global Impact on Supply Chains.* Retrieved from: www.ismworld.org/supply-management-news-and-reports/research-resource-centers/covid-19-resource-center/ Available [March 9, 2022].

International Monetary Fund. (2022). *Rising Caseloads: A Disrupted Recovery, and Higher Inflation.* Retrieved from: www.imf.org/en/Publications/WEO/Issues/2022/01/25/world-economic-outlook-update-january-2022 Available [March 9, 2022].

Jarzębowski, S. (2012). Zarządzanie procesami w łańcuchu dostaw. [Process management in the supply chain]. *Logistyka, 2,* 681–688.

Jones, R. W., & Kierzkowski, H. (1990). The role of services in production and international trade: A theoretical framework. In: R. W. Jones & A. Kruger (eds.), *The Political Economy of International Trade* (pp. 31–48). Oxford: Blackwell.

Jones, R. W., & Kierzkowski, H. (2000). *A Framework for Fragmentation.* IIFET 2000 Proceedings (pp. 1–9), Retrieved from: http://citeseerx.ist.psu.edu/viewdoc/download?doi=10.1.1.457.1636&rep=rep1&type=pdf Available [December 15, 2021].

Kaplinsky, R. (2000). *Spreading the Gains from Globalisation: What Can Be Learned from Value Chain Analysis?* Brighton: Institute of Development Studies (IDS).

Kaplinsky, R., & Morris, M. (2002). *A Handbook for Value Chain Research.* Ottawa: International Development Research Center (IDRC).

Klepacki, B., & Wicki, L. (red.). (2014). *Systemy logistyczne w funkcjonowaniu przedsiębiorstw przetwórstwa rolno-spożywczego* [Logistic Systems in the Conduct of Agri-Food Processors]. Warszawa: Wydawnictwo SGGW.

Kornai, J. (1971). *Anti-Equilibrium: On Economic Systems Theory and the Tasks of Research.* Amsterdam: North-Holland.

Kraemer, K.-L., Linden, G., & Dedrick, J. (2011). *Capturing Value in Global Networks: Apple's iPad and iPhone.* PCIC Working Paper.

Landefeld, S. (2014). *Implications and Challenges Associated with Developing a New System of Extended International Accounts, Discussion paper, International Conference on the Measurement of International Trade and Economic Globalization.* Aguascalientes, Mexico, September 29–October 1. Retrieved from: https://unstats.un.org/unsd/trade/events/2014/mexico/New%20System%20of%20Extended%20International%20Accounts%20-%20Steve%20Landefeld%20-%2018%20Sep%202014.pdf Available [March 9, 2022].

Lazzarini, S. G., Chaddd, F. R., & Cook, M. L. (2001). Integrating supply chain and network analyses: The study of netchains. *Journal of Chain and Network Science, 1,* 7–22.

Lund, S., Manyika, D. C. J., Woetzel, J., Barriball, E., Krishnan, D. C. M., Alicke, K., Birshan, M., George, K., Smit, S., Swan, D., & Hutzler, K. (2020). *Risk, Resilience, and Rebalancing in Global Value Chains.* McKinsey Global Institute. Retrieved from: www.mckinsey.com/business-functions/operations/our-insights/risk-resilience-and-rebalancing-in-global-value-chains Available [March 9, 2022].

Macneil, I. R. (1985). Relational contract: What we do and do not know. *Wisconsin Law Review, 3,* 484–525.

Meadows, D. H. (2008). *Thinking in Systems: A Primer.* White River Junction: Chelsea Green Publishing.

North, D. C. (2011 [1990]). *Institutions, Institutional Change and Economic Performance* (31st printing). Cambridge: Cambridge University Press.

Odersteijn, C., Wijnands, J., & Hurine, R. (2004). The economics of chains and networks. In: T. Camps, P. Diedered, G. J. Hofstede, & B. Vos (eds.), *The Emerging World of Chains and Networks: Bridging Theory and Practice* (pp. 235–250). Den Haag: Red Business Information,

O'Leary, L. (2020). The modern supply chain is snapping. *The Atlantic,* March 26.

Oliver, R. K., & Webber, M. D. (1982). Supply chain management: Logistics catches up with strategy. In: M. Christopher (ed.), *Logistics: The Strategic Issues* (pp. 63–75). London: Chapman and Hall.

O'Neil, S. K. (2020). How to pandemic-proof globalization: Redundancy, not re-shoring, is the key to supply-chain security. *Foreign Affairs*, April 1. Retrieved from: www.foreignaffairs.com/articles/2020-04-01/how-pandemic-proofglobalization Available [March 9, 2022].

Porter, M. E. (1998 [1985]). *Competitive Advantage: Creating and Sustaining Superior Performance* (with a new Introduction). New York: The Free Press.

Pszczołowski, T. (1978). *Mała encyklopedia prakseologii i teorii organizacji* [A Small Encyclopedia of Praxeology and Organizational Theory]. Wrocław: Ossolineum.

Raikes, P., Jensen, M. F., & Fonte, S. (2000). Global commodity chain analysis and the French Filière approach: Comparison and critique. *Economy and Society, 29*(3), 390–417.

Senge, P. M. (2006). *The Fifth Discipline: The Art: And Practice of the Learning Organization* (2nd ed.). London: Random House.

Shih, W. (2020). Is it time to rethink globalized supply chains? *MIT Sloan Management Review*, March 19. Retrieved from: https://sloanreview.mit.edu/article/is-it-time-to-rethink-globalizedsupply-chains/ Available [March 9, 2022].

Simon, H. A. (1962). The architecture of complexity. *Proceeding of the American Philosophical Society, 106*(6), 467–482.

Słojewska, A. (2022). *Rynek półprzewodników. Bruksela bierze się za chipy* [Semiconductor market: Brussels takes on the chips]. *Rzeczpospolita*. Retrieved from: www.rp.pl/biznes/art35649961-rynek-polprzewodnikow-bruksela-bierze-sie-za-chipy Available [March 9, 2022].

Smith, A. (2003 [1776]). *The Wealth of Nations* (reprint based on 5th ed.). New York: Bantam Books.

Stamm, A. (2004). *Value Chains for Development Policy: Challenges for Trade Policy and the Promotion of Economic Development*. Eschborn: Deutsche Gesellschaft für Technische Zusammenarbeit.

Sterman, J. D. (2000). *Business Dynamics: Systems Thinking an Modeling for a Complex World*. Boston: Irwin McGraw-Hill.

Stigler, G. J. (1951). The division of labor is limited by the extent of the market. *Journal of Political Economy, 59*, 185–185. https://doi.org/10.1086/257075

Storey, J., Emberson, C., Godsell, J., & Harrison, A. (2006). Supply chain management: Theory, practice and future challenge. *International Journal of Operations & Production Management, 26*(7), 754–774. https://doi.org/10.1108/01443570610672220

Sturgeon, T. J. (2008). *From Commodity Chains to Value Chains: Interdisciplinary Theory Building in an Age of Globalization*. Industry Studies Association Working Papers WP-2008–02. Retrieved from: http://isapapers.pitt.edu/84/1/2008-02_Sturgeon.pdf Available [December 15, 2021].

Sturgeon, T. J, & Lee, J. (2001). *Industry Co-Evolution and the Rise of a Shared Supply-Base for Electronics Manufacturing*. Globalization Study Working Paper 01–002. Industrial Performance Center, Massachusetts Institute of Technology.

Supply Chain Management Terms and Glossary. (2013). *Council of Supply Chain Management Professionals*. Retrieved from: https://cscmp.org/CSCMP/Educate/ SCM_Definitions_and_Glossary_of_Terms.aspx Available [December 15, 2021].

Sweeney, E. (2011). Towards a unified definition of supply chain management. *International Journal of Applied Logistics*, *2*(3), 30–48. https://doi.org/10.4018/ jal.2011070103

Sweeney, E., Grant, D. B., & Mangan, J. (2018). Strategic adoption of logistics and supply chain management. *International Journal of Operations & Production Management*, *38*(3), 852–873. https://doi.org/10.1108/IJOPM-05-2016-0258

Taleb, N. N. (2012). *Antifragile: Things That Gain from Disorder*. New York: Random House.

Vorst, van der J. G. A. J. (2004). Supply chain management: Theory and practices. In: T. Camps, P. Diederen, G. J. Hofstede, & B. Vos (eds.), *The Emerging World of Chains and Networks: Bridging Theory and Practice* (pp. 105–128). Den Haag: Reed Business Information.

Wallerstein, I. (1974). *The Modern World-System I. Capitalist Agriculture and the Origins of the European World-Economy in the Sixteen Century*. New York: Academic Press.

Wallerstein, I. (2004). *World-Systems Analysis: An Introduction*. Durham: Duke University Press.

Zielonka, J. (2020). Has the coronavirus brought back the nation-state? *Social Europe*, March 26. Retrieved from: https://socialeurope.eu/has-the-coronavirus-brought-back-the-nation-state Available [March 9, 2022].

Zschäpitz, H. (2022). "Black Swan"-Moment—so groß sind die Preisschocks bei Gas, Öl und Weizen. ["Black Swan" moment: That's how big the price shocks are for gas, oil and wheat]. *Die Welt*. Retrieved form: www.welt.de/finanzen/ver-braucher/plus237359463/Rohstoffe-Benzin-Weizen-Mais-Der-Preisschock-durch-den-Krieg.html Available [March 9, 2022].

Chapter 6

Intelligent Solutions in the Supply Chains: Challenges for 3PL Providers

Helga Pavlić Skender, Elizabeta Ribarić,
and Petra Adelajda Zaninović

University of Rijeka, Croatia

Contents

6.1 Introduction

In the last two decades, third-party logistics providers (hereinafter: 3PL) represent one of the most important factors in supply chains and international trade. 3PL providers play an important role in creating a competitive advantage for retailers and manufacturers. 3PL functions are transportation, warehousing, inventory management, order fulfillment, and information systems within which 3PLs have various activities (Sink et al., 1996 in Pavlić et al., 2016). These functions and activities are crucial for the smooth functioning of supply-chain networks. However, technological advancements and market uncertainties force 3PL providers and supply chains to increase their flexibility and efficiency.

The next step in technological advancement for 3PL providers, as well as supply chains, could be the use of autonomous vehicles. Autonomous vehicles are already being used in logistics, but their use is limited to private, controlled locations such as warehouses, ports, manufacturing plants, etc. The next stage that most 3PL providers anticipate is the deployment of autonomous vehicles in public places, such as highways. Implementation of autonomous vehicles on public roads could solve some challenges such as shortage of skilled drivers, cost of human labor, reduction (elimination) of human error, the risk to human life, congestion relief, reduced number of road accidents, and the inefficiency of global supply chains in unforeseen situations (e.g., COVID -19 situation). According to European Commission (2021), there are more than 40,000 deaths on the roads in the EU; and more than 90% of all accidents are caused by human error. The purpose of autonomous vehicles is to protect human life, and reduce traffic accidents, energy consumption, and consequently pollution and congestion while increasing traffic accessibility (Bagloee et al., 2016).

The aim of this paper is to investigate the implementation of autonomous vehicles in global supply chains using selected global 3PL leaders and to determine the main benefits of implementing autonomous vehicles in supply chains. The research question that emerges is: What are the key phases of autonomous-vehicle implementation that leading 3PL providers are dealing with? Our research is based on desk research and case-study analysis of the world's leading 3PL providers following the Armstrong and Associates' Top 50 Global 3PLs.

The paper consists of five parts. The introduction gives an insight into the topic, the research question, and the aim of the research. In the second part, a detailed explanation of the supply chain and 3PL providers, is given. In the third part, the phases of autonomous-vehicle deployment are explained, and innovative technologies from selected 3PL providers are analyzed. In the fourth part, advantages and possible concerns regarding the implementation of autonomous vehicles on public roads are given. The fifth part of this paper is a conclusion.

6.2 Definition and Characteristics of the Supply Chains and the 3PL Providers

The supply chain is a complex system with many parties within it, i.e., organizations, people, activities, information, and resources involved in the delivery of a product or service to a final consumer. 3PL providers play an important role in the efficient functioning of supply chains. The following part provides an overview of the current state of knowledge regarding supply chains and 3PL providers.

Supply Chain

The first literature explanation of the supply chain dates back to 1982 and is attributed to authors Oliver and Webber (Carter et al., 2015; Ellram & Cooper, 2014; Gibson et al., 2005). The supply chain is a set of processes associated with the flow of goods, information, and money between companies. It includes processes from raw-material supply to production, distribution, consumption, and recycling. Authors Min et al. (2019) define a supply chain as the long-term coordination of business functions within the company, but also between them, to achieve better results. The supply chain can be considered as a network (because it consists of lines and nodes), a flexible but complex system (because it involves a large number of participants), and an individual system (because it is unique to each product) (Carter et al., 2015). A supply chain can be defined as a system that provides the flow of materials, semifinished products, and finished products, from the manufacturer to the customer (Prasad et al., 2014).

Supply-chain management can be described as a tool to optimize the supply chain through integrated management (Sanchez-Flores et al., 2020). Supply-chain management includes several functions such as raw-material supply, production, transportation, inventory management, information systems, ordering processes, material handling, customer management, and customs clearance (Tezuka, 2011). Mentzer et al. (2001) define supply-chain management "as a group of three or more entities (organizations or individuals) directly involved in upstream and downstream flows of products, services, finances, and/or information from a source to a customer." Carefully designed supply-chain management can help reduce costs and improve financial performance. Supply-chain management represents the efficient integration of suppliers, manufacturing companies, and distributors (Dadashpour & Bozorgi-Amiri, 2020). Given growing globalization, supply-chain management is making significant efforts in terms of accountability and sustainability (Gurzawska, 2019).

Advances in technology, environmental standards, customer requirements, organizational structures (e.g., mergers and acquisitions, outsourcing) and the introduction of new and/or innovative products are leading to increasing complexity in supply chains. Sustainable supply chains (SSC) can be defined as complex systems that consider social, environmental, and economic impacts in addition to managing goods from suppliers to customers and vice versa (Barbosa-Póvoa et al., 2018; Alkhuzaim et al., 2021). The goal of the sustainable supply chain is to improve the company's internal processes through environmental and social practices, as well as improve the supplier process (Wang & Dai, 2018). Authors Kuik et al. (2011) stated that the supply chain can be improved through the process and product design. Process improvement includes reuse, recycling, and remanufacturing, while product design includes reduction, recovery, and redesign.

Sustainable-supply-chain management (SSCM) can be a strategic component that increases a company's effectiveness and competitiveness, achieves better customer service and can increase profitability (Tseng et al., 2015). Compared to standard supply-chain management, sustainable-supply-chain management is more focused on environmental and/or community issues (Gloet & Samson, 2020).

3PL Providers

A 3PL provider represents a company that has logistics expertise (know-how). 3PL providers have integrated, contact-based, and consultative functions (Tezuka, 2011). "A 3PL covers all services to effectively plan, store, and manage every type of product, service, and information flow from the beginning to the end of the supply chain" (Faruk Gürcana et al., 2016, p. 227). 3PL providers are also responsible for turnover, assembly, labeling, loading, unloading, repackaging, and distribution (Batarlienė & Jarašūnienė, 2017). They are increasingly oriented toward the e-commerce and retail sectors. 3PL providers can impact (reduce) the logistics and inventory costs of companies (Dadashpour & Bozorgi-Amiri, 2020). A 3PL provider picks up shipments from manufacturers, consolidates shipments at distribution centers, and transports them to customers (Jung, 2017). The 3PL providers are often referred to as supply-chain designers.

6.3 Case-Study Analysis of 3PL Provider's Implementation of Autonomous Vehicles

It is commonly known that autonomous vehicles have been used in logistics for decades. However, so far they have only been used in controlled environments such as manufacturing plants, ports, and distribution centers (Van Meldert & De Boeck, 2016; Flämig, 2016; Shah & Arengo Piragine, 2018). 3PL service providers offer a wide range of services and are now faced with the challenge of operating more efficiently, flexibly, and sustainably. Therefore, the topic of using autonomous vehicles in the 3PL business is receiving more and more attention from the business and academic communities. In the following part, the main features of autonomous vehicles are presented and analyzed on a global scale using case studies of leading 3PL service providers.

Main Features of an Autonomous Vehicle

An autonomous vehicle is a type of vehicle that drives itself. According to Van Meldert and De Boeck (2016), an autonomous vehicle is "a set of hardware and complex software technologies that together form the system that enables autonomy." "It relies on three elements: sensors for sensing the environment and its movement, on-board computers, and actuators for vehicle control" (Luettel et al., 2012, p. 1832). To achieve accurate environment sensing, it is necessary to use RADAR (Radio Detection and Ranging) and LIDAR (Light Detection and Ranging). They are both image-based sensors, but with one major difference: RADAR uses radio waves and LIDAR uses lasers or LED light. GPS is used to estimate the movement of the vehicle. The onboard computer and all sensors must be calibrated and work as a unit. All processing onboard the vehicle must be done in real-time. The purpose of the actuator is to close the control loop, e.g., vehicle control, braking, etc. (Luettel et al., 2012; Shah & Arengo Piragine, 2018). Authors Shah and Arengo Piragine (2018) mention that vehicle-to-vehicle (V2V) communication is being added in more and more automated vehicles. The purpose of

V2V communication is to exchange information between vehicles. All the technology mentioned above is used to detect other vehicles, traffic signs, traffic lights, and pedestrians.

An autonomous vehicle does not require the active absence of the driver. Autonomous vehicles may be able to make quicker decisions at a critical moment. In other words, an autonomous vehicle could increase road safety and thus protect human lives. By using GPS and V2V communication, the autonomous vehicle receives information about the busiest routes and traffic jams. In this way, it can select less busy roads and adjust its driving according to the movements of other vehicles. According to Van Meldert and De Boeck (2016), logistics operations throughout the supply chain, from raw-material extraction and intermediate transportation to operations in warehouses, distribution centers, and manufacturing plants, to the last-mile bridging system, can be influenced by the use of AVs, creating the potential for new business models while ending the prospects of existing ones.

Autonomous vehicles can be used in four segments: Indoor logistics, outdoor environment, long-distance transportation, and last-mile delivery. Autonomous vehicles are most commonly used in indoor logistics, where controlled conditions and predefined routes exist (Van Meldert & De Boeck, 2016; Shah & Arengo Piragine, 2018). The use of autonomous vehicles can make the process more flexible, efficient, and fast. As mentioned earlier, autonomous vehicles work indoors in ideal conditions, but the goal of the logistics industry is to use them outdoors, in an unsafe environment. Autonomous vehicles have already been deployed in private, controlled outdoor conditions such as seaports, airports, and logistics yards (Shah & Arengo Piragine, 2018). Similar to previous targets, the goal of AVs is to reduce (eliminate) the possibility of human error, ensure accurate and precise driving, continuously monitor the goods and vehicles, and reduce fuel consumption and human-labor costs (Van Meldert & De Boeck, 2016).

Uncontrolled outdoor transportation can be divided into several parts: The first mile, the line haul, and the last mile. The first mile and the last mile are similar in terms of transportation manipulation since they take place in urban areas. On the other hand, line-haul transportation is the longest part of the transportation route which is more predictable and easy (Shah & Arengo Piragine, 2018). Line haul transportation implies driving autonomous vehicles on public roads and highways. The participation of autonomous vehicles in this part of transportation can be risky in terms of traffic accidents. Autonomous vehicles are not yet advanced enough to be able to follow and react to the behavior of other vehicles in traffic. It's important to note that the technology that could change the long-haul transportation industry has introduced the concept of platooning, also called road trains. Platooning is the formation of two or more vehicles where the first vehicle (leader) determines the driving of the second vehicle (follower). Thanks to automation technology and V2V communication, the vehicles can drive at a smaller distance compared to the situation where the driver controls the vehicle. According to Agility (2017), "the goal of platooning is to improve safety, efficiency, and congestion, primarily due to existing speeds between vehicles." Platooning could affect all stakeholders, especially developers, users, policymakers, and regulators involved in the process of navigation and transportation (Janssen et al., 2015). The challenge faced by 3PL providers is last-mile delivery. Last-mile delivery involves transportation to reach local stores and customers. It is complex due to transportation with slower speed, narrow roads, smaller consignments of goods, and the greater number of manipulations with goods (Van Meldert & De Boeck, 2016). The environment is also more complex because it includes different types of subjects, from pedestrians and cyclists to different types of vehicles (Shah & Arengo Piragine, 2018).

Implementation of Autonomous Vehicles

Implementation of autonomous vehicles has several stages to be taken. According to the United States Department of Transport, NHTSA (2021), there are six levels of automation: From zero to five (Table 6.1).

In level zero, humans do all the driving. In the first level of automation, an advanced driver-assistance system (ADAS) as part of the vehicle can assist the driver in steering or braking/accelerating (only one operation is possible at a time). In the second level of automation, an advanced driver-assistance system (ADAS) can control steering and braking/acceleration under certain circumstances. The driver must pay full attention the entire time. In the third level of automation, an automated driver system (ADS) can handle all aspects of the driving task (steering, braking, accelerating), but only under certain conditions. The driver must be able to take control at any time. The driver must continue to monitor the environment. In the fourth level of automation, an automated driving system (ADS) can take over all driving tasks and monitor the environment, but the driver's attention is still required. In the fifth level of automation, an automated driving system (ADS) can perform all driving tasks, regardless of the driving conditions. At this level, the human is only the passenger and does not need to intervene in the driving process.

Table 6.1 Levels of Automation.

Level of automation	Characteristics
0	■ No automation ■ the driver performs all the driving tasks
1	■ Driver assistance ■ the driver controls the vehicle; some driving-assist features may be included in vehicle design
2	■ Partial automation ■ vehicle has some automated functions (accelerating, steering, braking); driver stays engaged with driving task and monitors the driving environment
3	■ Conditional automation ■ driver is not required to monitor the vehicle and driving environment, but needs to be prepared to take over control of the vehicle at any time
4	■ High automation ■ the vehicle is able to perform driving entirely by itself, in certain conditions; the driver has the option to control the vehicle
5	■ Full automation ■ the vehicle is capable of controlling all the driving in all conditions; driver may participate in controlling the vehicle

Source: Authors' elaboration based on NHTSA (2021).

According to SAE (2014) in Di Febbraro and Sacco (2016), automation levels could be divided into two classes: Class one represents level zero, level one, and level two where the human monitors the driving environment, while class two represents level three, level four, and level five where the automated driving system (autonomous vehicle) monitors the driving environment.

The analysis of the implementation of autonomous vehicles is based on the case study methodology. This method is widely used in logistics and supply-chain research (Pavlić Skender & Zaninović, 2020). The case-study methodology is used because it allows for numerous ways of obtaining data and is methodologically unconstrained in terms of data analysis (Yin, 2009; Cudzilo & Voronina, 2020). The analysis compares three cases of global top 3PL providers based on Armstrong and Associates' official website from 2020's list of top 3PLs (Logistics Management, 2020). Namely, the case-study analysis is conducted on DHL Supply Chain & Global Forwarding, Nippon Express, and DB Schenker.

DHL Supply Chain & Global Forwarding

DHL is a German, leading global 3PL service provider. It offers a wide range of services, from technical solutions for companies and transport organizations to finding new technological solutions and improving existing ones (DHL, 2021a).

DHL presented an automobile warehouse of the future, which includes advanced technological solutions such as warehouse automation, autonomous vehicles, unmanned aerial vehicles (drones), wearables, augmented reality, the Internet of Things, and Big Data. Since the focus of this article is on autonomous vehicles, only these will be discussed in more detail. Autonomous vehicles are suitable for transporting large and heavy parts. This is because they can support autonomous-parts picking, full-pallet picking, and the filing process (DHL, 2021b). DHL has developed several autonomous vehicles for in-house use (warehouse):

1) Narrow-aisle robots—primarily intended for slow-moving warehouses with limited shelf-location changes; they can autonomously drive and pick or dispose of the correct packages, and simultaneously adjust to the required shelf height;
2) bin focus—appropriated for larger warehouses and fast-moving warehouses with small items; it can autonomously navigate the warehouse; operators can add items while the vehicle is moving toward a specific place;
3) pallet focus—appropriate for larger and fast-moving warehouses where operators need to cover long distances; autonomous vehicle transport pallets in the warehouse;
4) bin focus—appropriate for large warehouses with high output and product range; they can navigate the way to every product that is needed to be transported;
5) pallet focus—intended for central-distribution warehouses; operators drive the vehicle to the picking location, and then step to activate "follow-me" mode; an operator can then put focus on the picking process;
6) goods-to-person robot—appropriate for aftermarket warehouses for picking small items with high turnover (e.g., e-commerce); it can move shelves to the operator;
7) Meerkat inventory robot—appropriate for large fast-moving warehouses that store pallets; its purpose is to check the stock and analyze each location while using several technologies such as cameras, lasers, and scanners;
8) automated inventory system—appropriate for construction inventory facilities or urban distribution centers; it uses robots and bins to quickly process small items and orders;

9) cleaning robot—it cleans the space during quiet times; the operator gives the instructions regarding starting and ending position; the operator is also needed to position and refill the robot.

According to DHL (2021c), one of the most important future implementations (five- to ten-year technology trend) is self-driving vehicles (autonomous vehicles), which are planned for implementation in long-distance trucking and the last-mile (Figure 6.1). Autonomous vehicles have entered common and public spaces, including highways, sidewalks, and ports. Right now, autonomous vehicles cannot drive autonomously on roads for legal, safety, and operational reasons. In other words, a human driver is still needed.

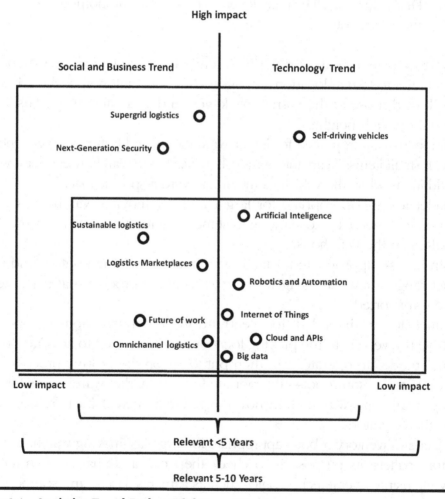

Figure 6.1   Logistics Trend Radar (High Impact).

Source: Authors' elaboration based on DHL (2021c).

Figure 6.1 shows that in less than five years, big-data analytics, the Internet of things, cloud and APIs, robotics and automation, and artificial intelligence will have a major impact on logistics. In the next five to ten years, the focus will be on autonomous vehicles, next-generation security, and super-grid logistics.

In 2019, a truck autonomously delivered butter from California to Pennsylvania (that's a distance of 4,500 km). The delivery would normally take nine days, but by using an autonomous vehicle, the goods were delivered in three. It's important to note that the weather conditions were not good. DHL also started working with a California startup, Ike, to increase the safety and efficiency of transportation on highways. On local roads and near facilities, the absence of a human driver in a vehicle is required. On long-distance transport (highways), the vehicle could drive autonomously (DHL, 2021c).

Nippon Express

Nippon Express is the third-best 3PL provider in the world and Japan's largest global logistics company. It provides solutions for warehousing, transportation, and local distribution of goods. In 2020, Nippon Express implemented a smart warehouse. The advanced technology includes (Tao, 2020):

1) AutoStore—robot storage system whose purpose is to maximize storage efficiency;
2) EVE—an automated transport robot;
3) Rack fork auto—an automated forklift that does not need the presence of a human;
4) AGV—an automated guided vehicle;
5) Thouzer—a target-guided autonomous vehicle;
6) Projection picking system—a digital picking system employing image-processing technology;
7) RFID Tunnel Gate—a device that uses RFID tags to improve the efficiency of inspection work.

In 2019, Nippon Express began nighttime, unattended operations to prepare for shipping. Automated forklifts and automated vehicle convoys were used. In 2019, a joint experiment on level-four automated vehicles was conducted on a public road (Nippon Express, 2019). Work is underway to develop the crawler type of automated driverless vehicle, which could reduce energy consumption and ensure better safety of human life at workplaces such as terminals. Also, the effectiveness of manned-truck platooning is being ana-lyzed (Nippon Express, 2020).

DB Schenker

DB Schenker is one of the world's largest 3PL providers in Denmark. It offers a wide range of services such as transportation, labeling, packaging, warehous-ing, and distribution (DB Schenker, 2021).

The first autonomous all-electric vehicle is being tested on a public road in Sweden. Permission to drive on a public road is granted by the Swedish Transport Agency. The autonomous vehicle, named T-Pod, is a self-driving vehicle that will drive the route between two locations of DB Schenken. The route includes a public road in parts. T-Pod is monitored by an operator who can remotely control the vehicle if necessary. With one load, the vehicle can travel about 200 km, carrying about twenty tons of cargo (DB Schenker, 2019).

In 2020, DB Schenker introduced an autonomous forklift vehicle in ware-house logistics. The forklift vehicle is equipped with a height-adjustable forklift. It can be used to lift and lower containers (Gill, 2020). Among the analyzed 3PL providers, it can be seen that autonomous vehicles are the near future of supply chains. The analyzed providers are already testing autono-mous vehicles on public roads. Regarding the level of automation, in indoor logistics, level four is already implemented and in use, and full implemen-tation of level five is expected shortly. In outdoor logistics (public places), some successful tests have been conducted, but the full implementation of autonomous vehicles might not be possible in the next five years.

6.4 Benefits and Potential Challenges of Implementation of Autonomous Vehicles

According to Flämig (2016), "from a microeconomic point of view, a shortage of drivers, an energy-saving driving style, high reliability, and accident avoid-ance are key reasons for the use of autonomous systems in the freight-transport chain." The implementation of autonomous vehicles in the supply chain can bring benefits such as cost efficiency, safety, flexibility, and environmental friendliness (Sell et al., 2019), minimization of waste streams and damaged goods, energy optimization, minimization of human errors, and increased safety of human lives (Bechtsis et al., 2018). According to Shah et al. (2019) and Pendleton et al. (2017), the benefits of automated vehicles include reduced labor costs (eliminating the need for human workers), increased safety standards (use of high technology in automated vehicles reduces the possibility of accidents), maximized accuracy and productivity (minimizing errors and mistakes in production lines), and ease of expansion and upgrade (companies can easily update the process). Themplementtation of autonomous vehicles by 3PL providers (as part of the supply chain) could change drivers' roles. As the driver is not responsible for driving the vehicle, he could take over other tasks during the transport process, e.g., route planning, documentation, and other administrative tasks, or he could rest Flämig (2016). Since autonomous vehicles are electrically powered, another benefit could be that noise emissions are reduced even at lower speeds and light emissions are reduced. The use of autonomous vehicles could speed up the delivery of goods to the customer (reduced delivery time), as the ordered package can be delivered to the customer's doorstep at any time (day or night) (Hörl et al., 2016).

On the other hand, there are several disadvantages, such as high initial costs (autonomous vehicles are cost-effective only when long-term investments are made), equipment-maintenance costs (maintenance of automated vehicles can slow down the process), unsuitability for non-repetitive production lines (autonomous vehicles are cost-effective only when economies of scale are involved), and inflexibility of operation (autonomous vehicles can perform only one task at a time) (Shah et al., 2019). In addition to the aforementioned disadvantages, Litman (2021) notes additional accidents due to system failures, platooning, increased overall vehicle mileage, invasion of privacy (hacking risk), increased infrastructure costs, possible reduction in alternative mobility such as walking and biking, reduced employment, and also optimistic predictions about autonomous vehicles could reduce interest in other transportation improvements. Autonomous vehicles could bring new safety issues. It is thought that people would feel safer in traffic and reduce the use of seat belts. One of the main benefits is the elimination of human error, but that does not mean the elimination of machine error at the same time. Due to the lack of subjectivity, a moral dilemma arises in the event of a traffic accident (self-interest of autonomous vehicles to protect cargo or socially beneficial decision to protect other participants) (Taeihagh & Min Lim, 2019).

6.5 Conclusion

The autonomous vehicle is a vehicle that, with the help of advanced technological solutions, analyzes the environment in which it is moving and adjusts its driving accordingly (accelerates, decelerates, brakes, stops). Autonomous vehicles on public roads could be the next step in the evolution of the transportation system. 3PL providers could play an important role in this process as they are creators (designers) of supply chains. 3PL providers represent companies that have various important functions in the transportation system, such as warehousing, inventory management, and information systems. Autonomous vehicles are mainly used in indoor logistics (e.g., warehouses) and outdoor logistics (e.g., private ports, airports). In other words, they are used under controllable and predictable conditions.

The companies analyzed represent the world's most advanced 3PL providers according to the Armstrong & Associates' Top 50 Global 3PLs. The 3PL providers analyzed are DHL Supply Chain & Global Forwarding (Germany), Nippon Express (Japan), and DB Schenker (Denmark). All observed 3PL providers have already fully implemented automation level four in indoor logistics. The implementation of level five could happen very soon. Several tests have been conducted in the outdoor logistics area. The biggest leap among the observed 3PL providers was made by DB Schenker, which is testing the first autonomous fully electric vehicle in outdoor logistics in Sweden.

Although there are many benefits of autonomous vehicles such as cost efficiency, safety, flexibility, reduction of pollution and energy consumption, reduction of congestion (in the long run), protection of human life, and reduction of traffic accidents, there are certain challenges that slow down the implementation of autonomous vehicles. These challenges could be laws, high initial costs, maintenance costs, increase in traffic accidents at the beginning of the implementation (due to the participation of classical—driver-controlled—and autonomous vehicles in traffic), increase in infrastructure costs, hacking risks, etc. The implementation of autonomous vehicles could speed up the delivery process, especially when it comes to long-distance and last-mile deliveries, but it is important to note that even autonomous vehicles cannot solve the challenge of the bottleneck between long-distance and last-mile deliveries.

It must be acknowledged that the literature and data on this topic are limited, as intelligent technology and autonomous vehicles are at an early stage of development.

This research contributes to the existing literature by recognizing the importance of implementing intelligent solutions in the supply chain, especially from an autonomous-vehicle perspective. The results of the research can serve as valuable information and guidelines for the managers and logistics operators to make further decisions regarding the technology and intelligent solutions.

References

Agility. (2017). Supply chain leaders are forced to get smart. *Tech Wave*. Retrieved from: https://logisticsinsights.agility.com/future-of-logistics/tech-wave/ Available [May 3, 2021].

Alkhuzaim, L., Zhu, Q., & Sarkis, J. (2021). Evaluating emergy analysis at the nexus of circular economy and sustainable supply chain management. *Sustainable Production and Consumption, 25*, 413–424. DOI: 10.1016/j.spc.2020.11.022

Bagloee, S. A., Tavana, M., Asadi, M., & Oliver, T. (2016). Autonomus vehicles: Challenges, opportunities, and future implications for transportation policies. *Journal of Modern Transportation, 24*(4), 284–303. Retrieved from: https://link. springer.com/article/10.1007/s40534-016-0117-3 Available [May 3, 2021].

Barbosa-Póvoa, A. P., Da Silva, C., & Carvalho, A. (2018). Opportunities and challenges in sustainable supply chain: An operations research perspective. *European Journal of Operational Research, 268*, 399–431. DOI: 10.1016/j.ejor.2017. 10.036

Batarlienė, N., & Jarašūnienė, A. (2017). "3PL" service improvement opportunities in transport companies. *Procedia Engineering, 187*, 67–76. https://doi.org/10.1016/j. proeng.2017.04.351

Bechtsis, D., Tsolakis, N., Vlachos, D., & Singh Srai, J. (2018). Intelligent autonomous vehicles in digital supply chains: A framework for integrating innovations towards sustainable value networks. *Journal of Cleaner Production, 181*, 60–71. DOI: 10.1016/j.jclepro.2018.01.173

Carter, C. R., Rogers, D. S., & Choi, T. Y. (2015). Toward the theory of the supply chain. *Journal of Supply Chain Management, 51*(2), 89–97. Retrieved from: https://onlinelibrary.wiley.com/doi/10.1111/jscm.12073 Available [May 15, 2022].

Cudzilo, M., & Voronina, R. (2020). Improving the efficiency of planning and execution of deliveries with the use of a location register based on GLN identifiers. In: A. Kolinski, D. Dujak, & P. Golinska-Dawson (eds.), *Integration of Information Flow for Greening Supply Chain Management* (pp. 47–62). Berlin, Heidelberg, DE: Springer.

Dadashpour, I., & Bozorgi-Amiri, A. (2020). Evaluation and ranking of sustainable third-party logistics providers using the DAnalytic hierarchy process. *International Journal of Engineering, 33*(11), 2233–2244. DOI: 10.5829/IJE.2020.33.11B.15

DB Schenker. (2019). Retrieved from: www.dbschenker.com/co-en/innovation-/einride Available [May 3, 2021].

DB Schenker. (2021). Retrieved from: www.dbschenker.com/dk-en/about Available [May 3, 2021].

DHL. (2021a). Retrieved from: www.dhl.com/global-en/home/about-us.html Available [May 6, 2021].

DHL. (2021b). Retrieved from: www.dhl.com/global-en/home/insights-and-innovation/thought-leadership/brochures/auto-mobility/warehouse-of-the-future.html Available [May 3, 2021].

DHL. (2021c). Retrieved from: www.dhl.com/global-en/home/insights-and-innovation/insights/logistics-trend-radar.html Available [May 7, 2021].

Di Febbraro, A., Sacco, N. (2016). Open problems in transportation engineering with connected and autonomous vehicles. *Transportation Research Procedia, 14,* 2255–2264. DOI: 10.1016/j.trpro.2016.05.241

Ellram, L. M., & Cooper, M. C. (2014). Supply chain management: It's all about the journey, not the destination. *Journal of Supply Chain Management, 50*(1), 8–20. Retrieved from: https://onlinelibrary.wiley.com/doi/full/10.1111/jscm.12043 Available [May 7, 2021].

European Commission. (2021). Retrieved from: https://ec.europa.eu/transport/themes/its/road_it Available [May 5, 2021].

Faruk Gürcana, O., Yazıcı, I., Faruk Beycac, O., Yavuz Arsland, C., & Eldemire, F. (2016). Third party logistics (3PL) provider selection with AHP application. *Procedia: Social and Behavioral Sciences, 235,* 226–234. DOI: 10.1016/j.sbspro.2016.11.018

Flämig, H. (2016). Autonomus vehicles and autonomus driving in freight transport. In: M. Maurer, J. Gerdes, B. Lenz, & H. Winner (eds.), *Autonomous Driving.* Berlin, Heidelberg, DE: Springer. DOI: 10.1007/978-3-662-48847-8_18

Gibson, B. J., Mentzer, J. T., & Cook, R. L. (2005). Supply chain management: The pursuit of a consensus definition. *Journal of Business Logistics, 26*(2), 17–25.

Gill, D. (2020). Retrieved from: www.logistics-manager.com/db-schenker-implements-driverless-forklift-truck/ Available [May 2, 2021].

Gloet, M., & Samson, D. (2020). Knowledge and innovation management to support supply chain innovation and sustainability practices. *Information Systems Management, 39*(1), 3–18. Retrieved from: DOI: 10.1080/10580530.2020.1818898 Available [May 2, 2021].

Gurzawska, A. (2019). Towards responsible and sustainable supply chains: Innovation, multi-stakeholder approach and governance. *Philosophy of Management, 19,* 267–295. DOI: 10.1007/s40926-019-00114-z

Hörl, S., Ciari, F., & Axhause, K. W. (2016). *Recent Perspectives on the Impact of Autonomous Vehicles.* Research collection, ETHzürich, Working paper. DOI: 10.13140/RG.2.2.26690.17609

Janssen, R., Zwijnenberg, H., Blankers, I., & Kruijff, J. (2015). *Truck Platooning: Driving the Future of Transportation.* Retrieved from: http://resolver.tudelft.nl/uuid:778397eb-59d3-4d23-9185-511385b91509 Available [June 26, 2021].

Jung, H. (2017). Evaluation of third party logistics providers considering social sustainability. *Sustainability, 9*(5), 777. DOI: 10.3390/su9050777

Kuik, S. S., Nagalingam, S. V., & Amer, Y. (2011). Sustainable supply chain for collaborative manufacturing. *Journal of Manufacturing Technology Management, 22*(8), 984–1001. https://doi.org/10.1108/17410381111177449

Litman, T. (2021). *Autonomus Vehicle Implementation Prediction Implication for Transport Planning.* Victoria Transport Policy Institute. Retrieved from: www.vtpi.org/avip.pdf Available [June 26, 2021].

Logistics Management. (2020). Retrieved from: www.logisticsmgmt.com/article/top_50_us_and_global_third_party_logistics_2020 Available [June 26, 2021].

Luettel, T., Himmelsbach, M., & Wuensche, H.-J. (2012). Autonomous ground vehicles: Concepts and path to the future. *Proceedings of the IEEE, 100,* 1831–1839. DOI: 10.1109/JPROC.2012.2189803

Mentzer, J. T., DeWitt, W., Keebler, J. S., Min, S., Nix, N. W., Smith, C. D., & Zacharia, Z. G. (2001). Defining supply chain management. *Journal of Business Logistics*, *22*(2), 1–25. Retrieved from: https://onlinelibrary.wiley.com/doi/abs/10.1002/j.2158-1592.2001.tb00001.x Available [October 25, 2021].

Min, S., Zacharia, Z. G., & Smith, C. D. (2019). Defining supply chain management: In the past, present, and future. *Journal of Business Logistics*, *40*(1), 44–55. Retrieved from: https://onlinelibrary.wiley.com/doi/full/10.1111/jbl.12201 Available [October 25, 2021].

NHTSA. (2021). *United Stated Department of Safety, National Highway Traffic Safety Administration*. Retrieved from: www.nhtsa.gov/technology-innovation/automated-vehicles-safety Available [May 25, 2021].

Nippon Express. (2019). Retrieved from: www.nipponexpress.com/press/release/2019/19-Jul-19-1.html Available [May 25, 2021].

Nippon Express. (2020). Retrieved from: www.nipponexpress.com/pdf/about/csr/social/Innovation-Based-on-Collaborating-and-Co-creation.pdf Available [May 25, 2021].

Pavlić Skender, H., Host, A., & Nuhanović, M. (2016). The role of logistics service providers in international trade. In: Z. Segetlija et al. (eds.), *Business Logistics in Modern Management, Proceedings of the 16th International Scientific Conference* (pp. 21–37). Osijek: Faculty of Economics.

Pavlić Skender, H., & Zaninović, P. A. (2020). Perspectives of blockchain technology for sustainable supply chains. In: A. Kolinski, D. Dujak, & P. Golinska-Dawson (eds.), *Integration of Information Flow for Greening Supply Chain Management* (pp. 77–92). Berlin, Heidelberg, DE: Springer.

Pendleton, S. D., Andersen, H., Du, X., Shen, X., Meghjani, M., Eng, Y. H., Rus, D., & Ang, M. H. (2017). Perception, planning, control, and coordination for autonomus vehicles. *Machines*, *5*(1). DOI: 10.3390/machines5010006

Prasad, K. G. D., Subbaiah, K. V., & Rao, K. N. (2014). Supply chain design through QFD-based optimization. *Journal of Manufacturing Technology Management*, *25*(5), 712–733. Retrieved from: www.emerald.com/insight/content/doi/10.1108/JMTM-03-2012-0030/full/html Available [May 25, 2021].

SAE. (2014). Retrieved from: J3016_201401: Taxonomy and Definitions for Terms Related to On-Road Motor Vehicle Automated Driving Systems—SAE International Available [May 20, 2021].

Sanchez-Flores, R. B., Cruz-Sotelo, S. E., Ojeda-Benitez, S., & Ramirez-Barreto, E. (2020). Sustainable supply chain management: A literature review on emerging economies. *Sustainability*, *12*(17). DOI: 10.3390/su12176972

Sell, R., Rassolkin, A., Wang, R., & Otto, T. (2019). Integration of autonomous vehicles and industry 4.0. *Proceeding of the Estonian Academy of Sciences*, *68*(4), 389–394. Retrieved from: https://kirj.ee/public/proceedings_pdf/2019/issue_4/proc-2019-4-389-394.pdf Available [May 25, 2021].

Shah, S., & Arengo Piragine, M. (2018). *Reality of Autonomous Transportation Technologies in Global Supply Chains: The Consumer Driven Demand Chain*. International Conference on Operations and Supply Chain Management. Retrieved from: www.researchgate.net/publication/339178905_Reality_of_

Autonomous_Transportation_Technologies_in_Global_Supply_Chains_The_ Consumer_Driven_Demand_chain Available [May 25, 2021].

Shah, S., Logiotatopouloh, I., & Menon, S. (2019). Industry 4.0 and autonomous transport: The impacts on supply chain management. *International Journal of Transportation Systems, 4,* 45–50. Retrieved from: www.researchgate.net/ publication/339178688_Industry_40_and_autonomous_transportation_the_ impacts_on_supply_chain_management Available [May 25, 2021].

Taeihagh, A., & Min Lim, H. S. (2019). Governing autonomous vehicles: Emerging responses for safety, liability, privacy, cybersecurity, and industry risks. *Transport Reviews, 39*(1), 103–128. DOI: 10.1080/01441647.2018.1494640

Tao, M. (2020). *Nippon Express opens "Cutting-Edge, Showroom-Style" Logistics Facility.* Retrieved from: https://roboticsandautomationnews.com/2020/08/26/ nippon-express-opens-cutting-edge-showroom-style-logistics-facility/35614/ Available [May 25, 2021].

Tezuka, K. (2011). Rationale for utilizing 3PL in supply chain management: A shipers' economic perspective. *IATSS Research, 35,* 24–29. DOI: 10.1016/j.iatssr.2011.07.001

Tseng, M. L., Lim, M., & Wong, W. P. (2015). Sustainable supply chain management a closed-loop network hierarchical approach. *Industrial Management & Data Systems, 115*(3), 436–461. DOI: 10.1108/IMDS-10-2014-0319

Van Meldert, B., & De Boeck, L. (2016) *Introducing Autonomous Vehicles in Logistics: A Review from a Broad Perspective.* Working Papers of Department of Decision Sciences and Information Management. Retrieved from: https://core.ac.uk/ download/pdf/45289932.pdf Available [July 23, 2021].

Wang, J., & Dai, J. (2018). Sustainable supply chain management practices and performance. *Industrial Management & Data Systems, 118*(1), 2–21. DOI: 10.1108/ IMDS-12-2016-054

Yin, R. K. (2009). *Case Study Research: Design and Methods.* Thousand Oaks: SAGE Publications.

Chapter 7

Sustainability Requirements for Micro and Small Food-Processing Companies

Marko Lukavac and Dejan Miljenović
University of Rijeka, Croatia

Contents

7.1 Introduction

Constant modernization of supply chain and logistics in almost any sector leads to higher efficiency, lower cost, and competitive advantages (Lu & Borbon-Galvez, 2012). According to the authors, supply-chain and logistics modernization should not be the source of non-competitiveness for micro and small companies. Sustainability strategies and regulations went on high standards, especially in specific industries like energy, pharmaceutical, health in general, food production, and food processing. Logistics services of the named sectors got a chance during the COVID-19 pandemic to improve efficiency and effectiveness. Sustainable food processing and logistics derive from supply chains made considering several micro and small-scale suppliers. Big retail chains (retailers) "love to brag" with a supply of domestic products, eco-friendlier than those being massively imported. There is a question of how much they are motivated in the context of being socially responsible, but at the beginning of the COVID-19 pandemic, micro and small domestic suppliers represented much safer sources of supply than foreign suppliers. This was the case with retailers in Croatia; to manage a more sustainable supply chain, big retailers engaged small food-processing and -providing companies. However, these small companies were then challenged with the economy-of-scale issue—to provide multiple retailers with the same quantity-quality ratio. This defines a logistical problem in the area of sustainability where small food-processing companies have the objective to achieve standard effective distribution while optimally adapting to different retail chains and large logistics subjects on the market. Usually, food assortment in stock requires controlled temperature, humidity, and very specific technical handling conditions. That is a necessary condition, especially in the case of perishable and frozen food. This chapter discusses specific problems of contemporary logistics efficiency, describing three logistic business models with an analysis based on the usual business environment, but concerning COVID-19 influence; the chapter offers a sustainable distribution model in the food supply chain as food processing can be noted as a national strategic branch. Therefore, this chapter also gives answers to actual research questions:

1) How does one identify the main effects of retailers and wholesalers on the logistical effectiveness of micro and small companies as food suppliers?
2) How does one optimize distribution and adapt the supply chain of small companies, the food suppliers, to large retail and wholesale stores?
3) To what extent is the logistical mismatch described previously a result of idiosyncratic shortcomings of micro and small companies, the food suppliers, in achieving sustainable and adaptive supply-chain management?

The research objective is to analyze the positive impact of implementing optimal logistics models in and for micro and small companies so that they can provide logistic services to retail businesses and create sustainable value in the food industry. The scientific contribution of the chapter is reflected in the logistics business model that leads to the harmonization of logistics business processes, which mostly leads to the adjustment of logistics business processes of large business entities in the field of trade and logistics services to micro and small entities to whom growth and development place the greatest emphasis on EU budgetary policies. Adoption of new technologies, enabling infrastructure, digitalization, and development of new products by micro and small business entities based on EU funds seems futile, if ultimately, in the context of this paper, the business model in the field of logistics is a source of non-competitiveness, i.e., one of the elements of the unsustainability of micro and small entities as suppliers to traders and users of outsourced logistics services.

This chapter provides literature review and presentation of research methods for different case studies of logistic services. Main research results indicate that in a case of a micro/small food supplier for large retailers as users of logistics services assortment requires highly controlled conditions. Discussion of similar contemporary research is given from the context of economic sustainability. Implications of the research for theory and practice are elaborated in the last part of the chapter before the conclusion.

7.2 A Critical Review of the Literature

Dealing with sustainability issues is not a simple task, as the value of economic sustainability of all links in the supply chain still does not seem to be recognized as the most important. Still, this leads to issues of environmental and social sustainability versus economic sustainability in the context of social economy and not the sustainable profits of only one company in the long term.

The authors of this chapter find inspiring work with similar views on economic problems in the research of Saleh and Roslin (2015), where the idea of integrative relationships through effective communication and coordination among food supply-chain partners enables firms to control the entire food-delivery process, allowing them to meet customers' expectations and maximize customers' value; it also provides numerous benefits to the firm either in the form of economic or noneconomic value. A review of the literature of that paper has directed the authors toward papers indicating that, in Malaysia, the food-processing industry played a significant role in Malaysian economic growth (Ahmed, 2012). According to the Companies Commission of Malaysia (cited from Saleh & Roslin, 2015), many firms were urged to close due to supply-chain performance problems, which can be supported by the research of Tukamuhabwa (2011) using the example from Uganda, too. Integrative relationships through the food supply chain represents a solution, but as 70% of supply-chain relationships tend to fail according to Sambasivan et al. (2011), it is vital to identify factors that influence the failure or success of supply-chain partnerships or integration initiatives from the perspective of soft behavioral attributes (Saleh & Roslin, 2015).

This paper, with a topic on the field of logistics, shows how food logistics play a crucial role in the management of the food supply chain. Lazarides (2011) defines it as a system that aims at efficient production, processing, and distribution to protect quality, assure safety, promote the fair and transparent distribution of created value, enhance consumer access to wholesome and healthy food at reasonable prices, and support the sustainable development of rural communities. In the domain of ensuring quality and food safety as imperatives, Mu et al. (2021) notice the importance of a practical supply chain that can adapt to be resilient to food-safety shocks. The proposed logistics model, by making the logistic process more synchronized, reduces the number of steps in deliveries and lowers the risk of inconsistencies in food-safety terms, especially when the source of supply is perishable or frozen food that requires controlled delivery conditions.

Further, in the context of sustainable-supply-chain management, the importance of "systems thinking," a higher degree of collaboration and effective communication as a result of interdependencies across the supply chain in the context of lowering the costs and uncertainty, are recognized by Hobbs (2021). The COVID-19 pandemic partially encouraged supply-chain factors to identify key sources of risks in logistics, and to define more sustainable supply strategies. The authors analyze the logistics models based on DSD (direct-to-store delivery) and CWD (central-warehouse delivery) through a practical prism, but the contribution of the work stems primarily from the newly proposed logistics model. Authors do not find direct basis for the proposed logistics model, aptly named the Inclusive & Partly Circular Model, in the literature. Nevertheless, the authors point out that it can be conceptually placed in the domain of the so-called circular-economy (CE) framework. In the CE segment, significant growth of scientific research is noticeable but much more in the primary domain that CE propagates. According to Geissdoerfer et al. (2017), CE is seen as "a regenerative system in which resource input and waste, emission, and energy leakage are minimized by slowing, closing, and narrowing material and energy loops." Hazen et al. (2020) discuss how supply-chain processes can support the successful implementation of CE, while Bernon et al. (2018) address the issue of retail reverse logistics, placing it in the frame of CE. Given the proposed circular supply process that contributes to sustainability, leaving the hitherto exclusively linear model, the authors recognize the link of contribution to CE and indicate how CE can and should be seen through the perspective of developing micro and small suppliers in the food supply chain. That is merged with the inseparability of economic sustainability from environmental and social sustainability, and with findings that circular business and circular supply chains help in realizing sustainability ambitions Geissdoerfer et al. (2018).

Lastly, the authors of this chapter agree with the extended visions of Fernie and Sparks (2018) stating how holding stocks just in case they may be needed is a highly costly activity. This refers to situation when warehouses and distribution centers are also expensive if not being efficiently used with all their infrastructure (vehicles, package handling services) on a high operational level. Consequently, the necessity of efficient as well as environmentally sensible logistics operations arises, but the authors, using a case study, point out in this chapter the exclusive focus that traders have on their own efficient and sustainable performance, which impairs efficiency and sustainability at the level of the entire supply chain.

7.3 Research Method

Using descriptive, correlative, causal, and so-called field methods, the authors describe, predict, and explain observations in real-world settings, combining science and practice, using their own experiences in the academic community and experiences in addressing logistical challenges within the active management of companies in the food-processing industry. Using a qualitative approach, the authors quantify observations with data from a primary source.

Primary data consist of the accounting documentation and parts of contracts of the company (which was differently classified by size during the last decade, from small to the micro producer in the domain of the food processing industry), with logistic companies, retailers, and wholesalers in the Republic of Croatia. Even the case is done according to the data of the company from the food-processing industry, specifically with frozen assortment, problems, and mismatches, which will be presented and can be observed as the problems and mismatches of the most micro and small suppliers to the main retail and wholesalers in the Republic of Croatia, regardless of the segment of supply. After all, a case based on the food-processing industry with data and conditions based specifically on the frozen assortment that requires controlled temperatures can enhance other research in the context of the topic that would contribute to the findings of this chapter, and make this topic generalized and not only limited to the food-processing-industry suppliers, i.e., the food supply chain.

Primary data are used with the consent of the authorized person representing the company in the food-processing industry with a product line requiring controlled-temperature conditions. The authors recognize the company's problems related to logistics. Considering the research approach, which uses many years of experience in the field of logistics, all descriptions, predictions, and explanations are considered to be the result of the so-called experimental method, too.

Considering the company's assortment requiring controlled-temperature conditions, a long tradition of more than three decades, the company's presence on the national market of the Republic of Croatia, the company's business success related to product quality, the share of highly qualified management, stable financial position, and success in obtaining funds from EU funds, the authors think that that the presented research results can be generalized about the selected company, i.e., that all negative aspects related to the described research problem, given other characteristics of the company, cannot be considered only as its idiosyncratic shortcoming. The company statement and profile, a document that proves authors were allowed to do and publish the research and main data of the company, is available upon request.

7.4 Results

In the context of this chapter, emphasis is placed on micro and small producers in the domain of the food-processing industry with a final product that requires controlled-temperature conditions to preserve the health and safety of the product. So, this is a business that requires a refrigerated or frozen regime when using logistics services. The focus is on this group of producers, given that retail or wholesale channels are usually the only way to market such products (perishable fresh and frozen food), given that direct sale between producers and end consumers are prevented by the lack of adequate delivery of postal packages to send perishable fresh and frozen food or the price's non-competitiveness of such deliveries.

The accuracy of the previous statements is confirmed by the high concentration in the domain of the food-processing industry in the Republic of Croatia, where the largest national companies dominate the placement of food products on the shelves of traders. This is especially pronounced in the domain of frozen assortment as the most demanding segment that shows the need for impeccable maintenance of the cold chain during logistics processes from production to place in the store, in which companies registered for production and distribution of frozen food have an almost monopolistic position.

This confirms the ultimate intention of large trade entities to operate with large food suppliers, especially in the domain of fresh perishable or frozen food, which requires a special temperature regime upon delivery and which requires special storage conditions in the placement in the store. It is clear that the developed outbound logistics of the largest business entities for the production and distribution of fresh perishable or frozen food assumes DSD is a key source of competitive advantage over micro and small suppliers in the same segment that rely on outsourcing of logistics operations.

Analyzing the contracts of the company in the food-processing industry with a frozen assortment and the largest traders, with the aim of understanding and then creating an optimal logistic model to support the business model, the authors defined and described limiting factors for optimizing logistics processes of micro and small food suppliers whose assortment requires controlled storage and delivery conditions.

Major maladjustments of large trade entities to do business with micro and small suppliers of food that require controlled conditions of storage and delivery are:

1) Impossibility of combining Central Warehouse (CW) and DSD.
2) Systematization of stores and assortment according to the store size.
3) JIT optimized orders by traders, at a given place on a specific date of delivery according to the administered logistical conditions of transport pallets and packaging.

Detected negative impacts for micro and small food suppliers following major maladjustments of large trade entities are as follows:

1) Small producers, as suppliers of food that require controlled logistics conditions, rely on outsourcing of outbound logistics due to capital constraints and non-specialization in the logistics services to operate on a national level. Due to the limited service and high prices of DSD of national logistics based on the cost of delivery by location and not only by weight or volume of delivery, as a consequence of the narrow range and failure to achieve economies of scale when delivering to a single point of sale (store), small producers can most often serve stores on a

national level only through delivery at the CW of national traders, relying later on traders' inbound logistics.

At the same time, inefficiency comes to the fore when producers are far from the location of the CW. For example, at the expense of the manufacturer, i.e., the supplier from his place of production and storage, the goods are transported 300 kilometers and more to the CW of the trader and then delivered by the inbound logistics of the trader, again at the supplier's expense. Returns in-store bear the production or storage of the supplier, where they can be independently serviced promptly and for a lower cost on a DSD basis by the supplier.

2) A barrier has been created in the supply of small-format stores due to the underdevelopment of inbound logistics of national traders, which is also partly based on the outsourcing of logistics services to national logistic entities. Neither national traders nor national logisticians have an extensive network of distribution logistics centers, which makes it difficult and often impossible to make store deliveries of goods from CWs to small-format stores that are usually located in crowded locations, i.e., by itself with significant consumption, but often with inadequate infrastructure to absorb the logistic suprastructure.

3) The business policy of retailers is that stores are systematized according to the size of the store, according to which the assortment range is defined. More specifically, a small supplier will get the opportunity to place its products "on the shelves," but only in stores of the largest formats scattered throughout the Republic of Croatia. Such a model introduces the issue of logistics for national distribution, but also potentially reduces stock turnover because certain products, especially the so-called supporting products to the basic product of a certain brand, are not equally characteristic for different geographic areas, which is especially evident in the Republic of Croatia where there are significant differences in consumer preferences depending on the climate of living or origin.

The determination of the assortment range by store size is also driven by the limitations detected under point 2. Also, within this point, the problem is more related to retailers than to wholesalers as a result of the fact that the sales centers of wholesalers are the largest formats with a strong infrastructure, which allows the assortment range to be adjusted to the regional needs of businesses. The business of wholesalers is based on the B2B model, which assumes serving a limited number of customers whose needs significantly affect the business policies of wholesalers in the context of the diversity of the assortment range.

4) Orders to traders' CWs under the JIT model do not take into account the significant logistical constraints of micro and small food suppliers. According to Hobbs (2021), the food-retail sector operates on a JIT delivery system which accounts for normal supply and demand trends. In the context of COVID-19 impacts on the Republic of Croatia, in the pandemic's first wave the JIT model was usually supported by the management forecasts for up to two months to ensure normal functioning of the food supply chain which would be useful to suppliers on regular basis, too. Micro and small suppliers have low bargaining power when negotiating business terms with national traders and, most often as suppliers of a narrow assortment range, cannot afford to set minimum-order conditions that would presuppose at least pallet deliveries. In the continuation of the chapter, it will be explained why neither the so-called combined pallet delivery is sometimes not a solution to optimize the cost of delivery, due to the nonacceptance of combined pallets to the CWs of traders. In this regard, the detected problem of requiring transport packaging with a single transport EAN code arises, which makes it difficult to organize the production of small and microenterprises, but eliminates the risk of mismanagement and mishandling in the CWs of traders. Purchasing IT systems are set up for automatic orders according to consumption and the time required to deliver goods by inbound logistics from the CW to the store. In this way, automatic orders are frequent and of smaller quantities, arising the advantages of JIT models for traders. IT systems did not incorporate the risk of non-delivery by the supplier, but the risk of non-delivery by the supplier as a shortcoming of the JIT model is most often penalized by a separate item of the contract between the supplier and the trader. Consequently, micro and small suppliers do not optimize their logistics processes when delivering to traders' CWs, but must sometimes find completely uncompetitive solutions to complete CWD. Additional restrictions arise from a given delivery date that assumes a steady "ad hoc" delivery when the opportunity arises, rather than in the context of supply by micro and small entities in the product domain requiring controlled logistical conditions. A special delivery problem was also detected when the place of delivery, i.e., the location of the CW, was located outside the routes, i.e., the directions of other CWs and the place of usual deliveries.

Major maladjustments of large logistic service entities to do business with micro and small suppliers of food that require controlled conditions of storage and delivery are:

1) Inadequacy of pricing models of large logistics entities.
2) Non-adaptation of vehicles to micro-locations of delivery and collection of goods.

Detected negative impacts for micro and small food suppliers in accordance with major maladjustments of large logistic entities include:

1) How the inadequacy of the pricing models of large logistics companies is mostly reflected in the defining of outsourced DSD prices according to the distance of the delivery location from the logistic main warehouse, with the determination of limit values of mass or volume of the delivery. In this way, micro and small suppliers with a narrow assortment range do not achieve higher weights or delivery volumes, which ultimately results in expensive smaller deliveries, i.e., an astronomically high cost of outsourced DSD that exceeds the supplier's margin, i.e., makes the supplier's business completely economically unsustainable. This problem is especially pronounced when the subjects of delivery are cheaper goods because then the relative cost of delivery in the cost price is particularly high. It should be noted that the analyzed delivery cost is only one component of the total logistics cost of the supplier, which is additionally included in the cost of pallet delivery of goods from the supplier to the logistic main warehouse, storage cost, and the cost of handling and administration of delivery notes. In addition, the cost of handling can be multiple in situations where the logistics operator operates on the principle of distribution centers in local areas and transfers the same goods within their warehouses until the final delivery to the store.

   This model was assessed as economically unsustainable in the company and it was concluded that it is a much more appropriate logistic business model that provides for deliveries to the CW of traders, relying on their much more efficient inbound logistics. In this way, the logistical costs of store delivery were reduced by an average of 50%, but were largely offset by the cost inefficiency of suppliers' deliveries to traders' CWs and lost revenue due to the reduced number of stores served due to the inability to combine DSD and CWD.

2) Another factor of the unsuitability of large logistics companies arises from the model of defining the cost of a pallet storage place according to an individual item in the warehouse, as a rule additionally with an individual lot number. This reduces the risk of expiration of the supplier's goods because the goods with the shortest shelf life are issued first and

additionally ensures accurate traceability, which is imperative in quality control and correctness of goods but is a major source of cost. That is the largest source of cost for the so-called supporting items to the basic product that has lower stock turnover. Due to the stated established logistical practice, when receiving goods at the CWs of traders, deliveries are limited to the so-called two sandwich pallets, i.e., with a maximum of two items in total per one pallet place, which increases the cost of delivery.

3) In the example of the company, a discrepancy was detected in vehicles commonly used in the distribution of frozen assortment adapted to DSD with vehicles of logisticians for the same purpose. Typical vehicles are those with side doors, while logisticians use classic trucks with back doors without a ramp, and with temperature regulation. From that, one can read how the logistics model of logistic companies relies on pallet-delivery care to larger stores with strong infrastructure and superstructure rather than on combined micro deliveries at micro-locations.

All the positive and negative impacts are profound to the authors for proposing higher efficiency models in research, and in relation to the following discussion, as well as implications for theory and practice. The chapter uses the example of the company's business analysis in the field of food processing and distribution of frozen assortment to show the logistical challenges that micro and small suppliers with an assortment that requires controlled logistical conditions face when placing their products. In the example of the company, logistics is recognized as a source of non-competitiveness, and solutions are offered below in written implications so that logistics not only ceases to be a price source of non-competitiveness, but also an eliminating factor for market presence. The solutions are reflected in the adaptation of all links in the supply chain.

In the context of answering the third question defined in the introduction, the task of the supplier in the current circumstances is to follow the trends in the context of modernization of production-logistics-accounting processes (EDI, ERP); the adjustment of logistics is reflected in the adjustment of the superstructure and organization of work, i.e., adapting the collection and delivery of goods at micro-locations, but the authors recognize traders as key links in achieving competitiveness and economic sustainability of micro and small food suppliers. The strategic decision of traders to partner with micro and small suppliers and to be transparent to achieve cost efficiency in the field of logistics is a necessity.

In the example of the company, it is evident that the choice of delivery to the CW (Central Warehouse) of traders is a better choice than the outsourced DSD of national logisticians done for micro or small suppliers. The solution in the context of supplier inefficiency in shredded deliveries to the CWs of traders is reflected in the analysis of the costs of shredded deliveries of suppliers against the storage costs of traders and the availability of their storage space. In a specific case in the Republic of Croatia, the issue of agreed larger deliveries of suppliers that exceed the needs of traders by their JIT automatic purchasing systems, usually set for a shorter period of seven days, records the problem of cash gaps for traders if they adapt the model of larger orders to micro and small suppliers to achieve logistical efficiency in the supply chain of their goods. The Law on Prohibition of Unfair Commercial Practice in Food Chain 117/17, published in the Official Gazette (2017), determines the payment of goods to the supplier within 30–60 days from the day of delivery. Furthermore, enabling a combination of CWD (central-warehouse delivery) and DSD in the supplier's arrangement, until the logistics are adjusted to the deliveries at the micro-location, is a prerequisite for achieving positive effects due to assortment in stores according to geographical model or maximum-projected-consumption model.

The combination of deliveries opens the possibility of cooperation between micro and small suppliers in different geographical areas to provide logistics services and may result in the final inclusion of micro suppliers in certain geographical areas as centers of distribution for national logistic entities or traders themselves. In addition, the optimal solution is reflected in the combination of inbound logistics processes of traders in the supply of their stores with the collection of goods at the micro-location of the supplier. In this way, efficient automated systems of traders based on JIT purchasing should not be made less efficient to achieve greater efficiency in the second fields, but inbound traders' logistics would be used as outbound supplier logistics. In certain situations, the supplier may deliver the goods to the largest format store of an individual trader in the geographical area (DSD).

7.5 Discussing the Results of Other People's Research

Given the scarcity of literature in the field of solving challenges in the cooperation of micro and small food suppliers and large traders in the context of logistics, this chapter's section should be viewed within the papers with scientific contribution of creating a macro perspective on business sustainability with an emphasis on the primary economic aspect.

The retail and wholesale market in the Republic of Croatia is extremely highly concentrated, i.e., a small number of business entities holds a significant market share. Segetlija et al. (2015) state that the concept of concentration can be seen not only in the context of total revenue but also in the context of the number of larger or smaller stores. In recent years, there has been a tendency to further increase national and local market concentration, especially in the retail market in the Republic of Croatia. The latter is particularly pronounced in the context of local-store exits, or the takeover of local retail chains with a smaller market share but a bigger number of local stores by retail chains that operate nationally. This poses a threat to the survival of micro and small supplier companies in the food-processing industry, which had their profitable niches in doing business with smaller local retailers by adapting the business model to them by performing direct-store delivery (DSD) to their stores at the micro-level. Despite the intention of the largest retail and wholesale entities to prefer food products of domestic micro and small suppliers in the context of the range offered, the practice shows that the procedures of the largest traders on the Croatian market are unsuitable for doing business with micro and small companies (from assortment inclusion to logistics assumptions). This showcases the intention to promote domestic production; business with micro and small food suppliers is mostly used for marketing purposes and to ensure a much more stable source of goods during the COVID-19 pandemic, which builds on the finding of Hobbs (2021) on how dispersed, smaller-scale firms with shorter supply chains may be more adaptable to COVID-19 requirements. In the context of all the above, it is interesting to refer to the research of Meinen and Raff (2018), who in direct import, find a source of competitive advantage in the Danish retail sector for large retailers compared to smaller local retailers who do not import. Smith (2019) concluded how the direct imports of large retailers in the US have played an important role in increasing concentration in the retail sector, too. The author assumes that the data should not be viewed in the context of the breadth of the assortment range but in the context of final-price competitiveness resulting from cheaper inputs and a supportive logistics model. Furthermore, Smith and Diaz (2020) find that the increase in markups implied by rising local concentration had a modest effect on retail prices due to the cost advantages large retailers have. Thus, traders behave much more like monopsonists, and less like monopolists, and the described policy of traders is certainly to the detriment of domestic production in the context of its representation and returns generated by its placement under increasingly poor sales conditions. This issue needs to be considered in the context of economies of scale because Linden (2016) states that one of the sources of lowering the average cost lies in lower input prices in terms of large purchases. Large, integrated purchases are characteristic of highly concentrated markets and dominant supply-chain players, thus gaining a competitive advantage at the expense of supplier positions. Considering the issue in such a broader sense, the chapter leads to the issue of economic sustainability, with many authors focusing on examining the negative effects of the so-called unfair trade practices in the food supply chain.

The issue of unfair trade practices is particularly characteristic of the European Union, and research is mostly related to the segment of primary agricultural production. According to Markou et al. (2020), unfair trade practices between food-chain companies, in the case of Cyprus, have a significant impact on supply-chain stakeholders and the environment, i.e., the cost of unfair trade practices is reflected in as much as 32% of the income of the negatively affected. Furthermore, Swinnen et al. (2019) deal with the issue of unfair trade practices, but also unfair prices from the perspective of suppliers in the food supply chain as a consequence of the growth of market concentrations. Finally, Blizkovsky and Brendes (2017) deal with a similar topic but introduce the notion of economic unfairness in the form of unfair distribution of added value created in the food supply chain.

Looking back at the latter, the authors note that in the framework of other scientific papers, they are engaged in research on the topic of the economic sustainability within the food supply chain in which they point out the importance of the fair financial distribution of added value or risk sharing in product development, and product placement in relation to micro and small producers with large traders who control the placement of goods, to achieve economic sustainability of small and microenterprises and direct their business in social and environmental responsibility frames, too. However, the author's view is that a greater degree of integration between micro and small food producers and traders in the field of logistics, according to the postulates of the circular economy (CE), can positively affect the economic sustainability of the first ones.

As already pointed out in the review of the literature, strongholds are found in the literature of Saleh and Roslin (2015) and Geissdoerfer et al. (2017, 2018).

7.6 Implications for Theory and Practice

Based on previous research and elaborated supply-chain issues of DSD and CWD, in the context of practical implications authors propose and analyze the structural effectiveness of three Logistics Models Analysis combinations (LMAC) depending on the delivery options, as follows: Direct-store model (DSM), central-warehouse model (CWM), and inclusive and partly circular model (IPCM).

Figure 7.1 represents the direct-store model (LMAC 1) originally based on DSD. DSM is for micro-/small-supplier arrangement that usually opens the possibility of wider product-range availability. However, indifferent to original DSD, a DSM becomes a significant source of non-competitiveness in a situation where the supplier does not rely on its outbound logistics processes (outsourced DSD) due to a narrower assortment range of suppliers and a lower turnover of supporting items, e.g., optimized orders of each store.

The central-warehouse model (Figure 7.2., LMAC 2, based on CWD) significantly reduces the cost of delivery from the trader's CW (by combined deliveries)

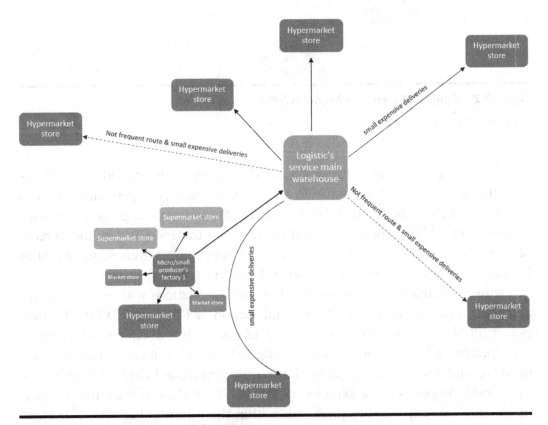

Figure 7.1   Direct-Store Model (DSM).

Source: Author's elaboration.

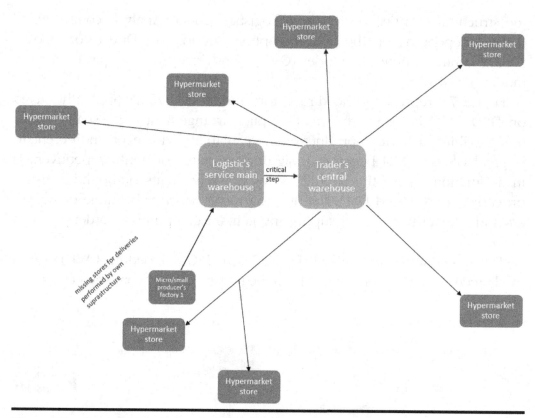

Figure 7.2   Central-Warehouse Model (CWM).

Source: Author's elaboration.

to an individual store (up to as much as 50% compared to individual deliveries from the main logistics warehouse to an individual store), but generally excludes the option of DSD and reduces the availability of assortment range of micro/small suppliers. In addition, non-optimized orders from traders' CWs, in the context of micro/small suppliers, result in a source of non-competitiveness in deliveries between the logistics main warehouse and retailers' CWs.

Figure 7.3 contains more complex effectiveness relations within the inclusive and partly circular model (LMAC 3; combination of DSD and CWD). The proposed IPCM assumes a strategic decision of traders in the context of adapting and optimizing logistics processes to increase their efficiency and the efficiency of micro and small food suppliers that require controlled delivery conditions. The model proposes a combination of DSD and CWD as well as the inclusion of supplier's supply-logistics processes within the inbound logistics of traders. The model is additionally suitable because it opens the possibility of relying on the traders for the performance of logistics processes performed by micro/

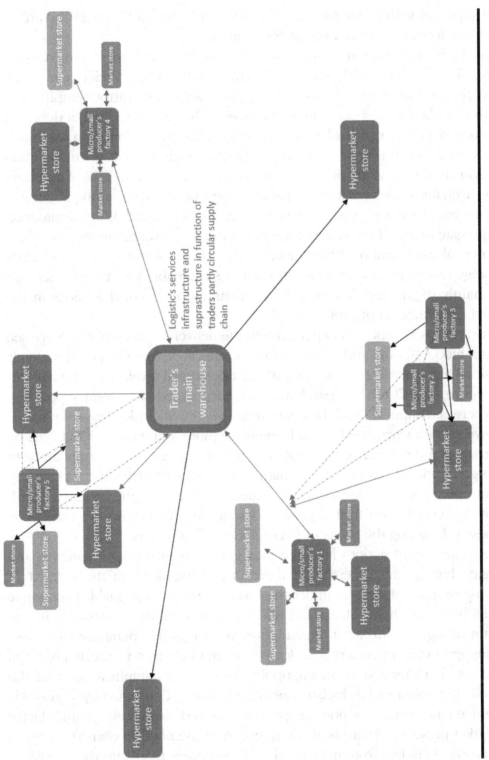

Figure 7.3 Inclusive and Partly Circular Model (IPCM).

Source: Author's elaboration.

small suppliers with a developed logistics infrastructure and superstructure in micro-locations, in a certain geographical area.

The basis for research analysis is a development content between three given LMACs (DSM, CWM, and IPCM). This results in the efficiency increase in the direction from model 1 to model 3, but it should be further emphasized that in models 2 and, 3 compared to model 1, the supplier remains deprived of market data that can lead to a decline in sales, in the long run. As much as models 2 and 3 reduce costs in the field of logistics and documentation (e.g., sometimes invoicing only one invoice for delivery to the CW of a trader), model 1 enables sales tracking at a single point of sale without the additional involvement of sales representatives. Further, models 2 and 3, in the situation of aggregate financial invoicing of the buyer (trader), require the sharing of the commercial information of the buyer (trader) to the supplier to better adapt the range assortment to micro-locations and sustainability of the partnership, e.g., mainly of the supplier to stay in the supply chain of the trader in the context of realization of projected sales.

The analysis is done and dependent on the delivery options of the proposed logistics model (IPCM), and fully includes the effects of the COVID-19 pandemic that small and microenterprises face at the operational level. From the author's perspective, the COVID-19 pandemic has encouraged short-term rapprochement between suppliers and traders to reduce economic risks. However, as the negative consequences of the pandemic leave more and more visible traces on business, in the context of the relationship of micro and small suppliers with the largest national traders (this primarily applies to retailers), the relationship cannot be longer characterized as a partnership. Retaining the short-term profitability of retailers and further growth despite declining turnover in the trade business is breaking the backs of micro and small suppliers.

Micro and small entities are seen as a generator of economic growth and diversity, but on the other hand, there is nothing done in the context of ensuring product placement under the business model that enables economic sustainability for them. Micro and small food-processing companies in the domain of logistics are left to maladjustment of logistic operations of traders and inappropriate price terms of logistician markets that in the Republic of Croatia is characterized as an oligopoly. Also, the geographical form of the Republic of Croatia makes logistic operations harder. Consequently, logistics is recognized as a source of non-competitiveness and also an eliminating factor for market presence. There is also a question of the need to change access to purchasing of traders from micro and small suppliers to ensure the economic sustainability of micro and small companies in the supply chain. That should be an obligation, which is also provided by the stakeholder theory of corporate social responsibility, to corporations in doing business with micro and small suppliers.

Educational programs and science often neglect the business challenges of micro and small business entities and are more focused on improving business processes characteristic of large companies that define the conditions for survival in the so-called free-market competition. The policy encourages the start-up of entrepreneurship, but it also does not address the limitations of their business. Neither the education system, politics, nor the scientific community contribute to the creation of relationships and business culture between business entities in the market. Economic sustainability of the business is the least represented in research subjects compared to social and environmental sustainability. In the framework of economic sustainability, it is rarely focused on the economic sustainability of suppliers in the supply chain to achieve economic sustainability of society; there is always expired economic sustainability of one company.

Given the importance of the topic, i.e., the possible threat to the business of small and microenterprises, it is recommended to explore other industrial areas to detect and eliminate inefficiencies in terms of logistics processes. In addition, the chapter refers to research aimed at finding efficient logistics processes or models of co-financing the cost of procurement and shipment of micro and small, but also medium and large, suppliers of traders whose place of production is located on islands or geographical areas with reduced business activity, too. Great efforts are being made in the development of less developed areas, the development of islands, and ultimately decentralization in general, but the next step from such policies may result in price non-competitiveness of companies while ordering their goods from such areas.

This is disastrous if the economy is based on the lowest costs, i.e., the added value of a cheaper product to enable the consumer within his budget as much variety of consumed goods and services. It is equally important to achieve economic fairness in product placement, i.e., to satisfy the correct distribution of added value in the financial context and the distribution of share risks in product placement. It is evident how this chapter, with such a strong practical implication, can also be seen from the perspective that contributes to the triple bottom line (TBL) theory of social responsibility in the domain of achieving economic sustainability, but of a sequence of companies in the supply chain, as well as to the stakeholder theory of corporate governance in the context of integration of stakeholders in the field of logistics on assumptions of circular economy (CE).

7.7 Conclusions

Technological solutions in the field of logistics under controlled-temperature conditions are mostly aimed at further risk and cost reduction in achieving economies of scale, while micro and small companies focus their business on value-added products characteristic of niche markets due to the impossibility of price competitiveness in this area. This is characterized by lower inventory turnover, and tighter, shallower product availability, which pose the risk that placement is not possible due to logistical constraints; on the other hand, the price calculation of micro and small producers is completely nullified due to the inability of traders and logisticians related to logistics, and suppliers from the food industry with an assortment that requires controlled-temperature conditions.

This leads to the fact that the micro and small companies in the food industry, i.e., with an assortment that requires controlled-temperature conditions, come to mutual cooperation, which is primarily due to the coverage of the need for logistics services, which can be understood as a kind of sharing economy in the B2B sector. It should be noted that the CWM that assumes CWD is not always available to all suppliers. In this situation, to lower the costs of outsourced DSD, cooperation between micro and small suppliers is a "life-saving" solution. Also, it enables product placement of different small and micro food producers in regional retail chains. Previous research in this area confirmed the whole lucrativeness of the logistics business, characterized by a high degree of market concentration as opposed to traditional distribution, which, due to the market pressure caused by the high level of supply and the predatory tendency of traders, can no longer cumulatively include a sufficient margin to finance logistics costs and all other sales and marketing costs, as well as making sales and payment risks.

Qualitative analysis proves how the major maladjustments of large trade entities to do business with micro and small suppliers of food that requires controlled conditions of storage and delivery in the Republic of Croatia show the impossibility of combining CWD and DSD, systematization of stores and assortment according to the store size, and JIT-optimized orders by traders, at a given place on a specific date of delivery according to the administered logistical conditions of transport pallets and packaging. Further, recognized major maladjustments of large logistics service entities to do business with micro and small suppliers of food that requires controlled conditions of storage and delivery in the Republic of Croatia are inadequacy of pricing models of large logistics entities and non-adaptation of vehicles to micro-locations of delivery and collection of goods. However, authors recognize traders as key links in the supply chain in the context of achieving competitiveness and economic sustainability of micro and small food suppliers. The strategic decision of traders to partner with micro and small suppliers and to be transparent to achieve cost efficiency in the field of logistics is necessary. Appropriately, the proposed logistics model which assumes the cooperation of micro and small suppliers and traders in the field of logistics is developed by the authors and named the Inclusive & Partly Circular Model (IPCM).

Limitations of the chapter arise from the inductive reasoning based on the case study as well as solving problems from the supplier's side through the food supply chain. Consequently, the chapter gives a lot of space for future research—from the point of view of testing problems and solutions in other markets and in other segments of the industry to upgrade the IPCM with the involvement of logisticians and traders in adapting it to their potential limitations not seen from the perspective of suppliers.

References

Ahmed, E. M. (2012). Malaysia's food manufacturing industries productivity determinants. *Modern Economy*, 444–453.

Bernon, M., Tjahjono, B., & Ripanti, E. (2018). Aligning retail reverse logistics practice with circular economy values: An exploratory framework. *Production Planning & Control, 29*, 483–497.

Blizkovsky, P., & Brendes, V. (2017). *Economics of Fairness within the Food Supply Chain in Context of the EU*. Applied Studies in Agribusiness and Commerce, Center-Print Publishing House, Debrecen.

Fernie, J., & Sparks, L. (eds.). (2018). *Logistics and Retail Management: Emerging Issues and New Challenges in the Retail Supply Chain*. London and Philadelphia, PA: Kogan Page Publishers.

Geissdoerfer, M., Morioka, S., de Carvalho, M., & Evans, S. (2018). Business models and supply chains for the circular economy. *Journal of Cleaner Production, 190*, 712–721. DOI: 10.1016/j.jclepro.2018.04.159

Geissdoerfer, M., Savaget, P., Bocken, N. M. P., & Hultink, E. J. (2017). The circular economy: A new sustainability paradigm? *Journal of Cleaner Production, 143*, 757–768.

Hazen, B. T., Russo, I., Confente, I., & Pellathy, D. (2020). Supply chain management for circular economy: Conceptual framework and research agenda. *The International Journal of Logistics Management*. https://doi.org/10.1108/IJLM-12-2019-0332

Hobbs, J. E. (2021). The Covid-19 pandemic and meat supply chains. *Meat Science*. Epub ahead of print. PMID: 33602591. DOI: 10.1016/j.meatsci.2021.108459.

Lazarides, H. N. (2011). Food processing technology in a sustainable food supply chain. *11th International Congress on Engineering and Food Procedia Food Science, 1,* 1918–1923.

Linden, G. (2016). *Economies of Scale.* London: The Palgrave Encyclopedia of Strategic Management.

Lu, M., & Borbon-Galvez, Y. (2012). *Advanced Logistics and Supply Chain Management for Intelligent and Sustainable Transport.* 19th World Congress on ITS (pp. 22–26), Vienna.

Markou, M., Stylianou, A., Adamides, G., & Giannakopoulou, M. (2020). *Unfair Trading Practices in the Food Supply Chain: The Case of the Cyprus Region.* Agricultural Research Institute, Cyprus.

Meinen, P., & Raff, H. (2018). International trade and retail market performance and structure: Theory and empirical evidence. *Journal of International Economics, 115,* 99–114.

Mu, W., Asselt, E. D., & Fels-Klerx, H. J. (2021). Towards a resilient food supply chain in the context of food safety. *Food Control, 125.* ISSN 0956–7135. DOI: 10.1016/j.foodcont.2021.107953.

Official Gazette. (2017). Law on Prohibition of Unfair Commercial Practice in Food Chain 117/17.

Saleh, Z. M., & Roslin, R. (2015). Supply chain integration strategy: A conceptual model of supply chain relational capital enabler in the Malaysian food processing industry. *Procedia: Social and Behavioral Sciences, 172,* 585–590.

Sambasivan, M., Siew-Phaik, L., Mohamed, Z. A., & Leong, Y. C. (2011). Impact of interdependence between supply chain partners on strategic alliance outcomes: Role of relational capital as a mediating construct. *Management Decision, 49*(4), 548–569. DOI: 10.1108/00251741111126486

Segetlija, Z., Mesarić, J., & Dujak, D. (2015). Distributive trade's significance for national economy. *Logforum Scientific Journal for Logistics, 11*(3), 217–225. DOI: 10.17270/J.LOG.2015.3.1

Smith, A. D. (2019). *Concentration and Foreign Sourcing in the U.S. Retail Sector.* Meeting Papers 1258, Society for Economic Dynamics.

Smith, A. D., & Diaz, O. S. (2020). The evolution of the US retail concentration, US department of labor, US bureau of labor statistics. *Office of Prices and Living Conditions.*

Swinnen, J., Olper, A., & Vandevelde, S. (2019). From unfair prices to unfair trading practices: Political economy, value chains and 21st century agri-food policy. *Agricultural Economics, special issue: "Trade, FDI and GVCs".*

Tukamuhabwa, B. R. (2011). A conceptual model for explaining supply chain performance in Uganda's SMEs. *Information Management and Business Review, 3*(6), 336–344.

Chapter 8

Sustainable Transport in the Fruit and Vegetable Supply Chain

Andrej Udovč and Sandra Bonča

University of Ljubljana, Slovenia

Contents

8.1 Introduction

In this chapter, we discuss sustainability-related issues connected to the increasing transport of fresh fruits and vegetables, especially the problem of assessing the external costs of their transport, which are not included in the retail price, and how their internalization would affect existing material flows in the case of Slovenia.

Fresh fruits and vegetables are an important part of a healthy diet, and regular consumption is widely supported by public health programs (e.g., the "five-a-day" campaign in the United Kingdom). Yet, such goods are highly perishable, often requiring special transport conditions, particularly when transported over long distances (e.g., specialized refrigerated vehicles and packaging), adding to the "externalities" issue.

The increase in the transport sector in the last decades is connected with a rise in negative impacts on the environment and society. For example, this refers to air pollution, noise, traffic accidents, soil and water pollution, and global warming. Mostly, these impacts are not reflected in the price of transport, but moving transport towards better sustainability is a long-term tendency. More sustainable use of transport is a crucial policy issue at a national, international and global level.

In the presented research, we were interested in analyzing the Slovenian market for fresh fruit and vegetables by looking at the sustainability of freight transport. Thus, the research question we followed was whether all fruit-and-vegetable transport that occurs internationally and nationally is actually justified and necessary from the point of view of sustainable development, and to estimate how the external costs of freight-transport internalization would reflect on total transport costs.

In the following subchapters, we first present a critical review of existing literature, followed by a description of the methods used. In the results subchapter, we present the obtained results on a systematic literature review of the external cost of transport on selected routes and their simulation into retail-crop prices. We conclude the chapter with a discussion of the obtained results and suggestions of some possible implications for theory and practice.

8.2 A Critical Review of the Literature

In the last few decades, the transport sector has grown dramatically, with the greatest increase observed in transport by road (the European Commission, 2012). This has contributed to an increased negative impact on the environment and on society, including air pollution, climate change, noise, accidents, congestion, soil and water pollution, effects on nature and the landscape, effects of upstream and downstream processes (Maibach et al., 2008), and infrastructural impacts on the environment (Beuthe et al., 2002; Forkenbrock, 1999; Marquez Diaz, 2009; Piecyk & McKinnon, 2007). These impacts are generally known as negative externalities and represent external costs neither paid by the consumer nor the transport service provider, but are imposed on the environment and society. According to Essen et al. (2020), road transport contributes to up to 83% of all external costs when compared to other transport modes.

If the food production of a country is not sufficient, the country must import the difference (the deficit). We are talking about the self-sufficiency of a country, where the level of self-sufficiency reflects the extent to which domestic production is sufficient for domestic consumption. Plut (2012) emphasizes that the production of food for one's own needs is even more strategically and existentially important if the country is not a geopolitical force, which is the case for Slovenia. Perpar and Udovč (2010) also add that a country's own food production is an important strategic issue. Slovenia is characterized by a low level of self-sufficiency in food and is a net importer of food. According to reports, this share is expected to be around 50% (Plut, 2012; Pestotnik, 2014). In the case of vegetables, it was 36.5% in 2011 and 34% in 2012 (SURS, 2015). As every import, as we have already mentioned, is related to transport, the country, consequently, also has a great need for transport. To achieve sustainable development, there is increasing emphasis on local food chains. It is food that is grown, processed, distributed, and consumed locally, but there are several different definitions of the locality.

Borec (2015) states that local food is freshly grown food in a local environment, which travels the shortest time from the field to the plate, and considers a local food chain as a market, which is up to 60 kilometers (km) away from the local environment. A similar definition is given by Nash (2003, in Thomson et al., 2006), who considers local food to be one that grows 64.4 km in diameter from the place of production. A longer distance of 161 km is suggested by Smith (2003, in Thomson et al., 2006), who considers that "local" means delivery on the same day the crop was harvested. Isensee (2003, in Thomson et al., 2006) proposes a more precise division, namely that the distance of up to 1.6 km defines the neighborhood, 1.6 to 16.1 km defines the city, 17.7 to 40.2 km defines the local area, and 41.8 to 161 or 241.4 km defines the region. Due to the geographical size of Slovenia and the mentioned definitions, we understood the distance of up to approximately 50 km as the local food chain, approximately 50.1 to 150 km as the regional food chain, and over 150.1 km as the national food chain.

At present, external costs of freight are not fully reflected in the market price of produce. Setting the right price for services (i.e., a full-cost price) is very important in freight transportation, as price setting has always been considered an important area of the marketing mix (Podnar et al., 2007). As Grewal and Compeau (1999) point out, the fusion of price as a "strategic marketing variable" and a "public welfare concern" is long overdue in the market. To make freight transport better aligned with the principle of sustainability, "full-cost pricing" would be required, through the internalization of "external costs" (i.e., incorporating the negative external effects).

In recent years, interest in researching this internalization has increased substantially (e.g., Baum et al., 2008; Márquez & Cantillo, 2013; Christidis & Brons, 2010; Janic, 2007; Janic, 2008; Macharis et al., 2010; Maibach et al., 2008; Marquez Diaz, 2009), but the method of calculating external costs has been very complex and remains incomplete (Nash, 2003; Quinet, 2004; Schreyer et al., 2004). Thus, we would like to emphasize that the money-market regulations through transport policy are not the only policy instruments available and, here, we defend the position that transport could also be made more sustainable using social marketing (Bonča et al., 2017).

In the presented research, we were interested in analyzing the Slovenian market for fresh fruit and vegetables by looking at the sustainability of freight transport. Recognizing the normative dimension that is inherent in the concept of sustainability, we aim to reflect on the potential benefits that sustainable transportation could make on the Slovenian fresh- fruit and -vegetable market, including its freight-transport use.

The distance between the manufacturer (or grower) and the points of sale, where the goods are available to final consumers, is extremely important, as external costs arise due to transport along these routes, which can vary greatly, for example in terms of the length, the mode of transport (road, rail, ship, air), the type of transport (e.g., van, small truck, semitrailer truck, trailer truck, train, ship), the driving time (e.g., during rush hour, at night) and the area (e.g., in the city, in the countryside). Most of these costs are currently not covered by existing market prices for goods and services. The question arises as to whether all this transport is actually justified and necessary from the point of view of sustainable development. We mention the fact that in certain cases the same type of goods is imported and exported (hereinafter exports also mean the intra-EU supply). Thus, Norberg-Hodge et al. (2013) report that most countries import and export a worryingly similar amount of the same types of goods. They give the example of the United States of America (USA), which annually exports a similar quantity of potatoes (365,350 tons of imports, 324,544 tons of exports), beef (953,142 tons of imports, 899,834 tons of exports), and coffee (41,209 tons of imports, 42,277 tons of exports) as it imports. The situation is similar in the United Kingdom in the case of milk (114,000 tons of imports, 119,000 tons of exports), eggs (21,979 tons of imports, 30,604 tons of exports), and pork (158,294 tons of imports, 258,558 tons of exports). As a result, more transport is performed than would be required given the production and consumption of each country.

There is a noticeable trend towards setting fairer and more efficient prices for goods and services, i.e., those that will reflect the external effects of transport on the environment and society. Here, fairness represents the improvement of cost distribution through ethical considerations (European commission, 1996; Christidis & Brons, 2010), and efficiency encompasses the economic views of pricing to maximize economic prosperity, including direct and indirect benefits for both transport users and for society as a whole (Proost et al., 2002; Christidis & Brons, 2010). On the one hand, the existing evaluation of freight transport only covers internal costs, which include labor costs, the depreciation of vehicles, tires, insurance, tolls, financing, administrative and sales costs, as well as fuel costs (Forkenbrock, 1998; Forkenbrock, 2001; Beuthe et al., 2002; Hočevar, 2008). Some internal costs, such as the cost of fuel, already include an environmental tax, which is relatively negligible in terms of the extent of the negative consequences that transport has on the environment (Fuel price movements, 2011; CURS, 2015). As transport also has external costs, and with the current policy and current legislation the transport user does not cover these, or only partially covers them through environmental duties and taxes, it is assumed that there are unrealistic prices of goods and services on the market. Christidis and Brons (2010) argue that the market price of a good that requires transportation on its way from the manufacturer to the point of sale (e.g., a supermarket) is underestimated. The latter affects everyone involved in this chain (e.g., producers, consumers, traders, carriers). However, there may also be an unequal position of local goods compared to goods of more distant origin. Setting the right price, the full-cost price, including the external costs of transport, is becoming increasingly important in the transport sector. To better align freight transport with the concept of sustainable development, external-cost internalization of transport would be needed (the inclusion of monetary externalities in the price of transport).

Thus, our research problem stems from the fact that most external costs of transport are neither covered by existing market-transport prices nor by fresh- fruit and -vegetable prices, which may lead to market inefficiencies and possible wrong purchasing decisions by consumers, as well as wrong decisions by other operators in the supply chain (e.g., growers, freight forwarders, carriers, distributors, traders, importers, exporters). Because the selling or purchase prices of crops do not reflect the external costs of transport, this may also have consequences in the unequal position of local crops compared to crops of distant origin. The consequence can also be reflected in the deviation of real transport needs from current ones and in the volume of imports and exports. Since it would be possible, to achieve the lowest possible external effects and external costs of transport or by internalizing them, to influence the volume of transport, imports, and the food self-sufficiency of countries and, thus, approach the concept of sustainable development, we wanted to gain a broader insight into the field of external costs of transport and assess pricing through the internalization of external costs of transport as an important indicator of sustainable transport (Litman, 2021).

This study focused on the freight transport of fresh fruits and vegetables and the choice of Slovenia as a case for further analysis. The aim was to appraise pricing through the internalization of external costs of transport as an important indicator of sustainability, assess the market situation, and present possible solutions for better sustainability. For our empirical case, we selected four typical Slovenian products (i.e., apples, pears, carrots, cabbage). On this basis, secondary data collection and analysis of material-flow accounts were used to analyze self-sufficiency, import and export features, and transport needs from 2005 to 2012, followed by a sustainability analysis of freight transport. Material-flow accounts included national transport accounts, where we derived information from the data about the quantity of current and real transport needs. Sustainable transport was understood as transport that is provided to satisfy current people's needs in the frame of consumption sufficiency without causing any effects on the environment, enabling a better life for people in time and location.

8.3 Research Methods

The use of the scientific method of the systematic literature review is relatively new in the field of transport and, as far as we know, has not yet been carried out for the purpose of researching calculations of the external costs of freight. The same applies to the external costs of the transport sector. Despite the fact that the method dates back to the 90s, it has long only been applied in the field of medicine, where it was originally developed and where the most significant advances in the method have been made (Davis et al., 1995; Cook et al., 1997; Booth, 2001; Hemsley-Brown in Oplatka, 2006). Only a few years ago, however, its applicability was also accepted in physical sciences (Dybå & Dingsøyr, 2008; Walia & Carver, 2009) and social sciences (Petticrew & Roberts, 2006). In the latter, examples are known from the fields of marketing (Aspelund et al., 2007; Birnik & Bowman, 2007), tourism (Morad, 2007; Gjerald

& Øgaard, 2008; Zhang et al., 2009), and strategic innovation (Edwards et al., 2004; Knoben & Oerlemans, 2006; Bartels & Reinders, 2010). Such a review of literature has been used in the field of transport, but only in the last few years (Fraser & Lock, 2011; Ginieis et al., 2011; Perego et al., 2011; Ginieis et al., 2012; Thomas, 2012; Mathisen & Hanssen, 2014). The literature found addresses other topics such as air transport (Ginieis et al., 2011, 2012), intermodal freight transport (Mathisen & Hanssen, 2014), logistics and freight transport (Perego et al., 2011), traffic safety (see Thomas, 2012), promoting active transport on the way to school (Chillón et al., 2011), and the active transport of children (see Pont et al., 2009), none of which addresses all forms of transport.

First, we surveyed selected scientific literature and other reports ($N = 32$), where a systematic literature review was undertaken. Totally, our sample included a review with 404 variables. Here, a comprehensive dataset of external costs for all transport modes was collected, allowing for detailed insight into this field. We also searched data about external costs per vehicle kilometer for a trailer truck with a payload of 24 tons.

When analyzing material-flow accounts, we obtained long-term data, from the Statistical Office of the Republic of Slovenia (SORS), concerning the production and consumption of selected produce, along with data about volumes imported and exported. The quantities of products being exported and imported were also the quantities transported to and from the country. We assumed that at a national level, only transport, which is really necessary, should be carried out, i.e., the volume of net import or export of produce. This we called the sustainability paradigm. As such, they represented "current transport needs" (export plus import). Further, we compared this data with "real transport needs," which is understood as a country's net import or net export and represents the physical trade balance. In this case, the real transport needs of the country are sufficient. Also, the external impacts and external costs of transport are the lowest and the difference between current and real transport needs represents any impacts on the environment. Every import and transport which is not a consequence of the deficit of the produce in the country and every export and transport which is not the consequence of the surplus was considered an unsustainable activity.

Building from the mentioned secondary source, we also obtained information concerning the place of origin of the crops (from 2005 to 2012).

In order to find out the product origin, the prices of domestic and non-domestic produce, retailer practices, and consumer consciousness on transport impacts, we conducted a primary data survey. It represented data collection in retail ($N = 8$) and two questionnaires where we interviewed the retailers ($N =$

2) only using open types of questions, and consumers, (N = 135) where questions were mostly of the closed type (only three were open). This information formed the basis for simulating the internalization of external costs into market prices of products that were, according to the data collection in retail, delivered to Ljubljana (this revealed the produce origin). The simulation was conducted for 27 selected cases of transport of produce on nineteen different transport routes (i.e., two inside of Slovenia, seventeen international) with the final destination being Ljubljana (confirmed also from retailer practice). For these routes, we calculated the distances in kilometers using a professional route planner: PTV Map&Guide internet (2013). Throughout the calculation to internalize the external costs of transport we considered the principles of economics (e.g., determining purchase produce prices from their retail prices, anticipating inflation in the product prices, and taking into account the exchange rate for the currency conversion).

Finally, a SWOT analysis was carried out to analyze transport with internalized external costs. Here, we considered sustainability indicators (economic, environmental, and social) and a measurement scale. Based on the principles of a perfectly competitive market with flexible supply and demand, and assuming that taxes and charges (representing the external costs of transport) are imposed on the users of transport, which, in the long term, results in lower demand and also a lower supply size, we found out, through the measurement scale, in which direction sustainability indicators moved. We compared the market situation when prices included internalized external costs with the current situation when these costs were not internalized. With the aim to set possible strategies for the better sustainability of transport we used the TOWS matrix.

8.4 Results

To internalize external costs into market prices of produce, we selected (based on calculations derived from reviewing 32 literature sources) 27 transport routes which were extracted based on the collected data in retail. We presumed Ljubljana to be the target destination and took into account a refrigerated trailer truck, as it is, according to the retailers' most-used practices, with a net cargo weight of twenty or sixteen tons. These data were part of our calculations, showing both scenarios for different weights. We found that marginal external costs are 0.0862 EUR/km in the case of twenty tons being transported, and 0.0820 EUR/km in the case of sixteen tons (i.e., 3.39 EUR/ton for twenty tons and 4.06 EUR/ton for sixteen tons of net cargo weight). The significant result is in the difference in external costs per kg in the case of different net cargo weights, where this cost per kg is higher for bigger tonnage. External costs per km are lower in the case of lower cargo weight (i.e., sixteen tons). When we compared differences between market prices, obtained from our primary data survey, and prices, to which we internalized external costs, it resulted in a price rise and was in line with our preliminary expectations. On average, this increase is negligible because it is 0.46 % for twenty tons of net cargo weight and 0.54 % if the net cargo weight is sixteen tons.

A systematic review found that existing studies address the field of calculations of external costs differently, which is reflected in the diversity of coverage of externalities and types of costs, their cost-component and monetary-valuation method, and their focus on different areas, means of transport, and time. Existing studies mostly (i.e., on average 87.5%) address the same types of externalities (i.e., air pollution, accidents, noise, congestion, and climate change), but also other effects (i.e., on nature and the landscape, on ecosystems and biodiversity, effects due to urban fragmentation and congestion, the impact on the infrastructure, the impact on sensitive areas and the pollution of soil and water), but they omitted addressing other areas directly, such as ecosystem services. The greatest diversity is characteristic of cost components, which have many different variables by type of cost (e.g., nineteen for accidents, seventeen for congestion, sixteen for air pollution, ten for external costs of other externalities, and nine for the external costs of construction and decommissioning of transport system elements). Regarding the monetary-valuation method, we found a similar situation, as they are also characterized by different possible evaluation methods, reflected in the existence of a large number of possible variables (e.g., eighteen for air pollution, thirteen for noise, six for external costs of disasters and six for external costs of climate change). However, we found that there is a difference between the sets of possible cost-component and monetary-valuation-method variables, which are less numerous for the latter. As a result, there is greater diversity in the calculation of external costs originating from the cost-component than that derived from the monetary-valuation method.

By simulating the internalization of external costs of transport into crop prices, we found that the impact on crop prices is negligible (on average increasing by 0.46% for twenty tons and 0.54% for sixteen tons of net cargo weight) and is significantly smaller than initially expected.

We found that the underestimation of the prices of imported products (on average 0.55%) is higher than that of Slovenian products (on average 0.06%)

and that it is not true that the underestimation of imported products always increases with the distance of the origin of products. If external costs are not internalized in the price of crops, on average, the prices of imported products on the Slovenian market are underestimated for shorter transport lengths, but not in all cases, and, on average, it is higher for longer and the highest for the longest journeys. It makes almost no difference whether twenty or sixteen tons of crops are transported. In general, however, this underestimation is greater in the case of transport lengths from 926 km onwards (the only exception is the route with a length of 389 km). In connection with the proportionality between the increase in the length of the journey and the underestimation of the prices of imported products on the Slovenian market, we proved that proportionality does not exist in all cases.

The secondary data collected about the volumes of apples, pears, carrots, and cabbage produced, consumed, imported, and exported from 2005 to 2012 suggest that Slovenia had a surplus in the production of apples, while the other three crops had a deficit. The average self-sufficiency in this period was 112.49% for apples, 87.88% for cabbage, 75.37% for pears, and 35.75% for carrots. The data indicate that self-sufficiency for all crops decreased during that period.

Within each year all produce was exported and imported, but, in the whole period, the export of apples was 81.8% higher than the import. In all other cases, the imports exceeded export (i.e., pears 203.2%, carrots 513.21%, and cabbage 2,685.73% higher import vs. export). The highest level of export vs. import was for apples in 2007 and the lowest was for cabbage in 2005, 2006 and 2009.

As a consequence of export and import, the total transported quantity of produce (export plus import) was 451,918 tons, which represents "current transport needs"—while the physical trade balance showed that net import was 184,692 tons of produce, which would have needed to be transported, i.e., "real transport needs." Thus, during the whole period, 59.13% of the transport was used "unnecessarily." The transportation usage for apples was 244.71% higher than necessary, followed by the transport of pears at an excess of 98.42%, carrots at 38.97%, and cabbage at 7.45%.

The highest transport need was for apples, because of high export and also high import. It is interesting to note that the imported quantity was more than half (55.01%) of that exported for the same period.

Imports of the four selected crops come mainly from neighboring countries (Italy, Austria, Croatia, etc.), while a minority come from more distant locations (the Netherlands, Spain, Belgium, Germany, Israel, etc.). However, 3,862 tons (1.7% of total imports) were imported from distant countries including

Israel, Egypt, South Africa, Argentina, and Chile. It is of interest to note that, according to the data obtained from SORS, Slovenia exported the same types of products to some countries (Austria, Bosnia and Hercegovina, Belgium, the Czech Republic, Germany, Egypt, Spain, France, Croatia, Hungary, Italy, Macedonia, the Netherlands, Poland, Serbia and Montenegro, Serbia, Slovakia, and Turkey) as are imported from those same countries. From 2005 to 2012, the share of Slovenia's net imports of selected crops from those countries was 18 % of total imports (i.e., imported 223,031 tons, exported 182,867 tons). This rate would be even higher if we were not to include the "surpluses," such as with apples, in this case.

Primary data gathered concerning 145 items (78 cases of apples, 21 cases of pears, twenty cases of carrots, and 26 cases of cabbage) in eight retail markets confirm the place of origin from SORS data. This data indicated that apples had Slovenian origin in 60.26% of cases while in 39.74% they were from countries of the European Union (EU). In 42.31% of cases, cabbage was from Slovenia, while 57.7% was from EU countries. On the other hand, pears were from Slovenia in only 19.05% of cases, while 61.91% were from EU countries. In 19.05% of cases, pears were from very distant countries, i.e., from the Republic of South Africa and China. Also, carrots are mostly imported from other EU countries with only 10% being of Slovenian origin. Most of these crops were produced by conventional agriculture, while about one-third were organically produced.

Imported produce was, in all cases, more expensive than Slovenian produce, except for organic pears (22.84% cheaper). On average, the selected imported crops were 38.19% more expensive than domestic crops. The price for all produce was, on average, lower for produce from shorter distances and higher from the most distant locations. On average, it was 0.86 EUR for produce transported for distances of 128 to 393 km, 1.64 EUR on routes from 394 to 493 km, and 2.13 EUR per kg on routes from 926 to 1,275 km.

The data collected with the questionnaire administered to retailers confirmed that fresh fruit and vegetables are transported by road in refrigerated truck trailers, mostly with a maximum payload of 24 tons (i.e., sixteen or twenty tons of net weight). Respondents stated that they set cost prices during negotiations, often depending on weather conditions, which varied daily. They also affirmed that there was no difference between cost prices for domestic and non-domestic produce, and the same was indicated by retail prices, which they said depended on cost prices. The results show that retailers purchased crops in Slovenia first, but that in cases of shortage they had to buy from abroad. The respondents stated that the share of the transport price in the cost price depended on the kilometers traveled, increasing for more distant locations. In general, retailers chose the place of purchase according to the principle of least distance, seeking the shortest and quickest path from producer to the final consumer.

8.5 Discussion

A broader view of the results of the considered cost component and monetary-valuation method revealed an important finding, namely that the studies citing these items go in two directions. Thus, some mostly cover a single variable (Christidis & Brons, 2010), while others mostly combine variables (OECD, 1998; Eriksen, 2000; Beuthe et al., 2002; Nash, 2003; Maibach et al., 2008), where the combinations are used more often in the cost component (on average in 61.94% of sources) than in the monetary-valuation method (on average 71.96% of sources deal with an individual variable). Among the twelve sources used for the internalization of external costs, both individual variables and combinations of variables are used the most, but the total cost component is dominated by several combinations of variables (i.e., 80% of sources), and for the monetary-valuation method individual variables (i.e., 70%), which differs from the previously mentioned data for all 32 sources to a greater extent, only in the case of the cost component. Since these are costs, the principle of "more is better than less" could be applied, as the transport user should cover them in full. In this case, it would be useful to capture as many variables as possible, i.e., combinations. However, this finding raises a new question, namely, which of the specific variables or combinations of the cost-component and monetary-valuation-method variables should be covered to reflect the costs actually incurred in transport and be fully covered by the transport user. For example, among existing studies, Maibach et al. (2008) cite only the best practice, which does not provide an answer about the best set of variables or combinations of variables of the cost component and monetary-valuation method.

Combining the findings, we can confirm that the existing external costs of transport calculations indicate the complexity as well as the shortcomings of the area. While other studies have already mentioned the complexity of the calculation of external costs and point to certain shortcomings (e.g., Baum et al., 2008; Jakob et al., 2006), in our study, we have systematically presented the individual external costs of transport items with their variables. For example, for all sources, we presented their geographical coverage for which external costs of transport calculations have already been made, thus identifying which areas remain geographically uncovered and which would be needed to implement external-cost internalization more accurately for selected transport-route cases. We also found that to better integrate the external costs of transport into crop prices, we would need data for a refrigerator truck. We have demonstrated that studies citing items on external-cost calculations go in two directions (i.e., the first covers an individual variable, the second covers combinations of variables), with 80% of the sources included in the internalization covering combinations of cost-component variables. The latter has a positive connotation if we consider the "more is better than less" principle, as more costs are covered in the internalization than in the case of the inclusion of a single variable, which may result in better internalization. Precisely due to shortcomings in the field of the external costs of transport calculations, the implementation of the internalization of external costs of transport was made difficult and we, therefore, had to apply the previously mentioned adjustments. For this reason, our internalization of external costs of transport into prices of selected products that were available on the shelves of Slovenian retailers in Ljubljana (i.e., 27 examples of crops from nineteen different places of dispatch) does not reflect the correct actual costs caused by transport to the environment and society but covers the best external-cost data offered by the existing literature and adapted to the needs of our empirical case.

As mentioned, our analysis shows that the underestimation of prices of imported products is higher than that of Slovenian products, and it is not true that the underestimation of imported products always increases with the distance of the origin of products. Similar findings were made in the study by Christidis and Brons (2010), who argue that the impact on product prices is negligible and that in situations where it is a low-cost product with high weight or when the load has a characteristic of low weight, but large volume, the price change is greater. Our result is very similar to the findings of Christidis and Brons (2010) (the average change in the price of the final product is a maximum of 0.5%), but it should be noted that this is due to everything we included in the calculation, namely the included external costs of transport based on the existing sources considered, the inflation rate and the exchange rate. However, the biggest impact has the included external costs of transport. As already mentioned, we found that these indicate complexity and shortcomings. Thus, the external-cost calculations and the resulting adjustments that we had to make (e.g., calculations for a truck and not for a truck with a refrigerator, the use of a nearby corridor instead of a precisely selected transport route) have the greatest impact on our result. Despite the obtained negligible influence of the external costs of transport on the price of crops, we found a difference between situations where the truck is loaded with twenty or sixteen tons of crops (the change in price for the case of sixteen tons is higher in all cases compared to the twenty-ton net weight). This difference stems from the fact that the same external costs were considered in both cases, as the existing literature does not provide separate external costs of transport for different truckloads and, therefore, in the case of transporting sixteen tons of crops, the same external costs are distributed at a lower weight than in the case of twenty tons. The latter is also reflected in the value of external costs/km of transport performed.

8.6 Implications for Theory and Practice

Based on a SWOT analysis of transport with internalized external costs and a TOWS matrix, we found that quite a few possible strategies relate to greater support for the local economy, which, in the case of Slovenia, can include supplies at a local, regional, and national level. To cover the external costs of transport, the principle of "more is better than less" would apply, which, with an understanding in the opposite direction, means that these costs should be avoided as much as possible. Priority supplies at a local level would make a positive contribution to achieving this and, in the event of a shortage (e.g., of goods), they would be extended to increasingly remote locations. This would require the additional awareness of consumers or transport users, where social marketing campaigns could play an important role, both at a state level and in local communities, as individual orientation would be crucial.

Greater sustainability of transport could also be achieved using other forms of transport of fresh fruit and vegetables, which we have not considered because in Slovenia road transport is mostly used for these purposes. An alternative could be rail transport, but as these are perishable goods, intermodal transport might be a better option. Of course, all the conditions required for the transport of fresh produce should be given. The field of finding alternative modes of transport is certainly interesting for further consideration.

The contribution of our analysis is in the rigorous review of the calculation of external costs of freight transport, which was done through the scientific method of systematic literature review and has not been used before in such depth as here. Our review shows how current literature deals with individual variables with a good level of detail and reveals, in this way, the imperfections of this field. There is a reason why the internalization of external costs of transport is difficult and could not reflect exact real costs, which are a consequence of transport on the environment and society. We prove that imperfections result in using the current data of external costs, which refer to a lack of geographical coverage, uncertainties about included taxes and charges, an inaccuracy of the transport mode, and obsolescence. Our contribution is also in finding that studies that address cost components and the method of monetary validation go in two directions, and that this is an area that should be improved with clearly defined guidelines about the information on which individual variables or combinations of variables would best reflect the real ecosystem services of transport. For the Slovenian case, we showed that transport done as a consequence of deliveries of fresh produce from other countries to Slovenia is unsustainable when considering the external effects and external costs. It means that this transport does not satisfy people's needs in the frame of consumption sufficiency (it is a surplus), which causes effects (negative) on the environment and does not enable a better life for people. Additionally, it means that this transport does not justify the principles of sustainable development. However, the internalization of external costs would lead to greater harmonization of prices of domestic products with the prices of products from the more distant origin and could also benefit towards better sustainable development.

8.7 Conclusions

The study results in information that Slovenia had a surplus only in the case of apples, but all other products had to be imported in the period from 2005 to 2012. Despite this, the country exported and imported all four selected produce and, if we compare import and export quantity for all products together, the quantity is nearly the same. Additionally, there were cases when Slovenia exported some types of products to countries from which these same types were also imported. Consequently, the country had higher transport needs than it would have with consideration of the definition of transport sustainability. Further, we studied whether transport in such a scope as it was currently would be necessary and justified if the concept of the sustainability of transport were considered. We concluded that the transport of produce had a potential for sustainable development and reducing high imports on account of lower export.

We discussed the use of a systematic literature review and obtained data. The study found that current calculations of external costs indicate complexity and imperfections. This calls for further research with a focus on certain specifics (e.g., micro locations, technical features of the vehicles). Retrieving data from the internalization of external costs, we confirmed the underestimation of imported-produce prices in the case when external costs are not internalized in comparison with Slovenian produce, but the underestimation does not rise proportionately according to the distance of the origin. We also confirmed that the transport of fresh fruits and vegetables from other countries to Slovenia is unsustainable when external effects and costs are taken into account. Firstly, transport routes in Slovenia are linked with lower external effects and costs in comparison with transport routes from abroad where mentioned effects and costs are higher. Secondly, we figured out that Slovenia also had unnecessary transport, and not just one which originates in net import or net export. However, we confirmed that the transport of produce in the case of import to Slovenia is unsustainable, but internalization could work towards better sustainable development.

The main limitation to our research we see in the selected data-collection method for the external-cost calculation is the systematic literature review, which is, despite the rigorous review of the existing calculation of external costs of freight transport, limited to the existing and available research reports and data. The existing studies do mostly address the same types of externalities (i.e., air pollution, accidents, noise, congestion, and climate change), and also some other effects (i.e., on nature and the landscape, on ecosystems and biodiversity, effects due to urban fragmentation and congestion, the impact on the infrastructure, the impact on sensitive areas and the pollution of soil and water), but more complex areas, such as ecosystem services, were mostly omitted, so our calculated marginal external costs are undervalued. This limited scope of external-cost calculation we see as the major topic for future research, whereby we are also aware of its complexity and interdisciplinarity, so the main research strategy for finding answers to these issues should be the development of the respective interdisciplinary and transdisciplinary research projects.

References

Aspelund, A., Madsen, T. K., & Moen, Ø. (2007). A review of the foundation, international marketing strategies, and performance of international new ventures. *European Journal of Marketing*, *41*(11/12), 1423–1448.

Bartels, J., & Reinders, M. J. (2010). Consumer innovativeness and its correlates: A propositional inventory for future research. *Journal of Business Research*, (64), 601–609.

Baum, H., Geißler, T., Schneider, J., & Bühne, J. A. (2008). *External Costs in the Transport Sector: A Critical Review of the EC-Internalisation-Policy.* Institute for Transport Economics, University of Cologne. Retrieved from: http://z-f-v. de/fileadmin/archiv/hefte-2008_1_2_3/2008-2/ZfV_2008_Heft_2_02_Baum%20 Gei%DFler%20Schneider%20B%FChne%20-%20External%20Costs%20 of%20Transport%20%96%20A%20critical%20review%20of%20the%20EC%20 Internalisation%20Policy.pdf Available [June 1, 2021].

Beuthe, M., Degrandsart, F., Geerts, J. F., & Jourquin, B. (2002). External costs of the Belgian interurban freight traffic: A network analysis of their internalization. *Transportation Research, Part D*, (7), 285–301. DOI: 10.1016/S1361-9209(01)00025-6

Birnik, A., & Bowman, C. (2007). Marketing mix standardization in multinational corporations: A review of the evidence. *International Journal of Management Reviews*, *9*, (4), 303–324.

Bonča, S., Rodela, R., & Udovč, A. (2017). A social marketing perspective on road freight transportation of fresh fruits and vegetables: A Slovene case. *Ekonomska istraživanja* [Economic Research], *30*(1), 1132–1151. DOI: 10.1080/1331677X.2017.1314820.

Booth, A. (2001). *Cochrane or Cock-Eyed? How Should We Conduct Systematic Reviews of Qualitative Research? Qualitative Evidence-Based Practice Conference, Taking a Critical Stance*, Coventry, 14–16. Maj. Coventry University. Retrieved from: www. leeds.ac.uk/educol/documents/00001724.htm Available [September 22, 2015].

Borec, A. (2015). *Lokalne prehranske verige in male kmetije* [Local Food Chains and Small Farms]. Maribor: Univerza v Mariboru, Fakulteta za kmetijstvo in bio-sistemske vede. Retrieved from: www.kgzs.si/Portals/0/Gradiva/04%20Borec. pdf Available [August 25, 2015].

Carinska uprava Republike Slovenije (CURS). (2015). *Environmental Duties.* Retrieved from: www.fu.gov.si/fileadmin/Internet/Davki_in_druge_dajatve/Podrocja/ Okoljske_dajatve/Opis/okoljske_dajatve.pdf Available [June 15, 2015].

Chillón, P., Evenson, K. R., Vaughn, A., & Ward, D. S. (2011). A systematic review of interventions for promoting active transportation to school. *International Journal of Behavioral Nutrition and Physical Activity*, (8), 10.

Christidis, P., & Brons, M. (2010). *Impacts of the Proposal for Amending Directive 1999/62/EC on Road Infrastructure Charging: An Analysis on Selected Corridors and Main Impacts.* Working Papers on Energy, Transport and Climate Change. N.3, Office for Official Publications of the European Communities, Luxembourg.

Cook, D., Mulrow, C., & Haynes, R. (1997). Systematic reviews: Synthesis of best evidence for clinical decisions. *Annals of Internal Medicine, 126* (5), 376–380.

Davis, D. A., Thomson, M. A., Oxman, A. D., & Haynes, R. B. (1995). Changing physician performance: A systematic review of the effect of continuing medical education strategies. *JAMA, 274*(9), 700–705.

Dybå, T., & Dingsøyr, T. (2008). Empirical studies of agile software development: A systematic review. *Information and Software Technology, 50* (9/10), 833–859.

Edwards, T., Battisti, G., & Neely, A. (2004). Value creation and the UK economy: A review of strategic options. *International Journal of Management Reviews, 5*(3/4), 191–213.

Eriksen, K. S. (2000). Calculating external costs of transportation in Norway: Principles and results. *EJTIR, 0*(0), 9–25. DOI: 10.18757/ejtir.2000.0.1.3491

Essen, H., Fiorello, D., & El Beyrouty, K. (2020). *Handbook on the External Costs of Transport: Version 2019–1.1,* European commission (2020). Directorat General for mobility and transport, Publications Office. DOI:10.2832/51388

European Commission. (1996). *Towards Fair and Efficient Pricing in Transport: Policy Options for Internalizing the External Costs of Transport in the European Union.* European Commission. Retrieved from: http://europa.eu/documents/comm/green_papers/pdf/com95_691_en.pdf Available [June 1, 2021].

European Commission. (2012). *EU Transport in Figures: Statistical Pocketbook 2012.* Luxembourg: Publications Office. DOI: 10.2832/52252

Forkenbrock, D. J. (1998). *External Costs of Truck and Rail Freight Transportation.* University of Iowa, Public Policy Center. Retrieved from: http://ir.uiowa.edu/cgi/viewcontent.cgi?article=1001&context=ppc_transportation Available [August 10, 2011].

Forkenbrock, D. J. (1999). External costs of intercity truck freight transportation. *Transportation Research, Part A,* (33), 505–526. DOI: 10.1016/S0965-8564(98)00068-8

Forkenbrock, D. J. (2001). Comparison of external costs of rail and truck freight transportation. *Transportation Research, Part A,* (35), 321–337.

Fraser, S. D., & Lock, K. (2011). Cycling for transport and public health: A systematic review of the effect of the environment on cycling. *European Journal of Public Health, 21*(6), 738–743.

Fuel price movements. (2011). *Petrol.* Retrieved from: www.petrol.si/na-poti/za-vozilo/goriva-q-max/gibanje-cen-goriv Available [December 17, 2011].

Ginieis, M., Sánchez-Rebull, M. V., & Campa-Planas, F. (2012). The academic journal literature on air transport: Analysis using systematic literature review methodology. *Journal of Air Transport Management,* (19), 31–35.

Ginieis, M., Sánchez-Rebull, M. V., Hernandez, A. B., & Campa-Planas, F. (2011). The air transportation sector and the interest in the scientific community: A systematic literature review. *Sustainable Tourism: Socio-Cultural, Environmental and Economics Impact,* 5. September. Tourism in South East Europe, 81–93. Retrieved from: http://ssrn.com/abstract=2165240 Available [September 22, 2015].

Gjerald, O., & Øgaard, T. (2008). Why should hospitality management focus more on the construct of basic assumptions? A review and research agenda. *Scandinavian Journal of Hospitality and Tourism, 8*(4), 294–316.

Grewal, D., & Compeau, L. D. (1999). Pricing and public policy: A research agenda and an overview of the special issue. *Journal of Public Policy & Marketing, 18*(1), 3–10.

Hemsley-Brown, J., & Oplatka, I. (2006). Universities in a competitive global marketplace: A systematic review of the literature on higher education marketing. *International Journal of Public Sector Management, 19*(4), 316–338.

Hočevar, M. (2008). *Kalkulacija stroškov tovornega (kamionskega) prometa* [Calculations of the Freight Trafic Costs]. Ljubljana: Univerza v Ljubljani, Ekonomska fakulteta.

Isensee, M. (2003, August 18). *What Does Locally Grown and What Does Family Farm Mean?* Message posted to comfood-l@listproc.tufts.edu

Jakob, A., Craig, J. L., & Fisher, G. (2006). Transport cost analysis: A case study of the total cost of private and public transport in Auckland. *Environmental Science & Policy,* (9), 55–66.

Janic, M. (2007). Modelling the full costs of an intermodal and road freight transport network. *Transportation Research, Part D* (12), 33–44. DOI: 10.1016/j.trd.2006.10.004

Janic, M. (2008). An assessment of the performance of the European long intermodal freight trains (LIFTS). *Transportation Research, Part A* (42), 1326–1339. DOI: 10.1016/j.tra.2008.06.008

Knoben, J., & Oerlemans, L. A. G. (2006). Proximity and inter-organizational collaboration: A literature review. *International Journal of Management Reviews,* 8(2), 71–89.

Litman, T. (2021). *Well Measured: Developing Indicators for Sustainable and Livable Transport Planning.* Victoria Transport Policy Institute. Retrieved from: www.vtpi.org/wellmeas.pdf Available [August 1, 2021].

Macharis, C., Van Hoeck, E., Pekin, E., & Van Lier, T. (2010). A decision analysis framework for intermodal transport: Comparing fuel price increases and the internalisation of external costs. *Transportation Research, Part A* (44), 550–561.

Maibach, M., Schreyer, C., Sutter, D., Van Essen, H. P., Boon, B. H., Smokers, R., Schroten, A., Doll, C., Pawlowska, B., & Bak, M. (2008). *Handbook on Estimation of External Cost in the Transport Sector: Version 1.1.* Delft, European Commission, DG TREN. Retrieved from: http://ec.europa.eu/transport/themes/sustainable/doc/2008_costs_handbook.pdf Available [August 10, 2011].

Márquez, L., & Cantillo, V. (2013). Evaluating strategic freight transport corridors including external costs. *Transportation Planning and Technology,* (36), 529–546.

Marquez Diaz, L. G. (2009). Estimating marginal external costs for road, rail and river transport in Columbia. *Ingenieria E Investigacion,* 31(1), 56–64.

Mathisen, T. A., & Hanssen, T. E. S. (2014). The academic literature on intermodal freight transport. *Transportation Research Procedia,* (3), 611–620.

Morad, T. (2007). Tourism and disability: A review of cost-effectiveness. *International Journal on Disability and Human Development,* 6(3), 279–282.

Nash, C. (2003). *Unification of Accounts and Marginal Costs for Transport Efficiency (UNITE): Final Report for Publication.* Leeds: Institute for Transport Studies, University of Leeds. Retrieved from: www.its.leeds.ac.uk/projects/unite/paris/nash.pdf Available [July 1, 2021].

Norberg-Hodge, H., Gorelick, S., & Page, J. (2013). *The Economics of Happiness: Discussion Guide and Companion to the Film.* International Society for Ecology and Culture. Retrieved from: www.localfutures.org/wp-content/uploads/the_economics_of_happiness_discussion_guide.pdf Available [August 25, 2015].

OECD. (1998). *Efficient Transport in Europe: Policies for Internalisation of External Costs.* Paris, European Conference of Ministers of transport, OECD Publications Service Retrieved from: http://internationaltransportforum.org/pub/pdf/98efficient.pdf Available [August 10, 2011].

Perego, A., Perotti, S., & Mangiaracina, R. (2011). ICT for logistics and freight transportation: A literature review and research agenda. *International Journal of Physical Distribution & Logistics Management, 41*(5), 457–483.

Perpar, A., & Udovč, A. (2010). Realni potenciali za lokalno oskrbo s hrano v Sloveniji [Real potentials for local food provision in Slovenia]. *Dela*, (34), 187–199.

Pestotnik, J. (2014). *Prehranska samooskrba Republike Slovenije v okviru Evropske unije* [Food self-sufficiency of the Republic of Slovenia within the European Union]. Undergraduate thesis, University of Ljubljana, Faculty of Social Sciences, Ljubljana. Retrieved from: http://dk.fdv.uni-lj.si/diplomska_dela_1/pdfs/mb11_pestotnik-jure.pdf Available [June 1, 2021].

Petticrew, M., & Roberts, H. (2006). *Systematic Reviews in the Social Sciences: A Practical Guide*. Malden: Blackwell Malden.

Piecyk, M., & McKinnon, A. (2007). *Internalising the External Costs of Road Freight Transport in the UK*. Edinburgh: Heriot-Watt University. Retrieved from: www.alanmckinnon.co.uk/uploaded/PDFs/Papers/Internalisation%20of%20external%20costs%20of%20UK%20road%20freight%20(Piecyk%20-%20McKinnon%202007)%20(final).pdf Available [June 1, 2021].

Plut, D. (2012). Prehranska varnost sveta in Slovenije [Food safety in the world and in Slovenia]. *Dela*, (38), 5–23. DOI: 10.4312/dela.38.1.5-23

Podnar, K., Molj, B., & Golob, U. (2007). How reference pricing for pharmaceuticals can increase generic share of market: The Slovenian experience. *Journal of Public Policy & Marketing, 26*(1), 89–101. DOI: 10.1509/jppm.26.1.89

Pont, K., Ziviani, J., Wadley, D., Bennett, S., & Abbott, R. (2009). Environmental correlates of children's active transportation: A systematic literature review. *Health & Place, 15*(3), 849–862.

Proost, S., Van Dender, K., Courcelle, C., De Borger, B., Peirson, J., Sharp, D., Vickerman, R., Gibbons, E., O'Mahony, M., Heaney, Q., Van den Bergh, J., & Verhoef, E. (2002). How large is the gap between present and efficient transport prices in Europe? *Transport Policy*, (9), 41–57.

PTV Map&Guide internet: Test now for free. (2013). Retrieved from: www.mapandguide.com/en/home/ Available [May 15, 2013].

Quinet, E. (2004). A meta-analysis of Western European external costs estimates. *Transportation Research, Part D*, (9), 465–476. DOI: 10.1016/j.trd.2004.08.003

Schreyer, C., Schneider, C., Maibach, M., Rothengatter, W., Doll, C., & Schmedding, D. (2004). *External Costs of Transport: Update Study*. Zürich/Karlsruhe: INFRAS/IWW, University of Karlsruhe. Retrieved from: http://habitat.aq.upm.es/boletin/n28/ncost.en.pdf Available [June 1, 2021].

Smith, J. (2003, August 15). *What Does Locally Grown and What Does Family Farm Mean?* Message posted to comfood-l@listproc.tufts.edu

SURS. (2015). *Self-Sufficiency Rate (%) by Different Agricultural Products, Yearly*. Ljubljana, SURS. Retrieved from: www.stat.si/StatWeb/pregled-podrocja?idp=84&headerbar=9#tabPodatkislovenija,letno Available [September 15, 2015].

Thomas, M. J. W. (2012). *A Systematic Review of the Effectiveness of Safety Management Systems*. Canberra, Australian Transport Safety Bureau. Retrieved from: www.atsb.gov.au/media/4053559/xr2011002_final.pdf Available [September 22, 2015].

Thomson, J. S., Radhakrishna, R. B., Maretzki, A. N., & Inciong, L. O. (2006). Strengthening community engagement toward sustainable local food systems. *Journal of Extension*, *44*(4), Feature Articles, 4FEA2. Retrieved from: http://archives.joe.org/joe/2006august/a2.php Available [June 1, 2021].

Walia, G. S., & Carver, J. (2009). A systematic literature review to identify and classify software requirement errors. *Information and Software Technology*, *51*(7), 1087–1109.

Zhang, X., Song, H., & Huang, G. (2009). Tourism supply chain management: A new research agenda. *Tourism Management*, *30*(3), 345–358.

Chapter 9

The Application of the Concept of Sharing Economy in the Supply Chain

Helga Pavlić Skender, Zoran Ježić,
and Petra Adelajda Zaninović

University of Rijeka, Croatia

Contents

DOI: 10.4324/9781003304364-11

9.1 Introduction

The ongoing drive to reduce greenhouse-gas (GHG) emissions and changing customer preferences to be more sustainable and environmentally friendly are putting a lot of pressure on the supply-chain industry. Supply-chain business is constantly looking for innovative methods and practices to improve business processes in a sustainable way. In order to be sustainable, supply chains need to simultaneously meet economic, social, and environmental aspects in the sense of the concept of the triple bottom line (Elkington, 1998 in Ocicka & Wieteska, 2017). The use of new technologies, especially network technologies in supply-chain business, can help companies meet these requirements. What new technologies can also do is provide the opportunity to work according to the concept of the "sharing economy." This concept is not new, but as technology develops, the sharing-economy model is spreading rapidly across a growing number of industries and markets worldwide (Owyang et al., 2013). The sharing economy can be beneficial for companies involved in supply chains as it allows them to share costly physical assets such as machinery, vehicles, and warehouses, and share information more easily.

The aim of this chapter is therefore to examine the concept of the sharing economy and its impact on economic growth and development with a particular focus on the supply-chain industry. In addition, this research evaluates the challenges and opportunities of implementing the sharing economy into supply-chain business operations through a three-case-study example of transport- and warehouse-sharing business practices. Research on the sharing economy is still in its infancy (Lee et al., 2018), and there is a gap in the literature regarding the relationship between sharing-economy practices and supply-chain business. These issues are particularly important in the era of challenges related to the COVID-19 pandemic, the growth of e-commerce, and the desire to reduce greenhouse-gas (GHG) emissions. The findings of the research can serve as a recommendation for companies involved in supply chains, and policy makers.

The rest of the chapter is organized as follows. Section 2 presents the theoretical background of the sharing-economy concept. Section 3 describes the materials and methods used in the analysis, while Section 4 presents the results of the case study. Section 5 concludes the chapter.

9.2 Theoretical Background

The sharing economy has gained attention among academics and businesses over the past decade, largely because consumers began to adapt a new model of consumption offered by a small digital company using only a mobile interface. Because of this, the concept of the sharing economy has the potential to grow and transform many businesses, including the supply-chain industry. Kathan et al. (2016) state that the sharing economy is characterized by "non-ownership, temporary access and redistribution of material goods or less tangible assets such as money, space or time." Miller (2016) agrees that the term "sharing economy" can also be described as collaborative economy or access-based economy and that it is radically affecting and changing the economy. The key difference between the sharing economy and the traditional business approach is that the main idea behind the sharing economy is to be able to "use something" rather than to "own something." The main hypothesis behind this is that in many cases (though not all) people are interested in using or accessing products or services and not necessarily in owning them (Bonciu & Balgar, 2016, p. 40).

The term "sharing economy" is often used together with many other terms such as "platform economy," "gig economy," "collaborative economy," and "on-demand economy" (United Nations, 2020). Sharing economy includes the buying and selling of temporary access to goods or services, usually mediated through a digital platform. According to Hunt (2018), sharing economy is becoming an important source of revenue in global economy and is led by companies like Uber and Airbnb.

The characteristics of the sharing economy are illustrated in Table 9.1. In addition to the characteristics of the sharing economy already mentioned, Table 9.1 also shows the characteristic of shifting the typical organizational and hierarchical structure of the company, that is, economy and better use of underutilized assets. These characteristics make sharing economy a more sustainable business model. However, although the United Nations "equally weight" all the characteristics, Table 9.1 reflects that some characteristics can be entirely attributed to the sharing-economy concept (column 1) while other characteristics cannot entirely be attributed to the sharing economy (column 2), as for example the characteristic "better use of under-utilized assets" is not always the case in sharing economy.

Table 9.1   Sharing-Economy Characteristics.

(1)	*(2)*
Flattened organizational hierarchies—workers receive instructions from algorithm	Digital platforms matching supply and demand at a large scale
Temporary access through renting or borrowing	Better use of under-utilized assets
Peer-to-peer exchange, among strangers	

Source: Author's work based on United Nations, 2020.

9.2.1 The Relationship Between the Sharing Economy, and Economic Growth and Development

According to Tabcum Jr. (2019), the sharing economy represents an economic system in which businesses and workers rent or share assets and services instead of owning them. For the "sharing system" to work, technology is needed. Technology, among other factors, is also responsive to economic development (Ježić, 2015). Technology serves as a way for businesses to connect to the digital world to share or rent their assets. Indeed, smartphones and tablets, combined with networking technology, apps, and social media, are enabling the sharing economy and making it popular in the business world (Benkler, 2006). Companies that operate on the principle of "sharing" rely on a network-based business model, using software and algorithms to manage the customer experience around a particular object (DHL, 2017).

However, in the literature and in public discourse, there is debate about the positive and negative effects of the sharing economy on the economy and its development as a whole. Bachnik (2016) and Nica and Potcovaru (2015) agree that the sharing economy drives sustainable development from an environmental, social, and economic perspective. Sharing-economy companies are growing exponentially (Avital et al., 2015) and are transforming the economy, although the positive or negative impact is yet to be seen. According to Bonciu and Balgar (2016), the sharing approach nowadays encompasses almost all types of economic activities (R&D, product design, production, ICT, marketing, consumption) and can ensure a better standard of living as it reduces the cost of living and labor while reducing the consumption-oriented lifestyle. The results of the fixed-effects regressions conducted by Dabbous and Tarhini (2021) suggest that the positive effects of the sharing economy on sustainable economic development and energy efficiency exist and have the potential to stimulate them further (Dabbous & Tarhini, 2021). Table 9.2 presents possible positive and negative impacts of the sharing economy from environmental, social, and economic perspectives.

The United Nations has created seventeen sustainable-development goals (SDGs) as a tool and guide for countries and individuals. Boar et al. (2020) conducted a content analysis of 74 articles from the Web of Science database on the relationships between the sharing economy, sustainability, and the SDGs, and their results show that the SDGs can be achieved through the implementation of the sharing economy (Boar et al., 2020).

Table 9.2 Possible Impacts of Sharing Economy.

Negative Impacts	Positive Impacts
ENVIRONMENTAL EFFECTS	
■ encourage unsustainable consumption patterns, such as less public transportation use	■ encourage sharing arrangements that reduces environmental footprints
ECONOMIC EFFECTS	
■ worsen economic security by entrenching people in uncertainty ■ low-pay employment with limited rights	■ better use of assets ■ improve economic security by providing extra income sources
SOCIAL EFFECTS	
■ commodify everyday life and undermine genuine forms of sharing	■ rebuild trust "one review at a time"

Source: Author's work based on United Nations (2020).

Avital et al. (2015) argue that companies that enable the sharing economy through digital platforms face two problems: A cooperation problem and a coordination problem, meaning that they have to "build trust and contract mechanisms that prevent someone from raiding an apartment rented through Airbnb (cooperation problem) and ensure that an Uber driver is in the right place at the right time to pick up a passenger (coordination problem)." The sharing economy relies on digital platforms to facilitate interactions between individuals and/or businesses, however, collaborative, long-term relationships are foundational to supply chains and sharing-economy relationships demand greater flexibility (Atkins & Gianiodis, 2021).

Finally, the rapid evolution of technology and consumer preferences are shaping new business models. The sharing economy represents an emerging trend that is transforming society and business today (Lee et al., 2018). The sharing economy has turned many industries upside down in the last decade. Companies need to rethink their business in the context of the sharing economy. Although the model has its positive and negative side effects, it can benefit many industries and economies in a sustainable way. Based on the scientometric review of a dataset of 2,229 scholarly publications from the Web of Science on the sharing economy, Klarin and Suseno (2021) suggest that further research should focus on examining the value creation of the sharing economy in terms of business models, and examine the sharing economy in other industries and sectors. In line with this statement, we examine the sharing economy in the supply-chain industry in the rest of the chapter.

9.2.2 The Relationship Between the Sharing Economy and the Supply-Chain Industry

Given the current economic situation and globalization, supply chains are becoming increasingly complex (Varma et al., 2006). The sharing-economy approach to supply chains offers many opportunities. First, it is necessary to shift the focus from the corporate level to the supply-chain level and also to align organizational goals with sustainability goals to address rising environmental and social concerns (Gold et al., 2010a, 2010b). From a business perspective, companies could engage in comanaged collaboration, which means sharing employees or physical assets, sharing technology, and sharing data or reports to meet customer demand in a more effective and timely manner. From an environmental perspective, supply-chain sharing could reduce greenhouse-gas emissions. A company could also partner with third-party delivery services to achieve same-day delivery or find new solutions to unsold inventory, such as renting to businesses and collecting data on which items are most popular to better meet the needs of future customers (Hunt, 2018).

In a recent study on the relationship between sharing economy and supply-chain management by Atkins and Gianiodis (2021), the supply-chain network is depicted, which includes a focal company as the central node and the sharing-economy companies (central dots). The customer companies are downstream, while the supplier and logistics companies are upstream. Logistics companies offer the transport, handling, and storage services from logistics networks, while supplier companies such as manufacturers and "procurement marketplaces" (Atkins & Gianiodis, 2021) form supplier networks. Downstream, from the central node is a customer network that consists of retail companies that connects sellers with a wide network of customers, auction companies, rental companies, and customer-service companies. The companies within and between networks use advanced software solutions and/or digital platforms to operate in a sharing-economy manner.

Depending on its position in the supply chain, the focal company may engage in the sharing economy as a service provider and look downward to a network of customers, or it may engage as a service user and look upward to networks of suppliers or logistics service providers. Indeed, depending on the perspective, one company's supplier network is another company's customer network (Figure 9.1).

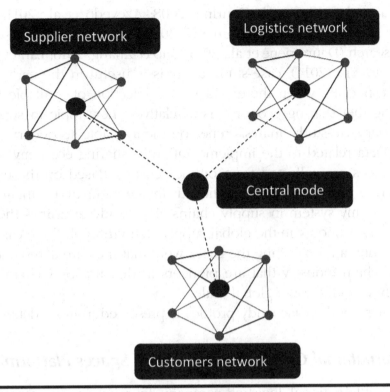

Figure 9.1   Sharing-Economy Supply-Chain Network.
Source: Author's work based on Atkins and Gianiodis (2021).

Logistics providers such as 3PL and 4PL are the main drivers of the sharing economy in the supply chain as they offer sharing services to their customers, such as higher utilization rates of transport vehicles, better utilization of warehouse space, reduced logistics costs and/or a lower carbon footprint (O'Byrne, 2020).

9.3 Materials and Methods

The aim of this chapter is to examine the concept of sharing economy, with special focus on the supply-chain industry. To achieve this, an analytical framework has been constructed based on previous literature on the sharing economy. The theoretical framework of the study helped the authors better understand the characteristics of the sharing economy and its unique features. Next, a case-study analysis is conducted, which is commonly used in supply-chain-related research (Seuring, 2008; Azevedo et al., 2011; Pagell & Wu, 2009; Pavlić Skender & Zaninović, 2020) as well as sharing-economy-related research (Daunorienė et al., 2015; Gao & Zhang, 2016; Lan et al., 2017). According to Yin (2014), case-study analysis is useful in the early stages of research, especially when there is a scarce selection of available literature. Considering that sharing economy is a relatively new topic in supply-chain research, our case-study analysis relies on the available secondary data from the field. Data related to the implementation of sharing economy in supply-chain practices are collected from online sources. Based on these data, we qualitatively analyze and discuss the advantages and disadvantages of the sharing-economy system in supply chains. This study examines the concept of the sharing economy in the global supply chain through three case studies. The main criteria for selecting the cases were that they are companies within the supply-chain industry that are pioneers in digital supply-chain solutions and that they operate on a global scale.

A summary of the case study profiles is presented in more detail below.

DHL International GmbH (Product: DHL Spaces Platform)

DHL is an international logistics company founded in the year 1969 and employs more than 400,000 people in over 220 countries. With more than 1.61 billion parcels delivered each year, DHL is a global leader in logistics. The company is divided into six divisions: Post and Packages, DHL Express, DHL Global Forwarding, DHL Freight, DHL Supply Chain, and DHL Parcel. The company uses advanced technology to shape, remodel, and facilitate the modern supply-chain industry. DHL is a leader in innovative business solutions and one of the first companies to adopt the sharing-economy business model. DHL is working on its "Strategy 2025—Delivering Excellence in a Digital World," that aims to connect people, and be both sustainable and technologically advanced (DHL, 2021a).

Uber Technologies Inc. (Product: Uber Freight Platform)

Uber Technologies Inc. is a technology company founded in the year 2009 and based in the United States. The company is known as Uber and is headquartered in San Francisco, California. Uber is present in over 900 cities around the world. Uber is a fast-growing global company that seems to be successful in adopting high-tech/innovative business models (PwC, 2015). Its services include ride-hailing, meal delivery, package delivery, courier services, freight transportation and, through a partnership with Lime, electric-bike and motorized-scooter rentals. Uber is also known as one of the largest and most popular companies in the sharing economy (Uber, 2021). Uber is an appropriate case-study model for the sharing-economy analysis due to its popularity (Lee et al., 2018).

Amazon (Product: Amazon Flex Platform)

Amazon was founded in the year 1994 as a small online company. Amazon.com, Inc. is a US multinational technology company focused on e-commerce, cloud computing, digital streaming, and artificial intelligence. Together with Google, Apple, Microsoft, and Facebook, Amazon presents one of the most successful and popular companies in the U.S. information-technology industry.

Amazon is a novel digital sharing-economy platform because it is changing the business ecosystems (Gong et al., 2019). The company has been called "one of the world's most influential economic and cultural forces" as well as the world's most valuable brand. Although Amazon's core business is online retail, the company offers many different transportation services under the Amazon brand to deliver packages, such as Amazon Air, Amazon Logistics, Amazon Prime Air, and Amazon Flex, which is one of the shared-economy services (Amazon, 2021).

9.4 Research Results and Discussion

The sharing-economy model is gaining more and more importance in business practice nowadays. It has positive implications for the business relationship in supply chains between potential market competitors. The sharing economy in the supply chain determines the requirement to manage the potential of companies and the relationships between them in a revolutionary way. In the supply chain, transportation and warehousing represent the most important sharing processes (Ocicka & Wieteska, 2017).

Warehouse Sharing—DHL Spaces Case Study

Warehouse sharing is a practice that is becoming increasingly popular in modern supply-chain business, especially in e-commerce. Shared warehouses are actually public warehouses used by many customers. Different customers share the warehouse space and all associated costs, such as space costs, warehouse-worker costs, equipment costs, and technology costs. Shared warehouses offer many advantages, for example, small businesses can enter new markets without having to make large investments in warehouses and long-term contracts. Shared warehouses are flexible in terms of supply-chain requirements; companies can use several small warehouses in different locations instead of running a large and central distribution center and are not forced to fill the entire warehouse capacity, but only the space they need. In this way, they avoid high fixed costs and risks. But besides that, it has other strategic advantages as it allows companies to store their inventory closer to their clients, speed up their velocity, and reduce their CO_2 emissions. For companies that sell seasonal products and need a lot of storage capacity at short notice, shared warehousing can be beneficial.

Shared warehousing is the ability to expand companies' product offerings, shorten delivery times, and enter new markets without incurring additional costs or time. Shared warehousing represents a cost-effective, nonbinding, and flexible business model (Ready Spaces, 2021). The shared-warehousing business model requires a platform that provides information about available warehouses, their location, capacity, and the ability to book the warehouse. DHL recognized the need for a platform that enables the practice of shared warehousing and invented the DHL Spaces platform. It is a digital warehouse locator that allows users to search for warehouse spaces in Europe, Middle East, and Africa. DHL Spaces shows users the location of the warehouse space, how many square meters are available, and provides contact information for booking the warehouse space (O'Byrne, 2020). Warehouse Locator is offered to existing DHL customers and expanding businesses. Users can find a variety of existing and newly developed space offerings in all sizes for short-, medium-, and long-term use (DHL, 2021b). Figure 9.2 illustrates the shared-warehouse business model.

Transport Sharing—Uber Freight and Amazon Flex Case Studies

The business model of shared transportation has already been put into practice in the supply chain. In order to meet demand while remaining profitable, logistics companies have developed solutions in which they combine small shipments (less than truckload—LTL) into one large shipment (full truckload—FTL) at consolidation centers (Mason & Harris, 2019, p. 18).

Before the consolidation point, smaller and more frequent deliveries were made by empty vehicles, while after the introduction of the consolidation point in the earlier phase of transport, deliveries were made in fuller vehicles

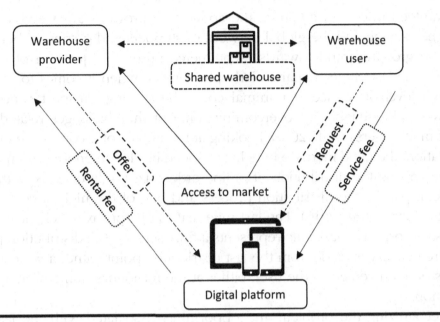

Figure 9.2 Shared-Warehouse Business Model.

Source: Authors' work based on DHL (2017).

and in a more economical and environmentally friendly way. However, this type of consolidation center involves a one-to-one "split": Two suppliers working together to set up and operate the consolidation center together. In many cases, other neighboring suppliers also had to be involved, and the location of the consolidation center was not always ideally located for the incoming customer, raising the question of how optimal the arrangements were.

The development of digital technology has created new opportunities for better utilization of all modes of transport and more optimized transport operations. Digital platforms allow providers and users better connections and access to information. Freight sharing offers opportunities to reduce/control costs while improving the level of service required for "last-mile" delivery. Numerous innovative examples are being brought forward and offered commercially (Mason & Harris, 2019), among which are Uber Freight and Amazon Flex services.

Uber Technologies Inc. launched Uber Freight in 2017 to match truck drivers with carriers, similar to how the company's ride-hailing app connects passengers seeking a ride with available drivers. The advantages of using Uber Freight are numerous, as the application offers the possibility to book transport 24 hours a day; it offers intelligent suggestions and transparent and guaranteed prices. In addition, the application provides an overview of live freight tracking and the global network of shippers and carriers (Uber, 2021).

The growing trend towards e-commerce raises the question of the "last mile." The "last mile" is particularly problematic when it comes to achieving a high level of service at minimal cost. The sharing-transport concept has shown to be suitable for overcoming some of the challenges related to the "last mile" (Joerss et al., 2016). Looking at the impact of e-commerce on transportation, the rapid increase in delivery speed has led to enormous challenges in organizing the distribution of online orders. Last-mile delivery is the most difficult part of the distribution process and one of the highest cost components (Joerss et al., 2016). The last mile makes up approximately 30% of total logistics costs. The last mile represents a final stage in the distribution process where delivery is made from the last distribution point, either a warehouse or a distribution center, to the user, either at the recipient's home or at a pickup location.

Recognizing the problem and opportunity associated with the last mile, Amazon Inc. launched a service called Amazon Flex in 2015. Amazon Flex works in such a way that actually anyone who owns a car can deliver an Amazon Prime product to homes or businesses. Amazon is turning to independent contractors in this way to handle their last-mile deliveries. Amazon Flex is known to handle some of the company's last-mile deliveries, which is beyond the capabilities of standard delivery companies with about 5 billion items shipped each year (O'Byrne, 2020).

9.5 Conclusion

The aim of this chapter was to examine the concept of the sharing economy in general, namely its possible positive and negative effects on economic growth and development. In addition, this research provides a specific insight into the current practice of the sharing economy in the supply-chain industry and assesses the challenges and opportunities of implementing the sharing economy in supply-chain business operations through three case-study examples from the transportation and warehousing businesses. There is obviously a gap in the literature dealing with the sharing-economy business model in the supply-chain industry. The reason for this is actually the immaturity of the application of the sharing-economy practice. The idea of sharing economy is not new, people have shared and rented goods for a long time, but the new business practice of sharing economy based on digital platforms and social technology is in its birth phase. The sharing economy was first introduced in urban transportation and hospitality, with Uber and Airbnb leading the way. Nowadays, however, it can be seen that the sharing-economy business model can be applied to many industries, although it has been shown to be particularly taken up in industries with large assets, such as mobility and hospitality.

Both the public and private sectors are undergoing dramatic change, and evaluating new business models is critical to achieving the triple bottom line, i.e., economic, social, and environmental concerns. The concept of the sharing economy could be the template for this; however, it is too early to confirm. Some positive impacts of applying the sharing economy are the use of underutilized resources, more efficient distribution of resources, flexible business models, and positive environmental impacts in terms of greenhouse-gas reduction. On the other hand, there are also negative sides of the sharing economy, such as lack of transparency and underpaid employers with limited rights, and lack of economic security. The analysis of the three case studies shows that the sharing-economy model has already been implemented in the supply-chain industry—especially in transportation and warehousing—but to a lesser extent. Sharing warehouses and transportation is based on digital platforms and offers many benefits to the business as it solves some crucial issues such as the high cost of renting an entire warehouse, location decision, and size of the warehouse. Warehouse sharing allows for better utilization and solves some inventory-management issues. In conjunction, transportation sharing also benefits from the high cost of investing in the fleet and all the additional costs associated with it. Transportation sharing also solves the high cost of last-mile delivery. Although case studies show positive examples, underpaid drivers and related transparency problems are present.

Finally, the positive patterns of the concept of sharing economy are evident, and it is expected that with the development of digital platforms, sharing in the supply chain will take its upswing. Its further implementation and development should have multiple impacts on supply-chain business and economic development as a whole. Although some positive patterns of the sharing-economy concept can be seen, it is not possible to draw accurate conclusions due to the short period of analysis and data limitations. Further research could be extended with interviewing different stakeholders in the supply-chain industry regarding their opinion on the future of the sharing economy. This research fills the gaps in the literature on the connection between sharing economy and the supply-chain industry. This work contributes to the existing body of knowledge by providing new insights into the best practices of the sharing economy and its positive and negative characteristics. The findings can guide future business decisions for policy makers, as well as supply-chain managers and founders of digital start-ups.

Acknowledgments

This paper was founded under the project line ZIP UNIRI of the University of Rijeka, for the project ZIP-UNIRI-130–9–20 (E-)education and Human Resources Development.

References

Amazon. (2021). Retrieved from: www.aboutamazon.com/?utm_source= gatewayandutm_medium=footer Available [September 1, 2021].

Atkins, R., & Gianiodis, P. (2021). An investigation at the intersection of the sharing economy and supply chain management: A strategic perspective. *International Journal of Logistics Research and Applications*. DOI: 10.1080/13675567.2021.1911970

Avital, M., Carroll, J. M., Hjalmarsson, A., Levina, N., Malhotra, A., & Sundararajan, A. (2015). The sharing economy: Friend or foe? In: T. Carte, A. Heinzl, & C. Urquhart (eds.), *Proceedings of the International Conference on Information Systems* (Vol. 36, pp. 1–8). Retrieved from: http://aisel.aisnet.org/cgi/viewcontent. cgi?article=1698&context=icis2015 Available [September 1, 2021].

Azevedo, S. G., Carvalho, H., & Cruz Machado, V. (2011). The influence of green practices on supply chain performance: A case study approach. *Transportation Research Part E: Logistics and Transportation Review*, 47(6), 850–871. DOI: 10.1016/j.tre.2011.05.017

Bachnik, K. (2016). Sustainable consumption through the sharing economy. *Research Papers of Wrocław University of Economics*, *423*, 35–44. DOI: 10.15611/pn.2016.423.03

Benkler, Y. (2006). *The Wealth of Networks: How Social Production Transforms Markets and Freedom*. New Haven and London: Yale University Press.

Boar, A., Bastida, R., & Marimon, F. (2020). A systematic literature review: Relationships between the sharing economy, sustainability and sustainable development goals. *Sustainability*, *12*(17), 1–14. DOI: 10.3390/su12176744

Bonciu, F., & Balgar, A. (2016). Sharing economy as contributor to sustainable growth, an eu perspective. *Romanian Journal of European Affairs*, *16*(2), 36–45. Retrieved from: https://heinonline.org/HOL/Page?collection=journalsa ndhandle=hein.journals/rojaeuf16andid=131andmen_tab=srchresults Available [September 1, 2021].

Dabbous, A., & Tarhini, A. (2021). Does sharing economy promote sustainable economic development and energy efficiency? Evidence from OECD countries. *Journal of Innovation & Knowledge*, *6*(1), 58–68. DOI: 10.1016/j.jik.2020.11.001

Daunorienė, A., Drakšaitė, A., Vytautas, S., & Valodkienė, G. (2015). Evaluating sustainability of sharing economy business models. *Procedia: Social and Behavioral Sciences, 213*, 836–841. DOI: 10.1016/j.sbspro.2015.11.486

DHL. (2017). Retrieved from: www.dhl.com/content/dam/downloads/g0/about_us/logistics_insights/DHLTrend_Report_Sharing_Economy.pdf Available [September 2, 2021].

DHL. (2021a). Retrieved from: www.dhl.com/global-en/home/about-us.html Available [September 2, 2021].

DHL. (2021b). Retrieved from: https://spaces.dhl.com/ Available [September 2, 2021].

Elkington, J. (1998). *Cannibals with Forks: The Triple Bottom Line of the 21st Century Business.* Stoney Creek, CT: New Society Publishers.

Gao, S., & Zhang, X. (2016). Understanding business models in the sharing economy in China: A case study. In: Y. Dwivedi, et al. (eds.), *Lecture Notes in Computer Science: Vol. 9844. Social Media: The Good, the Bad, and the Ugly* (pp. 661–672). Switzerland: Springer. DOI: 10.1007/978-3-319-45234-0_59.

Gold, S., Seuring, S., & Beske, P. (2010a). The constructs of sustainable supply chain management: A content analysis based on published case studies. *Progress in Industrial Ecology: An International Journal, 7*(2), 114–137. DOI: 10.1504/PIE.2010.036045

Gold, S., Seuring, S., & Beske, P. (2010b). Sustainable supply chain management and inter-organisational resources: A literature review. *Corporate Social Responsibility and Environmental Management, 17*(4), 230–245. DOI: 10.1002/csr.207

Gong, D., Liu, S., Liu, J., & Ren, L. (2019). Who benefits from online financing? A sharing economy E-tailing platform perspective. *International Journal of Production Economics, 222*(C). DOI: 10.1016/j.ijpe.2019.09.011

Hunt, E. (2018). *The Sharing Economy: An Effective Model for Supply Chain Management?* Retrieved from: www.kinaxis.com/en/blog/the-sharing-economy-an-effective-model-for-supply-chain-management Available [July 24, 2021].

Ježić, Z. (2015). Važnost tehnologije, istraživanja i razvoja i inovacija u konkurentnome gospodarstvu zasnovanome na znanju [The importance of technology, research and development and innovation in a competitive knowledge-based economy]. In: V. Kandžija (ed.), *Razvoj gospodarske konkurentnostu Republike Hrvatske kao članice EU* [Development of Economic Competitiveness of the Republic of Croatia as a Member of the EU] (pp. 59–71). Ekonomski fakultet u Rijeci. Retrieved from: www.bib.irb.hr/823573 Available [July 24, 2021].

Joerss, M., Schröder, J., Neuhaus, F., Klink, C., & Mann, F. (2016). *Parcel Delivery: The Future of Last Mile.* Retrieved from: https://bdkep.de/files/bdkep-dateien/pdf/2016_the_future_of_last_mile.pdf [September 2, 2021].

Kathan, W., Matzler, K., & Veider, V. (2016). The sharing economy: Your business model's friend or foe? *Business Horizons, 59*(6), 663–672. DOI: 10.1016/j.bushor.2016.06.006

Klarin, A., & Suseno, Y. (2021). A state-of-the-art review of the sharing economy: Scientometric mapping of the scholarship. *Journal of Business Research, 126*, 250–262. DOI: 10.1016/j.jbusres.2020.12.063

Lan, J., Ma, Y., Zhu, D., Mangalagiu, D., & Thornton, T. F. (2017). Enabling value co-creation in the sharing economy: The case of mobike. *Sustainability, 9*(9), 1–20. DOI: 10.3390/su9091504.

Lee, Z. W. Y., Chan, T. K. H., Balaji, M. S., & Chong, A. Y.-L. (2018). Why people participate in the sharing economy: An empirical investigation of Uber. *Internet Research, 28*(3), 829–850. DOI: 10.1108/IntR-01-2017-0037

Mason, R., & Harris, I. (2019). Retrieved from: https://assets.publishing.service.gov.uk/government/uploads/system/uploads/attachment_data/file/777699/fom_freight_sharing_economy.pdf Available [September 2, 2021].

Miller, S. R. (2016). First principles for regulating the sharing economy. *Harvard Journal on Legislation, 147*, 149–202. Retrieved from: https://core.ac.uk/download/pdf/217442016.pdf Available [September 2, 2021].

Nica, E., & Potcovaru, A. M. (2015). The social sustainability of the sharing economy. *Economics, Management, and Financial Markets, 10*(4), 69–75.

O'Byrne, R. (2020). *Boom Time for the Shared Economy within Supply Chain.* Retrieved from: www.logisticsbureau.com/boom-time-for-the-shared-economy-within-supply-chain/ Available [July 27, 2021].

Ocicka, B., & Wieteska, G. (2017). Sharing economy in logistics and supply chain management. *LogForum Scientific Journal of Logistics, 13*(2), 183–193. DOI: 10.17270/J.LOG.2017.2.6

Owyang, J., Tran, C., & Silva, C. (2013). *The Collaborative Economy.* A Market Definition Report. Retrieved from: www.altimetergroup.com Available [July 24, 2021].

Pagell, M., & Wu, Z. (2009). Building a more complete theory of sustainable supply chain management using case studies of 10 exemplars. *Journal of Supply Chain Management, 45*(32), 37–56. DOI: 10.1111/j.1745-493X.2009.03162.x

Pavlić Skender, H., & Zaninović, P. A. (2020). Perspectives of blockchain technology for sustainable supply chains. In: A. Kolinski, D. Dujak, & P. Golinska-Dawson (eds.), *Integration of Information Flow for Greening Supply Chain Management* (pp. 77–92). Switzerland: Springer International Publishing. DOI: 10.1007/978-3-030-24355-5

PwC. (2015). Retrieved from: pwc-consumer-intelligence-series-the-sharing-economy.pdf Available [July 27, 2021].

Ready Spaces. (2021). Retrieved from: https://readyspaces.com/case-study/what-is-shared-warehousing/ Available [July 27, 2021].

Seuring, S. (2008). Assessing the rigor of case study research in supply chain management. *Supply Chain Management, 13*(2), 128–137. DOI: 10.1108/13598540810860967

Tabcum Jr., S. (2019) *The Sharing Economy Is Still Growing, And Businesses Should Take Note.* Retrieved from: www.forbes.com/sites/forbeslacouncil/2019/03/04/the-sharing-economy-is-still-growing-and-businesses-should-take-note/?sh=5dc321f74c33 Available [July 27, 2021].

Uber. (2021). Retrieved from: www.uber.com/hr/en/about/ Available [September 2, 2021].

United Nations. (2020). Retrieved from: www.un.org/development/desa/dpad/wp-content/uploads/sites/45/publication/FTQ_Feb2020.pdf Available [September 2, 2021].

Varma, S., Wadhwa, S., & Deshmukh, S. G. (2006). Implementing supply chain management in a firm: issues and remedies. *Asia Pacific Journal of Marketing and Logistics, 18*(3), 223–243. DOI: 10.1108/13555850610675670/full/html

Yin, R. K. (2014). *Case Study Research: Design and Methods (Applied Social Research Methods)* (5th ed.). Thousand Oaks, CA: Sage Publications.

SUSTAINABLE LOGISTICS

Applications and Challenges

Chapter 10

Smart Logistics: Sustainable Distribution in the Age of the Internet of Things

Maria Bajak

Cracow University of Economics, Poland

Contents

10.1 Introduction

The main objective of this chapter is to analyze and evaluate the implementation of the concept of sustainable distribution using solutions offered by the

DOI: 10.4324/9781003304364-13

Internet of Things. The undertaken discussion comprises a review of world literature on the subject and an analysis of nine projects in the area of land, water, and air transport. The presented considerations relate to SMART logistics and sustainable development.

Undoubtedly, the development of information and communication technologies (ICT) has had a major impact on the contemporary world. The dynamic development of computer networks, which link everybody and everything (M. Castells' information-technology paradigm), facilitates more effective planning, organization, and management of logistics resources in the area of distribution. Digital technologies play a crucial role in increasing the productivity of vehicles and improving supply-chain-management processes, allowing for the development of more economical, safe, and environmentally friendly transport systems (Carrasco-Gallego & Moreno-Romero, 2010 Liu et al., 2019). The mass-scale development of SMART tools (e.g., applications, sensors, artificial intelligence) strengthens horizontal and vertical integration between particular links of supply chains (Schrauf & Berrtram, 2016; Kayikci, 2018). The use of information and communication technologies facilitates the development of networks of interrelated devices referred to as the Internet of Things (Kortuem et al., 2010; Dobbs et al., 2016; Buntak et al., 2019). The extension of this concept, which consists of managing the transport of people and goods using integrated IT infrastructure, facilitating its automatization and control, can be referred to as SMART logistics.

10.2 The Triple Foundation of Sustainable Development vs. Logistics

Presently, sustainable development is a significant concept in conducting economic activities. The World Commission on the Environment and Development defines it as development "which meets the needs of the present generation without compromising the ability of future generations to meet their needs" (Omri & Ben Mabrouk, 2020). Its practical implementation relates to various economic and social processes including those in the field of logistics.

The specificity of the TSL sector, particularly its great development potential, openness to innovation, and impact on the effectiveness of the economy and the quality of life, contributes to its special position in the area of sustainable development. Sustainable distribution refers to the concept and principles of sustainability (Portney, 2015; Thiele, 2016; Filho et al., 2019), and can be defined as an effort aimed at adapting the functions, processes, and practices of delivering goods and services to economic, social, and environmental requirements. This approach to distribution corresponds to the concept of the triple bottom line, developed by J. Elkington (1994). According to this concept, sustainable development relies on three elements: The people, the planet, and profit. These elements can be defined as economic, social, and environmental factors, which should be considered in designing sustainable solutions (Agrawal & Singh, 2019). These components can be referred to as logistics processes:

Economic [Profit]

This element refers to the use of effective and innovative solutions in transport and shipping, aimed at considerably cutting costs during the entire life cycle of vehicles, machines, and buildings (Ang et al., 2017; Tiwong et al., 2019). It relates to all outlays including the following:

1) Implementation costs—they are incurred in connection with developing solutions, testing, and implementation processes (Gonzales-Feliu, 2018);
2) costs of use—all outlays related to the use of a solution and possible servicing (Digiesi et al., 2015);
3) disposal costs—expenditure resulting from conducting recalls, liquidations, or processing (Gupta, 2016).

Social [People]

This component refers to ensuring the comfort, ergonomics, and safety of implemented solutions. A special role is played in cooperation with other elements of space, the comfort of recipients and third parties, as well as an aesthetic approach to infrastructure and means of transport (Eden et al., 2017; Garau & Pavan, 2018, Hurtová et al., 2018). The issues of key significance relate to the following:

1) The approval of a project—considering the social reception of an implemented solution and the interests of its future users (Hickson & Owen, 2015);
2) the availability of the infrastructure—ensuring an appropriate level of user safety and adjusting a solution to user needs (Regiani, 2019; Laasch, 2021);
3) the social impact—integrating a project with the environment, mitigating its negative effects, and providing benefits across society (Filho, 2021).

Ecological [Planet]

This refers to mitigating a negative impact of supply chains on the natural environment and climate. It is mainly related to the use of ecological solutions, including the use of innovative materials and technologies (Sarkis et al., 2002; Cosimato & Troisi, 2014) as well as logistics-process organization, distribution route optimization, and the so-called "traveling-salesman problem," identified in econometrics and operational research. A special role is played by adapting projects in the following areas:

1) Energy efficiency—reducing the use of natural resources, energy recovery, adapting to external conditions (Hasanuzzaman & Rahim, 2019; Yang, 2019);
2) emission reductions—controlling and reducing pollution, minimizing the effects of noise, light, and odors (Mulligan, 2019; Fortuński, 2020);
3) reducing waste—the effective use of available resources, ensuring recycling processes (Lemaire & Limbourg, 2019);
4) protecting natural resources—coexistence with an ecosystem, mitigating the negative effects of implemented solutions on flora and fauna (Grant et al., 2017).

The concept of the triple bottom line is strongly correlated with the UN 2030 Agenda for Sustainable Development. The document identifies seventeen goals that set directions for implementing the concept of sustainable development. It should be noted that despite the fact that the Agenda's particular goals can be referred to as the particular pillars of sustainable development (Table 10.1), they also, in practice, support the implementation of the remaining elements of the triple bottom line. In the first place, attention should be given to the double meaning of transport and shipping in this area. On the one hand, logistics can independently achieve sustainable-development goals (through its proper functioning), but, on the other hand, it supports the activities of market institutions from other industries (through the efficient delivery of materials and other resources).

10.3 Smart Solutions in Logistics

Digitalization is inseparably linked to the development of transport and shipment systems. Technological development plays a crucial role in the context

Table 10.1 Sustainable Development Goals vs. the Triple Bottom Line and Logistics.

The main component of the Triple Bottom Line	*The sustainable development goal according to the United Nations*	*Description of the goal*	*Reference to logistics*
Economic [profit]	(8) Decent Work and Economic Growth	Increased organizational efficiency, the promotion of economic development, and job creation.	Reduced costs of transport and warehousing, corporate development and modernization, and employing staff.
	(17) Partnerships for Goals	Ensuring access to effective public institutions, and cooperation between organizations.	Joint achievement of sustainable goals with partners, and cooperation with the social and economic environment.
Social [people]	(1) No Poverty	Fighting poverty and ensuring decent living conditions for everybody.	Job creation, offering decent compensation to employees.
	(2) Zero Hunger	Eliminating hunger, ensuring access to high-quality food, and stabilizing food prices.	Improvements in food supply chains, and food-inventory-management optimization.
	(3) Good Health and Well-Being	Providing universal access to medical services, and increasing people's safety.	Ensuring the safety of adopted solutions, reducing accident rates, and improvements in the supply of medical equipment.
	(4) Quality Education	Increasing levels of education in society and providing opportunities for its development.	Enlarging employees' knowledge, and developing their skills and competencies.
	(5) Gender Equality	Eliminating gender discrimination.	Employment and equal treatment of genders.
	(9) Industry, Innovation, and Infrastructure	Increasing the quality and reliability of infrastructure, supporting R&D and innovation.	The use of modern materials and technologies, the use of innovative solutions aimed at improving the movement of goods and ensuring safety.

(Continued)

Table 10.1 *(Continued)* **Sustainable Development Goals vs. the Triple Bottom Line and Logistics.**

The main component of the Triple Bottom Line	The sustainable development goal according to the United Nations	Description of the goal	Reference to logistics
	(10) Reducing Inequality	Reducing discriminatory laws and practices, and closing social gaps.	Providing access to goods in transport-excluded areas, ensuring equal employment opportunities.
	(11) Sustainable Cities and Communities	Creating safe and sustainable living spaces, adjusted to social needs.	Optimizing the movement of people and goods, supporting city and regional development through an integrated logistics network.
	(16) Peace, Justice, and Strong Institutions	Creating effective and responsible institutions, and improvements in legislation.	Supporting socially important values and the decent treatment of stakeholders.
Ecological [planet]	(6) Clean Water and Sanitation	Reducing water pollution and the generation of waste, increasing water-management effectiveness.	Mitigating the negative impact of supply chains on water resources and the effective management of water resources.
	(7) Affordable and Clean Energy	Rationalizing energy management and the use of renewable energy sources.	The use of ecological energy sources, energy recovery, and reduced use of energy by logistics networks.
	(12) Responsible Consumption and Production	Promoting responsible consumption and production, and a circular economy.	Balancing supply chains, reducing waste, the recovery of raw materials, and implementing reverse logistics.
	(13) Climate Action	Mitigating the impact of climate change.	Reducing exhaust emissions, mitigating the negative effect of transport and warehousing on the climate.

Table 10.1 *(Continued)*   Sustainable Development Goals vs. the Triple Bottom Line and Logistics.

The main component of the Triple Bottom Line	*The sustainable development goal according to the United Nations*	*Description of the goal*	*Reference to logistics*
	(14) Life Below Water	Protecting maritime and coastal ecosystems, reducing water pollution.	Reducing water pollution by supply chains and reducing ship accidents and breakdowns.
	(15) Life On Land	Reducing the devastation of land spaces, protecting the flora and fauna, and supporting biodiversity.	The sustainable use of ecosystems, reducing environmental degradation resulting from transport and warehousing.

Source: Author's research based on the United Nations (2015); Elkington (1994).

of sustainable development and in implementing the concept of the triple bottom line. It provides opportunities for introducing SMART solutions, which result from the development of networks of interrelated devices integrating buildings, companies, or entire cities. A special function in this area is performed by the Internet of Things systems (IoT). They represent another step towards social and economic digitalization (Rose et al., 2015), in which interrelated objects and devices collect and analyze data, as well as control and optimize processes in all areas of human life and economic activity (Dobbs et al., 2016). The "always connect" paradigm is a significant characteristic of the Internet of Things. It is of key significance to logistics, enabling the monitoring of the current status of transported goods (Tadejko, 2015) and coordinating demand-and-supply time-related factors. In such systems, sensors and IoT elements exchange information via wired and wireless communication channels. It allows for the efficient exchange of information, which translates into logistics process harmonization, thus creating a new dimension of integrating IT systems and networks (Yu et al., 2020).

Transport solutions that make use of complex IoT networks and other advanced IT solutions, such as artificial intelligence mechanisms, are commonly referred to as SMART. The functioning of this system is controlled and optimized, allowing it to achieve economic, social, and ecological benefits (Jia et al., 2019). ICT technologies in logistics systems facilitate intermodality and ensure the effectiveness of all supply-chain stages (Carrasco-Gallego

& Moreno-Romero, 2010; Tadejko, 2015), contributing to the practical implementation of the sustainable-development concept. The major benefits of implementing SMART logistics include cost cutting, reduced delivery time and failure rates, greater reliability and flexibility (economic benefits), safety and accessibility (social benefits), and reductions in waste and pollution (ecological benefit) (Kayikci, 2018).

The development of SMART logistics has an impact on the entire process of the movement of goods and their components. Benefits of implementing integrated IT systems relate to six areas:

1) Production—process optimization, an adaptation of processes to market needs, and a reduced generation of waste (Zhou & Piramuthu, 2013);

2) transport and procurement—the identification and optimization, and reduction in costs and risk, of increased process effectiveness (Shin & Eksioglu, 2015; Kamble et al., 2019), as well as improvements in the movement of goods and more effective control and coordination of supply chains (Ben-Daya et al., 2019);

3) warehousing—reduced costs, increased safety, process accuracy and productivity, the detection of errors (Sagaya-Selvaraj & Anusha, 2021), and the identification and monitoring of resources aimed at optimizing space management (Kamali, 2019);

4) customer service—improvements in supply chains aimed at better satisfying customer needs (Gružauskas et al., 2018), the integration of physical and information streams, the coordination of production and promotion activities (Bertolini et al., 2013), the analyses of data collected by systems to create innovation, increasing brand competitiveness and brand loyalty (Öztayşi et al., 2009);

5) transfer of data—increasing the effectiveness of the exchange of data between partners, leading to increased trust and collaboration (Piramuthu et al., 2015; Feng et al., 2020), the increased identifiability of goods, and the transparency of operations (Attaran, 2020; Merkaš et al., 2020), stimulating logistics processes based on forecasts (Gu & Liu, 2013);

6) recycling—implementing reverse logistics, improving and optimizing the movement of goods from the beginning to the end of a supply chain (Asif, 2011; Usama & Ramish, 2020), estimating the value and utility of residual products (Condea et al., 2010; Kongar et al., 2015), and process integration as part of a closed-loop supply chain (CLSC) (Gu & Liu, 2013; Hu et al., 2021).

The implementation of integrated IT solutions can contribute to changes in the interpretation of logistics and focus the business on intelligent, productive, and sustainable systems of digital logistics (Schrauf & Berrtram, 2016).

10.4 The Research Method

The main objective of this chapter is to analyze and assess the implementation of sustainable distribution using the Internet of Things solutions. The achievement of this objective is based on an analysis and assessment of the actual implementation of systems that use SMART solutions in land, water, and air distribution. The analysis is based on case research—an in-depth analysis of empirical material (using primary and secondary data) to explore relevant processes and their context (Rashid et al., 2019). Because of the character of the researched problem, the analysis is based on the combination of nine different case studies—not on one case as is frequently practiced. It allows for identifying differences and similarities between particular cases. Correlations are presented in tables, which is a common practice in this method of research (Miles et al., 2019). It serves to deepen the presented findings, and identify links between the researched cases (Halkias & Neubert, 2020). In this chapter, correlations between the analyzed cases allow for creating a model of SMART solutions in implementing the principles of sustainable distribution.

Because of the dynamic development of technologies related to the Internet of Things and their numerous implementations in logistics, the analysis is based on selected projects from the perspective of the main research goal. The selection of information about specific projects was preceded by the search of websites aimed at finding ecological competitions and institutions granting sustainable-development certificates. The following criteria were adopted:

1) Spectacular cases of implementing sustainable-development concepts;
2) the use of the Internet of Things;
3) the possibility of disseminating employed solutions by other institutions;
4) prospects for further improvements of the presented system.

Finally, three case studies were conducted for each type of distribution—by land, water, and air. For each area, one of the three components was selected: A handling terminal, a vehicle, and a logistics operator. In the first place, the analysis focused on the benefits of the use of IoT in implemented solutions as well as the main objectives of implemented systems. The analysis was conducted using available secondary sources. It comprised selected distribution systems and their technical specifications. The analysis was also based on available scientific and specialized literature, interviews, articles, and expert opinions. The particular cases were also analyzed from the perspective of their compliance with the United Nations 2030 Agenda for Sustainable Development. It allowed assessing the main areas of implementing sustainable-development concepts in supporting distribution systems with SMART solutions.

10.5 The Results

The study comprises nine carefully selected projects representing land distribution (Getafe Terminal Logistics Centre, IVECO S-Way Np 460, DB Cargo UK), water distribution (Port of Le Havre, MV Yara Birkeland, Hamburg Süd), and air distribution (Dallas Fort Worth International Airport, Boeing 777F, Air France-KLM Cargo). Each mode of transport is referred to as one significant component of a distribution system: One handling terminal, a vehicle, and a logistics operator (Table 10.2). A synthetic representation of the specificity of the selected cases is based on the description of the main objectives of implementing the Internet of Things systems in particular cases. They refer to the main reasons for which organizations decide to use SMART solutions, and they are identified based on available documentation and seasonal reports. Moreover, attention is given to the characteristic features of projects, which results indirectly from the use of intelligent systems, e.g., granted certificates or prizes.

The conducted analysis also aimed at finding out whether the adopted solutions met the criteria of UN sustainable goals as a result of the use of IoT technologies (2016). On average, the analyzed cases fulfill the requirements of nine sustainable-development goals, and the difference between the smallest and the largest number of achieved goals is four (Table 10.3). However, it is not possible to indicate that the analysis translates to a general degree of sustainability of the particular solutions. Some of them are focused on achieving a smaller number of goals, while others comprise a wider spectrum of functionalities, but are less dedicated to meeting specific criteria. The average number of achieved goals for inland transport (8), water transport (9.67), and air transport (9.33) are similar. However, it is possible to identify specific goals corresponding to the particular areas of distribution. A significant role in land and air transport

Table 10.2 **Review of Analyzed Solutions.**

Number of the Project	Name	Country	Type	Main objectives of implementation	Characteristic features
				Land distribution	
1.	Getafe Terminal Logistics Centre	Spain	Handling terminal	—reduction in CO_2 emissions —integration with the environment —mitigating negative effects on the environment	—holder of BREEAM Excellent certificate
2.	IVECO S-Way Np 460	Italy	Vehicle	—lower fuel consumption —reduced gas emissions —driver support and safety	—winner of "Sustainable Truck of the Year 2021" —the widest range in this category of vehicles
3.	DB Cargo UK	United Kingdom	Operator	—use of ecological fuels and reduced CO_2 emissions —cargo location detection —the more effective management of carriages and improved handling operations	—winner of the competition including "Best Rail Freight Operator" in 2018, and "Rail Freight and Logistics Excellence Award" in 2021
				Water distribution	
4.	HAROPA, Port of Le Havre	France	Handling terminal	—mitigating the impact of port and industrial activities on the environment —integration with the social environment —improvements in supply chains	—several world prizes were awarded for implemented solutions including The AFLAS Award (2015, 2016, 2017, 2020—Best Green Seaport); IBJ Award (2012, 2013, 2016—Best Solid Bulk Port)
5.	MV Yara Birkeland	Norway	Vehicle	—emission-free and autonomous container transport —use of all-electric drive —reduction in noise, NO_x, CO_2, and waste	—the first emission-free commercial ship in the world —winner of many prizes including The Norwegian Industry Climate Prize (2018), Green Award—Special Prize (2019)

(Continued)

Table 10.2 (Continued)   Review of Analyzed Solutions.

Number of the Project	Name	Country	Type	Main objectives of implementation	Characteristic features
6.	Hamburg Süd	Germany	Operator	—remote container monitoring and management —reduction in greenhouse gases and pollution —increased energy efficiency	—winner of The AFLAS Award (2019, 2020)—Best Green Shipping Line; Supplier Excellence Award (2019); Global Freight Award—Environment (2018)
				Air distribution	
7.	Dallas Fort Worth International Airport	The United States of America	Handling terminal	—protection of natural resources and increased operating potential —use of natural energy sources —strengthening employee competencies and potential	—the first Carbon Neutral Airport in North America, the largest in the world —holder of the highest rank (Transition) in Airport Carbon Accreditation
8.	Boeing 777F	The United States of America	Vehicle	—reduction in CO_2 emissions and pollution —productivity and safety optimization —intelligent route adjustment, —automated cockpit adjustment to cargo and external factors	—the first carbon-neutral cargo flight
9.	Singapore Airlines Cargo	Singapore	Operator	—reduced consumption of energy, waste generation, and CO_2 emissions —increased effectiveness of air operations, —integration of supply-chain management	—the world's most frequently awarded airline: The AFLAS Award (2020, 2019)—Best Green Airline; ACE Awards, Top Carriers—Gold (2019); ACSA Feather Awards—Best Cargo Airline (2018).

Source: Author's research based on AFLAS Awards (2020); Boeing (2020); DB Cargo (2020; 2021); DFW Airport (2020); Goodman (2021); Hamburg Süd Line (2021); Haropa Ports (2021); Iveco (2021); Singapore Airlines (2021), Yara (2021).

Table 10.3 Achievement of Sustainable-Development Goals Resulting from Implemented Solutions in Case Research.

Sustainable Development Goals by United Nations	Number of the Project								
	1	2	3	4	5	6	7	8	9
(1) No Poverty	-	-	-	-	-	-	-	-	-
(2) Zero Hunger	-	-	-	-	-	-	-	-	-
(3) Good Health and Well-Being	✓	✓	✓	✓	-	✓	✓	✓	✓
(4) Quality Education	-	-	-	-	-	-	-	-	-
(5) Gender Equality	-	-	-	-	-	-	-	-	-
(6) Clean Water and Sanitation	-	-	-	✓	✓	✓	-	-	✓
(7) Affordable and Clean Energy	✓	✓	✓	✓	✓	✓	✓	✓	✓
(8) Decent Work and Economic Growth	✓	✓	✓	✓	✓	✓	✓	✓	✓
(9) Industry, Innovation, and Infrastructure	✓	✓	✓	✓	✓	✓	✓	✓	✓
(10) Reducing Inequality	-	-	-	-	-	-	✓	-	-
(11) Sustainable Cities and Communities	✓	-	✓	✓	-	-	✓	-	✓
(12) Responsible Consumption and Production	✓	✓	✓	✓	✓	✓	✓	✓	✓
(13) Climate Action	✓	✓	✓	✓	✓	✓	✓	✓	✓
(14) Life Below Water	-	-	-	✓	✓	✓	-	-	-
(15) Life On Land	✓	✓	✓	✓	✓	-	✓	-	✓
(16) Peace, Justice, and Strong Institutions	-	-	-	-	-	-	✓	-	-
(17) Partnerships for Goals	-	-	✓	✓	✓	✓	✓	✓	✓

Legend:

✓ compliance with SMART solutions with sustainable-development goals,
- failure to achieve a sustainable-development goal as a result of SMART solutions

Source: Author's research.

is played by integration with the social environment (Sustainable Cities and Communities), and also, in the case of land transport, the concern with flora and fauna (Life On Land). Water distribution, on the other hand, focuses on water and its life (Clean Water and Sanitation; Life Below Water).

The analysis indicates that five of the UN sustainable-development goals (Figure 10.1) are achieved by all the analyzed solutions: Affordable and Clean Energy; Decent Work and Economic Growth; Industry, Innovation, and Infrastructure; Responsible Consumption and Production; and Climate Action. On the other hand, the analyzed cases do not meet any of the requirements related to four UN goals: No Poverty; Zero Hunger; Quality Education; Gender Equality. However, the fact that a given goal is not achieved despite the use of SMART solutions does not indicate that the analyzed entities disregard this goal. In many cases, goals are achieved as part of other institutional policies which are not directly related to IoT solutions. Moreover, the analysis of the

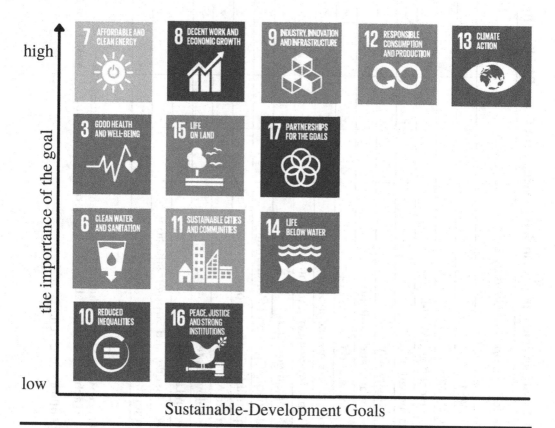

Figure 10.1 The Importance of the Goals.

Source: Author's research.

organizations which deal with the transport of both goods and passengers focuses only on cargo-related solutions.

The significance of UN sustainable-development goals is different in particular analyzed cases. Despite a small number of goals regarded as fully related to the economic component, it is they that are the most significant in SMART distribution (level of implementation = 88.9%) among the analyzed solutions. Also, a crucial role in corporate activities is played by ecological goals (level of implementation = 75.93%). It should be noted that this area of activity attributes great significance to goals related to reductions in energy consumption and the use of materials (Affordable and Clean Energy; Responsible Consumption and Production). The achievement of such goals translates to a company's long-term financial savings. Social goals play the least significant role in distribution (level of implementation = 29.63%). Interestingly, also, in this case, the most significant goal relates to development and increased effectiveness (Industry, Innovation, and Infrastructure), which is strongly linked to an organization's economic benefits. However, from the perspective of logistics, it can be expected that despite a low level of achieving social goals in the distribution of goods (29.63%), in the case of passenger transport, the performance of this task is much more significant—cargo movements do not much rely on interactions with people.

10.6 Discussing the Results of Other People's Research

These considerations combine three important areas: Distribution, sustainable development, and SMART technologies. There is still a lack of publications on this topic in the literature—most articles touch upon two of the indicated topics at most. However, there is no doubt that the development of digital systems and their implementation in supply chains, on the one hand, contribute to the expansion of the logistics industry (Buntak et al., 2019; Witkowski, 2017) and, on the other hand, support its sustainability (Liu et al., 2019; Ghahremani Nahr et al., 2021). When analyzing the digitalization of distribution processes, resources, practices, and functions, it should be pointed out that the role of systems from the Internet of Things area revolves around their monitoring, automation, control, and optimization (cf. Heppelmann & Porter, 2014). It is possible through the functions of IoT programs, such as the identification and tagging of objects, their location and positioning management, autonomous system management, data collection and analysis, an adaptation of processes to current conditions, as well as error capture, repair, and prevention (cf. Miller, 2018, Chbaik et al., 2021).

These tasks can be performed at any stage of the distribution process and concern any of its elements (Ferreira et al., 2010; Golpîra et al., 2021). To implement them, various technologies are used, as well as data-transmission standards, such as, for example, Wi-Fi, NFC, BLE, UWB, LoRaWAN, and ZigBee (Pundir et al., 2019; Ding et al., 2020; Machaj et al., 2021), including systems that are a combination of these solutions (Tabaa et al., 2020). Such integration strengthens their innovativeness and allows for the better acceleration of their potential. As a result, it is aligned with market needs in the areas of profitability, society, and the environment and are, therefore, more sustainable.

The multitude of advantages of IoT systems in distribution is somewhat counterbalanced by certain risks associated with the use of SMART technology in supply chains. First of all, this concerns the problem with privacy and exposure to hacking attacks (FBI, 2018; Gupta, 2019), but also the difficulties related to financing such investments (Chang & Zhu, 2019; Bajak, 2021). In addition, human-factor challenges are indicated regarding the need to acquire new knowledge and skills related to the operation of the systems (Guarda et al., 2017; Nagy et al., 2018). Despite some barriers, there is no doubt that the use of new technologies in distribution is a common and necessary phenomenon that affects the quality and efficiency of the supply chain. Indeed, the Internet of Things is the technology that, according to a McKinsey report, is expected to have the greatest impact on the functioning of organizations in the upcoming years, even overtaking artificial intelligence and cloud infrastructure (McKinsey, 2021). The implementation of such systems should, therefore, be actively supported, primarily through education and financial support. In this area, it is particularly important to point out the need for the government to support such sustainable projects. This assistance may be provided, for example, through subsidies, preferential loans, tax exemptions, as well as nonfinancial forms of support, such as substantive and legal support or as training and courses. As a result, it brings mutual benefits—on the one hand, it supports the development of enterprises and the economy and, on the other hand, it helps to achieve social and environmental goals.

10.7 Implications for Theory and Practice

The conducted research study indicates that from the perspective of the 2030 Agenda for Sustainable Development and SMART solutions, the implementation of projects is focused on their economic component. The analyzed organizations make efforts to increase the effectiveness of adopted solutions and generate savings, being simultaneously concerned about social and environmental issues. SMART solutions perform various functions in the analyzed entities. A detailed analysis indicates that the functions of SMART systems are related to process monitoring and facilitating their automatization. In the next step, specific activities are subjected to control and optimized with the use of relevant technologies. The full implementation of all tasks allows us to refer to them as autonomous solutions. The spectrum of the functionalities of SMART systems is inseparably linked to implemented logistics processes, available resources, corporate practices, and supply-chain functions. They, in turn, are determined by a type of distribution (land, water, or air). All these elements affect the scope and degree of achieving sustainable-development goals. These correlations allow for the development of a model for achieving sustainable-development goals in the context of the use of SMART systems in distribution (Figure 10.2).

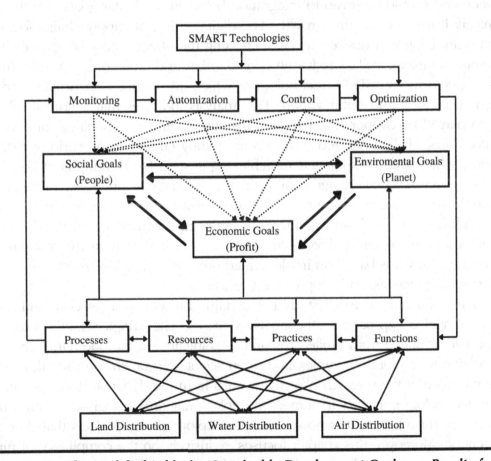

Figure 10.2 The Model of Achieving Sustainable-Development Goals as a Result of the Use of SMART Systems in Distribution.

Source: Author's research.

analyzed and evaluated from the perspective of their compliance with the goals identified in the 2030 Agenda for Sustainable Development. Correlations resulting from their achievement were identified and defined together with their strong links with economic organizations' business assumptions. Apart from cognitive results, the chapter presents the author's proposal of a model for achieving sustainable-development goals as a result of the use of SMART systems in distribution. It combines theoretical findings with the synthetic results of the conducted analysis.

The particular UN sustainable-development goals in economic, social, and environmental areas are interrelated, and the stronger their mutual links are, the greater their significance for institutions. In the context of the conducted analysis, attention should be given to the significance of the issue of profit, which is supplemented by considerations related to "planet" and "people." Also, consideration should be given to integration between particular goals, which ultimately leads to economic growth. The digitalization of supply chains focuses on optimizing logistics resources, increasing the effectiveness of vehicles and infrastructure as well as reducing consumption and emissions. It results from the specificity of SMART technologies, which are focused on process monitoring, control, and optimization. The analysis indicates that a crucial role is also played by cooperation between institutions and the exchange of experience. Most of the analyzed solutions are jointly employed by various institutions, which are also engaged in achieving sustainable-development goals. It should be noted that engagement in the issues related to profit, the planet, and people should be intensified in the course of achieving particular goals. The consolidation of goals in organizations' strategies increases achieved benefits and results in dynamic development. Therefore, it is fully justified to create integrated systems based on implemented processes, available resources, organizational practices, and supply-chain functions.

The conducted research study has certain limitations—a selective and nonrepresentative approach to the analyzed cases. The adopted methodological approach resulted from limited research possibilities on the one hand, and the intention to explore a complex and open scientific problem on the other. The significance of the research objective results from the dynamic development of IoT technologies and their numerous implementations in logistics. Within the scope of this chapter, it is not possible to explore all the projects that deserve attention. Moreover, this chapter focuses exclusively on the compliance of nine international cases with particular sustainable goals, not considering the degree of their implementation by particular systems. The title problem requires further research and discussion. Further explorations should be based on an in-depth

The achievement of sustainable-development goals is determined by an organization's strategy, specific policies, adopted assumptions, and business practices. A significant role is also played by exogenous factors such as significance attributed to sustainable development, the technological revolution, and the continuous process of the digitalization of the economy (Schwab, 2017) and all areas of social life (Skinner, 2018). A crucial role in market institutions is played by economic goals related to increased mid- and long-term market value and creating conditions for the stable financing of corporate operations and growth. Simultaneously, most processes supported by SMART systems are related to social and environmental goals. The achievement of such goals can lead to savings and increased revenue, but these effects are indirect and require adopting a long-term perspective. Organizations give priority to their expansion and economic benefits. It enables them to increase available resources and achieve their corporate objectives, including social and environmental ones, constituting a cause-and-effect sequence.

It should be noted that, because of the specificity of economic activities and their major impact on the planet, ecology is the area connected with the largest number of sustainable-development goals within the framework of the 2030 Agenda. This issue is of vital importance in the context of distribution, which considerably contributes to environmental pollution. The performance of ecological tasks is strongly correlated with increasing process effectiveness and improvements in supply chains. It is supply chains that are the targets of SMART functionalities of the analyzed logistics systems. It is possible to identify several correlations in this area between sustainable-development goals identified by particular institutions. They mainly concern the components of key significance to organizations: Affordable and Clean Energy; Decent Work and Economic Growth; Industry, Innovation, and Infrastructure; Responsible Consumption and Production; and Climate Action. The tasks representing these areas are related to all the analyzed solutions. Equally important goals include Good Health and Well-Being, Life on Land, and Partnerships for Goals, which are achieved by most of the analyzed entities.

10.8 Conclusions

The main objective of this chapter was to analyze and evaluate the implementation of sustainable distribution using the Internet of Things solutions. To achieve this objective, we analyzed nine international projects based on SMART systems in land, water, and air distribution. The particular cases were analysis of the specificity of projects related to SMART distribution, giving attention to the measurement of the degree of achieving particular sustainable-development goals. It would be advisable to apply advanced statistical techniques and carry out long-term observations. There is also a need for extensive international qualitative and quantitative research studies to analyze stakeholders' opinions on the adopted solutions and implementation strategies in developing international distribution channels. Such an approach will facilitate in-depth and methodologically supported assessments of the significance of SMART technologies in achieving sustainable-distribution objectives.

Acknowledgments

The publication was financed from the subsidy granted to the Cracow University of Economics.

References

Agrawal, S., & Singh, R. K. (2019). Analyzing disposition decisions for sustainable reverse logistics: Triple bottom line approach. *Resources, Conservation and Recycling, 150*, 104448. DOI: 10.1016/j.resconrec.2019.104448

Ang, J. H., Goh, C., Saldivar, A. A. F., & Li, Y. (2017). Energy-efficient through-life smart design, manufacturing and operation of ships in an industry 4.0 environment. *Energies, 10*(5), 610. DOI: 10.3390/en10050610

Asif, R. (2011). Reverse logistics: RFID is the key to optimality. *Journal of Industrial Engineering and Management, 4*(2), 281–300. DOI: 10.3926/jiem.2011.v4n2.p281-300

Attaran, M. (2020). Digital technology enablers and their implications for the supply chain management. *Supply Chain Forum: An International Journal, 21*(3). DOI: 10.1080/16258312.2020.1751568

Bajak, M. (2021). *Wykorzystanie beaconów w komunikacji marketingowej [Use of Beacons in Marketing Communication]*. Warszawa: PWE.

Ben-Daya, M., Hassini, E., & Bahroun, Z. (2019). Internet of things and supply chain management: A literature review. *International Journal of Production Research, 57*(15–16), 4719–4742. DOI: 10.1080/00207543.2017.1402140

Bertolini, M., Ferretti, G., Vignali, G., & Volpi, A. (2013). Reducing out of stock, shrinkage, and overstock through RFID in the fresh food supply chain: Evidence from an Italian retail pilot. *International Journal of RF Technologies Research and Applications, 4*(2), 107–125. DOI: 10.3233/RFT-120040

Buntak, K., Kovačić, M., & Mutavdžija, M. (2019). Internet of things and smart warehouses as the future of logistics. *Tehnički Glasnik, 13*(2), 248–253. DOI: 10.31803/tg-20190215200430

Carrasco-Gallego, R., & Moreno-Romero, A. (2010). *ICTs Contribution to Global Logistics Sustainability*. Proceedings of APMS 2010 International Conference—Advances in Production Management Systems, Cernobbio.

Chang, T., & Zhu, X. (2019). *A Research of Subsidies for the Internet of Things Enterprises Based on Signaling Game Theory*. 9th International Conference on Education and Social Science (ICESS 2019), Shenyang (pp. 874–877). DOI:10.25236/icess.2019.166

Chbaik, N., Khiat, A., Bahnsse, A., & Ouajji, H. (2021). The application of smart supply chain technologies in the Moroccan logistics. *Procedia Computer Science, 198*, 578–583. DOI: 10.1016/j.procs.2021.12.289

Condea, C., Thiesse, F., & Fleisch, E. (2010). Assessing the impact of RFID and sensor technologies on the returns management of time-sensitive products. *Business Process Management Journal, 16*(6), 954–971. DOI: 10.1108/14637151011093017

Cosimato, S., & Troisi, O. (2014). *The Influence of Green Innovation in Logistics Competitiveness and Sustainability. The DHL Case Study*. 17th International Conference Excellence in Services, Conference Proceedings, Toulon-Verona (pp. 95–112).

Digiesi, S., Mascolo, G., Mossa, G., & Mummolo, G. (2015). *New Models for Sustainable Logistics: Internalization of External Costs in Inventory Management*. Cham: Springer.

Ding, Y., Jin, M., Li, S., & Feng, D. (2021). Smart logistics based on the internet of things technology: An overview. *International Journal of Logistics Research and Applications, 24*(4), 323–345. DOI: 10.1080/13675567.2020.1757053

Dobbs, R., Manyika, J., & Woetzel, J. (2016). *No Ordinary Disruption*. New York: Public Affairs.

Eden, G., Nanchen, B., Ramseyer, R., & Evéquoz, F. (2017). Expectation and experience: passenger acceptance of autonomous public transportation vehicles. In: R. Bernhaupt, G. Dalvi, A. Joshi, K. Balkrishan, D. J. O'Neill, & M. Winckler (eds.), *Human-Computer Interaction—INTERACT 2017* (p. 10516). Cham: Springer. DOI: 10.1007/978-3-319-68059-0_30

Elkington, J. (1994). Towards the suitable corporation: Win-win-win business strategies for sustainable development. *California Management Review, 36*(2), 90–100. DOI: 10.2307/41165746

FBI. (2018). *Cyber Actors Use Internet of Things Devices as Proxies for Anonymity and Pursuit of Malicious Cyber Activities*. Retrieved from: www.ic3.gov/media/2018/180802.aspx/ Available [May 7, 2022].

Feng, H., Wang, X., Duan, Y., Zhang, J., & Zhang, H. (2020). Applying blockchain technology to improve agri-food traceability: A review of development methods, benefits and challenges. *Journal of Cleaner Production, 260*, 121031. DOI: 10.1016/j.jclepro.2020.121031

Ferreira, P., Martinho, R., & Domingos, D. (2010). IoT-aware business processes for logistics: Limitations of current approaches. *INForum*, 611–622.

Filho, W. L. (2021). *Integrating Social Responsibility and Sustainable Development: Addressing Challenges and Creating Opportunities*. Cham: Springer Nature.

Filho, W. L., Borges de Brito, P. R., & Frankenberger, F. (2019). *International Business, Trade and Institutional Sustainability*. Cham: Springer Nature.

Fortuński, B. (2020). Sustainable development and energy policy: Actual CO2 emissions in the European union in the years 1997–2017, considering trade with China and the USA. *Sustainability, 12*(8), 3363. DOI: 10.3390/su12083363

Garau, C., & Pavan, V. M. (2018). Evaluating urban quality: Indicators and assessment tools for smart sustainable cities. *Sustainability, 10*(3), 575. DOI: 10.3390/su10030575

Ghahremani Nahr, J., Nozari, H., & Sadeghi, M. E. (2021). Green supply chain based on artificial intelligence of things (AIoT). *International Journal of Innovation in Management, Economics and Social Sciences, 1*(2), 56–63. DOI: 10.52547/ijimes.1.2.56

Golpîra, H., Khan, S., & Safaeipour, S. (2021). A review of logistics Internet-of-Things: Current trends and scope for future research. *Journal of Industrial Information Integration, 22*, 100194. DOI: 10.1016/j.jii.2020.100194

Gonzales-Feliu, J. (2018). *Sustainable Urban Logistics: Planning and Evaluation.* Hoboken: Wiley.

Grant, D., Wong, C. Y., & Trautrims, A. (2017). *Sustainable Logistics and Supply Chain Management: Principles and Practices for Sustainable Operations and Management.* London: Kogan Page Publishers.

Gružauskas, V., Baskutis, S., & Navickas, V. (2018). Minimizing the trade-off between sustainability and cost effective performance by using autonomous vehicles. *Journal of Cleaner Production, 184*, 709–717. DOI:10.1016/j.jclepro.2018.02.302

Gu, Y., & Liu, Q. (2013). Research on the application of the internet of things in reverse logistics information management. *Journal of Industrial Engineering and Management, 6*(4), 963–973. DOI: 10.3926/jiem.793

Guarda, T., Leon M., Augusto, M. F., Haz, L., de la Cruz, M. T., Orozco, W., & Alvarez, J. (2017). *Internet of Things Challenges.* 12th Iberian Conference on Information Systems and Technologies (CISTI) (pp. 1–4). DOI: 10.23919/CISTI.2017.7975936

Gupta, A. (2019). *The IoT Hacker's Handbook: A Practical Guide to Hacking the Internet of Things.* New York: Apress Media.

Gupta, S. M. (ed.). (2016). *Reverse Supply Chains: Issues and Analysis.* Boca Raton: CRC Press.

Halkias, D., & Neubert, M. (2020). Extension of theory in leadership and management studies using the multiple case study design. *International Leadership Journal, 12*(2), 48–73. DOI: 10.2139/ssrn.3586256

Hasanuzzaman, M. D., & Rahim, A. D. (eds.). (2019). *Energy for Sustainable Development: Demand, Supply, Conversion and Management.* London: Academic Press.

Heppelmann, J. E., & Porter, M. E. (2014). How smart, connected products are transforming competition. *Harvard Business Review, 92*(11), 64–88.

Hickson, R. J., & Owen, T. L. (2015). *Project Management for Mining: Handbook for Delivering Project Success.* Englewood: SME.

Hu, Z., Parwani, V., & Hu, G. (2021). Closed-loop supply chain network design under uncertainties using fuzzy decision making. *Logistics, 5*(1), 15. DOI: 10.3390/logistics5010015

Hurtová, I., Sejkorová, M., Verner, J., & Kučera, M. (2018). Preference and area coordination of public transport in the modern city. *Engineering for Rural Development, ERD 2018*. DOI: 10.22616/ERDev2018.17.N345

Jia, M., Komeily, A., Wang, Y., & Srinivasan, R. S. (2019). Adopting Internet of Things for the development of smart buildings: A review of enabling technologies and applications. *Automation in Construction, 101*, 111–126. DOI: 10.1016/j.autcon.2019.01.023

Kamali, A. (2019). Smart warehouse vs. traditional warehouse—review. *CiiT International Journal of Automation and Autonomous System, 11*(1), 9–16.

Kamble, S. S., Gunasekaran, A., Parekh, H., & Joshi, S. (2019). Modeling the Internet of Things adoption barriers in food retail supply chains. *Journal of Retailing and Consumer Services, 48*, 154–168. DOI: 10.1016/j.jretconser.2019.02.020

Kayikci, Y. (2018). Sustainability impact of digitization in logistics. *Procedia Manufacturing, 21*, 782–789. DOI: 10.1016/j.promfg.2018.02.184

Kongar, E., Haznedaroglu, E., Abdelghany, O., & Bahtiyar, M. O. (2015). A novel IT infrastructure for reverse logistics operations of end-of-life pharmaceutical products. *Information Technology and Management, 16*(1), 51–65. DOI: 10.1007/s10799-014-0195-z

Kortuem, G., Kawsar, F., Fitton, D., & Sundramoorthy, V. (2010). Smart objects as building blocks for the internet of things. *IEEE Internet Computing, 14*(1), 44–51. DOI: 10.1109/MIC.2009.143

Laasch, O. (2021). *Principles of Management: Practicing Ethics, Responsibility, Sustainability*. Newcastle upon Tyne: SAGE.

Lemaire, A., & Limbourg, S. (2019). How can food loss and waste management achieve sustainable development goals? *Journal of Cleaner Production, 234*, 1221–1234. DOI: 10.1016/j.jclepro.2019.06.226

Liu, S., Zhang, Y., Liu, Y., Wang, L., & Wang, X. V. (2019). An 'Internet of Things' enabled dynamic optimization method for smart vehicles and logistics tasks. *Journal of Cleaner Production, 215*, 806–820. DOI: 10.1016/j.jclepro.2018.12.254

Machaj, J., Brida, P., & Matuska, S. (2021). Proposal for a localization system for an IoT ecosystem. *Electronics, 10*, 3016. DOI: 10.3390/electronics10233016

McKinsey. (2021). *The Internet of Things Catching Up to an Accelerating Opportunity*. Retrieved from: www.mckinsey.com/business-functions/mckinsey-digital/our-insights/iot-value-set-to-accelerate-through-2030-where-and-how-to-capture-it/ Available [May 7, 2022].

Merkaš, Z., Perkov, D., & Bonin, V. (2020). The significance of blockchain technology in digital transformation of logistics and transportation. *International Journal of E-Services and Mobile Applications, 12*(1), 1–20. DOI: 10.4018/IJESMA.2020010101

Miles, M., Huberman, A. M., & Saldana, J. (2019). *Qualitative Data Analysis: A Methods Sourcebook*. Thousand Oaks: SAGE Publications.

Miller, D. (2018). Blockchain and the Internet of Things in the industrial sector. *IT Professional, 20*(3). DOI: 10.1109/MITP.2018.032501742

Mulligan, C. (2019). *Sustainable Engineering: Principles and Implementation*. Boca Raton: CRC Press.

Nagy, J., Oláh, J., Erdei, E., Máté, D., & Popp, J. (2018). The role and impact of industry 4.0 and the Internet of Things on the business strategy of the value chain—the case of Hungary. *Sustainability, 10*(10), 3491. DOI:10.3390/su10103491

Omri, A., & Ben Mabrouk, N. (2020). Good governance for sustainable development goals: Getting ahead of the pack or falling behind? *Environmental Impact Assessment Review, 83*(7), 106388. DOI: 10.1016/j.eiar.2020.106388

Öztayşi, B., Baysan, S., & Akpinar, F. (2009). Radio frequency identification (RFID) in hospitality. *Technovation, 29*(9), 618–624.

Piramuthu, S., Rizzi, A., Vignali, G., & Volpi, A. (2015). Benchmarking of RFID devices for apparel applications: An experimental approach. *International Journal of RF Technologies: Research and Applications, 6*(2–3), 151–169. DOI: 10.3233/RFT-140064

Portney, K. E. (2015). *Sustainability.* Cambridge: MIT Press.

Pundir, A. K., Jagannath, J. D., & Ganapathy, L. (2019). *Improving Supply Chain Visibility Using IoT-Internet of Things.* IEEE 9th Annual Computing and Communication Workshop and Conference 2019 (CCWC), Las Vegas (pp. 0156–0162). DOI: 10.1109/CCWC.2019.8666480

Rashid, Y., Rashid, A., Warraich, M. A., Sabir, S., & Waseem, A. (2019). Case study method: A step-by-step guide for business researchers. *International Journal of Qualitative Methods, 18*, 1–13. DOI: 10.1177/1609406919862424

Regiani, A. (2019). *Accessibility, Trade, and Locational Behaviour.* Abingdon-on-Thames: Routledge.

Rose, K., Eldridge, S., & Chapin, L. (2015). *The Internet of Things (IoT): An Overview—Understanding the Issues and Challenges of a More Connected World.* Reston: Internet Society.

Sagaya-Selvaraj, A., & Anusha, S. (2021). RFID enabled smart data analysis in a smart warehouse monitoring system using IoT. *Journal of Physics: Conference Series, 1717*, 012022. DOI: 10.1088/1742-6596/1717/1/012022

Sarkis, J., Meade, L., & Talluri, S. (2002). E-Logistics and the Natural Environment. In: J. Park & N. Roome (eds.), *The Ecology of the New Economy. Sustainable Transformation of Global Information, Communications and Electronics Industries.* London: Routledge.

Schrauf, S., & Berrtram, P. (2016). *Industry 4.0: How Digitization Makes the Supply Chain More Efficient, Agile, and Customer-focused.* London: PWC.

Schwab, K. (2017). *The Fourth Industrial Revolution.* New York: Penguin Random House.

Shin, S., & Eksioglu, B. (2015). An empirical study of RFID productivity in the U.S. retail supply chain. *International Journal of Production Economics, 163*, 89–96. DOI: 10.1016/j.ijpe.2015.02.016

Skinner, C. (2018). *Digital Human: The Fourth Revolution of Humanity Includes Everyone.* Hoboken: Wiley.

Tabaa, M., Monteiro, F., Bansag, H., & Dandache, A. (2020). Green industrial Internet of Things from a smart industry perspectives. *Energy Reports, 6*, 430–446. DOI: 10.1016/j.egyr.2020.09.022

Tadejko, P. (2015). Application of Internet of Things in logistics—current challenges. *Economics and Management, 7*(4), 54–64. DOI: 10.12846/j.em.2015.04.07

Thiele, L. P. (2016). *Sustainability.* Hoboken: Wiley.

Tiwong, S., Rauch, E., Šoltysová, Z., & Ramingwong, S. (2019). *Industry 4.0 for Managing Logistic Service Providers Lifecycle.* 13th International Conference on Axiomatic Design 2019, Sydney. MATEC Web of Conferences, 301, 00014. DOI: 10.1051/matecconf/201930100014

United Nations. (2015). *Transforming our World: The 2030 Agenda for Sustainable Development.* Retrieved from: https://sustainabledevelopment.un.org/content/documents/21252030%20Agenda%20for%20Sustainable%20Development%20web.pdf/ Available [May 7, 2022].

Usama, M., & Ramish, A. (2020). Towards a sustainable reverse logistics framework typologies based on radio frequency identification (RFID). *Operations and Supply Chain Management, 13*(3), 222–232. DOI: 10.31387/OSCM0420264

Witkowski, K. (2017). Internet of Things, big data, industry 4.0—innovative solutions in logistics and supply chains management. *Procedia Engineering, 182,* 763–769. DOI: 10.1016/j.proeng.2017.03.197

Yang, P. (2019). *Cases on Green Energy and Sustainable Development.* Hershey: IGI Global.

Yu, L., Nazir, B., & Wang, Y. (2020). Intelligent power monitoring of building equipment based on Internet of Things technology. *Computer Communications, 157,* 76–84. DOI: 10.1016/j.comcom.2020.04.016

Zhou, W., & Piramuthu, S. (2013). Remanufacturing with RFID item-level information: Optimization, waste reduction and quality improvement. *International Journal of Production Economics, 145*(2), 647–657. DOI: 10.1016/j.ijpe.2013.05.019

Chapter 11

Digitalization in Transport: An Example of Transport Documents

Monika Roman, Piotr Pietrzak, and Sebastian Stolarczyk

Warsaw University of Life Science—SGGW, Poland

Contents

11.1 Introduction

Improving the flow of information in the supply chain is an important issue in modern logistics activities. Of particular importance is the implementation

DOI: 10.4324/9781003304364-14

of IT systems in the enterprise for faster data exchange and the automation of business processes (Gunasekaran et al., 2017; Ngai et al., 2008). Employees can perform more tasks during one working day, thanks to the support of their activities by various types of software (Gleissner & Femerling, 2013). The integration of technological solutions does not take place only within one company. Significant benefits are brought by combining the systems used in cooperating entities within one supply chain. This speeds up the decision-making process and allows one to effectively respond to unexpected changes in demand. In addition, it enables the reduction of costs and better cost control (Gulledge, 2006; Hahn, 2020).

The implementation of IT systems is often accompanied by the digitization of documentation in the enterprise. In addition to the benefits associated with supporting employee activities by systems, digitization brings savings in the time spent on preparing and handling paper documentation. This affects the time of servicing the means of transport in the process of loading and unloading goods. In transport and forwarding companies, delivering goods to the recipient in accordance with the 7R principle is a priority (Patcharawadee et al., 2021). The right time is of particular importance in this case, and the lack of administration of transport documentation significantly shortens it. The occurrence of any errors may result in the cargo not reaching the customer at the right time, which often results in various types of penalties. Therefore, shortening the delivery time is an opportunity to create a competitive advantage in the market for transport services.

This chapter presents the impact of digitization of transport documents on the information-flow processes in the supply chain using the example of the GreenTransit system. The main research problem of the work was to determine the benefits and barriers of the implementation of digitization systems in logistics companies. For this purpose, the example of the GreenTransit platform was used, which is used to digitize transport documentation in road transport, and above all the international consignment note (Convention Relative au Contrat de Transport International de Marchandises par la Route (CMR), which is proof of the conclusion of a contract for the transport of goods.

The chapter is organized as follows: Section 2 reviews the actual literature on digitalization in transport, Section 3 describes the methodology, Section 4 is dedicated to a case study describing the digital platform in transport documents, Section 5 discusses the implications derived from the study and addresses the limitations of this study and future research directions, and Section 6 presents concluding remarks.

11.2 Review of Literature

The last two decades described as "the digital age" (Hirt & Willmott, 2014) have fundamentally changed "the competitive dynamics of industries" (Cichosz et al., 2020, p. 210). New technologies and concepts such as cloud computing, big data, blockchain, artificial intelligence or self-steering processes and services have become increasingly important in economic processes. As a result, the phrase "industry 4.0" has been coined to describe the fourth industrial revolution (Fruth & Teuteberg, 2017).

The notion of digital transformation (DT) has recently gained a strong interest in both academia and practice. Although the early research on DT can be traced back to 1968, it was only after 2014 that the number of papers on this topic increased substantially (Reis et al., 2018). In 2016, 45% of the total number of articles are journal articles and 55% are conference proceedings (Reis et al., 2018). The United States of America, Germany, and the Popular Republic of China contributed the most to these publications, with 21%, 19%, and 5%, respectively (Reis et al., 2018).

As Kokkinakos et al. (2016) argue, state-of-the-art technologies, such as social software, and data analytics, revolutionize the day-to-day operations of modern organizations in every possible level and way, and as a result, it is expected that DT is going to soon become one of the most popular terms on the Internet; therefore, many authors have attempted to define and discuss the exact notion of DT. Nevertheless, it should be noted that they have not reached a consensus on how to define DT (Cichosz et al., 2020). Scholars view it as a process (Kondarevych et al., 2020; Zhang et al., 2021), a strategy (Hess et al., 2016; Albukhitan, 2020), and a business model (Kotarba, 2018; Vaska et al., 2021). It can be assumed that DT is the integration of digital technologies and business processes in a digital economy (Liu et al., 2011). In a more detailed approach, DT is viewed as the use of digital technologies to impact three organizational dimensions: External (improving the digital customer experience), internal (influence on business operations, decision making, and organizational structures), and holistic (impact on all segments and business functions and thus the emergence of completely new business models) (Kaufman & Horton, 2015; Schuchmann & Seufert, 2015). However, it should be pointed out that entrepreneurs are uncomfortable with DT in reality (Zhang et al., 2021). The slogan "waiting for death without transformation or dying faster from transformation" has been a prevalent view of digital transformation in recent years (Zhang et al., 2021). Table 11.1 presents selected definitions of digitalization.

**Table 11.1 Digitalization Definitions.
(Note: the definitions are presented in chronological order)**

Author(s), year, page(s)	Definition(s)
Maxwell & McCain, 1997, pp. 141–157	By transforming an analog signal into discrete pieces, digitalization makes it possible to manipulate information, text, graphics, software code, audio, and video in ways never before thought of, thus its information, transforming capabilities.
Valenduc & Vendramin, 2017, pp. 121–134	The term "digitalization" is not the irruption of a new revolution, but the pervasive synergy of digital innovations in the whole economy and society.
Eling & Lehmann, 2018, pp. 359–396	The integration of the analog and digital worlds with new technologies that enhance customer interactions, data availability, and business process.
Ringenson et al., 2018, p. 1278	Digitalization is about social life's restructuring around digital communication and media infrastructures.
Srai & Lorentz, 2019, pp. 78–98	Digitalization is defined as the way many domains of social life are restructured around digital communication and media infrastructures. In simple terms, digitalization may be defined as the use of digital technologies.
Reis et al., 2020, pp. 443–456	Digitalization is the phenomenon of transforming analog data into the digital language (i.e. digitization), which, in turn, can improve business relationships between customers and companies, bringing added value to the whole economy and society.

Source: Own elaboration.

DT has had a huge impact on many sectors, including logistics (Gulamov & Shermukhamedov, 2018). There are many practical examples in the literature of how digital technologies have revolutionized the functioning of this sector. Among them, the following can be pointed out:

1) RFID and sensor technology—intelligent features that allow identification, localization, communication, and sensing that will help optimize flows (Vural et al., 2020);
2) cloud logistics—a mediator between modal and actor interfaces to eliminate disruptions and facilitate interconnectivity (Haasis et al., 2015);
3) blockchain technology—a distributed database system that archives a variety of transactions along with other information and organizes all the data (Li et al., 2021);

4) big data—a large volume of data that is coming from different sources, generated by humans or machines at a high velocity (Kubáč, 2016);
5) automation technology—technologies that replace manpower with machine power in systems that control equipment and processes (Martín-Soberón et al., 2014).

Importantly, the number and types of digital applications in logistics are continuously increasing. However, it should be borne in mind that not all functional areas of logistics (inventory management, warehousing, packaging, transport) are supported to the same extent by digital technologies.

Only some authors present the effects of digitalization on transport (e.g., Kramers et al., 2018; Shaheen et al., 2020; Rodríguez et al., 2021). Very few publications deal with the impact of DT on the road (e.g., Pernestål et al., 2021), maritime (e.g., Sanchez-Gonzalez et al., 2019; Tijan et al., 2020), and air transport (e.g., La et al., 2021; Li et al., 2021). Broadly speaking, the application of digital technologies in the various modes of transport reduces human participation, which in turn results in higher control of processes, standardization of performance and service levels, minimization of uncertainty in response times, and cost savings from operations and human errors (Martín-Soberón et al., 2014).

Nevertheless, we can conclude that research in this area is still in its initial stages. There is a lack of "theoretical and empirical work as well as alternative explanatory approaches for appropriate recommendations for action and restructuring" (Fruth & Teuteberg, 2017, p. 3). The authors hope that this chapter will be an interesting starting point for future research.

11.3 Methodology

The object was purposefully selected for research. The selected company was established in 2019. It conducts activities related to the development and delivery of software for handling transport documentation—the GreenTransit system. The platform uses cloud-computing technology and is intended for all entities in the supply chain. The selection of the previously mentioned platform made it possible to achieve the set research purpose, which enables the presentation of digitization in the road-transport process, including the identification of benefits and threats.

The following data collection methods were used: The documentation method, the diagnostic-survey method with the interview-questionnaire technique, and participant observation. For this purpose, materials related to the GreenTransit platform were used, such as system-design documentation, pitch deck, information brochures, and in-house documents. The interviews were conducted with the company's employees and subcontractors providing services based on outsourcing. An important aspect of the research was passive and active participation in the process of creating the GreenTransit system and working on its implementation. This allowed identifying the most important functionalities and barriers of the system. The following methods were used to present the research results: Descriptive, graphical, and tabular.

11.4 Results

11.4.1 The Idea of the GreenTransit Platform

GreenTransit is a platform that supports the entire process of sharing data on the goods-transport process. During the creation of the platform, cooperation was established with the Institute of Logistics and Warehousing in Poznań, the Polish Chamber of Commerce for Electronics and Telecommunications, the Polish Road Transport Institute, and the GS1 Poland organization. On the basis of a contract, the service provider provides paid electronic services for a fee in the form of access to the GreenTransit platform. The services include the following:

1) Circulation of all transport documents in electronic form without the need to present them to control authorities in paper form;
2) exchange of information about transport, published by authorized users of the GreenTransit platform, to provide the contractor with information about transport and the provision of transport or forwarding services,
3) adding derivative users (subaccounts for employees);
4) generating and uploading documents;
5) security of transmitted data;
6) signing documents in electronic form;
7) access to the user database.

The GreenTransit platform is available on the website. The first registration concerns the user who creates the main company account that contains the data with the National Court Register or the Central Register and

Information on Economic Activity. It is used to manage the company profile, transport, and documents, as well as employee accounts. From the main account and accounts with permissions, the administrator can add a subaccount for employees with the administrator, dispatcher, driver, and warehouseman permissions. The functions available for the given employees are presented in Table 11.2.

Table 11.2 Functionalities Are Carried Out by Individual Actors.

Actors	Functionalities
Administrator	■ Adding accounts for employees; ■ deletion of a subaccount; ■ granting and changing user authorizations; ■ changing account settings; ■ adding a transport; ■ adding contractors; ■ sending and accepting invitations to cooperate; ■ generating, editing, downloading, and viewing documentation; ■ uploading PDF files; ■ signing documents using the GreenTransit system or SMS and on-screen methods; ■ adding and removing modes of transportation; ■ checking and updating modes-of-transportation availability status; ■ sharing links with access to a given transport; ■ access to all transports created or sent in a given enterprise; ■ ending of the transport process; ■ redirection to the hotline.
Dispatcher	■ Changing account settings; ■ adding a transport; ■ adding contractors; ■ sending and accepting invitations to cooperate; ■ generating, editing, downloading, and viewing documentation; ■ uploading PDF files; ■ signing documents using the GreenTransit system or SMS and on-screen methods; ■ adding and removing modes of transportation; ■ checking and updating modes-of-transportation availability status; ■ providing links with access to a given transport; ■ access to all shipments created or transmitted by the company; ■ ending the transport process; ■ redirection to the hotline.

(Continued)

Table 11.2 *(Continued)* **Functionalities Are Carried Out by Individual Actors.**

Actors	Functionalities
Warehouseman	■ Changing account settings; ■ adding a transport; ■ adding contractors; ■ sending and accepting invitations to cooperate; ■ generating, editing, downloading, and viewing documentation, ■ uploading PDF files; ■ signing documents using the GreenTransit system or SMS and on-screen methods; ■ access to all shipments created or transmitted by the company; ■ ending the transport process; ■ redirection to the hotline.
Driver	■ Changing account settings; ■ adding a transport; ■ adding contractors; ■ sending and accepting invitations to cooperate; ■ generating, editing, downloading, and viewing documentation; ■ uploading PDF files; ■ signing documents using the GreenTransit system or SMS and on-screen methods; ■ ending the transport process; ■ redirection to the hotline.

Source: Own elaboration based on the conducted research.

Figure 11.1 presents the functionalities of the system for individual entities that may participate in the supply chain. The figure shows the flow of information between the elements of the transport system. The owner of the company creates accounts for himself and his employees. This enables control over the flow of data to and from the enterprise. The information flowing from the forwarder to the driver is related to the given order. The main goal of the plan to eliminate paper documentation is to ensure the driver has the tools to confirm receipt and delivery, and to control the shipping documents by the inspection services. The sender and the recipient have the option of signing the documents; additionally, the sender has the option of uploading their files.

11.4.2 Benefits and Barriers Resulting from the Use of Electronic Transport Documents in GreenTransit

The implementation of electronic circulation of transport documentation brings several benefits. They are associated with a significant reduction in administrative issues for logistics operators, which is associated with cost

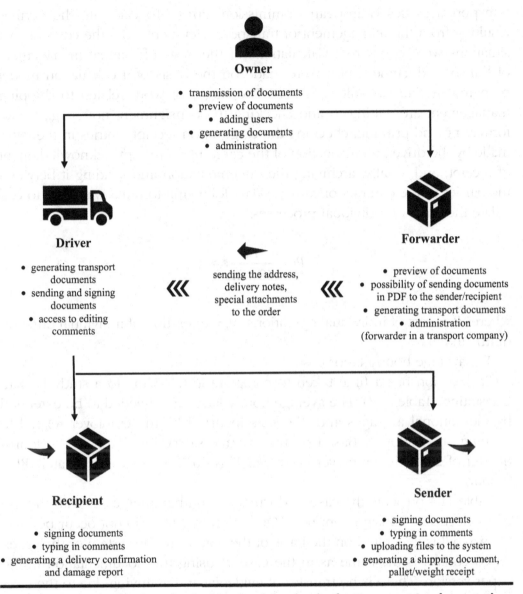

Owner

- transmission of documents
- preview of documents
- adding users
- generating documents
- administration

Driver

- generating transport documents
- sending and signing documents
- access to editing comments

sending the address, delivery notes, special attachments to the order

Forwarder

- preview of documents
- possibility of sending documents in PDF to the sender/recipient
- generating transport documents
- administration (forwarder in a transport company)

Recipient

- signing documents
- typing in comments
- generating a delivery confirmation and damage report

Sender

- signing documents
- typing in comments
- uploading files to the system
- generating a shipping document, pallet/weight receipt

Figure 11.1 Authorizations for Entities Participating in the Transport Implementation Process.

Source: Own elaboration based on the conducted research.

reduction. An additional advantage is the reduction of the emission of harmful substances to the environment resulting from the consumption of raw materials, processes occurring in the phase of paper production, and then wastepaper disposal. But most of all, the benefit is saving the employee's time, which he needs to handle documents in a paper version. Currently, paper documentation is used during at least one stage of about 99% of cross-border transport activities (European Commission, 2018). To calculate the savings resulting from the management of transport documentation, the costs of two situations were compared. Calculations of the costs of manual management of transport documentation were made on the basis of a calculation model prepared by Sira Consulting (2004). The stages of work related to shipping management are: Filling in and checking the consignment note (e.g., CMR), formatting and printing, checking the cargo upon receipt, entries in the letter made by the driver, an inspection of the cargo upon receipt, acknowledgment of receipt, and, finally, archiving the documentation and sending it between the parties to the contract of carriage. The following formula was used to calculate the costs of individual processes:

$$Pn = \frac{Tn}{60 \; min} * Y$$

where: P_n = cost of individual operations, T_n = operation of individual duration (min), and

Y = average hourly labor cost.

Each action has a time taken to complete it according to a study by Sira Consulting (Table 11.3). The average hourly labor cost needed to be extended by the national averages and the costs incurred by the employer related to keeping an employee. Based on the average salary in Poland in the fourth quarter of 2020, the employer's cost was PLN 40.72/hour (approximately EUR 9/hour).

Table 11.4 presents the case of documentation-handling costs with the use of an electronic consignment note. Operations 1 and 2 do not occur because the waybill is generated on the basis of the data from the system or the order. Cargo control is the same as in the case of using the documentation in the paper version. There is no transfer of evidence and archiving due to the electronic access to data by all participants of the transport process in real time. Thus, the time needed for the service decreased from 23 to nine minutes, which reduces the costs related to the handling of documentation from PLN 15.61(EUR 3.42) to PLN 6.11 (EUR 1.34).

Another advantage is the acceleration of payment deadlines by accessing the original documents by the client immediately after the transport. It also guarantees the security of stored data, quick access, and easy search. The use of an electronic consignment note will also allow for greater hygiene at work, as various germs and viruses can spread on paper transport documents (Zaborowski, 2020).

Table 11.3 Paper-Consignment-Note Administration Costs.

Operation number	Operation name	Time (T) (min)	Responsible person	Average labor cost (Y)(h)	Operation cost (P) (PLN)
1	Completion and inspection of the consignment note	5.0	Employee	40.72	3.39
2	Preparation and printing of the consignment note	1.0	Employee	40.72	0.68
3	Cargo control	4.0	Driver	40.72	2.71
4	Driver's entries on the consignment note	0.5	Driver	40.72	0.34
5	Cargo control	4.0	Driver	40.72	2.71
6	Confirmation of cargo delivery	0.5	Driver	40.72	0.34
7	Send confirmation	5.0	Employee	40.72	3.39
8	Document archiving	3.0	Employee	40.72	2.04
	Sum	23.0		Total cost	15.61

Source: Own elaboration based on the conducted research.

Table 11.4 Electronic-Consignment-Note Administration Costs.

Operation number	Operation name	Time (T) (min)	Responsible person	Average labor cost (Y)(h)	Operation cost (P) (PLN)
1	Completion and inspection of the consignment note	0.0	GreenTransit system	0.0	0.0
2	Preparation and printing of the consignment note	0.0	GreenTransit system	0.0	0.0
3	Cargo control	4.0	Driver	40.72	2.71
4	Driver's entries on the consignment note	0.5	Driver	40.72	0.34
5	Cargo control	4.0	Driver	40.72	2.71
6	Confirmation of cargo delivery	0.5	Driver	40.72	0.34
7	Send confirmation	0.0	GreenTransit system	0.00	0.0
8	Document archiving	0.0	GreenTransit system	0.00	0.0
	Sum	9.0		Total cost	6.11

Source: Own elaboration based on the conducted research.

The use of the GreenTransit system allows company owners to control their expenses. Receivables are charged for documents generated or uploaded to the system (PLN 0.5 per document, i.e., approximately EUR 0.11), and payment is made only after the end of the month. It is a cheaper option compared, for example, to the MobiCarnet platform (the platform was created on the initiative of the Ministry of Finance of Estonia). As far as this platform is concerned, generating an e-CMR document costs EUR 0.30 per document; there is also a monthly fixed fee of EUR 50 (MobiCarnet, 2021).

In addition, the system facilitates the organization of work. All documents are grouped and assigned to one transport, thanks to which one can find documents relating to a given transport very quickly. In addition, the system is transparent, compatible with the systems currently used in transport and warehouse companies. It works on tablets, phones, and computers.

One of the barriers to the development of electronic transport documentation in Poland and the use of the GrrenTransit system is the low level of innovation of enterprises. Polish entrepreneurs consider the implementation of innovations to be too capital-intensive and risky (Borowy et al., 2020). In addition, the fragmentation of the Polish transport industry poses a major challenge in implementing e-CMR. The benefits will be noticeable only when all entities in the supply chain use integrated documentation-digitization systems.

The second barrier is the fragmentation of legal acts in the EU countries. Therefore, it is necessary to standardize the control process as well as the required documents in international transport.

Another difficulty is the number of technological solutions used by companies in the transport-shipping-logistics (TSL) industry. In order to use an electronic consignment note and automate this process, there is a need to integrate the programs used or create a standard that allows data to be sent in a structured file. To this end, companies should invest in implementing information and communication platforms (e-FTI).

One of the barriers may also be training employees in the use of the new platform. According to the research conducted by the Polish Road Transport Institute (2021), as many as 63% of the surveyed logisticians and 79% of forwarders filled out the consignment note manually. However, if the CMR consignment note is filled out on a computer, it is usually done with the user's own software; in such cases, Office, enterprise-resource planning (ERP), or transport-management systems (TMS) are most often used. It is worth mentioning that over 80% of the surveyed employees expressed an opinion that using the e-CMR will result in fewer errors and shorten the time of filling in and handling the consignment note. Unfortunately, only 79% of logisticians, 51% of forwarders, and 63% of drivers expressed their willingness to work with the electronic consignment note, i.e., e-CMR. Thus, it is quite a significant barrier to the introduction of electronic transport documents.

11.5 Discussion

11.5.1 Contributions

Our study makes several contributions, both theoretical and practical. Firstly, the case study on the GreenTransit platform allowed us to indicate the benefits and barriers to the development of the electronic consignment note. Secondly, to our knowledge, there is no such detailed description of the functionality of such solutions in the literature. Moreover, many authors (e.g., Fruth & Teuteberg, 2017; Poliak & Tomicová, 2020) emphasize that there is a need for further research on the introduction of digitization-based solutions to improve transport processes.

11.5.2 Limitations

The limitations of the conducted research are related to the adopted research methodology. In the theoretical section of the chapter, the authors omitted some studies that could have been significant for some researchers with regard to digitization in transport. When selecting the literature, the authors considered availability and the reputation of a journal or publishing house to be of key importance. Moreover, an empirical section was prepared using the case study. The case study also has some weaknesses. The results concern only one platform for the digitization of documentation in transport. Therefore, it is not possible to generalize the results to a wider population.

11.5.3 Future Research Directions

The mentioned limitations also indicate further research directions. Firstly, studies on database security and the number of errors in data transmission between enterprises can be carried out to further analyze this issue. Secondly, an interesting direction of research could be to examine the problems arising from the implementation of such solutions in the supply chain. Thirdly, research can be carried out on the real benefits of introducing electronic documents and calculating the profits for enterprises. Another interesting study could be the recognition of opinions about users' trust in this type of solution.

11.6 Conclusions

This study attempts to determine the impact of the digitization of shipping documents on the information-flow processes in the supply chain usings the example of the GreenTransit system. The GreenTransit platform, created for companies from the logistics industry, enables data exchange between entities in the supply chain. The designed functionalities allow companies to add many different contractors to one transport so that each of them has access to documents in real time. Various types of permissions allow one to set access for employees depending on their positions and responsibilities. An additional improvement is the lack of the need for archiving, because all data is stored for five years with the option to change the period in the settings. The system allows users to sign documents using the platform and confirm them with a PIN code, a signature on the screen of a mobile device and a code sent to a telephone number. Each of these options allows the identity of the signer to be verified and, therefore, is recognized in court disputes.

Digitization facilitates the flow of information between entities participating in the performance of the contract. This leads to significant savings in connection with the employee's working time needed to prepare, service, and archive transport documentation. The results of the research showed that the remuneration on this account decreased by over 60%. The use of an electronic consignment note also has a positive effect on the natural environment by reducing the consumption of paper and the emission of carbon dioxide generated during its production.

One problem is the fragmentation of legal standards as each EU country has to adapt its rules to allow procedures to be put in place to control e-CMR. However, the key thing, as it turned out in the case of Poland, is to start work on introducing technological solutions that would enable verification of the presented data. Another aspect is the integration of systems used in the TSL industry. There are many ERP, TMS, WMS, etc., systems on the market that are used in enterprises. The exchange of information between them is a key issue to automate the process of sending documentation and related data.

The authors believe that this study is intended to serve as a basis and starting point for further discussion. Thus, digitalization in transport requires extensive research, especially empirical.

References

Albukhitan, S. (2020). Developing digital transformation strategy for manufacturing. *Procedia Computer Science, 170*, 664–671.

Borowy, M., Mażewska, M., & Rudawska, J. (2020). *Innowacyjność i internacjonalizacja przedsiębiorstw działających w polskich parkach i inkubatorach technologicznych w kontekście wyzwań Przemysłu 4.0 [Innovation and Internationalization of Enterprises Operating in Polish Technology Parks and Incubators in the Context of Industry 4.0 Challenges]*. Warsaw: WULS Press, 7.

Cichosz, M., Wallenburg, C. M., & Knemeyer, A. M. (2020). Digital transformation at logistics service providers: Barriers, success factors and leading practices. *The International Journal of Logistics Management, 31*(2), 209–238.

Eling, M., & Lehmann, M. (2018). The impact of digitalization on the insurance value chain and the insurability of risks. *The Geneva Papers on Risk and Insurance—Issues and Practice, 43*(3), 359–396.

European Commission. (2018). *Proposal for a Regulation of the European Parliament and the Council on Electronic Freight Transport Information*. COM(2018) 279 final. Retrieved from: https://eur-lex.europa.eu/legal-content/EN/TXT/?uri=CELEX%3A52018PC0279#footnote3 Available [September 15, 2021].

Fruth, M., & Teuteberg, M. (2017). Digitization in maritime logistics—what is there and what is missing? *Cogent Business & Management, 4*(1), 1411066, 1–40. DOI: 10.1080/23311975.2017.1411066

Gleissner, H., & Femerling, J. C. (2013). IT in logistics. In: *Logistics. Springer Texts in Business and Economics* (pp. 189–223). Cham: Springer. DOI: 10.1007/978-3-319-01769-3_9

Gulamov, S. S., & Shermukhamedov, A. T. (2018). „Digitalization" of logistics. *European Journal of Intelligent Transportation Systems, 1*(1), 3–6.

Gulledge, T. (2006). What is integration? *Industrial Management & Data Systems, 106*(1), 5–20. DOI: 10.1108/02635570610640979

Gunasekaran, A., Subramanian, N., & Papadopoulos, T. (2017). Information technology for competitive advantage within logistics and supply chains: A review. *Transportation Research Part E: Logistics and Transportation Review, 99*, 14–33.

Haasis, H. D., Landwehr, T., Kille, G., & Obsadny, M. (2015). Cloud-based eBusiness standardization in the maritime supply chain. In: J. Dethloff, H. D. Haasis, H. Kopfer, H. Kotzab, & J. Schönberger (eds.), *Logistics Management: Products, Actors, Technology* (pp. 265–276). Cham: Springer.

Hahn, G. J. (2020). Industry 4.0: A supply chain innovation perspective. *International Journal of Production Research, 58*(5), 1425–1441. DOI: 10.1080/00207543.2019.1641642

Hess, T., Matt, C., Benlian, A., & Wiesböck, F. (2016). Options for formulating a digital transformation strategy. *MIS Quarterly Executive, 15*(2), 123–139.

Hirt, M., & Willmott, P. (2014). Strategic principles for competing in the digital age. *McKinsey Quarterly, 5*(1), 1–13.

Kaufman, I., & Horton, C. (2015). Digital transformation: Leveraging digital technology with core values to achieve sustainable business goals. *The European Financial Review*, December–January, 63–67.

Kokkinakos, P., Markaki, O., Koussouris, S., & Psarras, J. (2016). Digital transformation: Is public sector following the enterprise 2.0 paradigm? In: A. Chuguno, R. Bolgov, Y. Kabanov, G. Kampis, & M. Wimmer (eds.), *Digital Transformation and Global Society. DTGS 2016. Communications in Computer and Information Science* (pp. 96–105). Cham: Springer.

Kondarevych, V., Andriushchenko, K., Pokotylska, N., Ortina, G., Zborovska, O., & Budnyak, L. (2020). Digital transformation of business processes of an enterprise. *TEM Journal, 9*(4), 1800–1808.

Kotarba, M. (2018). Digital transformation of business models. *Foundations of Management, 10*, 123–142.

Kramers, A., Ringenson, T., Sopjani, L., & Arnfalk, P. (2018). AaaS and MaaS for reduced environmental and climate impact of transport. *EPiC Series in Computing, 52*, 137–152.

Kubáč, L. (2016). The application of internet of things in logistics. *Transport Logistics, 16*(38/39), 9–18.

La, J., Bil, C., & Heiets, I. (2021). Impact of digital technologies on airline operations. *Transportation Research Procedia, 56*, 63–70.

Li, X., Lai, P.-L., Yang, C.-C., & Yuen, K. M. (2021). Determinants of blockchain adoption in the aviation industry: Empirical evidence from Korea. *Journal of Air Transport Management, 97*, 102139.

Liu, D. Y., Chen, S. W., & Chou, T. C. (2011). Resource fit in digital transformation: Lessons learned from the CBC Bank global e-banking project. *Management Decision, 49*(10), 1728–1742.

Martín-Soberón, A. M., Monfort, A., Sapiña, R., Monterde, N., & Calduch, D. (2014). Automation in port container terminals. *Procedia—Social and Behavioral Sciences, 160*, 195–204.

Maxwell, L., & McCain, T. (1997). Gateway or gatekeeper: The implications of copyright and digitalization on education. *Communication Education, 46*(3), 141–157.

MobiCarnet. (2021). Retrieved from: https://mobicarnet.eu/ Available [December 20, 2021].

Ngai, E. W. T., Lai, K. H., & Cheng, T. C. E. (2008). Logistics information systems: The Hong Kong experience. *International Journal of Production Economics, 113*(1), 223–234. DOI: 10.1016/j.ijpe.2007.05.018

Patcharawadee, T., Nattapong, T., Saravut, L., & Aumpol, K. (2021). Developing warehouse employee performance by applying the principles of 7R in logistics. *Turkish Journal of Computer and Mathematics Education, 12*(11), 4121–4126.

Pernestål, A., Engholm, A., Bemler, M., & Gidofalvi, G. (2021). How will digitalization change road freight transport? Scenarios tested in Sweden. *Sustainability, 13*, 304.

Poliak, M., & Tomicová, J. (2020). Transport document in road freight transport— paper versus electronic consignment note CMR. *The Archives of Automotive Engineering, 90*(4), 45–58.

Polish Road Transport Institute. (2021). *Elektroniczny list przewozowy E-CMR— badanie ankietowe [Electronic Consignment Note E-CMR—Questionnaire survey]*. Polish Road Transport Institute.

Reis, J., Amorim, M., Melão, N., Cohen, Y., & Rodrigues, M. (2020). Digitalization: A literature review and research agenda. In: Z. Anisic, B. Lalic, & D. Gracanin (eds.), *Proceedings on 25th International Joint Conference on Industrial Engineering and Operations Management—IJCIEOM. IJCIEOM 2019. Lecture Notes on Multidisciplinary Industrial Engineering* (pp. 443–456). Cham: Springer.

Reis, J., Amorim, M., Melão, N., & Matos, P. (2018). Digital transformation: A literature review and guidelines for future research. In: Á. Rocha, H. Adeli, L.P. Reis, & S. Costanzo (eds.), *Trends and Advances in Information Systems and Technologies* (pp. 411–421). Cham: Springer.

Ringenson, T., Höjer, M., Kramers, A., & Viggedal, A. (2018). Digitalization and environmental aims in municipalities. *Sustainability, 10*(4), 1278.

Rodríguez, M. V., Melgar, S. G., Cordero, A. S., & Andújar, J. M. (2021). A critical review of Unmanned Aerial Vehicles (UAVs) use in architecture and urbanism: Scientometric and bibliometric analysis. *Applied Sciences, 11*, 9966.

Sanchez-Gonzalez, P.-L., Díaz-Gutiérrez, D., Leo, T. J., & Núñez-Rivas, L. R. (2019). Toward digitalization of maritime transport? *Sensors, 19*, 926.

Schuchmann, D., & Seufert, S. (2015). Corporate learning in times of digital transformation: A conceptual framework and service portfolio for the learning function in banking organisations. *International Journal of Advanced Corporate Learning, 8*(1), 31–40.

Shaheen, S., Cohen, A., Chan, N., & Bansal, A. (2020). Sharing strategies: Carsharing, shared micromobility (bike sharing and scooter sharing), transportation network companies, microtransit, and other innovative mobility modes. In: E. Deakin (ed.), *Transportation, Land Use, and Environmental Planning* (pp. 237–262). Amsterdam: Elsevier.

Sira Consulting. (2004). Effectmeting administratieve lasten versobering vrachtbrief -Eindrapportage 1.0. TLN Report on the administrative burdens of consignment notes, Den Haag.

Srai, J., & Lorentz, H. (2019). Developing design principles for the digitalisation of purchasing and supply management. *Journal of Purchasing and Supply Management, 25*(1), 78–98.

Tijan, E., Jović, M., Aksentijević, A., & Pucihar, A. (2020). Digital transformation in the maritime transport sector. *Technological Forecasting and Social Change, 170*, 120879.

Valenduc, G., & Vendramin, P. (2017). Digitalisation, between disruption and evolution. *Transfer: European Review of Labour and Research, 23*(2), 121–134.

Vaska, S., Massaro, M., Bagarotto, E. M., & Dal Mas, F. (2021). The digital transformation of business model innovation: A structured literature review. *Frontiers in Psychology, 11*, 3557.

Vural, C. A., Roso, V., Halldórsson, Á., Ståhle, G., & Yaruta, M. (2020). Can digitalization mitigate barriers to intermodal transport? An exploratory study. *Research in Transportation Business & Management, 37,* 100525.

Zaborowski, H. (2020). E-dokument w codziennej pracy kierowców i firm magazynowych. *Logistyka, 2,* 66–68.

Zhang, J., Long, J., & von Schaewen, A. M. E. (2021). How does digital transformation improve organizational resilience?—findings from PLS-SEM and fsQCA. *Sustainability, 13,* 11487.

Chapter 12

Going Green: The Effects of Decarbonization on Container-Shipping Companies' Competitiveness

Leonardo Lovričić, Helga Pavlić Skender,
and Petra Adelajda Zaninović
University of Rijeka, Croatia

Contents

DOI: 10.4324/9781003304364-15

12.1 Introduction

While decarbonization is still far from being implemented across all industries, maritime shipping companies are the most likely to have made the leap towards its adoption, as they are the backbone of international trade. There is a great deal of interest in research circles on topics related to decarbonization, its implementation, and the impact on businesses and the economy. According to the Web of Science (2022) database, more than 40 research papers on decarbonization in the maritime industry were published from 2019 to 2022 alone. However, given the increasing importance of decarbonization, especially in light of ongoing economic shocks such as the post-COVID-19 era, high energy prices, European energy dependence, etc., there is a significant gap in the literature addressing the actual identification of the impact of decarbonization in the maritime industry, the necessary processes of its implementation, and best practices. Therefore, in this paper, both the opportunities and challenges were identified to answer the biggest question—how to remain competitive and market-relevant while adapting to the new environmental conditions. Theoretical and applied factors were analyzed and discussed with the aim of identifying the benefits of implementing an environmentally sustainable business model and its impact on shipping companies. Although the research was largely based on a case study with limited information details obtained through Internet research and the interview with A.P. Moller-Maersk employees, the results are encouraging and show the desired outcome—an overview of an adapted sustainable business model in relation to environmental regulations and market demands. In addition, the results of the analysis indicate that reducing greenhouse gasses is a challenge for the container-shipping industry and the competitiveness of shipping companies, but the right business model will allow them to remain competitive in the market. We also concluded that the concept of green and sustainable logistics is already being implemented due to the greenhouse gas regulation declared by IMO. Although there is a significant cost associated with future expansion, the benefits of doing so are far greater from a business-parameter perspective. Internal green practices increase the competitiveness of companies by enabling them to provide a contemporary sustainable end-to-end logistics service at the highest level of customer satisfaction and internal effectiveness. As detailed company reports and financial statements are required for a full analysis of competitiveness, this data is for internal use only, so understanding the full cost-effective background of the decarbonization journey could be challenging, but the general summary and basic initiatives can be easily outlined.

This chapter consists of five interrelated sections. Section 2 presents the theoretical background of the sustainable initiatives of IMO and the Paris Agreement. Section 3 presents the materials and methods of the research. Section 4 presents the findings of the Maersk case study. Section 5 presents the concluding remarks and contribution of the research.

12.2 Theoretical Background

As the world evolves and changes every day, especially in the last century, there is one thing that has a certain outcome: It is the negative impact on the environment that is becoming inevitable nowadays. Maritime transport is the most common way of transporting goods in the world, with container transport accounting for 70% to 80%. Considering this fact, the impact on the global environment through gas emissions, more specifically greenhouse-gas emissions, is immense, and new standardized regulations to minimize such shipping emissions have become mandatory today. There are many research papers dealing with decarbonization in the maritime industry (Psaraftis, 2019; Mallouppas & Yfantis, 2021; Halim et al., 2018; Romano & Yang, 2021; Farkas et al., 2021; Stopford, 2022), in which the importance of implementing decarbonization in the maritime industry and the relevance of this research area are consistent.

While carriers with a great sense of environmental sustainability have a competitive advantage, it also comes at a price. There are already certain climate targets, such as the net-zero target, the carbon-neutral target, the zero-carbon target, and the Paris target. The most important target for shipping companies is the Paris target, based on which the IMO has proposed maritime standards (Task Force on Climate-related Financial Disclosures, 2021). The sustainable initiatives, combined with modern trends such as automation and digitalization that help with traceability and transparency when it comes to the global-emissions footprint, form the basis for a competitive advantage in a fierce market run by a few big players. To adhere to both the UN and IMO pathway to mitigate CO_2 and other GHG emissions, as well as overall decarbonization, strategic partnerships and market collaboration are required, despite the obvious differences between value-chain participants. Based on guidelines provided by regulatory and governance bodies, market response and further implementation of decarbonized green logistics processes should be timely and cost-effective, as this matter affects everyone; not only business owners, related stakeholders, authorities, and value-chain partners, but all of humanity.

12.2.1 *International Maritime Organization (IMO)*

As the principal organization for international maritime trade and the body that regulates the terms of shipping, the IMO's contribution to the global fight against climate change is enormous. As the extended arm of the UN, when it comes to climate change, the UN Sustainable Development Goal 13, which aims to reduce greenhouse-gas emissions and other greenhouse gasses, was implemented immediately after the adoption of CO_2 reduction policy and decisive steps based on the international shipping industry. In 2018, IMO adopted an initial strategy to reduce GHG emissions, with the further goal of fully decarbonizing shipping (International Maritime Organization, 2021). The strategy was divided into three different segments, but with the same goal:

1) Short-Term Actions—from 2018–2023;
2) Mid-Term Actions—from 2023–2030;
3) Long-Term Actions—beyond 2030.

The main objective of the IMO GHG strategy was to reduce global CO_2 emissions by 40% by 2030, with the further intention of reducing them by 70% by 2050 compared to 2008 levels, while reducing other GHG emissions by at least 50% by 2050 (International Maritime Organization, 2021). These can be considered basic guidelines based on which the member states are operating and working towards the same goal. The revised strategy is expected to be adopted in 2023, with the expected milestone being the collected data of 5,000 ships based on fuel consumption and emission dating back to 2019.

12.2.2 *Paris Agreement*

In the period from 30 November to 12 December 2015, the Conference of the Parties 21 was held in Paris, based on the UNFCCC—UN Framework Convention on Climate Change—with the main objective of reducing greenhouse-gas emissions (Falkner, 2016). The reduction of greenhouse-gas emissions is to prevent human degradation of the environment, while in addition to the aforementioned goal, the main goal is to limit the raise of global temperature to 2 degrees Celsius above pre-industrial levels, with the future intention of limiting the global temperature to 1.5 degrees Celsius (The Intergovernmental Panel on Climate Change, 2019). Furthermore, the environmental treaty signed by 195 countries aims to support and assist all countries around the world with climate change and challenges, while strengthening climate resilience and keeping socioeconomic foundations intact (The United Nations Framework Convention on Climate Change, 2021). Looking at the treaty from the perspective of international trade, especially from the position of the maritime sector itself and the legally binding nature of the agreement (Bodansky, 2016), taking into account the global impact of maritime transport and its effects on both the global economy and the global climate, the treaty was seen as a challenging opportunity.

From the outset of the negotiations, the shipping industry has been excluded at the country level, acting through its own regulatory body, which in this case is the IMO—the International Maritime Organization, the crown body for regulating the conditions of international shipping. Between 9 and 13 April 2018, the 72nd session of the IMO's Marine Environment Protection Committee (MEPC) was held, where the first guidelines and strategy for the implementation of the Paris Agreement were adopted, aimed at reducing greenhouse-gas emissions from ships and, by extension, shipping itself. While the IMO reaffirmed its commitment to reduce GHG emissions, the reduction of the same is inevitable and marked as an urgent environmental task to be achieved within this century. The 2050 target to reduce GHG emissions by at least 50% from 2008 levels, with the further intention of decarbonization, should be addressed immediately (The United Nations Global Compact, 2018) and limit fossil-fuel consumption to below a quarter of total consumption by 2100 (Walsh et al., 2017). The previous MEPC meeting, held from 24 to 28 October 2016, resulted in the IMO 2020 Strategy, which aimed to reduce the sulphur content in the fuel used by ships. These two sessions, combined with the IMO's evident commitment to ensuring that shipping meets its environmental obligations, can easily be described as a significant step towards decarbonized logistics, the main aim of which is to enrich both the global economy and the health of humanity.

Green logistics means sustainable development when it comes to shipping, so the decarbonizing driver is the main task that must be accomplished to meet the environmental commitments made. While A.P. Moller-Maersk remains fully committed to the Group's intention and ambition to not only reduce but eliminate greenhouse-gas emissions, the company is working towards achieving the milestone of "net-zero emissions" through its maritime operations. As a significant 60% reduction in emissions from shipping compared to 2008 levels is likely to be achieved by 2030, net-zero emissions from the entire supply chain are the main driver that should cover all emissions aspects of the value chain (A.P. Moller-Maersk, 2020a).

12.3 Materials and Methods

For this research, a combination of case-study and interview method was used, with limited online access through Internet research for targeted data. In addition, secondary data from A.P. Moller-Maersk Group's public environmental sustainability report was used to complement feedback from an interview with the sustainability development manager and the sustainability analyst on the intention to decarbonize business and on the Group's strategy to reduce emissions from international shipping. Due to the long distance between the colleagues interviewed, the interview was conducted via online platforms with a particular focus on Sustainability Report 2020 to gain a broader understanding and knowledge of the data presented, which in combination with the case study resulted in an amazing overview of the decarbonization journey.

12.4 Research Results and Discussion

For A.P. Moller-Maersk, climate commitment and environmental sustainability measures are a strategic imperative, so the group has been reorganized accordingly to adhere to the environmental commitment and ensure that the necessary collaboration is in place across different business activities (A.P. Moller-Maersk, 2020a).

As shown in Figure 12.1 below, the main target is a 60% reduction in CO_2 emissions and a carbon-neutral ship in its operations by 2030, while a net-zero operation overall is targeted by 2050, highlighting the Group's continued progress inefficiency and the possibility of implementing net-zero solutions toward net-zero emissions in shipping throughout the timeframe proposed by the regulators and supervisors.

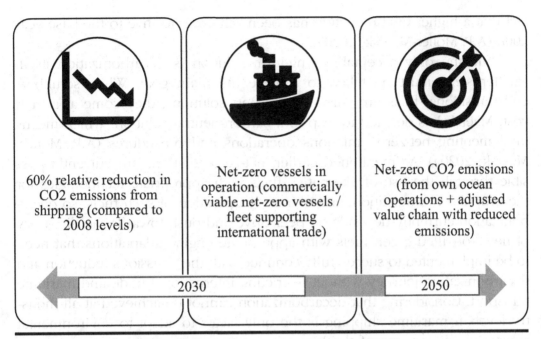

Figure 12.1 A.P. Moller-Maersk Decarbonization Action Plan.

Source: Authors' elaboration.

2020 was the key year when it came to decarbonization efforts. As the Group is labeled as an industry leader, pole position comes at a certain cost—in this case, that would be environmental obligations and associated duties, so the extra mile needs to be pushed to decarbonize business processes across the value chain. Decarbonization is the main goal when it comes to reducing GHG emissions (The Intergovernmental Panel on Climate Change, 2019), and there are several approaches to achieving this milestone. To reduce GHG emissions and eventually eliminate them completely, several approaches can be taken, from installing scrubbers to switching fuel use, to fully implementing new net-zero fuel techniques, and installing appropriate engines.

As the most important short-term goal is still to reduce CO2 by 60% compared to 2008 levels, the following graphs show Maersk's ambitions toward decarbonized shipping. The calculations are based on both the EEOI (Energy Efficiency Operational Indicator 2008) and the gCO2/ton-nm principle. While the EEOI formula has been updated and both the old and new versions have been used in the calculation, the new one shows even better performance in comparison and will continue to be used. The new calculation shows a higher value for the actual efficiency in gCO2/ton-nm, which is consistent with the fact that a higher CO_2 reduction has been achieved, relative to the base year 2008 (A.P. Moller-Maersk, 2020a).

While the only acceptable long-term solution is decarbonization itself, smaller steps must be taken to achieve the main goal. While scrubbers and transitional fuels are currently the best solutions, they come at a high cost. Maersk has decided to leap to a carbon-neutral solution, which means implementing net-zero emissions operations and procedures (A.P. Moller-Maersk, 2020a). As mentioned earlier, net-zero solutions are currently possible through the use of alternative fuels with appropriate technologies for the propulsion, innovation, and ultimately operation of such fuels, so decarbonization currently depends on peer drive and push towards the discovery of new so-called green fuels with appropriate engine adaptations that need to be implemented to successfully continue with the emissions reduction and decarbonization journey without restricting international trade and maritime transport. Considering that decarbonization cannot be achieved at all industry levels if maritime shipping is the only factor to adapt to environmental constraints, being one of the biggest contributors to climate change, every other aspect of logistics services based on an end-to-end solution must follow the ambitions of maritime shipping to achieve the ultimate goal of such international strategies.

12.4.1 Green Fuels

Based on the analyses carried out on numerous fuel technologies within the Maersk Group in recent years, four of them are mature enough to be pursued further. Throughout the deselection process, biomethane and liquefied natural gas, fuel cells, nuclear power, and onboard carbon capture have been abandoned due to concerns about one or more steps in the fuel conversion process. Biomethane and liquefied natural gas had high levels of methane emissions, while the overall investment resulted in marginal reductions in CO_2 emissions. For example, fuel cells have high production costs, which means they are not ready to be efficiently produced on a large scale (A.P. Moller-Maersk, 2020a). Due to environmental regulations, Maersk has decided to move directly to true net-zero-emission technologies, as transitional fuels and alternative technologies do not lead to a favorable outcome compared to decarbonized ones. More detailed information on the four priority fuels can be found in Table 12.1.

To achieve the decarbonization milestone, fuel transformation involves a supply chain in which tasks must be evenly distributed. Due to this fact, there

Table 12.1 Four Priority Fuels for Net-Zero Shipping.

Fuel	Key advantages	Key limitations/risks
Biodiesel	Can be used as drop-in fuel in existing vessels and engines.	Limited availability of biomass feedstock triggers scalability challenge. There is a significant price pressure due to high demand from competing industries.
Methanol (bio-methanol and e-methanol)	Already in operation used as marine fuel. Liquid at normal conditions. Existing engines and handling well known.	Bio-methanol: Scalability challenged by uncertainty by biomass availability. E-methanol: Availability of biogenic CO_2 source at production site, cost and maturity of electrolysis technology.
Lignin fuels (biomass residue and alcohols)	Potentially the most price-competitive net-zero fuel with the lowest price estimate, almost on a pair with fossil fuels.	In development stage, production needs to be scaled up in order to create new value chain and infrastructure for supply. Engine requirements would be the same as for methanol, but additional contaminant-handling might be required.
Ammonia (green ammonia)	Fully zero-emission fuel and can be produced at scale from renewable electricity alone.	There are significant safety and toxicity challenges, as well as infrastructure challenges at ports. Furthermore, cost depends on the future cost of electricity and cost/maturity of electrolysis technology.

Source: Authors' elaboration.

are still many obstacles that need to be overcome to execute a smooth fuel transformation from start to finish.

As mentioned above, numerous doubts and questions arise when it comes to the implementation of alternative fuels. Looking briefly at it, first of all, the biggest question mark remains on the availability of raw materials and their price, as well as the sustainability factor. If the analysis shows a positive answer to these questions, the implementation can proceed to the second of eight phases shown in Table 12.1. While production efficiency is important, transportation and storage, as well as port storage, is one of the most important logistics segments of the fuel supply chain, where proper handling and a smooth transition are very important to meet the highest environmental standards. The fifth phase raises many safety issues as bunkering is considered particularly harmful to the health of both humans and other environmental ecosystems with its sulphur emissions during the bunkering process and its very high toxicity and harmful characteristics. If all five aspects are met, the last three segments can be described as the shipping companies' efforts to fully implement the use of alternative fuels, making both fuel systems and ship engines the key factors when it comes to reducing emissions and decarbonization itself. As complicated as it is, none of the problems can be solved simply, so the following pages explain each threat in more detail.

Challenges can be divided into four major groups:

a) Fuel-Production Scaling

This has a lot to do with the closely related technology currently available on the market since the main obstacle to net-zero-emission ships is the unavailability of such fuel production on a large scale. This fact was the main reason for Maersk joining methanol and ammonia production projects and the LEO Coalition Foundation (lignin-ethanol oil), which focuses mainly on lignin and ethanol fuel production, together with its partners who are leaders in their respective businesses, such as Wallenius Wilhelmsen, BMW Group, H&M, Levi Strauss & Co., and Marks & Spencer. The LEO coalition, in combination with other fuel projects, aims to provide the power for Maersk Group's fleet, although fuel price may still be an obstacle to overcome (A.P. Moller-Maersk, 2020a). Acceptance will certainly mature over the years, but it is a process that will take time before we can talk about scaling green fuel production.

b) Fuel Infrastructure

Currently, there are no fueling infrastructure or fuel-supply-chain techniques that can handle net-zero-fuel transformations.

c) Safety Concerns

As described in Table 12.1, both methanol and ethanol are highly flammable substances, and this needs to be addressed before they can be used as operational fuels. In the case of ammonia, its toxicity is paramount, as there are still no suitable solutions for transport, bunkering, and operation as a pure marine fuel. The same applies to Maersk Mc-Kinney Centre, which is briefly described later in the text.

d) The Profitability Impacts

Green intentions with a particular commitment to decarbonization impact the cost picture, but at Maersk, the view is that the competitive advantage arising from such measures outweighs the costs and risks associated with the journey.

12.4.2 *Maersk Mc-Kinney Moller Centre for Zero Carbon Shipping*

Maersk launched the Maersk Mc-Kinney Moller Centre for Zero Carbon Shipping in 2020, primarily through the group's major shareholder, A.P. Moller Foundation (A.P. Moller-Maersk, 2021b). The research center itself, in conjunction with a bunch of industry champions, represents a significant step forward for environmental tasks and represents the strong commitments that the Group has previously acknowledged. Moreover, this intention will help A.P. Moller-Group to grow while helping its partners and customers to decarbonize their own logistics solutions end-to-end. Maersk's strategy implies that they will serve their customers' supply chains and work with both partners and customers when it comes to market standards and solutions to complete green logistics (A.P. Moller-Maersk, 2020a).

Working towards green solutions means that the Group is strengthening its responsible business practices, which further consolidates its market position as they are the foundations on which the Group operates. The challenges that arise throughout the operations and value chain are handled and addressed with the utmost care, guided by the Group's core values and its commitment to all stakeholders in the international shipping chain, from the environment itself, to investors, regulators, stakeholders, employees, and customers, with green logistics and sustainability being the main drivers. (A.P. Moller-Maersk, 2020a).

Every year, 300 million tons of fuel are consumed by 70,000 ships worldwide, making the shipping industry responsible for 3% of total global CO_2 emissions. To meet the maritime standards that have been introduced, the industry is expected to invest more than $6 trillion in the fight against greenhouse-gas emissions over the next few decades. The Centre itself is a non-profit, independent research-and-development center that provides industry-wide solutions to transition to net-zero shipping (A.P. Moller-Maersk, 2020b). It can also be considered a climate action that aims at high-efficiency environmental sustainability and implements decarbonized green-logistics solutions from end to end. As mentioned earlier, decarbonization is the vision of Maersk Mc-Kinney Centre, with a specific mission to be the driving force in the industry toward greener shipping. The Centre operates on a foundation of specialized knowledge based on industry-wide reach, combined with a research-and-development department that drives technology solutions and strategic guidance for net-zero transformation (A.P. Moller-Maersk, 2020b). In 2020, the world has seen that a simplified and unified supply chain equals a winning strategy. In contrast, decoupled value chains, autarky, and protectionism represent a flawed strategy as digitalization and automation, combined with business openness, signify consistency in the current uncertain world. Maintaining the vital flow of supply with an aspect of innovation and growth in these times is challenging to say the least, but for Maersk Group this has been an opportunity to define its leadership position while nourishing its business operations along with its green footprint. It can be concluded that climate change and climate action is a social and business imperative, a collective challenge that can be overcome by a collective act of supply-chain transformation with technological innovation, policy support, and strengthening the resilience of sustainable value chains through uncertain times (Hermwille et al., 2019). Decarbonization is thoroughly implemented in this group as it is a strategic imperative nowadays, especially for companies of this size and with such a significant industry reach. Looking at the current trends related to the green journey, some of them underline the urgency of decarbonization activities. The first is the idea of a logistics company without a proper decarbonization action plan, which means it risks becoming irrelevant in the market. The gap created by the lack of activity in the green-logistics segment creates increased costs for their partners and customers, as they will be the ones without the ability to weave this inadequate support into their offering. Maersk as an industry leader must lead the carbon-journey curve. The following trend correlates closely with the reality of climate change, and it represents policy. Slowly but gradually, supported by science as well as extreme environmental outbreaks and pressure from stakeholders, numerous mechanisms and disclosure requirements based on CO_2 emissions are being enacted to provide the basic framework for the shipping business. This can be seen as a government incentive to adopt environmental regulations in every aspect of human life. While taxes and similar pricing mechanisms partially mitigate the financial risk of climate change for companies, Maersk strongly supports the adoption of standardized CO_2 pricing systems, and the Group's mission and vision can easily be concluded with a fully transparent collaboration between decarbonized logistics intent, sustainability adjustments in the end-to-end offering, and responsible business practices as a whole. Green logistics is a modern name for sustainable-supply-chain values and practices, and can be elaborated as corporate activities with the main intention of contributing to improvement and ultimately benefiting individuals, communities, and the environment. The traceability of such intentions is the basis on which the ecological footprint is calculated and the positive impact on the environment is paramount to sustainable development. All of this contributes to the notion of the low-carbon economy, where the trend towards controlled and reduced emissions with sustainability as the primary factor in business practices is the cornerstone of the UN path to net-zero emissions.

12.4.3 ECO Delivery Product

So far, Maersk has partnered with Maersk Mc-Kinney Centre to launch ECO Delivery. It was launched in 2019 and is still one of the few carbon-neutral transport solutions on the market (A.P. Moller-Maersk, 2020a). Transitional fuels are currently not fully in line with green logistics as they do not enable carbon-neutral shipping and are not yet manufactured, so biodiesel processed from waste cooking oil remains the best fuel alternative on the market. Biodiesel powers the Maersk fleet's vessels to save CO2 emissions, and its uptake at launch has far exceeded the Group's expectations. Although the ECO Delivery product only covers a minority of the total containers shipped, the product is very promising and currently, key customers are considering the option to switch all their shipments to ECO Delivery. Maersk's ECO Delivery product plays a key role in this. To reach the decarbonization milestone, a much larger number of participating customers is needed, as the transition to decarbonization should be supported by overall demand and willingness to scale net-zero emissions, as well as international cooperation (Roelfsema et al., 2020).

Modern trends of urgent climate action, increased willingness to pay for sustainability, and market participants' desire to go the extra mile in adopting green solutions make the global market open to price volatility. Every aspect of the aforementioned commodity market contributes to the development of decarbonized solutions, which lowers the risk that transportation companies, in this case, A.P. Moller-Maersk, take when investing in research and development for decarbonization. Aligned with the needs of customers and their ambitions for decarbonizing, Maersk has introduced a multivariate value proposition for green logistics that is helping to develop the sustainable market of the future. As one of the largest assets of responsible business practices, combined with others, ECO Delivery Product is gaining big momentum with its biodiesel use when it comes to reducing unwanted gas emissions in international shipping.

12.4.4 Decarbonizing Footprint

The Maersk Group's efforts are aimed at full decarbonization, so the main challenge, in addition to operational and technical aspects, remains balancing customer needs, stakeholder requirements, and overall Group emissions with the development of a sustainable, efficient, and green value chain with a decarbonized end-to-end solution (A.P. Moller-Maersk, 2020a). The largest share of emissions comes from Maersk's maritime activities, with the curve expected to slowly move towards inland solutions and transportation.

The second-largest share comes from supply-chain activities, where the Group is largely dependent on its vendors and suppliers, so the aforementioned collaboration between all participants in the supply chain is a must when talking about green logistics.

The smallest part of the emissions comes from purchased electricity, which is also on Maersk's account. Net-zero solutions need to be embedded throughout the value chain, which includes end-to-end solutions from sea transport to land transport and warehousing to digitized solutions if a positive footprint is to be left. While Maersk has the largest ownership of its sea assets, the land part will require a slightly different approach as there is limited operational control over the assets which offer a different solution than at sea (A.P. Moller-Maersk, 2020a).

Collaboration, cooperation, and willingness to act together will be the main driver for the transformation of the shipping industry, therefore Maersk Group is working on integrating environmental sustainability into the procurement criteria in tenders (A.P. Moller-Maersk, 2020a). As mentioned earlier, despite competitiveness or different business strategies, a partnership between peers in the supply chain is the main driver when it comes to collective response and mutual ambition, i.e., mutual support is much needed if a positive impact on the global environment is to be achieved. Moreover, the compliance and commitment of all market participants are inevitable and must be followed in the coming years if the proposed path is to be achieved and a new market is developed.

As shown in Figure 12.2, the majority of A.P. Moller-Maersk's carbon footprint comes from its operations, 64% in total. Emissions in this group come from the group's financially controlled operations, while 96% of total Scope 1

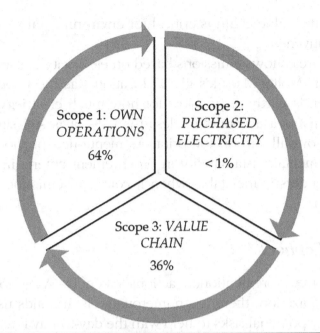

Figure 12.2   A.P. Moller-Maersk CO₂ Footprint.

Source: A.P. Moller-Maersk, 2020a

emissions in 2020 come directly from bunker fuel. The vast majority of total emissions within owned operations are from marine transportation, although this statistic will change as land transportation increases and the logistics and services portfolios expand.

The carbon footprint from value-chain activities is divided into five different material segments, such as upstream transportation and distribution, purchased goods and services, use of sold products, fuel- and energy-related activities, and capital goods (A.P. Moller-Maersk, 2020a). It is important to note that under Scope 3, the emissions considered for a calculation come from business activities in the value chain, as well as emissions from cargo transported under a ship-sharing agreement. As Maersk has a significant share of assets in the deep-sea segment, in the first scope, the company has a leading position in the decarbonization journey related to deep-sea activities and international maritime trade. Considering that inland activities will increase in the future and the structure of inland activities is somewhat different from maritime activities, A.P. Moller-Maersk will have limited operational control over inland assets, making the company highly dependent on logistics partners. The same is true for the higher level of collaboration required for end-to-end decarbonized logistics, and traceability between all participants in the value chain is critical for environmental sustainability and carrier competitiveness.

The second area shows emissions based on electricity consumption, which is related to A.P. Moller-Maersk's global locations, as the Group, as an electricity consumer, is partly responsible for how much electricity is used daily. Even though this area accounts for less than 1%, it is still significant when calculating the overall carbon footprint. As mentioned previously, the inclusion of environmental sustainability in procurement criteria in strategic partnerships and tenders is inevitable when it comes to emission reduction and decarbonization.

12.4.5 Star Connect

In addition to the aforementioned actions taken by A.P. Moller-Maersk to achieve decarbonization, there are numerous tools and aids used within the group to identify potential risks to help with the day-to-day intention of reducing GHG emissions and ultimately decarbonizing shipping. The most important of these is the Star Connect monitoring system, which is implemented in all the Group's vessels and helps to understand engine efficiency and calculate the most convenient sea voyage. It works on the principle of displaying real-life data visible to seafarers, who can instantly adapt to suggestions and new routes as needed, leading to CO2 reduction and better fuel efficiency (A.P. Moller-Maersk, 2020a).

A similar system is found on the Group's chartered vessels, which in turn helps with standby utilization and workflow optimization. Despite the above facts, the greatest need remains to be continued research and development into new fuels, implementation of modern engine technologies, and energy efficiency.

12.4.6 Emissions Dashboard

Maersk will implement Emissions Dashboard, a digital solution that will help consolidate emissions data across all transportation modes and help its customers establish a baseline and find opportunities to optimize their own emissions footprint. Overall, Emissions Dashboard is an analytical tool that gives customers a detailed overview of their carbon footprint, regardless of whether they transport their goods by ship or any other mode of transportation (A.P. Moller-Maersk, 2021a). The main purpose behind such a dashboard lies in the idea of complete transparency and visibility when it comes to emissions footprints, which should encourage customers to move forward with their decarbonization journey. The emissions dashboard works based on the GLEC (Global Logistics Emissions Council—a globally accepted methodology for emissions calculations) methodology, used to calculate emissions data. It is important to note that it also includes data from all other carriers, not just Maersk, that are involved in the end-to-end supply chain. This type of reporting is of great importance as the information obtained from it can be used in the company's sustainability reporting (A.P. Moller-Maersk, 2021a).

So far, the tool has been used by the Group's 100 largest customers, mainly those that have already developed and implemented clear policies for decarbonization actions in their value chains. The aim is to make it available to every single customer, which for Maersk is an indispensable part of its global-sustianability commitment and environmental duty when it comes to green logistics. Tracking CO2 emissions in international trade and shipping is a key aspect of controlling CO2 emissions when it comes to reducing them temporarily and mitigating them completely in the long term. As CO2 plays a crucial role in biological processes, it has key properties when it comes to radiative transfer as well as its contribution to total greenhouse-gas emissions worldwide. The ability to get a clear view of the CO2 footprint can lead to concrete mapping of the supply chain, as well as verification of the data and procurement of the expertise needed to implement the know-how to achieve decarbonization.

12.4.7 Carbon-Neutral Vessel

Due to increased customer demand, technological advances, and strong collaboration between peers involved in numerous projects, Maersk plans to launch its first, but more importantly, the world's first, carbon-neutral ship in 2023, meaning the group's intentions have been accelerated by seven years, in line with its original plan to have a carbon-neutral liner by 2030. Thereafter, all new buildings owned by A.P. Moller-Maersk will be equipped with dual-fuel technology, which will allow the vessels to run on either carbon-neutral or very-low-sulphur-fuel oil (VLSFO) (A.P. Moller-Maersk, 2020a).

The most interesting thing about the carbon-neutral ship is the fact that it will run on methanol and have a capacity of about 2,000 twenty-foot containers (TEU) while operating on the intra-regional network. As mentioned before, the ship will be equipped with a twin engine and will be able to run on VLSFO, but the idea is to run it on e-methanol or bio-methanol from the first day of deployment in a carbon-neutral way (A.P. Moller-Maersk, 2021b).

As mentioned in the first part of this chapter, the biggest challenge remains the proper supply of large-scale carbon-neutral methanol before the vessel's deployment, as well as the fuel supply chain, to adequately advance such a technology. Given the partnership with those responsible for fuel production and fuel-technology development, as well as with key collaborator Maersk Mc-Kinney Centre for Zero Carbon Shipping, which is active in numerous industries that support the development and implementation of new energy systems and technologies, the carbon-neutral ship is an achievable goal that will help scale and accelerate the implementation of new fuel technologies and energy consumption (A.P. Moller-Maersk, 2020a). Decarbonization requires a strong commitment to innovation, which is why A.P. Moller-Maersk will continue to research other carbon-neutral pathways, such as alcohol-lignin blends and ammonia, following the introduction of methanol feeders, as all three of the aforementioned carbon-neutral alternatives could become a standard for marine fuels.

12.5 Conclusion

Since the Paris Agreement's legal commitment to use new technologies to reduce CO2 and other GHG emissions to achieve full decarbonization in the long term, it has become one of the most important milestones in the global fight against climate change. While new technologies require significant investment, they can certainly contribute to greater fairness in the global market and help every participant in the supply chain. The benefits can be seen from various aspects such as traceability of emissions, better environmental activities, greater customer reach, and the like. Traceability and transparency are the main benefits of such a development, which is a must in the modern business world as the requirements and needs of the end customers have become more complicated. Certainly, decarbonization adds value to every stakeholder in the value chain, despite the price to be paid. As the case of A.P. Moller-Maersk shows, quick response and adaptation to global needs can be the key factor when it comes to market share and overall competitiveness, as A.P. Moller-Maersk can be considered a market leader. This paper provides an overview of decarbonization activities based on the Group's sustainability report with the mentioned legal framework for such activities. Although this study has certain limitations as it is mainly based on online data collection and interviews with certain colleagues, the findings contribute to the existing body of knowledge and can be of great value to both the academic and professional communities. This study presents the hottest topic at present from the perspective of the current leader in the shipping industry, especially when it comes to innovation. The increasing climate activities and research of the market players as well as their activities towards decarbonized logistics can go a long way in making this world a better place for all. With all of the above, from tracking the emissions footprint, to research and development of decarbonized solutions, to the final implementation of net-zero technologies, great success is achieved both for humanity on an individual level and for the ambitions of companies to save the environment in which they operate.

References

A.P. Moller-Maersk. (2020a). Retrieved from: www.maersk.com/about/sustainability/reports Available [March 25, 2021].

A.P. Moller-Maersk. (2020b). Retrieved from: https://zerocarbonshipping.com/#. Available [July 14, 2021].

A.P. Moller-Maersk. (2021a). Retrieved from: www.maersk.com/digital-solutions/emissions-dashboard Available [June 11, 2021].

A.P. Moller-Maersk. (2021b). Retrieved from: www.maersk.com/news/articles/2021/02/17/maersk-first-carbon-neutral-liner-vessel-by-2023 Available [February 20, 2021].

Bodansky, D. (2016). The legal character of the Paris agreement. *Review of European, Comparative & International Environmental Law, 25*(2), 142–150.

Falkner, R. (2016). The Paris agreement and the new logic of international climate politics. *International Affairs, 2*(5), 1107–1125.

Farkas, A., Degiuli, N., Martic, I., & Vujanovic, M. (2021). Greenhouse gas emissions reduction potential by using antifouling coatings in a maritime transport industry. *Journal of Cleaner Production, 295*, 126428. DOI: 10.1016/j.jclepro.2021.126428

Halim, R. A., Kirstein, L., Merk, O., & Martinez, L. M. (2018). Decarbonization pathways for international maritime transport: *A model-based policy impact assessment. Sustainability, 10*(7), 2243. DOI: 10.3390/su10072243

Hermwille, L., Siemons, A., Förster, H., & Jeffery, L. (2019). Catalyzing mitigation ambition under the Paris agreement: Elements for an effective global stocktake. *Climate Policy, 19*(8), 988–1001. https://doi.org/10.1080/14693062.2019.1624494 Available [June 10, 2021].

The Intergovernmental Panel on Climate Change. (2019). Retrieved from: www.ipcc.ch/site/assets/uploads/sites/2/2019/06/SR15_Full_Report_Low_Res.pdf Available [June 8, 2021].

International Maritime Organization. (2021). Retrieved from: www.imo.org/en/MediaCentre/HotTopics/Pages/Reducing-greenhouse-gas-emissions-from-ships.aspx Available [June 5, 2021].

Mallouppas, G., & Yfantis, E. A. (2021). Decarbonization in shipping industry: A review of research, technology development, and innovation proposals. *Journal of Marine Science and Engineering, 9*(4), 415. DOI: 10.3390/jmse9040415

Psaraftis, H. N. (2019). Decarbonization of maritime transport: To be or not to be? *Maritime Economics and Logistics, 21*(3), 353–371. DOI: 10.1057/s41278-018-0098-8

Roelfsema, M., van Soest, H. L., Harmsen, M., van Vuuren, D. P., Bertram, C., den Elzen, M., Höhne, N., Iacobuta, G., Krey, V., Kriegler, E., & Luderer, G. (2020). Taking stock of national climate policies to evaluate implementation of the Paris Agreement. *Nature Communications, 11*, 2096. Retrieved from www.ncbi.nlm.nih.gov/pmc/articles/PMC7190619/ Available [May 15, 2021].

Romano, A., & Yang, Z. (2021). Decarbonisation of shipping: A state of the art survey for 2000–2020. *Ocean & Coastal Management, 214*, 105936. DOI: 10.1016/j.ocecoaman.2021.105936

Stopford, M. (2022). Maritime governance: Piloting maritime transport through the stormy seas of climate change. *Maritime Economics and Logistics.* https://doi.org/10.1057/s41278-022-00227-9

Task Force on Climate-related Financial Disclosures. (2021). Retrieved from: https://assets.bbhub.io/company/sites/60/2021/05/2021-TCFMetrics_Targets_Guidance.pdf Available [May 28, 2021].

The United Nations Framework Convention on Climate Change. (2021). Retrieved from: https://unfccc.int/process-and-meetings/the-paris-agreement/the-paris-agreement Available [July 20, 2021].

The United Nations Global Compact. (2018). Retrieved from: https://d306pr3pise04h.cloudfront.net/docs/issues_doc%2FEnvironment%2Fclimate%2FGlobal-Climate-Action-Playbook-2018.pdf Available [July 7, 2021].

Walsh, B., Ciais, P., Janssens, I. A., & Peñuelas, J. (2017). Pathways for balancing CO2 emissions and sinks. *Nature Communications, 8*, 4856. DOI: 10.1038/ncomms14856

Web of Science. (2022). Retrieved from: www.webofscience.com/wos/woscc/summary/05f121b1-5949-4ab9-8a0c-007ac66eaed4-36e9c658/relevance/1 Available [October 5, 2022].

Chapter 13

The Organization of Transportation: City Rhythm and Communication in Times of Telematic Transformation

Irena Jędrzejczyk

University of Bielsko-Biala in Silesia, Poland

Contents

13.1 Introduction

An overview of the directions in the research on transportation systems friendly for the environment and inhabitants led to the identification of the following topics to the scientific debate:

DOI: 10.4324/9781003304364-16

1) The evolution of transportation systems in geographical space, including urban geographical space;
2) the economic effectiveness and technical efficiency of transportation systems;
3) the influence of transportation systems on urban development and environmental transformation;
4) human-transport behavior within the urban ecosystem;
5) innovativeness in urban transportation systems and the transport behavior of users of urban space.

The differences between big and medium or small cities constitute the justification of the topic. Particularly the latter two struggle with many development problems such as depopulation, a decrease in investment, and an exodus of family businesses to bigger urban hubs in the country or even abroad. In 2020, two Polish cities—Warsaw and Breslau—were placed in the ranking IESE Cities in Motion Index of the world's top 100 smartest cities. In the ranking IESE Cities in Motion Index for 2020, Warsaw was placed 69 and Breslau 95. Both cities were the top two in the "Polish Cities of the Future 2050" ranking prepared by the company Saint Gobain (Kaz´mierczak, 2021). In both rankings, the cities were rewarded for their mobility investments. In Breslau, the biggest number of projects related to the smart city concerned city mobility. One of the key projects was the Intelligent Transport System (ITS) launched in 2014. The system included, among others, the installation of 1,285 CCTV cameras in 159 intersections in Breslau. Moreover, nearly 650 tramways and busses were equipped with board computers and detectors cooperating with software. Similar systems were also launched in Warsaw, Krakow, Poznan, Białystok, Rzeszów, and Tychy. Currently, Katowice and Zielona Góra are also preparing for ordering similar systems. Certain big cities in Poland introduced the standards Smart City ISO 37120 as the cities friendly for inhabitants and for the environment, and in relation to the participation in the international initiatives such as the project Urban Lab, the project RUGGEDISED, and others.

Big cities were the subject of multiple scientific types of research and many proposals for project partnerships. Compared to this, the small cities and towns rarely are objects of scientific analysis. In the studies such as "IESE Cities in Motion: International urban best practices" or "Cities and Mobility & Transportation," the big cities are evaluated on the international level. At the same time, in Poland, the National Strategy of the Regional Development indicates the needs of the Areas of the Strategic Interventions:

1) The 139 medium cities out of 934 cities in Poland, which lose their economic function, and
2) 755 communes out of a total of 2, 477 (including urban, urban-rural, and rural communes) are at risk of permanent marginalization.

The urban space, which loses the socioeconomic functions and/or is threatened by permanent marginalization, faces challenges—including mobility challenges—much greater than big, rich, and well-organized cities. The small cities and towns face the challenges of the mobility organization in the context of the mobility conditions, maintaining the rhythm of the city and with the respect for the rules of the sustainable development of the mobility. These challenges are the objects of this analysis, as by the justification previously stated. "At the ecological level, habitation becomes essential. The city envelops it; it is form, enveloping this space of 'private' life, arrival and departure of networks of information and the communication of orders (imposing the far order to the near order). Two approaches are possible. The first goes from the most general to the most specific (from institutions to daily life) and then uncovers the city as specific and (relatively) privileged mediation. The second starts from this plan and constructs the general by identifying the elements and significations of what is observable in the urban. It proceeds in this manner to reach, from the observable, 'private', the concealed daily life: its rhythms, its occupations, its spatial-temporal organization, its clandestine 'culture', its underground life" (Lefebvre, 1996, p. 113).

The objective of the chapter is to recognize the changes in the mobility system designed to cover a scope of municipalities of various sizes. The changes were aimed to adjust the system to the rhythm of the small city, using the capacity of the telematic transformation.

The problem is to identify the solution to the disadvantages of the transit vehicular traffic for a small city located at the intersection of the numerous regional and national routes. The chapter does not comprise the evaluation by the indexes used in the rankings of IESE Cities in Motion.

The following hypotheses will be verified:

1) Moving the transit vehicular traffic from the area of the small city to its administrational borders reduces the disruptions of the life rhythm of the small city and eliminates the disadvantages sourced in the transit traffic;
2) the smart transit center located on the edge of the city by the railway station allowed outer transit traffic to not commute to schools and workplaces directed towards the urban area;

3) the traffic and schedules of public urban transport for commuters to schools and work and for tourists have been harmonized with the arrivals to the smart transit center from further and closer surroundings;

4) existing and new cultural, economic, and social interlinks emerge in the urban and suburban space of the isochrones of 25 km.

The aim of the chapter is the recognition of changes in the transportation system in the context of adjusting to the city rhythm using the capacity of telematics transformation. The Feasibility Study of the Smart Transfer Hub was based on the following assumptions:

1) The Center concentrates traffic in one point of the area but not in the city center;

2) the Center allows commuters to combine various means of transportation;

3) the Center does not interrupt the natural city rhythm.

For the feasibility study of the investment, field research was conducted for three cross-cutting characteristics:

1) As for the spatial profile, the location of the transport route within territorial units, the usage, and functions of the examined areas were analyzed;

2) as for usage, passenger traffic intensity was examined during the day and on chosen days of the week;

3) as for social patterns, passengers' behavior and their opinions regarding the effectiveness of transportation systems were analyzed;

4) as for the institutional profile, the organization of transport was analyzed based on the opinions of the people directly responsible for organizing transport in the city.

In the chapter, selected results of the research and analysis of the spatial and institutional aspects are presented. The source of the information is the query of the programme strategic documents on the national and local levels, operating planning documents, interactive websites of the Regional Data Bank of the Statistics of Poland, reports of investment implementation[1] as well as the information and data retrieved by the questionnaire, interview, and the participative observation.

13.2 The Organization of Transportation in the Urban Area Harmonized with the City Rhythm: The Choice of the Place of Research

Like all organisms, the city lives in its own rhythm. The cyclical, repetitive stages systemize the city's order. Observing a sequence of changes stabilize over time allowed for drawing the cycle of urban life. It is determined by passing time—the seasons of the year and times of day mark the meaning of particular urban intervals. The intensity of traffic, the presence of specific actors inside the urban space (inhabitants, tourists, trespassers, and others), and the mutability of points in space affected by this presence are all factors, which, when observed in a systemic manner, will deliver knowledge about the city rhythm.

The author assumes that big investments in the urban infrastructure, including transportation investments, have an impact on the organization of urban space and on the environment. According to the most recent information, transport is responsible for 25% of the air pollution in Europe. The speed of the growth of emissions from this source is terrifying—in 2018 compared to 1990, growth reached 29% (EEA, 2019). The choice of the research was deliberate and its main arguments were the level of air pollution, the density of the transport network, and the diversity of city functions and its regional neighborhood.

The pollution map of the entire area of Poland was analyzed, indicating the Silesian Voivodship as the most polluted area requiring urgent action for the improvement of air, including changes in transportation systems. An example of the problem of changes in the organization of transport and its adjustment to city-rhythm life during the telematic transformation is a small city located in the Silesian Voivodship: Pszczyna.

The quality of the air in the analyzed area in Poland using the synthetic air quality index is presented by Chief Inspectorate For Environmental Protection (Inspectorate for Environmental Protection, 2021). Air Quality Index (AQI) is the simplest way to define the level of air pollution. Its scale is from zero to 500—the higher the index is, the greater the air pollution. The assessment of the air quality includes primarily the level of the suspended particulates PM2.5 and PM10 and also selected gas pollutants sulfur dioxide (SO_2), ozone (O_3), nitrogen oxide (NO), carbon monoxide (CO), and benzene, which are most frequently the result of the combustion of fuels. AQI could be referred to the American, Chinese, and so-called Polish standards (relevant to the member countries of the European Union). The European standard is more restrictive than the American one, which can be observed in the example of Pszczyna. For this city, the air quality index is at the passable level, i.e., to the 150 µg/m³ of the PM2.5 according to the American standard and only to the level of 75 µg/m³ of PM2.5 by the more severe EU standards.

According to the Development Strategy of the City Pszczyna for the years 2015–2023, in the III strategic area, the activities are designed to lower the atmospheric pollution for AQI improvement from the passable level to the moderate level or even to the good level (Strategy of the City Pszczyna . . ., 2015, p. 84).

Pszczyna is an active city in the context of green and smart mobility and a multifunctional city. It includes settlements and offers touristic, industrial, craft, and commerce functions. The city is said to be an important transportation hub following the big investment in the transport infrastructure. Pszczyna belongs to the group of Polish cities affected by the significant decrease of the population pictured also by the author's own calculations based on the data of the Statistics Poland (interactive websites of the Regional Data bank). In the years 1995–2016 a population decrease of 25% was observed, from 34,675 inhabitants in 1995 to 25,980 inhabitants in 2016.

In 2021, Pszczyna was inhabited by 25,833 citizens on an area of 22.5 km², with an average population density of 1,148.5 inhabitants per km². For the Pszczyna region, the urbanization rate amounted to 23.5%. According to data from the National Heritage Institute, as of December 15th, 2017, the 63 historical buildings and objects listed in the register of monuments were registered (Pszczyna w liczbach, 2017). There were areas of forest greenery and so-called Pszczyna forests surrounding the city in its direct proximity, giving shelter to wisents (the European bison) as a protected species (Sopot-Zembok & Cempura, 2020).[2]

The following places had substantial meaning for the gravity of the city's traffic structure: The City of the second half of the 13th century, i.e., the market square and the layout of the buildings surrounding it. The Castle from the 18th to 19th centuries (by today's 1 Ksawery Dunikowski St.) is also known as the Pszczyna Palace. There are five public roads of a voivodship category or higher, cutting through the city of Pszczyna, including the No. 1 state Road (DK1) and the regional roads DW 931, DW 933, DW 935, and DW 939. Two railway tracks lead through Pszczyna. They were used both for passenger and freight traffic, namely railway lines No. 139 Katowice-Zwardoń (LK 139) and railway No. 148 Pszczyna-Rybnik (LK 148) (Pszczyna w liczbach . . ., 2021).

The major transport gravity points, sorted by their meaning, were as follows:

1) The neighborhood of the historical city walls of Old Town;
2) the Castle Museum located in the Castle from the 18th to 19th centuries—the palace of the von Pless family;
3) the railway station.

The implementation of big infrastructure investment, which was the transformation of the railway station and its surroundings, and the construction of a bus transport hub (busses, coaches, minibusses) to the Transfer Hub altered the gravity of urban-space traffic. It has now become the central focus point for the new localization of business undertakings and new settlements of some offices and institutions.

According to the research questionnaire conducted after the investment had been completed, the majority of responders indicated that Pszczyna was a transportation hub. That differs from the previous questionnaire research which had been carried out when the most frequent answer was that Pszczyna is the hub of culture and tourism. Two essential questions arise:

1) Is the city rhythm regulated by the times of arrival and departure from and to other cities and districts of Pszczyna from the transfer hub?
2) Does Pszczyna lack one central point, which would serve typical functions (Wallis (1990), i.e., the function of the urban space with its natural rhythm?

If, following the result of the questionnaire research, Pszczyna is an important transportation hub, the traffic of pedestrians and cars is regulated by the cycle of traffic lights. During the week, in the morning and afternoon, the traffic lights stop hundreds of cars and pedestrians. In this aspect, the city fulfills this function practically all day long. The city changes in the late evening when the traffic loses its intensity, so it does not need to be regulated with lights. With the seasons changing throughout the year, the time of turning on the streetlamps, shop lights, and boards changes. In the summertime, urban space starts being lit with the illumination at about 9 PM and the light is turned off at about 4 AM.

Indicators such as the time of turning the streetlamps on and off, the length of the cycles of traffic lights, and the lights on or off in the windows of buildings all describe the city rhythm.

13.3 An Example of an Urban Profile and the Types of Arrangement of Urban and Suburban Space

The analysis of the arrangement of areas located in the transport layout of Pszczyna based on the county land registry and the Statistics Poland data was carried out by the author. Based on the analysis, six types of areas that generate traffic streams and passenger streams in various ways and on various levels could be distinguished. The proportions between the forms of land use, the density of buildings and their character, and the level of intensity of coverage of terrain with transport and settlement networks were the criteria of the type of space arrangement.

The urban and transport profile of the area intensity responded to the following types:

1) Type I: An urban area with investments represented by Pszczyna, Tychy, Goczałkowice, and Czechowice-Dziedzice; these were places with a very intense density of buildings and a high concentration of various services in a relatively small area with a high concentration of the population;

2) Type II: Invested-in suburb areas with a mixed habitation and service structure, and a limited production function; apart from farm properties, the services of craft, commerce, and random production grounds were located here; the functional diversity typical for suburban areas was characterized by a concentration of land arrangement and population concentration, which are above average;

3) Type III: Invested-in suburb areas with a mixed habitation and service structure, and holiday functionalities; farm households, single random services, and holiday resort estates were intertwined. The types of functions were characteristic of suburban areas, the type of buildings was characterized by an average intensity of land use with a seasonal population concentration fluctuating during a year;

4) Type IV: Invested-in rural areas of the settlement function and holiday resort estates; farm buildings dominate. The area arrangements were of average intensity with an average level of population concentration. The population concentration demonstrates seasonal population concentration fluctuating during the year, similarly to Type III;

5) Type V: Rural areas dominated by farm fields; mostly covered by arable fields and meadows; the terrain was of a low level of space arrangement and low population density;

6) Type VI: Forests with a minimal level of space usage; not populated by permanent inhabitants.

Based on the comparison of the areas generating the road and passenger traffic shared by the City Council of Pszczyna and the author's research on the land management in the communication context in Pszczyna and its neighborhood, the new convergences were identified. The results identified the new transport routes and new stops for the collective transport of the city and commune of Pszczyna. The generated passenger traffic justifies the investment "Integrated Transfer Hub in Pszczyna."

Within the urban profile, each type of area described previously can be assigned to a different level of generating road traffic, including passenger traffic.

Type I was characterized by a very strong and permanent capacity to generate passenger traffic. Type II generated strong passenger traffic with a periodic seasonal increase in the number of participants in such traffic. Types III and IV generated average passenger traffic, while V and VI generate passenger traffic only at a limited level.

The analysis of passenger traffic was conducted for random bus routes linked by a network with the Integrated Transfer Hub in Pszczyna. Three very serious constraints were interfering:

1) The decrease of the passenger traffic intensity due to the COVID-19 pandemic (administrational restrictions of sanitary authorities, recommendations of healthcare authorities, lockdown affecting employees' commutes);
2) the decrease of the railway links during the recent decade and more due to the drastic reduction of the railway network in Silesia caused by the decline of its profitability (railway lines operated were reduced from 2,155 km in 2010 to 1,912 km in 2020 (Statistics Poland, 2021);
3) the creation and successive growth of bike paths thanks to co-financing from the EU funds (bike paths increase their total length from nearly zero kilometers in 2010 to 726.3 km in 2015 and 1,194.9 km in 2020 (Statistics Poland, 2021).

The indicated research limitations showed that the identified passenger traffic was not a result of one factor but many factors coinciding. According to experts studied, one of the crucial factors was the launch of the Smart Transfer Hub.

The results of the analysis indicated that the heaviest used external routes (with consideration for acceptable borders due to the COVID-19 pandemic) were:

1) Pszczyna—Kobiór—Tychy;
2) Pszczyna—Goczałkowice—Czechowice-Dziedzice;
3) Pszczyna—Zakopane.

The route Pszczyna—Zakopane was characterized by seasonal fluctuation in passenger traffic due to the dominating tourist function of Zakopane—the resort in the Polish Tatra Mountains.

Additionally, the analysis presents ways to other external towns (beyond the Pszczyna county), however, with lower isochrones of distance from the Integrated Transfer Hub of average use (with consideration for acceptable borders due to the COVID-19 pandemic):

1) Pszczyna—Wola;
2) Pszczyna—Jawiszowice;
3) Pszczyna—Żory;
4) Pszczyna—Pawłowice;
5) Pszczyna—Strumień;
6) Pszczyna—Rybnik;
7) Pszczyna—Jankowice—Studience;
8) Pszczyna—Bieruń.

Among the routes crossing the administrational border linking Pszczyna with its suburban areas, the ones used most intensely were:

1) Pszczyna—Rydułtowice—Ćwiklice;
2) Pszczyna—Polne Domy;
3) Czarków—Pszczyna CP—Pszczyna Szpital;
4) Pszczyna—Czarnków Kościół via Stara Wies;
5) Pszczyna—Czarnków Skrzyżowanie via Piasek.

Further routes emerging as the most frequently used within city borders as a result of the analysis were:

1) F1 Pszczyna—Złoty Kłos;
2) F2 Pszczyna—Złoty Kłos;
3) A Pszczyna—Wisła Mała;
4) A Pszczyna Transfer Hub—Szymanowskiego Street.

The analysis of passenger traffic in the urban area by internal city routes and routes operating within the borders of the Pszczyna county led to interesting conclusions. The observations made on working days from 6 AM to 9 PM demonstrated a peak of transfers from 6 AM to 9 AM with a maximum between 7 AM and 8 AM. This significant domination in vehicle traffic intensity during the day was related to school and work commutes. Between 9 AM and 1 PM, traffic intensity falls by half. Smaller values noted in this time interval reveal the daily rhythm of urban life (before the meridian behavior related to having to be at work or school dominate visibly). Past 1 PM, slow growth of the number of passengers who start or end their work in the afternoon hours can be observed, with rush hours between 3 PM and 5 PM. After 5 PM, a gradual decrease in activities outside of the home among permanent Pszczyna inhabitants can be observed.

The fluctuation of the intensity of passenger traffic was related to the seasonal holiday period and the summer holidays at schools and colleges and results from repetitive cycles of lockdown during the pandemic crisis caused by COVID-19. It was observed that during the holidays a load of internal routes is half the load observed on working days.

The study of the intensity of passenger traffic was carried out, observing the sources in external areas and with the tourist-and-visitor stream passing through the Integrated Transfer Hub. The observation revealed flows towards Pszczyna Castle and the beautiful park surrounding the Castle. The stream's peak time was during the weekends and the summer holidays. The lowest traffic is observed on these routes in winter. The traffic intensity reveals the seasonal rhythm of the city fulfilling touristic and leisure functions.

13.4 Developing a Sustainable Transport System in the City Using New Investment Initiatives and Smart Telematic Solutions

The literature on the topic distinguishes at least three models of city relations with its neighborhood, which are (Guy & Marvin, 2001):

1) Redesigning the city model (RDC)—designed as a compact and energy-efficient municipality;
2) the externally-dependent-city model (EDC)—i.e., the city relying on external influences;
3) the self-reliant-city model—in which the city strives for the deep internalization of its economy and environmental activities as well as openness, integration, and cooperation with the ecosystem.

Big infrastructure investments, such as the Integrated Transfer Hub, allowed for the assessment of Pszczyna as a city aspiring to become a self-reliant city.

The initiative for the construction of the Integrated Transfer Hub was initiated by the Council of Pszczyna county in 2013. The studies and design works were carried out in 2016 when the ground was purchased from the Polish State Railways (PKP) for the construction of the Hub in 2017. The contract for co-financing from EU funds was signed, and with a financial outlay of PLN 17.8 million (ca. € 3.9 million), a modern Integrated Transfer Hub was created and opened in 2019. The Hub comprises, among others, 180 parking places for bikes and 200 parking places for cars.

Despite the research constraints, the statement was justified that the investment brought about many advantages for the city and the region, such as:

1) The improvement of the road infrastructure;
2) the opening of the city for its touristic values (cultural and natural) to tourists;
3) the integration of passenger streams and other transportation facilitations for inhabitants and visitors, including the passenger streams generated in the new areas of the mobility gravity area surrounding Pszczyna;
4) the introduction of new technological solutions, including the first telematic approach.

Despite the unquestionable predominance of opportunities over threats, a serious risk of the increase in harmful emissions appeared, particularly for the atmospheric air due to the multiplication of the transportation fleet using the Integrated Transfer Hub serving internal city routes, external suburb routes, and long-distance coaches. Currently, the Integrated Transfer Hub is used by 170 busses and other vehicles of collective passenger transport, serving the routes related to the Hub.

According to the Long-Term Financial Prognosis in the attachment The Inventory of the Undertakings to the Long-Term Prognosis, the position 1.1.2.1 lists the following undertaking: The Construction of the Integrated Transfer Center with a Necessary Infrastructure, construction of the bike paths—Improvement of the Mobility Quality in Pszczyna commune with the budget of PLN 28,699,539.00, including the limit for 2022 of PLN 7,588,377.35 (with the main expenditure: New technological solutions). In the position 1.3.1.7, the amount of PLN 100,860.00 with a limit of PLN 80,688.00 is dedicated to the Study of the Conditions and Spatial Planning of Pszczyna commune together with the forecasting of the impact on the environment and the preparation of the eco-physiographic study for the Pszczyna commune—the directions of the spatial development (Table 13.1).

Table 13.1 Mobility and Collective Passenger Transport in Pszczyna in 2021, in the Opinions of Experts, Users, and Contractors.

Sources generating the most passenger traffic (% of responses)	*Main factors defining the rhythm of the city (% of responses)*	*The mobility and technology priorities with the participation of the city (% of responses)*
— educational institutions and facilities—46% — culture, sport, and tourist locations and facilities—16% — administration and governmental offices—10% — workplaces—10% — open markets and shopping malls—9% — hospitals and the specialized clinics—4% — railway and bus stations—3% — external sources of the transit character 2%.	— the leading function of Pszczyna as a support mobility hub on the background of other functions—58% — the daily traffic rush hours as a leading indicator of rhythm of the city compared to other indicators—81% — the following months as the peak of the season related to the school year (sorted by the intensity): March, April, September, October—65% — the peak months for short tourist visits (sorted by the intensity): June, July, and August—55%.	— improvement of passenger care in the areas on the borders with other regions in Poland—43% — reinforcement of the national Silesia—Kraków schemes and links and Agglomerations of Bielsko-Biała and Rybnik with Ostrava—26% — improvement of the network of long-distance links with the South and southeast of Poland—26% — the implementation of the new technologies, including telematics—21%.

Main founders and collective transport providers cooperating with them in the urban space (% of indications)	*The assessment of the routes and courses (one-way and return) (% of responses)*	*The structure of the passengers by the origins, habits, personal features, and expectations of passengers of the collective transport in the city (% of responses)*
— the Mayor of the city of Pszczyna—81% — Pszczyna's chief administrative officer (Starosta)—11% — the Mayor of Tychy—3% — the Mayor of Żory—2% — the Marshal of the Silesian Voivodship—2% — the Marshal of the Lesser Poland Voivodship—2%.	— responders glad about the location of routes and stops—55%; responders proposing new stops—14%; remaining responders did not have an opinion — persons suggesting the higher frequency of the routes—30%, the higher density of the network—30%; happy about the schedules—25%; and with no opinion—15%; — using the public transport regularly from Monday to Friday—15%; regularly on Saturday and Sunday—5%; irregularly from Monday to Friday—29%; and infrequently—51%.	— the share of the citizens of Pszczyna in the passengers' structure is 22% among the thirteen municipalities — the shares of the youth from sixteen to twenty years old—the biggest share—82% among seven age intervals — the share of the passengers without a driving license—51%; passengers ecologically aware—22%; acknowledging the lower cost of the public transport—11% — the share of the expectations of the modern fleet, higher standards, and ecology standards—9%.

Source: Author's own elaboration.

The city aimed at shaping a sustainable transportation system, with major desired features—firstly, limiting the need to move and, secondly, shortening the distance the citizens have to overcome when commuting to work, schools, or shopping centers. The development of remote jobs and workplaces, digital sales channels, and the development of e-commerce platforms foster these pursuits. The environmental risk triggered by urban transport systems will be reduced by the purchase of electric vehicles and other technological measures, among them telematics.

Telematics is a way of limiting the loss ratio in the car fleet. The installation of the telematic system means caring for safety and economic driving, i.e., saving petrol, reducing car usage (Król, 2011; Merkisz-Guranowska et al., 2015; Neumann, 2017; Nowacki, 2008; Plusiński, 2017; Wydro, 2005; Wydro, 2008). Adaptive cruise-control sensors, eco-roll systems, retarders or MX, the collision-warning system with an emergency deceleration to zero, automatic car steering based on the tilts of the set, and the tire pressure sensor are just a few of many amenities offered to drivers.

An analysis of the usage correctness of solutions affecting safety and earth-bound parameters, such as the level of gas-pedal pressure or the way and time of the usage of a retarder and breaks will help to form an adequate transport policy in the city.[3] The automation of processes creates the possibility to increase work efficiency and optimize the time for the tasks of carriers and dispatchers. Thanks to the modern technology of TMS (transport-management systems), orders can be proficiently planned, shipped, delivered, and settled.[4] The city telematics platform, which delivers telematics services for such bodies as the Integrated Transfer Hub and related providers servicing particular routes, should be of interest to the city council. Górecka (2021) states that systemic solutions in public transport in cities depend on the adopted transportation strategy for the particular unit. The adoption of the sustainable strategy leads to limiting private car usage to the advantage of public transport and to actions for the protection of the natural environment including the air.

13.5 Conclusions

Green and smart mobility is a strategy with ecological and digital transformation at its basis. Its purpose is to increase the resilience of transportation in future crises. As indicated in the European Green Deal, thanks to the smart, competitive, and safe transportation system, which is accessible and cost-attractive for users, emissions can be lowered by 90% by 2050.

As national research indicates, Polish big and small cities join the ecological transformation and implement smart mobility. The analysis of the study case of Pszczyna leads to the following conclusions:

1) New infrastructure investments, such as the integrated Transfer Hub in Pszczyna, influence the activation of the suburb zone and the integration with other remote city hubs thanks to long-distance bus routes;
2) the intensity of passenger traffic reflects the rhythm of urban life, including seasonal changes;
3) the environmentally friendly city-transport policy aims to limit the human need to relocate, and it tries to shorten the distance;
4) the telematics, including the urban telematics platform, is a chance for the development of "a self-reliant city," including its vicinity and shaping the transport system sustainably in terms of the environment, organization, and technology.

Considerations within this chapter allowed us to verify the hypothesis formed at the beginning that the smart transfer center is an investment facilitating the organization of the sustainable transport in the city thanks to the concentration of traffic at one point in the area and also beyond the city center in line with the rhythm of urban life.

The integrated Transfer Hub located in the proximity of the railway station helps passengers to combine various transportation means, and encourages the usage of railways, which are, currently, the friendliest to the environment.

Notes

1 The project "The Construction of the Transfer Center in Pszczyna with the Necessary Assisting Infrastructure" and other materials acquired from the Marshal Office of the Silesian Voivodship, Department of Geodesy, Real Estate Management and Spatial Planning in Katowice, documentation of the contest "The Best Public Space of the Silesian Voivodship", The Management of the Silesian Voivodship in cooperation with the Polish Architects Association, Katowice Branch, edition 2020.
2 The story of the resettlement of wisents to Pszczyna forests originates in 1865 when wisents were brought to this area on the initiative of the Prince von Pless, Jan Henryk XI Hochberg. More on the topic can be found in the chronicles of Pszczyna.

3 The problem is discussed in more depth in texts in sector press such as "Motor Transport" and "Commercial Motor"
4 There are two types of TMS software available on the market: local and cloud based. In the first case, the software is installed on the local computer and is accessible by the user directly.

References

EEA. (2019). *The First and Last Mile—the Key to Sustainable Urban Transport. Transport and Environment Report*. EEA Report No 18/2019.

Górecka, A. (2021). Zarządzanie transportem miejskim aglomeracji Warszawy—kontekst środowiskowy [Urban transport management of the Warsaw agglomeration—environmental context]. In: W. Pizło (ed.), *Współczesne obszary zarządzania [Contemporary Areas of Management]* (pp. 55–70). Warsaw: Management Institute, WULS Publishing House.

Guy, S., & Marvin, S. (2001). Models and pathways: The diversity of sustainable urban future. In: K. Williams, E. Burton, & M. Jenks (eds.), *Achieving Sustainable Urban Forms* (pp. 9–18). London & New York: Spon Press.

Inspectorate for Environmental Protection. (2021). Retrieved from: https://powietrze.gios.gov.pl/pjp/current Available [March 26, 2021].

Kaźmierczak, M. (2021). *Smart city po polsku. Tak nasze miasta staja sie inteligentniejsze [Smart City in Polish: This Is How Our Cities Get Smarter]*. Retrieved from: www.bankier.pl/wiadomosc/Smart-city-po-polsku-Tak-nasze-miasta-staja-sie-inteligentniejsze-8242747.html Available [March 26, 2022].

Król, H. (2011). Telematyka transportu drogowego elementem bezpieczeństwa [Road transport telematics as an element of safety]. *Logistyka*, 3, 1389–1398.

Lefebvre, H. (1996). Seen from the window. In: H. Lefebvre, E. Kofman, & E. Lebas (eds.), *Writings on Cities*. Oxford: Blackwell Publishing.

Merkisz-Guranowska, A., Andrzejewski, M., & Stawecka, H. (2015). Przydatność telematyki transportowej w ocenie energochłonności ruchu pojazdów [Usefulness of transport telematics in the assessment of energy consumption of vehicle traffic]. *Prace naukowe Politechniki Warszawskiej*, 107, 86–91.

Neumann, T. (2017). Wykorzystanie systemów telematyki na przykładzie wybranych przedsiębiorstw transportu drogowego [The use of telematics systems on the example of selected road transport companies]. *Autobusy*, 3, 605–610.

Nowacki, G. (2008). *Telematyka transportu drogowego [Telematics of Road Transport]*. Warsaw, Poland: Wydawnictwo Instytutu Transportu Samochodowego.

Plusiński, R. (2017) Telematyka w paragrafach [Telematics in paragraphs]. *Truck & Business Polska*, 1, 28–30.

Pszczyna w liczbach. (2017). Retrieved from: www.polskawliczbach.pl/Pszczyna# formy-ochrony-przyrody Available [July 30, 2021].

Pszczyna w liczbach. (2021). Retrieved from: www.polskawliczbach.pl/Pszczyna# transport-i-komunikacja Available: [July 30, 2021].

Sopot-Zembok, B., & Cempura, G. (eds.). (2020). *Kroniki Pszczyńskie, Z4 [Pszczyna's Cronicles]*. Pszczyna, Poland: UM Pszczyna and Towarzystwa Miłośników Ziemi Pszczyńskiej.

Statistics Poland. (2021). *The Yearbook of the Silesian Voivodship for 2021*. Katowice: Statistical Office in Katowice.

Strategy of the City Pszczyna for 2015–2023. (2015). Retrieved from: https://bip. pszczyna.pl/zalacznik/20379 Available [October 15, 2021].

Wallis, A. (1990). *Socjologia przestrzeni [Sociology of Space]*. Warsaw, Poland: Niezależna Oficyna Wydawnicza.

Wydro, K. (2005). Telematyka—znaczenia i definicje terminu [Telematics—meanings and definitions of the term]. *Telekomunikacja i Techniki Informacyjne, 1–2*, 116–130.

Wydro, K. (2008). Usługi i systemy telematyczne w transporcie [Transport telematics services and systems]. *Telekomunikacja i Techniki Informacyjne, 3–4*, 23–32.

Chapter 14

Food-Sharing Economy: Analysis of Selected Solutions in the Warsaw Agglomeration

Agata Balińska

Warsaw University of Life Science—SGGW, Poland

Contents

14.1 Introduction

The sharing economy is an interesting socioeconomic trend manifesting itself mainly in large cities. As an economic phenomenon, sharing is usually analyzed in the area of transport services (e.g., city bikes, electric scooters, car sharing, Uber, BlaBlaCar) and lodging services (e.g., Airbnb). During the COVID-19 pandemic, the intensity of sharing various resources has been inhibited. The sharing-economy concept is also applicable in the area of the redistribution of surplus food and groceries. With this in mind, properly equipped and maintained local food-sharing points are being set up. There are public storage places,

DOI: 10.4324/9781003304364-17

where every individual can leave surplus food for others to take. Independently, mobile applications are being created that enable contact between stakeholders in the food-exchange process (i.e., the donor and the recipient). There are also several institutions in Poland (e.g., Polish Food Banks) that act as an intermediary between those in need and donors, primarily retail chains, individual shopkeepers, and food producers. Also, individuals can become donors by donating food to volunteers of Polish Food Banks in shopping centers and supermarkets during food-collecting actions.

This study focuses on local food sharing points and food- or meal-sharing mobile applications that enable donating and obtaining food on a noncommercial basis. They can be used by both senior citizens, who do not use digital technologies (local food-sharing points), and young people for whom new media is a natural way of communicating with the world. The reason for undertaking this research was the very idea of food sharing, which, firstly, limits food waste, and, secondly, enables the transfer of surplus goods to those in need (redistribution). When justifying the choice of this research problem, it is necessary to indicate the scale of food waste with which we are dealing. According to a new UN report (UNEP Food Waste Index Report, 2021), "around 931 million tonnes of food waste was generated in 2019, 61 percent of which came from households." The report points to the fact that "household per capita food waste generation is found to be broadly similar across country income groups, suggesting that action on food waste is equally relevant in high, upper-middle and lower-middle income countries." The figures on food waste and loss are particularly controversial due to the fact that approximately 690 million people worldwide are malnourished. Food waste is not only an ethical problem but also an environmental problem. The same report stated: "The fact that substantial amounts of food are produced but not eaten by humans has substantial negative impacts: environmentally, socially and economically. Estimates suggest that 8–10% of global greenhouse gas emissions are associated with food that is not consumed" (UNEP Food Waste Index Report, 2021, 2021). Food waste is not only discarding food products but also wasting water that was used in the process of growing crops, the production of fuels for agricultural-machinery means of transport, energy, and the water used in food processing. It is also the loss of forests, which in some regions of the world are cut on a large scale to enable expanding the area of banana, avocado, and maize plantations or pasture areas for livestock. These are just a few examples of the damage to the environment caused by the overproduction of food. If the discarded food were a country, it would be the third-largest emitter of carbon dioxide, right after China and the USA (Sobolak, 2021).

Table 14.1 Total Annual Food Waste Produced in Selected Countries.

Country	Food waste per year (in millions of tonnes)	Food waste per capita (kg)
China	91.6	64
India	68.8	50
the United States	19.4	59
Japan	8.2	64
Germany	6.3	75
France	5.5	85
the United Kingdom	5.2	77
Russia	4.9	33

Source: Based on www.statista.com (retrieved 20 December, 2021).

Food waste is not the only characteristic of rich countries. The highest figures for food waste, of course, are in countries with the largest populations. However, when food waste is calculated per capita, this ranking changes (Table 14.1).

Despite appearing to have a relatively high level of total food waste compared to other countries (Table 14.1), some nations discard less per capita, e.g., the Russians, while the French waste the most per capita but their total food-waste index is lower due to a smaller population. In Poland, according to the research of the Food Rationalization and Reduction Program (PROM) (Bank Żywności, 2021) we waste 4.8 million tonnes of food. So every second 153 kilograms of food end up in the bin. More than half (a minimum of 53%) of wasted and lost food comes from households, followed by processing (19%), gastronomy (12%), production (11%), and distribution (5%). In 2018, 42% of Poles admitted to throwing away food. The most commonly discarded products include bread (49%), fruit (46%), cold meats (45%), vegetables (37%), yogurts (27%), potatoes (17%), and milk (12%). The most frequently mentioned reason for throwing away food is exceeding the use-by date (29% of indications). The less frequently mentioned reasons include: Overbuying (20%), excessive meal portions (15%), purchasing poor-quality products (15%), and improper food storage (13%) (Bankier.Pl, 2021). The scale of the phenomenon of food waste prompted the European Parliament to adopt the document: P8_TA (2017) 0207 "Resource efficiency: reducing food waste, improving food safety, the European Parliament resolution of 16 May 2017 on the initiative on resource efficiency: reducing food waste, improving food safety (2016/2223 (INI))" (European Parliament, 2021). The same concern was behind the 2030 Agenda for Sustainable Development adopted by UN member states. Food loss and waste are covered by Goal 12 entitled "Sustainable Consumption and Production," and specifically by Target 12.3: "By 2030, half per capita global food waste at the retail and consumer levels and reduce food losses along production and supply chains, including post-harvest losses" (United Nations, 2021). Food-sharing solutions analyzed in this chapter refer both to the resolutions of the European Parliament and the United Nations Agenda for Sustainable Development. Taking into account the abovementioned facts and figures, there is a need for a reduction in food waste by end users, i.e., households. The largest concentrations of consumers are found in large cities. The scale of food waste is also particularly noticeable in large cities (Sapała, 2019; Lee, 2018; Warshawsky, 2019; Mugica & Rose, 2019).

Sharing solutions are also an important part of city logistics, as they work effectively primarily in densely populated areas, i.e., in cities. During the pandemic, food sharing has undergone some modifications, and new initiatives have emerged (e.g., the unpaid delivery of dishes from restaurateurs to doctors and nurses working in infectious-disease hospitals). Food-sharing solutions also fit in with the scope of shared consumption, and even the Smart City concept (How Food Waste Costs Our Cities Millions, 2021). As this is a relatively new phenomenon, it is still not sufficiently described in the literature. This study aims to contribute to the existing research gap.

The research presented in this chapter covers both food-shargin solutions that require the fairly free use of new media (mobile applications, e.g., Too Good To Go) and those that do not even require a mobile phone (local food-sharing points). The local food-sharing points are specially adapted places, equipped with a refrigerator and a closed cupboard, without architectural barriers. People can leave surplus food or leftovers in the fridge without fear that they will go off. On the other hand, people looking for food can come and take the products that suit them free of charge. The donor and the person in need do not meet. Wherever possible, the food-sharing points are arranged in such a way that both those who leave food and those who look for food can use them at any time, regardless of the working hours of any institution. Thus, they are located in public spaces, very often on the premises of municipal or city authorities and universities, etc. The originator (local authorities, a university, a housing community, etc.) takes on the obligation of keeping the infrastructure of the point clean. Information about local food-sharing points is placed on notice boards of local housing cooperatives, municipalities, cities, etc., and posted on the Internet. Whisper marketing is also important here. The participants of the sharing process do not meet. Moreover, the same person can simultaneously be in two roles, i.e., leave what they will not use (eat) and take what someone else has left. Recently, the food-sharing points have also been referred to as "social refrigerators" (Wezpomoz, 2021). This name results from the fact that refrigerators are part of the necessary equipment in such places, but the name also has a symbolic meaning. It indicates that the food there is stored under appropriate conditions and has a short shelf life. In public spaces, and especially in the mass media, information on the possibility of leaving surplus food in "social refrigerators" most often appears before Christmas and Easter. This is because the side effect of these holidays is, unfortunately, food waste at a scale even two or three times bigger than normal. Unfortunately, the research on the actual functioning of the food-sharing points and the roles of their users has been insufficient. The author's observations showed that this type of food-sharing facility is mainly used for seniors.

Mobile apps facilitate food sharing in a slightly different way. Depending on the application, natural persons, but very often shops or food outlets (restaurants, cafes, pizzerias, etc.) post information about products that they want to give away or sell at a reduced price at a given moment. A consumer who wants to take advantage of such an offer reserves it, pays if it is to be paid for, and collects it directly from the place where it is offered. Despite the fact that the information is transferred via the Internet, ultimately the parties meet at the arranged time and place (usually at the donor's). Unlike the food-sharing point, this process is not completely anonymous.

The aim of this study was to present the perceptions and experiences of consumers (the sample included Warsaw residents) using food-sharing points and food- or meal-sharing apps.

The following research questions were adopted:

1) To what extent are food-sharing points and food-sharing apps popular with respondents?
2) What are the motives behind the use of food-sharing solutions?
3) What are the barriers to the use of food-sharing solutions?
4) To what extent do sociodemographic variables influence the use of the analyzed forms of food sharing?

The choice of Warsaw as the place to conduct this research was deliberate. Due to the fact that it is the capital and the largest Polish city (with a population of 2 million inhabitants), various forms of sharing economy are being implemented in its area, including food-sharing initiatives.

There are 38 food-sharing points in Warsaw (Jadłodzielnie, 2021), and their greatest concentration is in the central districts of the city. Also, over 500 entities from Warsaw are registered in a database of the most popular food-sharing application Too Good To Go (Toogoodtogo, 2021). The mission of both the food-sharing points and the app is to save food and prevent the discarding of food.

14.2 Theoretical Background: Food Sharing as Part of the Concept of the Sharing Economy

The phenomenon of sharing is a socioeconomic system, which is based on the maximum use of resources owned by an individual by making them available to other people, including consumers, primarily through the use of massively available new technologies. It is a kind of consumer cooperation. Majchrzak (2016) points out that the sharing economy manifests itself on the market in various forms and structures, both nonprofit and generating profit for one of the parties. In the scientific literature, this concept is also referred to as collaborative consumption, the sharing economy, the collaborative economy, the access economy, or the peer economy (Burgiel, 2014). These concepts are not completely unambiguous but share many features.

Botsman (2013) points out that the collaborative economy is the broadest concept in the field of the sharing economy. It consists of a whole range of interrelationships of both individuals and communities in four areas: Production, finance, education, and consumption.

Botsman (2013) treats the sharing economy as an element of collaborative consumption (Figure 14.1). It can be defined as an economic model consisting of accessing various types of resources or people's property and sharing them by renting, swapping, bartering, or reselling both goods and services. One of the three systems[1] that make up collaborative consumption is collaborative lifestyles. The idea of the sharing economy concerns precisely this element of collaborative consumption. Collaborative lifestyles form a system based on people sharing their unutilized resources through mobile applications, websites, or in-common physical spaces with other members of the community. These resources include space, skills, free time, and food, which are analyzed in this chapter.

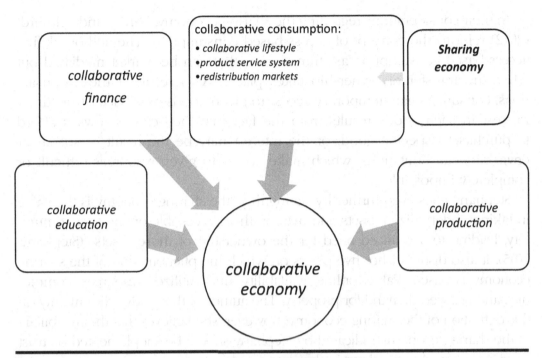

Figure 14.1 Components of the Collaborative Economy.

Source: Own visualization based on: "The Sharing Economy Lacks a Shared Definition," Fast Company. (2013). R. Botsman. www.fastcompany.com/3022028/the-sharing-economy-lacks-a-shared-definition

It is worth noting that communication within this system is based on direct interpersonal contacts, in the literature referred to as P2P (peer-to-peer) communication (Allen & Berg, 2014), Typically, it does not include intermediaries, although there are examples of intermediaries that play a managerial role (Ulug & Trell, 2020).

Belk, on the other hand, focuses on collaborative consumption, which he describes as "people coordinating the acquisition and distribution of a resource for a fee or other compensation," where other compensation is understood as a nonmonetary barter (Belk, 2014). It seems that, in the author's understanding, forms of sharing resources for which no compensation is provided, as it is in the case of surplus food left in local food-sharing points, do not count as collaborative consumption. It is difficult to agree with this approach. Even if we accept Belk's interpretation of barter exchanges, the benefits of the parties do not have to be the same. For the recipient, the benefit is free food, and for the donor, the benefit may be immaterial, e.g., a sense of agency, satisfaction, fulfilled duty, or meeting ethical or religious standards.

In their considerations regarding the sharing economy, Bardhi and Eckhardt (2012) refer to the concept of access-based consumption. The authors define access-based consumption as "transactions that can be market mediated but where no transfer of ownership takes place." As a result of these transactions, consumers gain temporary access to given goods or services. Consumer interest in such goods results from the fact that they cannot always afford to purchase a specific good, or the interest may be the result of spatial or environmental limitations, which make access to given resources difficult or completely impossible.

Stephany goes even further by stating that "the sharing economy is the value in taking underutilized assets and making them accessible online to a community, leading to a reduced need for the ownership of those assets" (Stephany, 2015). It also distinguishes five pillars on which the phenomenon of the sharing economy is based: Value, online availability, underutilized resources, community, and reduced demand for property. The author of this study relies mainly on this definition of the sharing economy; however, she believes that the five pillars of the sharing economy indicated by Stephany should be supplemented by trust as an indispensable mediator in the sharing processes.

Jaros (2016) lists a wide range of behaviors that are included in the sharing-economy concept. The list includes sharing, bartering, renting, lending, recycling, and repairing. This chapter focuses on local food-sharing points and mobile applications for food- or meal-sharing. The former can be classified as a locally based, neighbor-to-neighbor solution (Schwalb, 2020), while the latter is mediated by information technology. In the area of meal sharing, host-guest matching platforms and applications are becoming more and more helpful, and they are increasingly popular with young consumers. One of the most interesting is EatWith. The website is advertised as "the largest community in the world that offers culinary experiences with residents in over 130 countries" (Eatwith, 2021). EatWith connects chefs and cooking enthusiasts, residents of tourist destinations, and tourists—food lovers, looking for unique, authentic culinary experiences. People using the website have the opportunity to eat dinner in private homes or participate in cooking together. There were five offers from Poland on the website, all of them added by the same user (Eatwith, 2021).

Another example is the platform EatAway (Eataway.Com, 2021). Initially, the main idea was to post the hosts' offers for shared meals in their private homes. Then, the platform also began to provide the possibility of ordering meals from private individuals with personal pickup. At the end of 2020, it had over 500 hosts from 73 cities. The number of such applications is still growing, e.g., Ordinary Dinner, Too Good To Go, Meeatie, TasteAndSharePL.

It should be emphasized that sharing a meal requires mutual trust between hosts and guests. The hosts share their private space and put their culinary skills to evaluation. The guests, in turn, must trust that the meals are prepared under appropriately hygienic conditions, from good-quality ingredients, and that they will satisfy their culinary tastes. However, both parties may fear spending time with a stranger.

Many authors argue that food-sharing apps are a form of community self-organization aimed at replacing the anonymity of the food system with creating social relationships through sharing. The research of E.J. Veen also shows that users look for good value for money and expect the price to reflect the noncommercial nature of this initiative (Veen, 2019).

It is also worth noting that sharing food is a universal human trait that was a central component of economic and social life in hunter-gatherer societies. Socioeconomic development slowed down this phenomenon, especially in developed countries in the second half of the 20th century. Food sharing and limiting food-waste trends make donating surplus food to others and celebrating meals in a larger group a socially desirable behavior. As emphasized by Gurven and Jaeggi, research on this issue should take into account cross-cultural differences in sharing norms and behavior, and apply a variety of research methods to better combine the observed sharing patterns with the study of underlying social conventions and beliefs (Gurven & Jaeggi, 2015). The studies of Harvey et al. (2020) show that donor-recipient reciprocity and balance are rare. Most often, people are only donors or recipients. The research also shows that for the seamless functioning of the application, the location where the food is picked up is also important and should be comfortable for each party.

An interesting approach to technological solutions was proposed by Feenberg, who claims that technology is not an independent variable, but is co-constructed by social forces that it organizes and liberates (Feenberg, 2012). This perspective takes into account not only the technical components but also the material, personal, political, and social aspects of sharing mediated by technology that allows for food redistribution (Davies, 2019). Such solutions are also analyzed as part of an urban civic collective that facilitates local activities in the field of food-sharing initiatives (Ulug & Trell, 2020). The mobile applications used in this process are treated as an innovation in the food-sharing model but they are only one of the elements facilitating this process. This is a very important component, undergoing intensive development, which makes it the subject of analyses by many researchers (Rosenlund et al., 2020; Berketova & Volodina, 2020; Harvey et al., 2020).

14.3 Materials and Methods

The research process followed the stages presented in Table 14.2.

This study involved the analysis of source materials (publications) and computer-assisted web interviewing (CAWI). The survey questionnaire was prepared on the Survio platform. The following types of questions were used in the survey: Filtering questions, alternative questions, single-answer multiple-choice questions as well as ranking- and rating-scale questions. The link to the survey was shared on social media and other online platforms from September to October 2019. The survey was addressed to the residents of Warsaw; therefore the link was posted on social-media groups associating with the residents of the capital. To make sure that only Warsaw residents would participate in the study, the filtering question "Are you currently living in Warsaw?" was used. A positive answer made it possible to move on to the next part of the questionnaire, a negative one ended the participation in the study. In this way, the non-random-selection method of elimination was used (Mazurek-Łopacińska, 2005).

The actual research was preceded by a pilot study carried out in June 2019, which allowed for the improvement of the research tool.

550 people took part in the actual survey. The group was diverse in terms of gender, age, education level, and disposable income per person. The collected dataset was analyzed quantitatively and qualitatively. The statistical tools included: The Mann-Whitney test, the Kruskal-Wallis test, and Spearman

Table 14.2 Research Stages.

Step 1	Review of literature on food sharing
Step 2	Identification of food-sharing solutions implemented in Warsaw
Step 3	Setting research questions and objectives
Step 4	Designing the questionnaire
Step 5	Pilot study
Step 6	Pilot study data analysis and verification of the questionnaire design
Step 7	Main study—data collection
Step 8	Qualitative verification of the collected data
Step 9	Choosing statistical methods, processing data
Step 10	Interpretation of data

Source: Own research.

R. The research results have been presented in graphic, tabular, and descriptive forms.

The supporting technique was participant observation conducted at the food-sharing point located near the Warsaw-Ursynów district office, as well as online forums and thematic groups gathering people seeking and sharing knowledge and experience in the area of the sharing economy.

14.4 Research Results and Discussion

The survey involved a sample with the following characteristics: Regarding gender, the majority of the respondents (61.8%), were women. In terms of age, the structure of respondents was as follows: 38.2% were under 25; 21.2% were aged 26–35; 19.8% were aged 36–45; 14.5% were aged 46–55; and 7.3% were aged 56+. As for household size, the number of people per household was quite diverse; most people declared two-person households (36.4%), three- and four-person households (23.6% each), one-person households (9.1%), five and more persons (7.3%). The research plan also required the respondents to declare their net disposable income per person (i.e., "spare cash" left after bills like rent and mortgage, etc.). Respondents most often declared amounts over PLN 2,000 (approx. EUR 468.4)—34.5%; PLN 1,000–1,500 (approx. EUR 232.6–348.8)—25.5%; PLN 1,500–2,000 (EUR 348.9–468.3)—20.2%; and up to PLN 1,000 (EUR 232.5)—19.8%.

To begin with, the level of use and the respondents' attitude to food-sharing points and food-sharing applications were verified (Table 14.3).

The declared frequency of use of the analyzed food-sharing solutions was rather low (Table 14.3). It is worth noting, however, that a positive attitude

Table 14.3   Frequency of Use and the Attitude of the Respondents to Food-Sharing Points and Applications (in %).

Frequency of use	Food-sharing apps	Food-sharing points
Two to three times a month	4.4	0.5
A few times a year	13.6	12.7
Once in a few years	1.8	1.8
I don't use it but I believe it is needed	71	77.7
I don't use it and I believe it is not needed	9.2	7.3

Source: Own research.

towards them prevailed even among people declaring no experience with their use. A positive attitude towards food-sharing solutions was also confirmed in the research of other authors (e.g., Płaczek & Ziętara, 2021). Due to the relatively small share of people with experience in the use of food-sharing points and applications in the sample and a lack of significant differences in their responses, they will further be analyzed as one group.

The aim of this study was to verify the motives for using the analyzed forms of obtaining food. One of the initial research questions was: What are the motives behind the use of food-sharing solutions? The research was designed to verify the motives that most often appeared in the studies of other authors, media content, and declarations of associations and foundations operating in the area of food sharing.

The respondents were then asked to rank the reasons for using the food-sharing points and apps. The lowest rank (with a mean value of 5.3) was assigned to "cost reduction," followed by: "Care for the natural environment" (4.9), "the possibility of making contacts with people" (3.4), and "a sense of being active and useful" (3.0). The highest mean value was assigned to "curiosity and new experience" (2.9). The respondents had the opportunity to provide their reasons not included in the query. Some of them took advantage of this possibility and mentioned ethical and moral reasons, saving time, or the will to help others.

The reasons for using these solutions were correlated with the respondents' gender (Table 14.4) and the declared disposable income (including the amount spent on food)—Table 14.5. In the first case, the Mann-Whitney test was used, and in the second, the Spearman's rank correlation coefficient.

A statistically significant difference was demonstrated in the reasons for using food-sharing solutions between women and men (Table 14.4). Women ranked "care for the environment" higher (the mean value for women is 1.85) than men (the mean value for men is 2.57). This finding is consistent with the studies of other researchers who showed that care for the environment, not only at a level of declarations but also in concrete actions, is higher in the case of women than men (Antonetti & Maklan, 2014; Brough et al., 2016; Urena et al., 2008). It also seems important in the context of social and cultural changes, i.e., the increasing participation of women in political life, holding positions of responsibility in regional and national administrations as well as international organizations (Hessami & da Lopes, 2020).

Men ranked "curiosity and new experience" significantly higher than women (the mean value in the group of men was 3.52, while for women it was 4.38). In the case of other variables, no statistically significant relationships were found (Table 14.4).

Table 14.4 The Relationship between Reasons for Using Food-Sharing Facilities and Gender.

Variable	Mean		Mann-Whitney test	
	Women	Men	Z	p
Care for the environment	1.853	2.571	−2.117	0.034
Cost reduction	1.794	1.524	0.823	0.411
Possibility to make contact with people	3.412	3.857	−1.080	0.280
Sense of being active and useful	3.764	4.286	−1.852	0.064
Curiosity and new experience	4.382	3.524	2.820	0.004

Source: Own research.

Table 14.5 Disposable Income per Person and the Reasons for Using Food-Sharing Apps and Points (Spearman R).

Reasons for using food-sharing apps and points	Spearman R	p
Care for the environment	0.127	0.355
Cost reduction	−0.283	0.037
Possibility to make contact with people	0.189	0.166
Sense of being active and useful	0.0003	0.998
Curiosity and new experience	0.159	0.247

Source: Own research, p = statistical significance.

The research showed a statistically significant correlation only between the level of disposable income and the "cost reduction" factor, which seems logical and confirms the correctness of this study (Table 14.5). The lower the level of disposable income, the higher the rank of this factor (a greater need to reduce costs). It is worth noting that the economic factor is analyzed quite often in the literature. Some researchers emphasize that the interpretation of the reasons for using sharing solutions is not straightforward. Cost reduction as a motivation to participate in food sharing was indicated by Falcone and Imbert (2017). In their research, and also the research of Cappellini (2009), and Barnes and Mattsson (2016), both low- and medium-income consumers are ashamed of talking about their concerns regarding economic needs, even though they play a crucial role in their choices. Instead, they declare environmental considerations, which are almost a global trend. Thus, despite the growing public awareness of environmental issues and the focus of many scientists on the impact of such solutions on the environment, their research shows that, generally, consumers choosing sharing-economy solutions are mainly motivated by economic, not environmental, reasons. Also, when it comes to efforts to reduce food waste in households, the impact of environmental motivation seems to be less significant (Quested et al., 2013; Graham-Rowe et al., 2014). In turn, the leading role of the pro-environmental factor and commitment to sustainable development was indicated in the research by Ulug and Trell (2020). The research involved a case study of an initiative called Free Café, a citizen-driven collective in one of the academic cities of the Netherlands serving a free meal biweekly, using food that would otherwise be thrown away. A very large share of young people in the social structure of the town, the involvement of the authorities, and the engagement of other stakeholders made this particular food-sharing initiative feasible. This may explain the leading role of motives to promote pro-environmental and sustainable development. Although it is not the purpose of this chapter to assess to what extent the declared motives for using sharing-economy solutions coincide with actual ones, the previously mentioned doubts and cited discrepancies in research findings were intended to signal the complexity of this area.

Next, the Kruskal-Wallis test was used to verify the differences in the use of the analyzed food-sharing solutions depending on age, household size, and disposable income (Table 14.6).

Table 14.6   The Use of Food-Sharing Points and Applications by Selected Variables (Kruskal-Wallis Test).

Specification	Kruskal-Wallis test	p
Applications & Age	2.2396	0.524
Food-sharing points & Age	1.1809	0.758
Applications & Household size	1.3927	0.498
Food-sharing points & Household size	2.1013	0.350
Applications & Disposable income	3.4510	0.327
Food-sharing points & Disposable income	2.1318	0.546

Source: Own research.

There was no statistically significant difference between the use of food-sharing solutions and variables such as age, household size, and disposable income, which may result from the research method (an online survey accessed via social media).

The use of the food-sharing points and applications is limited by numerous barriers, which was also indicated by the authors cited in this study. These barriers may be: Technical (an inability to use the application and the broadly understood phenomenon of digital exclusion, especially of the elderly), sociocultural (shame, fear of being judged by others, limited trust in partners/collaborators in the process of the food exchange), and organizational (no such facilities available in the immediate vicinity). This study also verified the significance of various limitations to the use of food-sharing solutions.

The most important barriers mentioned by the respondents included: A lack of trust in the quality of this method of acquiring food (4.6 points on average, with a maximum value of five). This is especially true of food obtained from the food-sharing points. In this case, the donor is unknown; the freshness of the products can very often be verified only with the help of one's senses. In the case of multi-ingredient products (ready meals, salads, and cakes), it is also difficult to identify the ingredients by solely relying on the senses and avoid the ingredients that are not tolerated by the consumer (e.g., containing allergenic ingredients such as lactose, gluten, nuts, etc.). There is greater confidence in the case of pre-packaged products, preferably in transparent packaging.

The respondents also pointed to the fact that finding the right product (offer) requires time and energy (4.5). It takes time to reach the food-sharing point and there is no guarantee of finding the right products. Also, acquiring food through the app can be time consuming. Both searching for the right offer and picking up the product take time. And, even in this case, there is no guarantee that it will be what the consumer is looking for. Restaurants, bakeries, or other catering facilities often offer "food bags" without giving the details of what is inside them.

Another barrier was a lack of this type of offer in the place of residence (3.9), a lack of sufficient information about such solutions, i.e., an information barrier (3.5). As mentioned earlier, food-sharing applications and points operate primarily in large cities.

The fear of judgment by others (3.3) was the least important barrier indicated by the respondents. This is mainly because the inhabitants of large cities feel anonymous.

Table 14.7   Significance of Barriers to the Use of Food-Sharing Solutions by Gender (Mann-Whitney Test).

Specification	Gender	
	Z	p
Finding the right product (offer) requires time and energy	1.1169	0.264
Fear of judgment by others	0.3611	0.718
Lack of trust in the quality of this method of providing food	−0.8956	0.370
Lack of this type of offer in the place of residence	−1.6209	0.105
Lack of sufficient information about such solutions	0.5269	0.598

Source: Own research. Z = test value, p = statistical significance.

The respondents also had the opportunity to indicate their own limitations not included in the survey query. They mentioned: Habit, concern for the safety of others, and a lack of legal regulations, which makes it difficult to pursue one's rights in the case of possible damage to health. The legal aspects of obtaining food from one's neighbors and other individuals (even famous chefs), were discussed by Schwalb (2020) and Koch (2020).

This study also verified whether sociodemographic variables differentiate the importance of these barriers. It was checked whether the respondents' gender was the differentiating variable. For this purpose, the Mann-Whitney test (Table 14.7) was used.

There was no statistically significant difference between the aforementioned barriers and the gender of the respondents, as shown in Table 14.7.

Using Spearman's rank correlation coefficient, the relationship between the barriers and other variables was also verified (Table 14.8).

Also, in this case, no statistically significant correlation was found between age, household size, and barriers preventing the use of the analyzed food-sharing solutions. It should be emphasized that the analyzed barriers are mostly complementary.

Some scientific studies in this area focus on social barriers, including a lack of trust. Falcone and Imbert (2017) point to social barriers to food sharing. In turn, the research of Bielefeldt et al. (2016) shows that even if people have a positive attitude towards the sharing economy (distributed-use economy), many of them do not use any concrete solutions, which indicates a discrepancy between attitudes and actual behavior. This is an additional challenge for the researcher, as the research should not only focus on declarations but

Table 14.8 Significance of Barriers to the Use of Food-Sharing Solutions by Age, Household Size, and Disposable Income (Spearman R).

Parameters	Age		Household size		Disposable income	
	R	p	R	p	R	p
Finding the right product (offer) requires time and energy	−0.202	0.139	−0.052	0.708	−0.044	0.753
Fear of judgment by others	−0.078	0.569	−0.146	0.288	−0.129	0.349
Lack of trust in the quality of this method of providing food	0.183	0.181	−0.057	0.682	0.116	0.398
Lack of this type of offer in the place of residence	0.095	0.490	0.039	0.774	0.059	0.665
Lack of sufficient information about such solutions	0.075	0.587	0.215	0.115	−0.021	0.879

Source: **Own research.**

also investigate actual participation in the sharing process. However, because sharing solutions also function outside the official organizational system, it is difficult to obtain reliable secondary data.

Lazell (2016) and Farr-Wharton et al. (2014) indicated a lack of social relationships and a consequent lack of trust as the crucial barrier to food sharing. Saginova et al. (2021) went even further and pointed to the feeling of shame about using free food as a key barrier to participating in food sharing. Thus, the dissemination of the sharing economy not only requires the availability of pro-environmental solutions but, above all, the repositioning of this phenomenon in public awareness and a change in social attitudes.

14.4 Conclusions

This research has shown that both food-sharing points and applications are not very popular among the respondents. However, it is worth emphasizing that the respondents who did not use them still perceived them as positive solutions in the vast majority of cases. Cost reduction was the main reason for using local food-sharing points and mobile applications. The second reason was a concern for the environment. As it has been suggested in this chapter, this area requires further in-depth research. Despite the fact that the majority of respondents declared their acceptance of this type of solution, it does not mean that they participate in the food-sharing process. This study has shown that the main barrier preventing people from using food-sharing solutions is social, not technological, as it involves a lack of trust. Interestingly, the sociodemographic variables differentiated the reasons and barriers to using food-sharing points and applications only to a limited extent. The only statistically significant difference was found in the reasons for using the analyzed solutions between women and men. Women were more motivated than men by concern for the environment and less than men by the desire to experience something new. There was also a relationship between the level of disposable income and the desire to reduce costs, i.e., the lower the level of disposable income, the higher the need to reduce costs.

Research limitations: The limitation of this study was the uneven representation of all age groups in the research sample as well as a lack of representativeness of the research. Broader research on a representative sample of the largest cities' residents could provide better recognition of the current state of the art and allow for applicable conclusions regarding the desired directions of development of the sharing economy. Further research should be carried out both through ethnography methods (as new media and modern technological solutions are increasingly being used in the sharing economy), as well as in physical (real) space as not all consumers (especially the elderly) use mobile applications and, even if they do, ultimately the food is handed over/ picked up in real space. A limitation that should be eliminated in subsequent studies is the sole use of an Internet-based survey to collect empirical data as this tool excludes those groups of respondents who do not use the Internet or use it to a limited extent.

These findings provide the following insight for future research and possible applications: The dynamics of the development of the phenomenon of sharing practices, including food sharing, require the implementation of cyclical, interdisciplinary research employing various research methods and techniques. Future studies should use an experiment and the SERVQUAL method to find out to what extent the experiences of the respondents meet their expectations.

It would be beneficial to conduct cross-sectional research carried out at an international level, e.g., in EU countries, and incorporate appropriate solutions in consumer-protection legislation, or perhaps also in the common agricultural policy. A practical implication of these research findings is the need to improve the ways of communicating various opportunities to participate in food sharing to different groups of recipients. In the case of food-sharing applications, it is useful to develop clear and consistent recommendation systems. Balińska et al. (2021) showed that in the group of applications encouraging ecological behavior, including sharing practices, the application promoted in traditional media enjoyed the greatest recognition. This means that developing a functional application is only part of the success. It is extremely important to reach potential users with information about it and encourage them to use it.

Undoubtedly, activities aimed at improving consumer awareness of the possibility of sharing and taking advantage of surplus food are of primary importance. Without raising awareness and encouraging appropriate behavior in this area, neither food-sharing applications nor points will fulfil their functions.

Deriving from the available sources and the results of the author's own empirical research presented in this chapter, as well as taking into account specific cultural patterns and technological solutions, the following model of food sharing can be proposed (Figure 14.2).

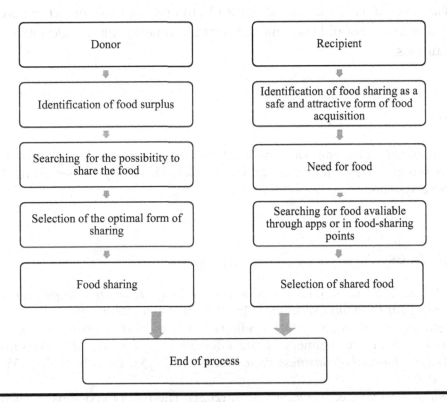

Figure 14.2   Model of the Food-Sharing Process.

Source: Own study.

The food-sharing model in Figure 14.2 should only be treated as an inspiration for further research. The development of food sharing can be inhibited by various factors. The presented research showed that the most important barrier is a lack of trust in the level of quality of the available food. Therefore, it is important to both develop a recommendation system and effectively promote food-sharing practices. In the process of selecting information channels to promote food-sharing solutions, potential users of different ages should be taken into account, i.e., traditional media, digital media, or public space should be used.

As indicated in this research report, the existing solutions in the field of food sharing (applications and food-sharing points) are developing in large cities. This does not mean that food waste in small towns and villages is not a problem and there are no people who would like to use such solutions. In subsequent studies, it would be valuable to analyze the problem of food sharing in small towns and villages. The development potential of the food-sharing system in such places should differ from that in large cities. The differences would not only refer to the logistic dimension of this type of behavior but above all to the social and cultural dimensions. Therefore, the planned research should take into account the unique cultural identity of local communities.

Note

1 Collaborative consumption consists of 3 systems: redistribution markets, a product service system and collaborative lifestyles. This study focuses on the last of these systems.

References

Allen, D., & Berg, C. (2014). *The Sharing Economy: How Over-Regulation Could Destroy an Economic Revolution.* Institute of Public Affairs, 36.

Antonetti, P., & Maklan, S. (2014). Feelings that make a difference: How guilt and pride convince consumers of the effectiveness of sustainable consumption choices. *Journal of Business Ethics, 124*(1), 117–134. DOI: 10.1007/s10551-013-1841-9

Balińska, A., Jaska E., & Werenowska, A. (2021). The role of eco-apps in encouraging pro-environmental behavior of young people studying in Poland. *Energies, 14*(16), 1–16. DOI: 10.3390/en14164946

Bankier.Pl. (2021). *Polska na 5. Miejscu w UE pod względem marnotrastwa żywności. [Poland Ranks 5th in the EU in Terms of Food Waste].* Retrieved from: www. bankier.pl/message/Marnowanie-zywnosci-Polska-a-5-place-in-UE-7719342. html Available [December 20, 2021].

Bank Żywności. (2021). *Nie marnujmy Perspektywy zapobiegania marnotrawstwu żywności w Polsce do 2030 roku Raport z badań, [Let's not waste. Prospects for preventing food waste in Poland until 2030. The research report].* Warszawa. Retrieved from: www.bankizywnosci.pl/wp-content/uploads/2021/07/Raport_ BadaniaDelfickie_PROM.pdf Available [December 20, 2021].

Bardhi, F., & Eckhardt, G. M. (2012). Access-based consumption: The case of car sharing. *Journal of Consumer Research, 39*(4), 881–898. DOI: 10.1086/666376

Barnes, S. J., & Mattsson, J. (2016). Understanding current and future issues in collaborative consumption: A four-stage Delphi study. *Technol Forecast Soc Change, 104*(C), 200–211. DOI: 10.1016/j.techfore.2016.01.006

Belk, R. (2014). You are what you access: Sharing and collaborative consumption online. *Journal of Business Research, 67*(8), 1595–1600. DOI: 10.1016/j.jbusres. 2013.10.001

Berketova, L. V., & Volodina, S. S. (2020). Food sharing—as an eco-friendly way to use food. *Bulletin of science and practice, 1,* 253–259. DOI: 10.33619/ 2414-2948/50/28

Bielefeldt, J., Poelzl, J., & Herbst, U. (2016). What's mine Isn't yours—barriers to participation in the sharing economy. *Die Unternehmung, the Swiss Journal of Business Research and Practice, 70*(1), 4–25. DOI: 10.5771/0042-059X-2016-1-4

Botsman, R. (2013). *The Sharing Economy Lacks a Shared Definition, Fast Company.* Retrieved from: www.fastcompany.com/3022028/the-sharing-economy-lacks-a-shared-definition/ Available [September 15, 2020].

Brough, A. R., Wilkie, J. E. B., Ma, J., Isaac, M. S., & Gal, D. (2016). Is eco-friendly unmanly? The green-feminine stereotype and its effect on sustainable consumption. *Journal of Consumer Research, 43*(4), 567–582. DOI: 10.1093/jcr/ucw044

Burgiel, A. (2014). Rozwój technologii informacyjnych jako determinanta adaptacji modelu konsumpcji wspólnej. [The development of information technologies as a determinant of the adaptation of the shared consumption model]. *Marketing i Rynek [Marketing and Market], 11,* 316–326.

Cappellini, B. (2009). The sacrifice of re-use: the travels of leftovers and family relations. *Journal of Consumer Behaviour, 8*(6), 365–375. DOI: 10.1002/cb.299

Davies, A. R. (2019). *Urban Food Sharing.* Rules, tools, and networks POLICY PRESSR, 67. Retrieved from: https://library.oapen.org/bitstream/handle/ 20.500.12657/25248/9781447349860.pdf?sequence=1&isAllowed=y/ Available [December 23, 2021].

Eataway. (2021). Retrieved from: https://eataway.com/ Available [December 27, 2021].

Eatwith. (2021). Retrieved from: www.eatwith.com Available [November 22, 2020].

European Parliament. (2021). *European Parliament Resolution of 16 May 2017 on Initiative on Resource Efficiency: Reducing Food Waste, Improving Food Safety (2016/2223(INI)).* Retrieved from: https://eur-lex.europa.eu/legal-ontent/EN/ TXT/?uri=CELEX%3A52017IP0207 Available [1December 18, 2021].

Falcone, P. M., & Imbert, E. (2017). Bringing a sharing economy approach into the food sector: The potential of food sharing for reducing food waste. In: P. Morone, F. Papendiek, & V. Tartiu (eds.), *Food Waste Reduction and Valorisation* (pp. 197–214). Cham: Springer. DOI: 10.1007/978-3-319-50088-1_10

Farr-Wharton, G., Choi, J. H.-J., & Foth, M. (2014). Food talks back: Exploring the role of mobile applications in reducing domestic food wastage. In: T. Robertson, K. O'Hara, G. Wadley, L. Loke, & T. Leong (eds.), *Proceedings of the 26th Australian Computer-Human Interaction Conference on Designing Futures: The Future of Design* (pp. 352–361). Sydney, Australia: Association for Computing Machinery (ACM). DOI: 10.1145/2686612.2686665

Feenberg, A. (2012). *Questioning Technology*. Abingdon, UK: Routledge.

Graham-Rowe, E., Donna, C., Jessop, D. C., & Sparks, P. (2014). Identifying motivations and barriers to minimizing household food waste. *Resour Conserv Recycl, 84*, 15–23. DOI: 10.1016/j.resconrec.2013.12.005

Gurven, M., & Jaeggi, A. V. (2015). Food sharing. In: R. Scott & S. Kosslyn (eds.), *Emerging Trends in the Social and Behavioral Sciences* (p. 1). Hoboken, NJ: John Wiley & Sons, Inc.

Harvey, J., Smith, A., Goulding, J., & Branco Illodo, I. (2020). Food sharing, redistribution, and waste reduction via mobile applications: A social network analysis. *Industrial Marketing Management, 88*. DOI: 10.1016/j.indmarman.2019.02.019

Hessami, Z., & Lopes da, F. M. (2020). Female political representation and substantive effects on policies: A literature review. *European Journal of Political Economy, 63*, 101896. DOI: 10.1016/j.ejpoleco.2020.101896

How Food Waste Costs Our Cities Millions. (2021). Smartcitiesdive. Retrieved from: www.smartcitiesdive.com/ex/sustainablecitiescollective/how-food-waste-costs-our-cities-millions/1065356/ Available [November 20, 2021].

Jadłodzielnie. (2021). Warszawa19115.Pl. Retrieved from: https://warszawa19115.pl/-/jadlodzielnie?redirect=%2Fhome Available [December 20, 2021].

Jaros, B. (2016). Sharing economy jako ważny trend w obszarze zrównoważonej konsumpcji [Sharing economy as an important trend in the area of sustainable consumption]. *Handel Wewnętrzny, 5*(365), 84.

Koch, R. (2020). Public, private, and the appeal to the common good: Practices of justification in a peer-to-peer economy. *Transactions of the Institute of British Geographers, 45*(2), 392–405. DOI: 10.1111/tran.12287

Lazell, J. (2016). Consumer food waste behavior in universities: Sharing as a means of prevention. *Journal of Consumer Behavior, 15*(5), 430–439. DOI: 10.1002/cb.1581

Lee, K. C. L. (2018). Grocery shopping, food waste, and the retail landscape of cities: The case of Seoul. *Journal of Cleaner Production, 172*, 325–334. DOI: 10.1016/j.jclepro.2017.10.085

Majchrzak, K. (2016). Ekonomia dzielenia się i jej przejawy w turystyce [The sharing economy and its manifestations in tourism]. *Ekonomiczne Problemy, 1* (33), 22.

Mazurek-Łopacińska, K. (2005). *Badania marketingowe. Teoria i praktyka*. [*Marketing Research. Theory and Practice*]. Warsaw: PWN.

Mugica, Y., & Rose, T. (2019). Tackling food waste in cities: A policy and program toolkit. *Report R:19–01-B, Natural Resources Defense Council.* Retrieved from: www.nrdc.org/sites/default/files/food-waste-cities-policy-toolkit-report.pdf Available [November 20, 2021].

Płaczek, E., & Ziętara, H. (2021). *Sharing Economy as a Concept of Solving the Problem of Food Waste* (No. 4918). EasyChair.

Quested, T. E., Marsh, E., Stunell, D., & Parry, A. D. (2013). Spaghetti soup: The complex world of food. *Resour Conserv Recycl, 79,* 43–51. DOI: 10.1016/j.resconrec.2013.04.011

Rosenlund, J., Nyblom, Å., Ekholm, H. M., & Sörme, L. (2020). The emergence of food waste as an issue in Swedish retail. *British Food Journal, 122*(11), 3283–3296. DOI: 10.1108/BFJ-03-2020-0181

Saginova, O., Zavyalov, D., Kireeva, N., Zavyalova, N., & Sagino, Y. (2021). Food-sharing in the distributed use economy. *E3S Web of Conferences 247,* 01016. DOI: 10.1051/e3sconf/202124701016

Sapała, M. (2019). *Na marne. [Wasted].* Wołowiec: Wydawnictwo Czarne.

Schwalb, E. (2020). McNeighbor? Legal barriers to a national food-sharing economy. *Barry Law Review, 25*(1). Retrieved from: https://lawpublications.barry.edu/barrylrev/vol25/iss1/5 Available [July 15, 2021].

Sobolak, J. (2021). *Ranking: tych 10 produktów wyrzucamy najczęściej. "Polacy mają się czego wstydzić" [Ranking: These 10 Products Are the Ones We Throw Away the Most. „Poles Have Something to be ashamed of"].* Retrieved from: https://wyborcza.biz/biznes/7,147743,26309257,ranking-tych-10-produktow-wyrzua-my-najczesniej-polacy-maja.html Available [December 27, 2021].

Statista. (2021). Retrieved from: www.statista.com/ Available [November 20, 2021].

Stephany, A. (2015). *The Business of Sharing, Making It in the New Sharing Economy.* London: Palgrave Macmillan.

Toogoodtogo. (2021). Retrieved from: https://toogoodtogo.pl/pl Available [December 27, 2021].

Ulug, C., & Trell, E. M. (2020). It's not really about the food, it's also about food': Urban collective action, the community economy, and autonomous food systems at the Groningen Free Café. *International Journal of Urban Sustainable Development Open Access, 12*(2), 127–1423. DOI: 10.1080/19463138.2019.1696804

UNEP Food Waste Index Report 2021. (2021). UNEP—UN Environment Programme. Retrieved from: www.unep.org/resources/report/unep-food-waste-index-report-2021 Available [December 30, 2021].

United Nations. (2021). *Sustainable Development Goals.* Retrieved form: www.un.org/sustainabledevelopment/sustainable-consumption-production Available [December 20, 2021].

Urena, F., Bernabeu, R., & Olmeda, M. (2008). Women, men and organic food: Differences in their attitudes and willingness to pay: A Spanish case study. *International Journal of Consumer Studies, 32*(1), 18–26. DOI: 10.1111/j.1470-6431.2007.00637.x

Veen, E. J. (2019). Fostering community values through meal sharing with strangers. *Sustainability, 11*(7), 2121. DOI: 10.3390/su11072121

Warshawsky, D. N. (2019). The challenge of food waste governance in cities: Case study of consumer perspectives in Los Angeles. *Sustainability, 11*, 847. DOI: 10.3390/su11030847

Wezpomoz. (2021). *Poznaj społeczną lodówkę. [Get to Know the Social Refrigerator].* Retrieved from: https://wezpomoz.pl/lodowka-spoleczna Available [December 30, 2021].

Index

Page numbers in *italics* indicate a figure and page numbers in **bold** indicate a table on the corresponding page.

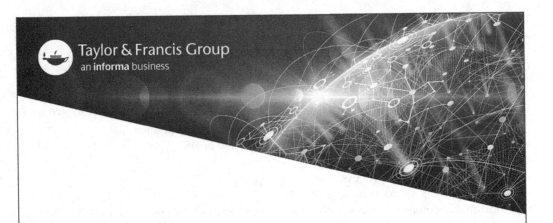